URBANIZATION AND ENGLISH ROMANTIC POETRY

Through an incisive analysis of the emerging debates surrounding urbanization in the Romantic period, together with close readings of poets including William Blake, William Wordsworth, and Samuel Taylor Coleridge, Stephen Tedeschi explores the notion that the Romantic poets criticized the historical form that the process of urbanization had taken, rather than urbanization itself. The works of the Romantic poets are popularly considered in a rural context and often understood as hostile to urbanization – one of the most profound social transformations of the era. By focusing on the urban aspects of such writing, Tedeschi re-orientates the relationship between urbanization and English Romantic poetry to deliver a study that discovers how the Romantic poets examined not only the influence of urbanization on poetry but also how poetry might help to reshape the form that urbanization could take.

STEPHEN TEDESCHI is Assistant Professor in the Department of English at the University of Alabama. His articles have appeared in *European Romantic Review, Keats-Shelley Journal, Essays in Romanticism*, and *Keats-Shelley Review*.

CAMBRIDGE STUDIES IN ROMANTICISM

This series aims to foster the best new work in one of the most challenging fields within English literary studies. From the early 1780s to the early 1830s a formidable array of talented men and women took to literary composition, not just in poetry, which some of them famously transformed, but in many modes of writing. The expansion of publishing created new opportunities for writers, and the political stakes of what they wrote were raised again by what Wordsworth called those "great national events" that were "almost daily taking place": the French Revolution, the Napoleonic and American wars, urbanization, industrialization, religious revival, an expanded empire abroad, and the reform movement at home. This was an enormous ambition, even when it pretended otherwise. The relations between science, philosophy, religion, and literature were reworked in texts such as *Frankenstein* and *Biographia Literaria*; gender relations in *A Vindication of the Rights of Woman* and *Don Juan*; journalism by Cobbett and Hazlitt; poetic form, content, and style by the Lake School and the Cockney School. Outside Shakespeare studies, probably no body of writing has produced such a wealth of comment or done so much to shape the responses of modern criticism. This indeed is the period that saw the emergence of those notions of "literature" and of literary history, especially national literary history, on which modern scholarship in English has been founded.

The categories produced by Romanticism have also been challenged by recent historicist arguments. The task of the series is to engage both with a challenging corpus of Romantic writings and with the changing field of criticism they have helped to shape. As with other literary series published by Cambridge, this one will represent the work of both younger and more established scholars, on either side of the Atlantic and elsewhere.

For a complete list of titles published, see the end of this book.

URBANIZATION AND ENGLISH ROMANTIC POETRY

STEPHEN TEDESCHI

University of Alabama

CAMBRIDGE
UNIVERSITY PRESS

University Printing House, Cambridge CB2 8BS, United Kingdom

One Liberty Plaza, 20th Floor, New York, NY 10006, USA

477 Williamstown Road, Port Melbourne, VIC 3207, Australia

314-321, 3rd Floor, Plot 3, Splendor Forum, Jasola District Centre, New Delhi - 110025, India

79 Anson Road, #06-04/06, Singapore 079906

Cambridge University Press is part of the University of Cambridge.

It furthers the University's mission by disseminating knowledge in the pursuit of education, learning and research at the highest international levels of excellence.

www.cambridge.org
Information on this title: www.cambridge.org/9781108402637
DOI: 10.1017/9781108235815

First published 2018
First paperback edition 2019

A catalogue record for this publication is available from the British Library

Library of Congress Cataloging in Publication data
NAMES: Tedeschi, Stephen.
TITLE: Urbanization and English Romantic poetry / Stephen Tedeschi.
DESCRIPTION: Cambridge ; New York : Cambridge University Press, 2017. |
Series: Cambridge studies in Romanticism ; 117 |
Includes bibliographical references and index.
IDENTIFIERS: LCCN 2017023995 | ISBN 9781108416092 (hardback)
SUBJECTS: LCSH: English poetry – 19th century – History and criticism. |
Urbanization – Great Britain – History – 19th century. | Urbanization in literature. | Romanticism – Great Britain.
CLASSIFICATION: LCC PR590 .T44 2017 | DDC 821/.709145–dc23
LC record available at https://lccn.loc.gov/2017023995

ISBN 978-1-108-41609-2 Hardback
ISBN 978-1-108-40263-7 Paperback

Contents

Acknowledgments

I am pleased to acknowledge the guidance, support, and inspiration I have received from many teachers, colleagues, and friends. Paul H. Fry and Christopher R. Miller guided this book from its inception with patience and kindness. Bill Ulmer was a generous listener, reader, and advisor through several long rounds of revision. Heather White, Deborah Weiss, and Fred Whiting helped me see it to completion. Linda Bree and James Chandler gave this book a chance and steered it through. The anonymous readers for the Press know how much their insightful reports have improved this book. Susan J. Wolfson and Jim Richardson taught me how to read and write. David Currell will read this book as a long letter from a friend written the day after a lively conversation. Sarah Mahurin has walked with me throughout, on summer afternoons and winter evenings. Alec Brookes, Sam Cross, Lucinda Currell, Joey Gamble, Julia Gardial, Erica McAlpine, Matt Mutter, and Carson Vines kept the fires burning. My family loved me and forgave me. Whatever value this book has derives from these people and from many others: its faults are my own. The thought that runs through these pages no more belongs to me than water belongs to a river or current belongs to a wire. As Wordsworth says, each particular thought hath no beginning. The academic world is small enough that I am sure my reader can trace these thoughts back to himself or herself or to books we both have admired. And I am confident that whoever reads this book outside the academic world knows the author well enough to have shaped his mind and heart. This book, reader, in words of reason deeply weighed, is for you. Part of the fourth chapter was originally published in *Keats-Shelley Journal*, vol. 63 (2014), pp. 102–22, and part of the second chapter appeared in *European Romantic Review* in February 2012 and is available online at www.tandfonline.com/doi/abs/10.1080/10509585.2012.653282. I am grateful to the editors of these journals for permission to use this material.

INTRODUCTION

Urbanization and English Romantic Poetry

During the three hundred years preceding the Romantic period, the portion of the population of England that lived in cities – largely in London but also in port cities, manufacturing towns, and regional trading and administrative centers – increased along with the expansion of the nation's commercial, manufacturing, and financial activity. This change in social geography shaped and was shaped by changes in the ways in which people thought about urbanization. During the eighteenth century, a discourse promoting the benefits of urbanization ascended to effective dominance in polite culture. In this discourse, developed in the work of several prominent moral philosophers of the eighteenth century, the growth of cities appeared as a natural and epochal step in the progressive development of civilization: the nation was changing from a predominantly agrarian rural society into a more advanced, more civilized, predominantly commercial urban society. This metamorphosis involved changes not only in political economy and social geography but also in culture: urbanization was understood to foster the development of more refined sensibilities and cultural practices. Conventional concerns about urban corruption, disorder, and disease persisted, but the dominant discourse represented urbanization as a sign and an engine of historical progress. At the end of the eighteenth century, however, conditions in the cities that this discourse could not adequately describe became more pressing: London's rookeries proved resistant to attempts at improvement; working-class districts in the manufacturing towns presented scenes of infernal squalor; and the possibility of uncontrollable urban popular violence – seen at home in the Gordon Riots and then indelibly associated with events in revolutionary Paris – haunted the collective imagination.

During the Romantic period changes in the conditions of the cities and in the form of urbanization provoked a reassessment of the prevailing discourse on urbanization. This reassessment involved a reexamination and revision of models of specifically urban forms of subjectivity, of the nature of the ties between urban society and the spirit of commerce, and of the notion that polite urban culture was the vanguard leading the advance of civilization. Out of this reassessment, alternative ways of thinking about urbanization emerged. These new ways of thinking were diverse and cohered only loosely: they did not constitute a new discourse that could succeed the prevailing discourse as dominant but rather remained emergent. They cohered negatively by responding to the established discourse and positively by sharing a common set of premises about urbanization and concerns about its present form. Among these common premises was the notion that the prevailing discourse and the form of urbanization it legitimated were not necessary and natural but historical and subject to reform. This recognition carries with it the crucial distinction between the current historical mode of urbanization and urbanization per se. Other kinds of urbanization and other kinds of cities were possible. While this emphasis on imagining alternative social structures gives the alternative discourse on urbanization an affinity with reform, the discourse was not confined to any political faction or closely associated with any specific ideology. Instead, the contest between the alternative and prevailing attitudes was negotiated throughout English culture, from the practices of everyday life to speeches in Parliament, and, in literature, from popular radical journalism to polite poetry.

The literature of the Romantic period was a forum for the explicit reassessment of the discourse on urbanization and, since urbanization was understood to have transformed the literary field, it was also one of the stakes of the debate. Urbanization changed the conditions of literary production by improving transportation, concentrating larger potential readerships in space, and fostering increased literacy rates. These changes in the conditions of the literary marketplace altered the relative standing of genres. Newspapers, journals, and magazines flourished as existing markets expanded and new markets emerged. Writers sorted out the shifting, fluid relations between genres of periodical prose, and this reworking of genres shaped prose writers' modes of articulating the alternative discourse on urbanization. The complex conjunctions of the urban environment, deep social and political transformations, and the form of the periodical essay play out in the works of canonical prose writers of the period, including Charles Lamb, Leigh Hunt, Thomas De Quincey, William Hazlitt, and, with a different perspective on the same questions, William Cobbett.[1] While poetry circulated more widely as the traffic in periodicals increased and while volumes by Sir Walter Scott, Lord Byron, and Robert Bloomfield were runaway commercial successes, poetic conventions nonetheless represented urbanization as antagonistic to poetry. By the end of the eighteenth century, the figural repertoires for the genres of poetry most used to represent social geography – such as pastoral, georgic, and locodescriptive – and the conventional poetic tropes for representing cities assumed in their organization an opposition between the conditions of urban life and the conditions for writing and reading polite, literary poetry. City life was too sordid, commercial, distracting, and alienating for poetry. Poets in the Romantic period who participated in the alternative discourse on urbanization and who recognized the historicity of forms of urbanization, however, revised these figural repertoires and distinguished between the hazards to poetry and society inherent in urbanization itself and those peculiar to the political, economic, and cultural dimensions of its current historical form. These poets imagined ways in which urbanization might be reformed, and considered not only the influence of urbanization on poetry but poetry's potential influence on urbanization.

In examining the relation between urbanization and English Romantic poetry, this book contributes to an ongoing scholarly inquiry into urban literary culture in the Romantic period. James Chandler and Kevin Gilmartin's 2005 collection *Romantic Metropolis* identified and encouraged this inquiry by explicitly demonstrating that several current critical methods and discourses, otherwise not necessarily overlapping, all shared an investment in urban social spaces and practices. Their introduction assembles the essays in the collection under the concept of "metropolitanism," which they define as "a sense of the urban site as at once capital to the provinces and point of contact with the wider world."[2] As it is used in their introduction, metropolitanism describes both a pattern of development in the social geography of imperial capitalism and the eclectic, bustling social environment of a major city. I aim to contribute to the lines of criticism this collection gathers together by considering different objects on both sides of the relation. Defining the object as urbanization rather than metropolitanism has considerable consequences for critical inquiry, not the least of which is its ability to describe the metastasis of urbanization in the Romantic period beyond London to the manufacturing towns and port cities. And while poets and individual poems regularly appear in studies of the Romantic metropolis, scholarly work on metropolitan culture often focuses primarily on periodical prose or on the spaces and practices of political and literary discourse rather than on the peculiar generic conventions of poetry or its place in the changing literary field.

While the concept of urbanization has rarely appeared explicitly in scholarly studies of Romantic-period literary culture, elements of the process of urbanization have been studied under different names. Recent work in this vein draws on two classic frameworks for describing the large-scale economic, social, and political determinations and effects associated with urbanization. First, Raymond Williams's landmark book *The Country and the City* inaugurates the project of considering the interrelations between the dynamic transformations of social geography and literary history. Williams demonstrates the utility to such a project of formations such as structures of feeling and the metropolitan pattern of development, a pattern in imperialist and capitalist development in which a metropolitan center oversees the economic, political, and cultural activity of a subordinated interior and a rural and colonial periphery.[3] Second, E. P. Thompson's *Customs in Common* describes a deep and pervasive change in culture during the Romantic period, with traditional ways of organizing daily life and labor confronting a movement toward standardization, rationalization, and the imposition of time discipline. Historians, including Peter Linebaugh, have tracked this shift in the cities in the reorganization of labor, redefinition of crime, and emergence of disciplinary apparatuses such as the police.[4] Simon Joyce's study of class and crime in London draws on both lines of inquiry, and Saree Makdisi's studies of representations of the metropolis cross the two with theories of empire. Makdisi examines how writers around 1800 redefined the discourses of Orientalism and Occidentalism in mapping the different neighborhoods and social groups of the metropolis and how institutions tested "[s]trategies and tactics of discipline, surveillance, and control" on local plebeian cultures.[5] In Makdisi's work, as in Daniel E. White's study of the mutual cultural exchange between the metropolitan capital and India, the metropolis itself evolves as it approaches, but never fully realizes, the hierarchical structure between center and periphery.[6]

While this literary scholarship understands urban environments to be mutable, its focus on specifically metropolitan relations defines a different, and in crucial ways narrower, scope than that defined by the concept of urbanization. Thinking in terms of urbanization can account for other forms of urban development in addition to the metropolitan – including the emergence of regional centers, manufacturing towns, port cities, and resort towns – and for various factors on urban development such as proximity to resources and interurban competition. The crucial difference between urbanization and metropolitan organizations is that the former defines a process and the latter a pattern within a process. In literary analysis, defining the object as the metropolis has the potential to shade into a study of representations of the eclecticism and bustle of the urban environment.[7] As a pattern within a process, the metropolitan organization informs the scene of literary activity, structures the imbalanced exchanges between domestic and foreign publics, and appears in literature in the forms of patterns of discourse, tropes, and figural repertoires. As a broad process, urbanization influences literature in all these ways and at the level of the literary field. It has a more direct relation to the development of provincial literary markets and their interactions with the market in the capital and to the changing relations between genres of literature.[8]

These approaches study how global, systemic, and abstract forces shape urban form and literary culture; another, complementary line of inquiry, gathered and advanced by Gillian Russell and Clara Tuite's 1998 collection *Romantic Sociability*, examines the social and cultural practices that constitute urban publics and shape urban spaces.[9] In his book on the crossovers between cultures of conversation and print in the Romantic period, Jon Mee notes that "polite conversation was not just a practice, but also an influence on the physical forms taken by the eighteenth-century urban renaissance," shaping the construction of open urban spaces such as coffeehouses, ballrooms, and theatres.[10] Kevin Gilmartin has studied the different spaces of polite and plebeian political speech, and Ian Newman has related Wordsworth and Coleridge's project in the *Lyrical Ballads* to popular ballads sung in London's taverns.[11] In his study of the Hunt circle, Jeffrey Cox remarks, "It is important always to stress the urban nature of the Cockney School," since its poets were defined "as being London – as opposed to Lake District – poets," though in practice the urban quality of the poetry quickly shades into "cosmopolitan urbanity." Cox's Cockneys "sought an image in their circle of the reformed world they imagined," creating a "community not limited by the divisions of class interest and distinction" but united by "affiliative relations."[12] In these studies, the city shapes social practices and social practices shape the city, but the concreteness of the analysis often leaves relatively underdeveloped the interaction between these practices and large-scale social determinations. For a study of urbanization and literature, both the concrete spaces and practices and the critical formations informing these analyses – such as the public sphere, the configuration of its spaces, and the literary field – no longer serve as objects of analysis in themselves but must be repositioned as intermediary formations, connecting specific literary practices and figures at one pole and opening a place for an understanding of urbanization at the other pole.

While recent work in Romantic literary studies has reexamined the relationship between urban life and Romantic literary culture from new perspectives, critical studies of representations of the city in Romantic literature, especially in poetry, have remained more or less consistent for the past thirty years. In these readings, the city appears as a phantasmagoria of sights and sounds, and this overwhelming commotion shapes distinctively urban sensibilities that anticipate Georg Simmel's diagnosis of the effect of the metropolis on mental life or the attitudes of Walter Benjamin's typical urban characters in his comments on the social and cultural logic of Baudelaire's Paris. Critics have used the same models of urban experience to discuss poetic representations of cities from the Renaissance to the present.[13] Collectively, these studies demonstrate that poetic conventions for representing cities stay remarkably consistent over centuries. But the more critics apply the models, the more the models lose their historical and local specificity and tend to naturalize a model of urban experience originally associated with specific phases of capitalist modernity. Sociologist and urban theorist Manuel Castells argues that the concept of a specific urban culture or sensibility is itself an ideological myth that naturalizes the effects of capitalism and mystifies the true source of its symptoms: "the writings on 'urban society' which are based directly on this myth, provide the key-words of an ideology of modernity, assimilated . . . to the social forms of liberal capitalism."[14] The dominance of ideologies directly implicated in capitalist modernization can by no means be assumed in the Romantic period among either radicals or conservatives; the alternative discourse on urbanization reopened the possibility of different forms of urban consciousness precisely by relating the prevailing form to present conditions.[15]

The work of literary criticism that most closely anticipates my conception of urbanization remains Williams's *The Country and the City*. Williams directly examines the dynamic, large-scale transformation of the social geography of England throughout history, connects changes in the city to changes in the country, and traces the imaginative and affective responses to these changes in literature. I aim to revise and refine Williams's reading of Romantic-period poets' responses to urbanization, a reading that in its outline of a general ambivalence still represents a critical consensus.[16] Williams sees Romantic culture simultaneously drawn to and repelled by the city. In Goldsmith's nostalgic pastoral *The Deserted Village* (1770), Williams discerns "with unusual precision, what we can later call a Romantic structure of feeling – the assertion of nature against industry and of poetry against trade; the isolation of humanity and community into the idea of culture, against the real social pressures of the time[.] . . . We can catch its echoes, exactly, in Blake, in Wordsworth, and in Shelley." These poets, that is, respond to urbanization with a "combination of protest and nostalgia." Yet at the same time, Wordsworth's poetry offers sharp, "direct observation of a new set of physical and sense relationships: a new way of seeing men in what is experienced as a new kind of society." Breaking from conventional perspectives on urban life, Wordsworth felt a "historically liberating insight, of new kinds of possible order, new kinds of human unity, in the transforming experience of the city."[17] The course of Romantic criticism has since challenged the representativeness and accuracy of the model of Romanticism behind Williams's description of the Romantic structure of feeling, and more recent criticism has proven that other ways of considering the relation between literature and society reveal a different sense of Romantic-period writers' relation to the urban environment.[18]

To revise Williams's analysis and develop his suggestive insights, I aim not only to use these more recently developed critical formations but also to sift the distinctions between the structures of feeling and organizing concepts that belong to a generic repertoire and those that belong to specific poetic utterances within or against that genre. The emergence of an alternative discourse on urbanization appears in poetry in part in subtle deviations from these generic repertoires. During this period of emergence, some conventional motifs, tropes, and modes survived; others were challenged or revised; and new ones were invented.[19] This balance of continuity and innovation, as Williams's argument recognizes, registers a specific affective response to the transformations in social geography and in social customs. But it also signals an argumentative and ideological response to the prevailing discourse on urbanization inherent within the configuration of conventional repertoires and shared with eighteenth-century moral philosophy, from David Hartley to Adam Smith and from David Hume to Edmund Burke. Examining the argumentative as well as the affective response allows for a fuller definition of the emergent alternative discourse on urbanization and for a finer description of those "new kinds of possible order" that Williams discovers in Wordsworth but that critics have since left unexplored.

In my attempt to reconstruct the understanding of urbanization in eighteenth-century and Romantic-period writing, I refer to and rely on modern urban theory. Modern urban theory helps to organize the often inexplicit connections within historical discourses that precede the emergence of the disciplines of urban theory, social geography, and, indeed, that precede the appearance of the word "urbanization." Genealogies of urban theory rarely reach back beyond Engels; in the Romantic period, scholarly interest in urban development took the form of a fashion for antiquarian histories of individual cities.[20] But the absence of a formal discipline of urban studies by no means implies that writers of the period had a naïve sense of the political, economic, and cultural determinations and consequences of urbanization. The work of David Harvey provides a framework for interrelating these determinations that can also, with a few adaptations, link a theory of urbanization to a post-Habermasian concept of publics and to Bourdieu's model of the literary field. Harvey conceives of urbanization as an inherent component and product of the process of progressive accumulation in capitalism: it both expedites the realization of surplus value by rationalizing the spatial and temporal coordination of the means of production (including labor), distribution, and consumption, and absorbs enormous amounts of surplus value into the physical and social environments of cities.[21] "Capital," Harvey summarizes, "represents itself in the form of a physical landscape created in its own image, created as use values to enhance the progressive accumulation of capital."[22] Far from professing a reductive economic determinism, however, Harvey regularly adverts to the complex political, social, and cultural tensions and pressures that shape conscious and unconscious decisions about social geography. Urbanization, Harvey argues, "means a certain mode of human organization in space and time that can somehow embrace all of these conflicting forces, not necessarily so as to harmonize them, but to channel them into so many possibilities of both creative and destructive social transformation."[23] This field of conflicting forces produces the historical form of urbanization. The poets of the Romantic period took up and shaped an alternative discourse on urbanization in order to help channel those conflicts creatively.

A graph of the proportion of the population in England that lived in towns would show a sweeping upward curve from the sixteenth century through the Romantic period. The curve would appear to be a sign of steady, progressive modernization. Around 1600, about 6 percent of the population lived in cities or towns, and the overwhelming majority of that urban population lived in London. Despite plagues, cholera epidemics, and the Great Fire of 1666, the population of London continued to grow both absolutely and relative to the rest of the nation. By 1700, its population had nearly tripled to 575,000; by 1800, the metropolitan area had around one million residents. Between 1801 and 1831, London gained another 800,000 people. At the same time, the populations of Liverpool, Manchester, and

Leeds expanded geometrically, and by 1851, half the population of England lived in cities.[24] But the continuous line of the curve evens out a series of uncertain shifts and interferences between dominant modes of production and regimes of political power, each with distinctive ways of regulating social tensions and influencing cultural expression; it blends together several historical forms of urbanization into one continuous process and masks that each point along the curve represents a tenuous balance between conflicting social pressures.

In retrospect, urbanization in the Romantic period appears as part of a broader process of capitalist modernization. Yet the teleological tendency in the concepts of urbanization and modernization obscures the range of futures once perceived as possible and, in doing so, reduces the range of positions available in Romantic-period culture to a one-dimensional binary of facilitating or resisting modernization rather than an open and multidimensional consideration of alternative possibilities. To absorb the history of urbanization into a narrative of capitalist modernization would be to miss the specific value of considering the alternative discourse on urbanization and to overlook both its perceptive diagnoses of the consequences of a historical form of urbanization and its imaginative intimations of alternative ways of organizing society and alternative urban sensibilities and cultures.[25] In the brief sketch of the history of urbanization in England that follows, I emphasize the influence of the pursuit of capital accumulation on the historical form of urbanization and the complicated interrelations between the equally dynamic economic, political, social, and cultural dimensions of urbanization. A change in any one dimension sets off changes in all other dimensions. The alternative discourse on urbanization emergent in the Romantic period represents this process as inequitable, prone to crises, and susceptible to active reform.

Harvey's theory of urbanization ties the production of space to the flows of capital, the evolution of the distribution of political power, and the ideological force of cultural production. In its restless motion in service of progressive accumulation, Harvey observes, capital must pass through the relatively immobile form of fixed capital. Fixed capital includes factors of production (such as heavy machinery and furnaces), the physical spaces of production (such as workshops and factories), the spaces of consumption (such as shops), and the physical infrastructure that facilitates transportation (such as turnpikes, canals, bridges, and docks). The organization of the built environment images the organization of capital circulation at a historical moment and represents the ongoing negotiations between residual, dominant, and emergent formations of economic activity.

The flow of capital ties urbanization to the wider economic processes reshaping social geography: as Williams so lucidly reveals, urban expansion and agricultural transformation were mutually enabling parts of a single process. Two large changes in the agricultural economy fed the gradual urbanization of England from the sixteenth to the early nineteenth centuries. First, during the sixteenth and seventeenth centuries, yeoman farmers gradually but substantially increased the yield per acre of the land through intensive labor and the adoption of best practices such as improved crop rotations. Yeomen held long leases and both tenants and landlords profited from higher yields. This increase in food production supported the growing population of the nation and of London in particular, which maintained the demand for food. As yields rose and trade increased, farming gradually shifted from a relatively subsistence economy to a largely capitalist enterprise. Second, as land became more productive and more valuable, landlords raised rents and shortened leases, merged smaller farms into larger ones, and extended their holdings through engrossment and enclosure. Agricultural labor was increasingly done not by tenants themselves but by wage laborers and became more productive.[26] A steady stream of laborers migrated from the country to the cities, where expanding trade, manufacturing, and demand for personal services created opportunities for employment.[27]

The growth of London integrated the national economy. The work of supplying the busy world of the metropolis marshaled much of the country's resources. London's constant demand for provisions encouraged regional agricultural specialization; its need for labor drew in deterritorialized rural laborers; its need for goods consumed in commerce (barrels, ships, brooms, nails, bottles) and in everyday life (boots, clothes, carriages) supported large metal works in Birmingham, shoemakers in Northampton, and artisan tradesmen in London; the maintenance and development of its built environment sustained a constant demand for timber, brick, and stone, and still more materials went into massive projects such as its bridges, docks, and canals; its demand for coal for domestic heating developed the heavy mining industry.[28] London drew raw materials and unfinished goods from the provinces and returned finished goods and capital. Throughout the eighteenth century, the metropolis was also the most important port for international trade.[29] These great flows of commodities and capital were coordinated through London's commercial and financial firms, and at the beginning of the Romantic period London was still the primary site of the urbanization of capital. But by integrating the national economy, London also created conditions that allowed an unprecedented spread of urbanization to the provinces.

The integration of the national economy required substantial improvements in transportation infrastructure, and the emergence of networks of canals and turnpikes transformed the flows of goods and people within cities and the economic relations between cities. Canals and turnpikes reduced transportation time and costs for commodities, people, and information, and were attractive investments that promised relatively high and secure returns.[30] Cobbett recognizes the connection between transportation, capital accumulation, and a form of urbanization that he vehemently opposes. To Cobbett, canals and turnpikes are so many profitable instruments for London's omnium eaters masquerading as a national good: "Talk of *roads* and *canals* and *bridges*! These are no signs of *national prosperity*. They are signs of *accumulated*, but not *diffused* property."[31] The improved infrastructure tightened interurban competition. The industrial manufacturing towns that mushroomed in the Romantic period arose near shipping routes, canals, and roads that gave them a competitive advantage over other towns by lowering the cost of factors of production such as coal and of distributing finished goods. Towns that could not compete contracted. "One estimate," Peter Borsay writes, "suggests that by 1770 perhaps as many as a third of the market towns of Tudor and early Stuart England had become extinct," largely because "the smaller towns were unable to compete with the superior commercial facilities offered to both buyers and sellers by their larger neighbours, a trend exacerbated by improvements in road and water transport."[32]

The integration of the national market and the tightening of commercial competition brought with them innovations in urban modes of production and reconfigurations of class relations. During the eighteenth century and into the Romantic period, employers sought to increase productivity by rationalizing the division of labor (as in Adam Smith's example of a pin factory), developing the industrial mode of production, and refining flexible labor arrangements such as the putting-out system. Different industries in different regions adopted different organizations of labor, and their influence on urban development and class relations varied by city. In the manufacturing towns, industrial production generated relatively stark class divisions, while in London and in the port cities, the greater variety of economic activities maintained complex fields of class relations. Industrialization, that is to say, was an important but not defining element of Romantic-period urbanization: as late as 1831, one-tenth of the male workforce was employed in industrial manufacture.[33] In London, guild restrictions and apprenticeship laws loosened as production moved outside the walls of the City; wage and piece labor became more common; and the intensification of the division of labor in handicrafts raised concerns about deskilling among the large artisan population. The flows of capital that drove the historical form of urbanization contributed to the coalescence of an urban working class. At the same time, the tasks of managing larger enterprises and coordinating ever-expanding commerce required lawyers, clerks, and bookkeepers and swelled the ranks of the professional middle orders.

In the Romantic period the movement of capital had a greater influence on the development of the built environment of British cities than it did on continental cities. The more closely an account of urbanization approaches specific examples of development, the more the abstract determinations are complicated by the chaotic interference of the contingencies of particular cases and by the wills of specific human agents. But even so, relative to the development of other major European cities, urban development in England during the Romantic period followed the play of private interests in the market without central planning. Among European capitals, London alone, John Summerson notes, was "raised by private, not by public, wealth"; it was, in Roy Porter's words, "above all the uncontrolled city."[34] The relative lack of central planning derives in part from the division between the commercial center of the City and the government seat in Westminster and in part from the fact that the city sprawled over a hodgepodge of administrative districts. Donald Low remarks that, while the City had a capable administration, the rest of London comprised "a kind of twilit administrative no-man's-land made up of over ninety parishes or precincts situated within the three counties of Middlesex, Surrey and Kent."[35] For much of London, there was no center that could coordinate a major plan.

As Francis Sheppard explains in his lucid histories of London, from the sixteenth century through the Romantic period, London was built primarily through speculative leaseholds.[36] Landowners leased their undeveloped property at low ground rents to developers for a set term – in the Romantic period, leases were usually for ninety-nine years. In most cases, the landowner and developer would agree on a plan for the property, giving some coherence to the estate.[37] With few exceptions, this was the scale of urban planning in London. The developer, often subcontracting with a builder, would oversee the development of the land and either run the property or sell the rights to the rents to another agent. At the end of the lease, the land and its improvements would revert to the possession of the landowner.

Developers had an incentive to build quickly and cheaply and move on to other projects; property managers had an incentive to maximize rents received – even if that meant building beyond the original plan and overcrowding – and to minimize maintenance near the reversion date. Under the leasehold system, developers often attempted to appeal first to affluent tenants, but buildings "often degenerated into slums within a decade or two of their erection," though, as Porter observes, "whether a particular zone rose or slid down-market depended upon hosts of local eventualities: the lie of the land . . . the savvy of landlords, the proximity of transport and industry – to say nothing of timing and luck."[38] By passing obligations through several hands, the leasehold system encouraged waves of speculative building; as Sheppard remarks, "it was in fact easier for a man to start speculating than to stop, and the result was excessive building followed by a slump."[39] Building advanced in cycles of boom and bust: the booms drove and were driven by economic expansions, while the busts coincided with recessions and financial crises. Between the 1780s and the 1810s speculation helped drive up the price of land in London by about 50 percent.[40]

Under the leasehold system, London's expansion was largely determined by the interaction of private interests. Construction of new bridges and the widening of London Bridge opened Southwark to residential and eventually industrial development; the population south of the river increased about sixfold between 1750 and the end of the century.[41] Building continued on the prestigious west end and in the northern suburbs, where rows of townhouses and detached cottages catered to the swelling and mobile professional classes. Cobbett, again thinking about the distribution of wealth, queries the assumption that the fine suburban houses "added to the Wen," that is, London, "are proofs of *growing prosperity*, are they? These make part of the *increased capital of the country*, do they? But, how is this *Wen* to be *dispersed*?"[42] This pattern of growth also bothers Edmund Burke, who contrasts the grand monuments of Rome, which present an ennobling image of collective aspiration, with the petty private interests manifest in London: "What is London? Clean, commodious, neat; but, a very few things indeed excepted, an endless addition of littleness to littleness, extending itself over a great tract of land."[43]

Urban development tended to reinforce residential segregation along class lines and to increase the disparity between living conditions. These divisions were starkest in the manufacturing cities. Engels notes that, in Manchester, "by unconscious tacit agreement, as well as with outspoken conscious determination, the working-people's quarters are sharply separated from the sections of the city reserved for the middle class."[44] The private interests of property owners strongly determined the form of these cities: the masters lived in suburbs, while laborers crowded in slums. The expansion of the laboring population far outpaced the passage of building regulations to ensure proper ventilation and drainage or the provision of public utilities and amenities such as sewage systems, parks, and hospitals.[45] Rosemary Sweet records that an "improvement bill in Liverpool, which proposed to close down all occupied cellars in 1802, was defeated by the property owners who stood to lose out on rent."[46] Disease spread rapidly in overcrowded working-class districts. Cities were known to be population sinks: Arthur Young cites Montesquieu to prove that depopulation results from "the number of people crowded into a close unwholsome [*sic*] spot," and Malthus lists urban growth among the positive checks on population growth.[47] In London a general division between classes held, with the laboring districts east of the City and the nobility to the west, though pockets of mid-rate housing and an archipelago of rookeries significantly complicated the general pattern. John Nash presented the design of Regent Street in London – the largest project of central urban planning in the Romantic period – not only as a thoroughfare to gratify the Regent's desire for a route from Carlton House to what would become Regent's Park untroubled by the relatively run-down neighborhoods of Soho but also as a public good that would improve sanitation in the area.[48] John Barrell notes that Regent Street was redeveloped "with the express intention of marking a grand symbolic boundary between east and west, or drawing, as Nash put it, a 'Line of Separation' between the 'Streets and Squares occupied by the Nobility and Gentry' and 'the narrow Streets and meaner houses occupied by mechanics and the trading part of the community.'"[49]

As a product in part of capital flowing through a variety of modes of production, circulation, and consumption, the historical form of urbanization in the Romantic period was inseparable from a concurrent realignment of class relations; changes in class relations were inseparable from changes in the ideological conceptions of the classes; and these ideological conceptions informed new political, social, and cultural practices. While urbanization further enriched aristocratic landowners by raising property values, the greatest beneficiaries, relatively, were the merchants, manufacturers, financiers, and professional classes. In the eighteenth century, as J. G. A. Pocock demonstrates, traditionally aristocratic political virtues of independence, intelligence, and worldliness came to be attributed to the man of commerce along with new virtues such as time discipline and enterprise.[50] The urban middle orders leveraged their social and ideological influence through the journals and coffeehouses of the public sphere and through the opposition within Parliament to push for a reform of the franchise and a redistribution of parliamentary representation. James Mackintosh argues in the *Edinburgh Review* that representation should be transferred from rotten boroughs to the new cities: "Villages have since sprung up into immense cities; great manufactures have spread over wastes and mountains; ease, comfort and leisure, have introduced, among the middling classes of society, their natural companions, curiosity, intelligence, boldness, and activity of mind. A much greater proportion of the collective knowledge and wealth of the nation has thus fallen to their lot."[51] Mackintosh links urbanization to the increasing wealth and political virtue of the middling orders and to the polite reform movement. A similar coordination between urbanization and calls for political reform appears in the commonplace association of Dissenters with urban commerce and oppositional politics.

The lower orders felt their social standing jeopardized or degraded by the historical form of urbanization and, being largely excluded from official channels for political action and for forming public opinion, exploited the improved means of organizing generated by urbanization. London artisans, long allied with Wilkesite opposition and City interests, found more radical and self-directed modes of political activity in the London Corresponding Society and among the Spenceans. Radical artisans opposed the dissection of labor processes and the liberal reduction of social relations to a competition among individuals; perceiving a realignment of class interests, they organized in working-class taverns with wage laborers, held large meetings in fields around the city, and, especially in the Regency, formed publics around their own newspapers.[52] Manchester weavers, organized by newspapers, common industry, and physical proximity, with no other means of political expression, turned to mass demonstrations and sought to coordinate with national networks of radicals. Haunted by memories of the Gordon Riots and revolutionary Paris, polite culture and political discourse remained wary of political activity among the urban lower orders.

The economic and political realignments worked by urbanization also reshaped class relations in the domain of culture. The wealth generated through urbanization helped to sustain demand for luxury goods, including polite culture. The demand for luxury goods helped sustain a "consumer society"; and one of the attractions of town life was that it offered access to scarce luxuries.[53] As Peter Borsay demonstrates, provincial towns invested in recreational facilities for the polite classes, building assembly halls, promenades, theatres, and racetracks in order to attract luxury spending. The luxury trade had a large footprint in London: in the late eighteenth century approximately 20 percent of London shops specialized in luxury goods.[54] A prominent current of eighteenth-century moral philosophy associated urban luxury with refined sociability and saw it as "part of a wider movement, an English enlightenment, whose underlying mission was to rescue the nation from barbarity and ignorance; in a word, to *civilize* it."[55] This civilizing process, as Gillian Russell argues, increased the social influence of women of the higher ranks. Polite women set the standards for fashionable consumption, managed the social calendar, and embodied the refinement of culture.[56] In an essay originally titled "Of Luxury," Hume correlates the progress of luxury, refined culture, and civilization:

> The more these refined arts advance, the more sociable men become; nor is it possible, that, when enriched with science, and possessed of a fund of conversation, they should be contented to remain in solitude, or live with their fellow-citizens in that distant manner, which is peculiar to ignorant and barbarous nations. They flock into cities; love to receive and communicate knowledge; to show their wit or their breeding.[57]

The ideal of refinement tended to separate polite and plebeian cultural spheres: among the higher orders, at least officially, lectures filled the place of cockfights. In order to receive, communicate, and display their learning, polite consumers supported a heavy trade in print materials, including journals, newspapers, and books. The urban renaissance faltered with the interruption of trade during the Napoleonic Wars, but it rekindled, however briefly, during the Regency.

This desire to "civilize" urban culture involved taking disciplinary action against popular culture. Makdisi, Newman, and Vic Gatrell have studied efforts to police and sanitize the morals and politics of plebeian culture in London, such as the work of the Society for the Suppression of Vice and the crackdown on ballad singing in city streets. Popular culture adapted. Literacy rates have historically been higher in urban areas, where print is ubiquitous, and Sunday schools – founded in part as a disciplinary reaction to the "misery and idleness" of "wretchedly ragged" children in manufacturing towns who "spend their time in noise and riot" – raised literacy rates higher still.[58] Periodicals and cheap editions of books appeared to supply this emerging market and to constitute its audiences. Lending libraries sprouted up in cities across the country and circulated books through the upper strata of the lower orders.[59] This new reading public, nascent in the 1790s, grew larger, more independent, and more conscious of its influence after Waterloo with the rise of Cobbett's two-penny trash.

The field of conflicting forces within Romantic-period urbanization generated a conflict between the dominant discourse on urbanization derived largely from eighteenth-century political economy and moral philosophy and an emergent, alternative discourse that dialectically focused on the empirically and ideologically questionable representations of the dominant discourse. This emergent discourse appears in the poetry of the period, refracted both by the conventions of a genre that represented itself as threatened by urbanization and by the intellectual backgrounds of individual poets. In the first chapter, I describe the nature and stakes of the emergent discourse on urbanization by recovering and contrasting the understandings of urbanization implicit in the different figural repertoires for representations of urban life in eighteenth-century poetry and Romantic-period poetry. In the chapters that follow, I focus on individual poets in order to account for the range of poetic expressions of the emergent discourse; for the idiosyncrasy of each poet's intellectual background, figurative logics, and discursive situations; and for the range of concerns associated with urbanization. These chapters – on Coleridge, Wordsworth, Shelley, and on Robinson and Barbauld – cover texts from the mid-1790s to the last years of the Regency and proceed in roughly chronological order. The emphasis of the alternative discourse on urbanization changes with the times, as the violence in Paris fades further into the past, the great manufacturing towns mushroom in the midlands, and cheap radical journals intensify the pressure for reform in urban centers. While these chapters model different critical approaches adapted to analyze different concerns in the works of different poets, they also share an interest in disclosing the ways in which each poet's treatment of each concern interconnects with the treatment of each other concern. The differences between the poets' perspectives indicate that their discourse is only emergent; the convergences reveal a set of tensions, questions, or positions characteristic of that discourse. This set of overlapping concerns gives rise to themes that thread through all the chapters, including a concern with the ability of societies actively to shape the urbanization of history, with the condition of the urban working classes, with the formation of urban publics, and with the place of poetry in an urbanizing society.

Where the dominant discourse represented urbanization as natural and necessary, the emergent discourse reopened the question of the role individual and conscious collective agency might have in shaping social geography and its associated cultural, social, and mental formations. Writing within the dominant discourse, Adam Smith argues that the autonomous operation of the market produces urbanization. The market drives the increasing division of labor, the integration of markets, and the improvement of commerce. This process, for Smith, naturally increases both the accumulated wealth of the nation and the quality of life for all its members. From this perspective, the degree of urbanization serves as an index of the progress of civilization: in stadial models of history, civilizations advance through a series of stages of development defined by different modes of production, patterns of development, and cultural formations, from savage hunting to pastoral husbandry to settled agriculture and finally to urban commerce. The history of urbanization becomes the urbanization of history. Wordsworth entertains this premise when he refers to London in Book 8 of *The Prelude* as "The Fountain of my Country's destiny / And of the destiny of Earth itself."[60] The emergent discourse on urbanization challenges the premise that urbanization is natural and considers in what ways and to what extent it may be responsive to individual and collective agency.

The alternative discourse no longer assumes that the historical form of urbanization is natural and beneficial, and it offers new and more sympathetic representations of the conditions of the urban working and artisan classes. Smith boasts that the lowliest worker in England enjoys greater material comforts than the richest savage king, while at the same time he warns that highly routinized labor stunts the development of the moral and intellectual capabilities of workers. In the alternative discourse, these conditions are represented as neither natural nor necessary: the impairments they produce appear partial, reversible, and susceptible to reform, and the potential for healthy social relations and cultural practices appears behind the obstacles to their realization. Proposals for reform fall along a spectrum from adjustments to political representation and labor practices that aim to relieve direct and potentially revolutionary social tensions to radical reimaginings of the fabric of the social order that would produce new labor relations, new mentalities, and a new social geography. Blake's radical vision of community fundamentally differs from the liberal premises shared by Coleridge, Wordsworth, Shelley, Robinson, and Barbauld, but these poets all appeal for more equitable systems for distributing wealth, political power, and opportunities to participate in culture, and all implicitly warn that, without some reform, the urban lower orders may express their discontent in violent or disruptive protest.

These Romantic-period poets came to this emergent discourse in part through their experience in reformist and radical coteries within urban publics. Various urban social and institutional conduits transmitted various radical discourses, ranging from seventeenth-century republicanism, to the culture of Dissent that absorbed Coleridge first in Cambridge and then in Bristol, to the circles of antinomian artisans in London that encompassed Blake. These conduits included print institutions such as Joseph Cottle's print shop in Bristol, Joseph Johnson's shop in London, Daniel Stuart's *Morning Post*, and Leigh Hunt's Hampstead cottage and London office. Considered more extensively, urban print production preserved these discourses and disseminated them throughout the country, facilitating the cross-pollination of intellectual traditions. The poets' experiences in urban scenes – Blake among London's artisans, Wordsworth in Paris, Coleridge in Bristol, and Barbauld in Hampstead – shape their sense of the effects of urbanization and the intellectual lenses through which they see it. These poets recognize in their works that the growth of cities magnifies the resources of political resistance and repression; they are especially interested in the formation of radical publics, with the contagious spread of opinion within them, and with their power to organize protest meetings, assemblies, and perhaps revolutions.

Finally, these poets share a common concern over the place of poetry in an urbanizing society. As Wordsworth notes in the Preface to *Lyrical Ballads*, the social changes correlative with urbanization changed the relative position of genres in the literary field. Wordsworth recognized that the novel and the periodical press enjoyed increased readerships. In his history of the novel, Ian Watt argues that the expansion of the reading public in the eighteenth century was largely confined to towns, which had a greater population of the literate middling sort who wished to read novels about lives like their own.[61] Newspapers saturated cities and penetrated into the country and were an important vehicle for and perceived threat to poetry. The readership for poetry grew both through its distribution in newspapers and periodicals and through sales of books.[62] In the terms of the dominant discourse on urbanization, the hurry and commerce of urban life were uncongenial to the kind of deliberate and collected reflection that poetry generically represented to itself as a condition of its production and reception or consumption. The emergent discourse on urbanization appears in poetry not only directly but also in generic, formal, and stylistic strategies for negotiating with a reading audience fractured along class lines and mentally conditioned by the historical form of urbanization. These poets theorize how poetry's unique repertoire of strategies and tactics and its specific adaptation to the transmission of feeling and the cultivation of imagination may directly or indirectly influence public discourse and the course of urbanization.

These themes weave throughout the following chapters and their relative prominence varies with the peculiarities of each poet's intellectual concerns and with the historical circumstances in which each poet writes. Within the roughly thirty-year sweep of this book, the material situation of urbanization changes in ways that reshape Romantic-period writers' engagements with it. As Kevin Gilmartin has demonstrated, radicalism sank down between 1790s, when the strongest current of radicalism came from groups of Dissenters and London artisans, and the postwar years, when radicalism became a far more plebeian phenomenon through the publication of Cobbett's *Political Register* and the emergence of working-class organizations.[63] By 1820 groups of democrats were wary of each other: liberals in the City or in suburban Hampstead were suspicious of the laboring radicals in Spitalfields.[64] At the same time, public and private opposition to democratic agitation had proven remarkably resilient and resourceful. After the French wars, the government financed a massive project to build more churches and barracks in London and the new towns to maintain order – "barracks there must be," Cobbett remarks, "or *Gatton* and *Old Sarum* must fall."[65] In the later Romantic period, the emergent discourse of urbanization acquires a sharper tone; it becomes more caustic and ironic as the obstacles to meaningful reform appear more obstinate and as conditions in the manufacturing towns draw more attention.

In designing this argument, I have sought to construct a conceptual framework capable of placing the works of other poets writing in and of other cities with different concerns in relation to broad cultural concerns. I seek to counteract the tendency toward abstraction in a reconstruction of a discourse and an examination of a process as pervasive and elusive as urbanization by rooting specific analyses in Coleridge's Bristol, Wordsworth's London, the Manchester of Peterloo, and the poetry office of London newspapers.

In my first chapter, I trace the evolution of constructions of specifically urban experience in eighteenth-century and Romantic-period poetry. I follow the fundamental insight of Castells that models of the effects of the urban environment on people's behaviors and attitudes – familiar in commonplace assumptions about urban alienation, anomie, and rationality and in academic essays such as Georg Simmel's "The Metropolis and Mental Life" – are historically mutable ideological myths that assign to the city effects produced by other factors, especially the conditions of production. John Gay in *Trivia* (1716) and William Cowper in *The Task* (1785) adapt the forms of the dominant urban ideology to the social pressures of their times, while the emergent discourse in the Romantic period, here represented by William Blake in "London" (1794) and *Jerusalem* (1815–20?) and William Wordsworth in *The Prelude* (1805), critically reveals the ideological work of these constructs and imagines instead alternative models of urban experience. The chapter establishes the distinction between the historical form of urbanization and urbanization per se in the dimension of mental and behavioral urbanization.

In the second chapter, in a study of Coleridge's work, the question of the relation between poetry and urbanization appears as a specific instance of the broader question of the relation between culture and society. On a theoretical plane, I connect Bourdieu's model of the literary field with Harvey's theory of the geography of capital. Coleridge recognizes that the social geography of the accumulative system has an inescapable influence on literary production and yet he tries throughout his career to imagine practical and theoretical ways to evade such determinations. During 1795–96, Coleridge tries to earn a living in the literary field in Bristol while arguing against urban commercial markets: his projected utopian commune, Pantisocracy, is both an image of an escape from urban markets and a stance within an urban market. In "Reflections on Having Left a Place of Retirement" and "This Lime-Tree Bower My Prison," Coleridge exposes independent retirement as a fiction and projects autonomy into epistemological terms. In his later prose and lectures, he continues to assert that works of genius may arise in cities, even as he concedes that cultivation depends on civilization for its means of action. His celebrations of an ideal autonomous culture always point back to the practical heteronomy of his present urban cultural production.

Wordsworth's poetry contains a searching analysis of the influence of urbanization in a wider social reorganization of structures of feeling. Wordsworth writes with an awareness of a broad transition from customary to market-driven modes of social relations – a transition later analyzed by E. P. Thompson – that detaches laborers from the land, regulates their work by the clock, and, by deskilling their labor, diminishes their investment in their work. Conditions that fostered the maturation of strong feelings yield to conditions that stunt the emotional and intellectual lives of laborers. In the Preface to *Lyrical Ballads*, Wordsworth entertains this line of thought, while also subverting its generalizations about the affects of urbanization. In his ambivalent pastoral *Michael*, Wordsworth speculates about the possibility of translating conventionally rural communal values into urban social relations, while in other urban lyrics he imagines how poetry, as the genre best adapted to communicate powerful feeling, might help affect this translation and subtly change the affective charge of class relations and defuse the potential for Jacobin violence.

Shelley's writings in the months after the Peterloo Massacre examine the political implications of urbanization. On a theoretical level, Shelley correlates a civilization's state of development with the extent of democratic liberty its institutions support, and his poetry is littered with images of cities ruined by tyranny as a warning to contemporary London. In *A Philosophical View of Reform*, Shelley analyzes how urbanization since the Restoration has helped to concentrate the resources of political representation in the hands of a wealthy few: the rich control parliamentary representation and control what can be made public and what cannot. To avoid the coming ruin, an unforeseeable change must take place, a change Shelley hopes to encourage by shaping the nation's response to the Peterloo Massacre. In *The Mask of Anarchy*, Shelley skeptically overlays various outcomes of the attempt to change the course of the nation through poetry: perhaps in present circumstances the poem cannot be published; perhaps it cannot be understood; or perhaps it can help light a spark that will retroactively reveal the previously invisible conditions that allow for the possibility of its publication and influence. Social progress depends on such constant redefinitions of the conditions of publicity and, as such, on the continuous reshaping of urbanization.

To conclude the study, I examine how Mary Darby Robinson and Anna Letitia Barbauld arrive at the alternative discourse on urbanization by negotiating the conflict between the conceptions of urbanization in the discourses of civic humanism and Enlightenment moral philosophy. I focus specifically on their use of the concept of luxury, a point of contradiction between the two discourses. While Robinson and Barbauld adopt the correlation in Enlightenment moral philosophy of luxury with urbanization, cultural refinement, sociability, greater opportunities for women, and historical progress, they also leverage the residual moral force of the civic humanist conception of luxury as a vice against the free hand Enlightenment moral philosophy gives to commerce and the historical form of urbanization that that discourse has underwritten. For Robinson and Barbauld luxury is a metonymy for both polite cultural consumption and the production and distribution of the surplus. Robinson celebrates luxury insofar as it supports the arts, but she criticizes the accelerating tempo and relentless mutability of fashions of commercial cultural production and consumption, which she encountered in an extreme form as chief poetic contributor for the *Morning Post* and which she saw systemically disadvantaging women writers. Barbauld similarly criticizes the encroachment of time discipline – and with it abstract conceptions of space and time and the wage relation – as a threat to the amiable sociability that radiates from the feminine intimate sphere and a possibly ruinous violation of the natural rhythms of producing the surplus.

1

Urban Ideology in Eighteenth-Century and Romantic Poetry

I noted in the Introduction that to think in terms of urbanization instead of metropolitanism or the city is to focus attention on a complex and dynamic social process that comprises demographic, geographic, structural, behavioral, and cultural transformations. Urbanization is a complex process in which a change in one of its dimensions produces changes in each other dimension. And yet, how changes carry and convert from one dimension to the others, what mechanisms mediate those mutual adjustments, and what relative gradients of convertibility define the structure of the process remain matters for critical analysis. The study of literature has proven to be a productive interdisciplinary interlocutor for urban theory, especially for its insight into historical understandings of the relation between the urban environment and particular forms of consciousness, behavior, and culture.

When literary critics examine this relation, however, they tend to rely on a line of urban theorists who argue that the urban environment determines a typical mentality, set of behaviors, and values. These theorists deduce the nature of urban mentalities and cultures out of the formal attributes of cities, such as the size or density of the population or the diversity of occupations within a relatively coherent area of development. The most commonly cited example of this determinist approach is Georg Simmel's "The Metropolis and Mental Life." Simmel famously associates the form of life in the metropolis – characterized by the diversity and intensity of its sensory stimuli, its tendency to replace social relations with monetary relations, and the pressures to fit into its refined division of roles – with a psychological profile of "metropolitan individuality."[1] The resident of the metropolis, Simmel claims, adopts a defensive, blasé attitude to screen out distractions, reduces qualitative distinctions to quantitative differences, emphasizes intellection over feeling, and pursues endless specialization in order to stand apart from the crowd of competitors. In his classic essay "Urbanism as a Way of Life," Louis Wirth cites Simmel approvingly and goes still further. From the size of the city, Wirth deduces a multiplicity of superficial social encounters, the loosening of community ties, the predominance of anonymity and superficiality, and the emergence of anomie and a "schizoid" character; from the highly differentiated urban social functions, he infers "Personal disorganization, mental breakdown, suicide, delinquency, crime, corruption, and disorder"; from the heterogeneity of urban social encounters, he deduces a tendency toward cosmopolitanism, relativism, and secularism.[2]

Even though urban sociologists have disputed the determinist approach on theoretical and empirical grounds and have emphasized the importance of other factors, such as group identities and subcultures, against ecological determinations, the determinist approach continues to resonate in the popular mind. "As we have often found to be the case," Claude Fischer remarks, "determinist theory and popular image are . . . quite similar."[3] Manuel Castells argues that this similarity arises because the deterministic theory attempts to explain and naturalize a deeply ingrained model of urban mentalities and cultures rather than question that model critically. He refers to theories of ecological determination as "urban ideology." This ideology, Castells observes, "is not confined to academic tradition"; it "has deep social roots" and "is, above all, in people's heads."[4]

For Castells, the urban ideology implies a philosophy of history that subjects the individual to abstract historical processes. He traces its academic genealogy back to Oswald Spengler and the early German sociologists and argues that it emerged out of "the ideological schema of a dualistic rural/urban, agricultural/industrial, traditional/modern society." The historical narrative associated with this familiar set of stark, reductive contrasts between conventional images of traditional rural life and modern urban life can in turn be traced back through the Romantic period to Enlightenment universal history. Like universal history, this schema relates social organization and culture to "the technico-natural conditions of human existence and, ultimately, to its environment."[5] For Simmel, the place of the abstract phases of history is filled by an equally abstract and determinative spirit of history: "The development of modern culture is characterised by the predominance of what one can call the objective spirit over the subjective; that is, . . . there is embodied a sort of spirit [*Geist*], the daily growth of which is followed only imperfectly and with an even greater lag by the intellectual development of the individual."[6] The historical spirit (*Geist*) realized in the physical environment develops in advance of and determines the historical form of the mental life (*Geistesleben*) of the individual. In both universal history and Simmel's spirit of history, the form of modern urban experience is determined by the process of modernization and follows a course determined by abstract laws of history. Castells criticizes these narratives of modernization as ideological masks for uneven development. The historical schema is, Castells argues, "strictly speaking, a myth, since it recounts, ideologically, the history of the human species. Consequently, the writings on 'urban society' which are based directly on this myth, provide the key-words of an ideology of modernity."[7] Urban ideology comprises both this historical schema and the theory of ecological determination.

The theory of ecological determination attempts to assign a set of cultural practices specifically to the urban environment rather than to other determinants operating either independent of the environment or through it. Castells claims that "A detailed analysis of each of the features that characterize it [urban culture] would show without difficulty the causal link, at successive levels, between the structural matrix characteristic of the capitalist mode of production and the effect produced on this or that sphere of behaviour."[8] By assigning responsibility for these characteristics to the urban environment rather than to the processes that determine the environment, the determinist perspective naturalizes the underlying processes, puts the nature of the social order out of the question and beyond the reach of individual or collective agency, and obscures how class, race, gender, and other social formations shape experience. In the eighteenth and early nineteenth centuries, urban ideology evolved to help channel the social pressures of the time.

Literature serves as a record and an instrument of urban ideology: it documents historical representations of putatively urban modes of consciousness, and it helps urban ideology sink into the popular mind by reproducing and disseminating attitudes, topoi, and images that condition the understanding of urban experience and urban experience itself. In *The Country and the City*, Raymond Williams shows how men become "accustomed to seeing their immediate environment through received intellectual and literary forms." Williams's argument implies that this contrast between country and city has had an ideological function since classical antiquity: Quintilian gives the contrast between country and city as his "first example of a stock thesis."[9] Studies of representations of cities have reached an effective consensus that within this long history the model of urban experience changes remarkably quickly and dramatically during the Romantic period. The change is often implied in the historical scope of an argument rather than explicitly analyzed: William Chapman Sharpe and critics of literary modernism trace the imagery, topoi, and perspective of twentieth- and twenty-first-century representations of urban experience back to the Romantics, while Max Byrd, Brean Hammond, and critics of eighteenth-century representations of the city end their studies by looking ahead to Blake and Wordsworth.[10] Williams devotes his central and pivotal chapters to literature of the Romantic period.

This chapter studies the urban ideology encoded within the genres, figures, styles, and perspectives of eighteenth- and early nineteenth-century poetry and traces how that ideology evolves along with changing social conditions. The key texts for such an inquiry are the poems that give the fullest and most influential accounts of the effects of the urban environment on mental and social forms and that most fully represent a specifically urban mode of experience. In the eighteenth century, this means John Gay's *Trivia* and William Cowper's *The Task*. These poems both anticipate elements of the modern constructs of urban mentalities, and to use Simmel and Wirth to analyze them would be to use a theoretical frame to analyze the texts from which that frame in part derives. The historical form of urban ideology in the eighteenth century takes shape in relation to the negotiation of the urbanization of the gentry and the gentrification of the urban. Gay's georgic instruction in the art of walking the streets of London seeks to unite the gentry in town for the season and the prosperous urban ranks within a shared system of manners and culture of consumption. The detached, quantitative, and intellectual aspects of the urban mentality appear in *Trivia* as attributes of an informed consumer. Gay imagines and naturalizes an ideal public order in harmony with private commercial interests and culture. By Cowper's time, however, the dominant theory of the urban mentality more fully represents a middle-class perspective. Cowper incorporates distraction and disorder into his model of the urban mind, and he uses the threat posed by the public space of the city to promote an ideal vision of suburban retirement and of the intimate domestic sphere. These middle-class spaces depend on the busy world of commerce but preserve the illusion of disengaged autonomy.

Critical commentary on representations of urban experience in Romantic-period poetry concentrates on Blake's "London" and on Books 7 and 8 of Wordsworth's *The Prelude*, and I discuss these texts, along with Blake's *Jerusalem*, less from a conviction of their representativeness than from an interest in placing my argument in relation to existing criticism on its own terms. Blake and Wordsworth show the influence of the alternative discourse on urbanization on the construction of urban ideology: conceiving of the forms of urbanization and urban experience as historical rather than natural, they recognize and imagine other forms of urban mentalities. Involved in London's radical artisan culture, Blake represents the dominant form of the urban mentality as a symptom of the present hegemonic commercial order of the city. In the working-class districts of the city, Blake finds alternative models of urban experience and community based on a model of the subject not as an individual pursuing private self-interest but as a part of a divine collective linked to others through ties of love and labor. Blake, like Wordsworth, recognizes the tendency in models of urban behavior to naturalize class relations. More closely affiliated with the milieu of polite London radicalism, Wordsworth tests the limits of generic representations of urban experience even as he reproduces them and subtly sketches a different way of seeing the city that recognizes the common humanity veiled by representations of class differences.

"Inur'd to City Ways": Gay's Instruction in Urban Experience

Once urban ideology has been recognized as a historical construct, representations of urban experience appear as various and as responsive to the ideological pressures of the time as the versions of pastoral. Drafted in 1714 and published in 1716, John Gay's *Trivia* offers a version of ecological determination calculated to negotiate and naturalize a common code of urban manners for the gentry and the middle class, reconciling the landed aristocracy with the values of urban commerce. These common manners posit and sustain a shared culture of competitive consumption, and "The Art of Walking the Streets of London" seeks to establish a set of behaviors that can maintain public order and allow commercial activity to flow uninhibited. This set of customs presupposes and constructs a form of subjectivity implicated in its vision of public order: individuals pursue their private interests in a society structured by commodity relations, and, if they assume that private interests depend on public order, they also assume that public order exists to support private interests. This order relies not only on common customs but on the ability to read people and situations; it requires its own disciplinary knowledge. While Gay presents this order as permanent, he allows that a disturbance might arise from what it excludes, from the unknown working-class quarters where polite people seldom stray.

Trivia carries on the general outline and social project of the urban ideology implied within the generic repertoires of urban poetry since the early seventeenth century. During the early seventeenth century, an expanding royal court, a fuller schedule of parliamentary sessions, and the financial business of estate management drew an increasing share of the landed gentry to London. "It was in this context," Francis Sheppard writes, "that in the early seventeenth century there developed a London 'season.'"[11] The acclimation of the landed grandees to urban life proceeded only gradually and, as Roy Porter notes, "involved no mean persuasion."[12] A robust market of luxuries and services eased the transition and, along with the emergence of a culture of competitive consumption, helped to generate a new pattern of urban life. Lawrence Manley argues that in Caroline London, "the social, literary, and ethical innovations of the urbanizing gentry helped to create a new technology of 'metropolitan' life," one that is "usefully illuminated by Georg Simmel's classic essay on the subject."[13] In the Horatian *vers de société* of the London season, Manley finds evidence of the blasé attitude, of the cultivation of distinction through differentiation, and of the reduction of qualitative to quantitative differences. Although the verse represents these habits of mind as the product of city life, they arise in early modernity not as a natural product of the environment of London but as affected attitudes inseparable from luxury consumption among the gentry. The aspiring merchant classes joined in the culture of consumption and adopted its mentalities and postures. Together the gentle ranks and urban commercial classes established an exclusive and inter-legitimating game of competitive consumption and display. Sociable verse became "an arena for debate between the two classes and parties that had emerged as contending forces in the nation's life."[14] Poetry participated in communicating the values and attitudes that allowed for the urbanization of the gentry and the gentrification of the urban.

As part of their rapprochement, the gentry and the urban commercial classes negotiated a reorganization of the relationships between public and private interests and spaces in the hope of establishing a new, stable order for urban society. As the influence of competitive commerce and the cash economy spread to more aspects of life, Richard Sennett writes, "The struggle for public order in the 18th Century [*sic*] city, and the tension between the claims of public and private life, constituted the terms of a coherent culture."[15] During the long eighteenth century, as John Brewer demonstrates, the scene of high culture shifted from the court to the city, and artists relied less on patronage and more on the market.[16] Cynthia Wall "situates the literature of Restoration and early Augustan England . . . within the historical and cultural contexts of the rebuilding of London after the Great Fire" and relates its concerns to the practical and philosophical questions about the relative claims of public and private interests in the task of rebuilding the city.[17] This negotiation created and took place in the public sphere, where private individuals met in a public forum; "the early periodicals such as *The Tatler* and *The Spectator*," Peter Stallybrass and Allon White argue, "had a central role in ... negotiating a cultural alliance between the gentry, the Court and the town through the formation of an inclusive, refined public gently coerced with a mixture of satire and example, into the ways of tolerance and good manners." Referring to Dryden's prefaces, Stallybrass and White remark how the public sphere's cultivation of refinement and civility sought "to make the audience reform and discipline itself by an internal transformation of its collective *and* individual identity." The new urban public, that is, required and created a new urban individual, someone self-interested, habituated to cash relations, and invested in an ethos of rational calculation. This consensus depends on the "relentless series of *exclusions*" by which polite urban society defines itself against the lower orders and against the vulgar entertainments of the past.[18]

These deep cultural and social tensions influence Gay's model of urban behavior, but its particular form of expression derives largely from the influence of the poetry of his friends and the state of the literary field. These influences overlap: critics tend to interpret Gay's social philosophy by triangulating it with Swift's and Pope's, and his poetry shares with the other Scriblerians the pressure of squaring aristocratic stability with middle-class dynamism.[19] In *Trivia*, Gay fuses georgic and satire, two genres favored by the Scriblerians that carry potentially contradictory attitudes and perspectives.[20] This generic tension is similar in kind to those in Pope's celebration of London's enduring commercial activity in the hybrid georgic and locodescriptive *Windsor Forest* (1713) and in his indirectly admiring mock epic satire on the dunces in *The Dunciad* (1728). Gay also writes of town life in town eclogues such as "Araminta" (1713) and "The Toilette" (1716). The Scriblerians' town eclogues, Markman Ellis notes, circulated first in manuscript and preserve the more intimate relation of author and audience found in older forms of *vers de société*: "the gentle irony of the town eclogue is socially integrative," among polite society, "laughing its readers together by gently exposing the follies of high society."[21] Gay gestures toward a wider public, however, both by publishing his town eclogues and by explicitly appealing in *Trivia* both for patronage and for a favorable placement for his book in the shop window. Gay's position as a professional poet during the economic transformation of the literary field depends on the class concord the poem projects.

Trivia departs from the rest of the poetry of the Scriblerians, however, and introduces a construction of an urban mentality that later texts will take up.[22] Like Swift's "A Description of a City Shower" (1710), *Trivia* presents the city from within. But in contrast to Swift, the speaker of *Trivia*, known in criticism as the Walker, moves about the city, organizes and interprets his observations, and appears as a character as well as an observer. Unlike the rest of Augustan poetry about the urban environment, *Trivia* offers a model of an urban mentality. Gay presents the Walker's patterns of thought and behavior as determined by the urban environment: Philip Carter argues that as a "record of urban experience, *Trivia* highlights how the perceived city shapes the behaviour of its citizens."[23] When Gay celebrates the knowledge of "Experienc'd Men, inur'd to City Ways," "Ways" ambiguously refers to both customs and paths, suggesting the close relation between the structure of the city and the behaviors it constructs.[24] These behaviors and forms of private consciousness participate in the broader cultural renegotiation of the terms of public and private and represent the internalization of the discipline required to maintain the established urban order.

Urban georgic implies a structural contrast or comparison between rural and urban domains, and in *Trivia*, Gay uses the juxtaposition to encourage the urbanization of the rural gentry. *Trivia* fictively instructs a gentleman coming to London for the season – the poem opens with the signs of late fall as "all the *Mall* in leafy Ruin lies" (1.27) and notes in its whimsical index "*summer* [is] *foreign to the Author's Design*" (179) – in the habits and manners proper to a life of leisure and consumption in the city. The generic contrast between rural and urban life generally remains in the background and comes to the fore primarily when Gay sees a chance to display his playful inventiveness by translating tropes of rural life into urban terms.[25] What Gay borrows from the *Georgics* is largely structural and independent of its rural setting. He instructs in useful skills; he uses a loose topical structure marked with description and varied with etiologies; he plays variations on the Orpheus myth; and he reworks descriptions of the weather. Gay chooses georgic instead for its resonance with the desires of polite society. As John Chalker argues, Dryden's translation of Virgil's *Georgics* (1697) had appealed to a nation ready for peace and economic growth by celebrating useful and productive knowledge, profitable arts of living, and national stability and power.[26] Gay transfers the source of stability and power to the commercial world of the city.

In this transference, virtue and vice are displaced into the terms of the legible order of consumer practices. He presents utility as his principle for selection. He contrasts the canes of the fops against that of the practical walker: "Be theirs for empty Show, but thine for Use" (1.68). But show is always part of the utility. When buying a coat, the Walker advises against fine, thin materials that do not stand up in the rain; but the rhetorical question, "Who would wear / Amid the Town the Spoils of *Russia*'s Bear?" (1.50) rules out what might otherwise be a warm winter coat because it is unfashionable. He recommends the "true *Surtout*" (1.58) be made "of *Kersey* firm, though small the Cost" (1.59). The "though small the Cost" implies that the known inexpensiveness of the material would ordinarily reflect poorly on the wearer. Gay's zeugma "Wrapt in my Vertue, and a good *Surtout*" (2.590) shows morality blending into commodified appearances; "miry Spots" can "thy clean Cravat disgrace" (1.78). Much of the art of walking consists in avoiding threats to one's clothes, preserving at once one's commodities and public character from depreciation.

The Walker presents his consumption as virtuously sober, avoiding both vulgarity and excessive luxury. But the goods he recommends are far too expensive for the majority of the population, and the threshold of excess conveniently retreats whenever approached. The Walker admires the luxuries he denounces and qualifies his condemnations.[27] Luxury slips from being a vice to being a symptom of vice. The terms of the contrast between the healthy, social pedestrian and the vicious, indolent rider in a chariot shift:

> See, yon' bright Chariot on its Braces swing . . .
> That Wretch, to gain an Equipage and Place,
> Betray'd his Sister to a lewd Embrace. . . .
> This next in Court Fidelity excells,
> The Publick rifles, and his Country sells.
> May the proud Chariot never be my Fate,
> If purchas'd at so mean, so dear a Rate. (2.573, 575–76, 585–88)

The chariot still represents pride, ostentation, and vice, but the fault lies not in owning the chariot – the virtuous wealthy can own one – but in getting one through dishonorable practices or even at too high a price.[28] The sin in this passage is not luxury but "mean Ambition" (2.569), breaking out of the appropriate order of etiquette or aspiring to a status beyond one's rank.

Gay's urban georgic not only seeks to facilitate the urbanization of the gentry and gentrification of the urban, it also seeks to present the pattern of behavior and city it creates as natural and stable. In Virgil's *Georgics*, the art of agriculture appears as ancient and permanent as the resistance nature poses to human endeavor. Natural rhythms – diurnal, seasonal, annual, biological – appear as eternal cycles stretching back before recorded history and forward into an indefinite future. Virgil claims such permanence for his own verse in teaching this art, performing its timelessness in a dense array of allusions to Lucretius, Callimachus, and Hesiod. Gay parodies Virgil's claims. Experienced Londoners, habituated to commercial cycles, "Need not the *Calendar* to count their Days" (2.406): the same goods have been sold on the same days and in the same seasons since before the Reformation. Walking is a permanent feature of urban life, and Gay jocularly claims that readers will "to my Verse their future Safeties owe" (2.568) and that his poem has made him "ripe for Immortality" (3.408). The poem acknowledges signs of historical change: it comments on the traffic of chariots and coaches, which had become more popular over the preceding century, and concludes with a scene of a fire. This veiled reference to the Great Fire of 1666 defends the pervasive investment in stability by associating change with catastrophe. Otherwise, the poem does not refer to London's rebuilding or expansion, and the historical form of the city appears natural and permanent.

In presenting the city as natural and permanent, Gay presents the art of walking its streets not only as an art but as a science. The environment demands from the Walker a vaguely empirical, analytical way of seeing and thinking. Dianne Ames argues that "the fatuousness of Gay's advice ... soon makes it clear that we will learn from *Trivia* how to exercise our minds rather than our legs"; that is to say, it teaches a way to think rather than a way to walk.[29] This instruction treats as universal the perspective of a polite, educated, white, male subject, who can view the city from the socially insulated vantage of a "professional observer."[30] The professional observer deduces and obeys the laws of the city. Gay invites the reader "From sure Prognosticks learn to know the Skies" (1.122) by providing "certain Signs" of "changing Weather" (1.133) based on observation and implores the reader to discount "All Superstition" (1.175) and "Let not such vulgar Tales debase thy Mind" (1.187). Knowing the city and its routines ensures everyone's safety and keeps traffic moving. The way to avoid scams is to know how they work (3.247–50), and the city appears like a labyrinth until "*Ariadne*'s Clue unwinds the Way" (2.86), and what was a physical thread in myth turns in *Trivia* into a set of directions and a mental map that discloses the straightforward path within what had appeared complicated.

This vision of the city as ordered by rules and patterns and of the Walker as the observer of these rules informs the structure of the poem. At the broadest level, the poem's organization resembles that of an almanac. Each book addresses a general topic; within each book, Gay offers advice on or descriptions of a variety of subtopics; and these subtopics comprise a series of images and witty morals built up in blocks of couplets. The logic of the order at each level can be hard to discern: even the connections between sentences and clauses can be elusive. Gay tends to organize his advice in parallel syntax, often using conditional phrases such as "if . . . then" or "when . . . then" constructs:

> When the *Black Youth* at chosen Stands rejoice,
> And *clean your Shoes* resounds from ev'ry Voice;
> When late their miry Sides Stage-Coaches show,
> And their stiff Horses thro' the Town move slow;
> When all the *Mall* in leafy Ruin lies,
> And Damsels first renew their Oyster Cries:
> Then let the prudent Walker Shoes provide,
> Not of the *Spanish* or *Morocco* Hide. (1.23–30)

The parallel syntax folds up in the procrustean bed of the closed Augustan couplet. In Gay's use, the couplets mark breaks between images. The connection between the images is formal and conceptual: the poem does not attempt to create an illusion of a consistent point of view, and the images do not necessarily succeed each other in time or appear within the same horizon of space. Woodman argues that Gay's handling of the couplet is "brisk" and "comes especially into its own here to represent the stops and starts of his own engaging curiosity, his short-lived, excited attention."[31] The images flash by, but since there is no sustained point of view, the city does not appear distracting. Instead, the specifically conceptual link between the images indicates that the flashes can be synthesized and can reveal the underlying order and rules of the city. The illegible sequencing of the subunits, however, may imply the need for a polite guide. Marginal glosses help to hold the work together and provide a guide to *Trivia* as the Walker provides a guide to London. Gay similarly invokes the goddess Trivia: "Thro' spacious Streets conduct thy Bard along; / By thee transported, I securely stray" (1.6–7).[32] The new wide streets give a more extensive field of view to the observer, and these streets as much as the goddess transport the Walker securely.

The Walker's assertion of order contains a persistent fear of disorder. He worries about getting lost in the labyrinth and straying without security into unknown regions. Philip Carter discerns an atmospheric darkness in the section on walking at night that implies an "equation of the unknown with danger."[33] While the Walker knows the hidden underside of London's polite society, traversing the back alley that connects the two worlds (2.271–84), regions of the city remain unknown to him, especially those working-class districts or what Donald Low calls thieves' kitchens with narrow streets, where he does not feel he can securely stray.

The Walker's system of manners serves a disciplinary function of preserving public order on the terms of the polite classes. Miles Ogborn argues that Londoners negotiated political and social issues not only in the Habermasian public sphere in the coffeehouses but also in the public space of the street. The streets hosted directly political acts of "'mob' riot and elite spectacle." The everyday manners that maintain order on the streets can also be "considered as part of the problematic constitution of new publics of privatised individuals."[34] The public of the street, like the public in the coffeehouse, codifies a set of practices organized around particular values, mentalities, and behaviors: in *Trivia*, Gay translates the putatively rational, polite, and liberal pursuit of private self-interest from the coffeehouse into the streets. The streets and street life are disciplinary apparatuses.

The Walker seeks a public order not for itself but as a condition of the pursuit of private interests. He generally pursues his self-interest – he focuses on the acquisition and preservation of commodities and status – but he nonetheless internalizes a deference to public interest and insists that "due Civilities be strictly paid" (2.45). A healthy male walker, for example, must yield to maids, the elderly, the overburdened, and the blind. But "due Civilities" also cover the scenes of the crowd catching a thief and of the fireman rescuing an infant. Gay's interest in the internalization of the claims of the public suggests his social philosophy resembles less that of Mandeville – whose *Fable of the Bees* (1714) is often cited as expressing a comparable viewpoint – than that of Shaftesbury.[35] Shaftesbury, Mandeville, and Gay all share an interest in relating private interests and public good; in Ogborn's words, they all "attempt . . . to rework the ways in which privatized (and acquisitive) individuals could be constructed and could construct a public."[36] All three would agree with Pope that ultimately "Self-love and Social be the same," but Mandeville absolves the individual from thinking about public interest and lets the mystery of divine wisdom transmute private vices into public good while Shaftesbury and Gay include public good as a factor in the assessment of true self-interest.[37]

True self-interest, for Gay, involves supporting the flow of commerce. In *Trivia*, Alison Stenton argues, Gay presents the relation between the individual and the urban system largely in terms of movement: his interest as a walker is to flow with the crowd.[38] Like commerce, pedestrians in the poem seek to avoid any obstacle to their motion. Interruptions, disturbances, and idleness are menacing threats. When the Thames freezes, its flow is "in icy Fetters bound" (2.360), and fear lingers beneath the carnival atmosphere. The scene opens with "The Waterman, forlorn along the Shore" (361), who "reclines upon his useless Oar" (362) and ends with the grim scene of Doll the fruiterer being decapitated as she falls through the ice. The flow of the streets and the flow of the Thames are inseparable from the flow of trade, and the cessation of the flow is deadly. Dryden opens *Annus Mirabilis* by scorning the Dutch for clotting the circulation of wealth: "Trade, which like bloud should circularly flow, / Stop'd in their Channels, found its freedom lost."[39] The system of manners in *Trivia* permits the continued flow of trade that benefits the private individual.

In the urban world organized around trade, social relations reduce to the superficial, formal, and impersonal encounters of commercial relations. The poem follows convention in quickly identifying people by profession and transforms varieties of social encounters into transactions to be expedited. Most interactions in the poem are specifically commercial. The "Watchmen" will conduct you home at night "with friendly Light" for "*Sixpence*" (3.307–10); the Walker finds himself "stor'd with friendly Bills" (2.540), or advertisements for doctors and tailors. Even Gay's effusive praise of Burlington is a petition for patronage. And when the Walker sets out on a walk with a friend, "the Tide / Tumultuous" (3.91–92), the bustling and irresistible crowd, immediately separates the two forever. The public order of the streets, he seems to imply, brooks no friendship.

The "due Civilities" unite the gentry and middle classes within a single system of manners and regulate the social order by assigning people to their proper roles. Tom Woodman notes that "manners were at the heart of Addison and Steele's whole enterprise of reconciling the upper classes and the commercial interest."[40] J. A. Downie observes, "Like many of his contemporaries, Gay had an ideal view of the way society should be structured and how it should operate" and this ideal must be defended against "*parvenus*" who are too aggressive "in the pursuit of their own advantage" outside of the acceptable channels for promotion.[41] The satirical dimension of *Trivia*, rather than criticizing urban society, gently enforces its proper order among the polite ranks.

Gay's representations of the lower orders project the unstrained class relations that his naturalization of the urban social order necessarily presupposes. The Walker's apparently sociable interactions with the lower orders in *Trivia*, which are more extensive than in poetry before or after, lead Dianne Dugaw to argue that Gay grants "sympathetic attention to the lower ranks" and "gives voice and subjectivity" to marginalized social groups including "children, women, [and] laborers."[42] But the poem assigns roles to the lower orders in a system of manners constructed for the gentry and middle classes and assumes that these roles are for their own and for the common good. The working classes and the destitute appear only in their professional roles as objects in tableaux, and even then they are often only dirty obstacles or hazards. Copley and Haywood observe that Gay "translate[s] the labours of others into decorative spectacle for the entertainment of his readers."[43] Indeed, Gay naturalizes working poverty: the gods have blessed the bootblack with the tools of his trade so that he can work "his destin'd Stand" (2.101). He moralizes on the "happy unown'd Youths" (2.145), those fortunate poor orphans who can bear exposure to the weather, "While the rich Infant ... Thirsts with each Heat" (2.147–48). The poor are bound by the system of manners that maintains order even as it keeps them poor. Gay asks his bookseller Lintott to put *Trivia* in the front window to attract buyers but also "So shall the Poor these Precepts *gratis* know, / And to my Verse their future Safeties owe" (2.567–68). In encounters with beggars, "Those who give late, are importun'd each Day, / And still are teaz'd, because they still delay" (2.459–60). This implies, implausibly, that beggars stop begging from those who give them money: the point of the tableau is instead that it allows those who gave money to think the beggar who renews his petition is violating proper decorum.

The greatest threat to the natural order of the city, Gay's imagery implies but never states, is the potentially unruly crowd. Clare Brant and Susan Whyman note that Tory politicians and clergymen had in 1710 and 1713 "mobilized popular sentiment that led to street demonstrations by what was perceived as a mob"; Tim Harris writes that "both Whigs and Tories actively cultivated support amongst the London masses" and tactically sought "to encourage demonstrations."[44] In the darker and more dangerous atmosphere of the third book, "Of Walking the Streets by Night," the Walker warns not to let the "Ballad-Singer's shrilling Strain / Amid the Swarm thy list'ning Ear detain" (3.77–78); any such pause is a threat to proper commercial circulation and leaves one vulnerable to pickpockets. The Walker imagines the crowd ebbing and flowing into the spacious streets from a network of narrow ways, its motion as irresistible and dangerous as the movements of the sea. When a coach passes through the crowd, "The Rabble part, in Shoals they backward run" (3.84), sweeping out of sight only to rush back in like a "Tide" (3.91). The rude crowd moves swiftly, violently, and with something like its own rhythm.

Gay closes *Trivia* with an image of a fire that recalls Dryden's depiction of the Great Fire in *Annus Mirabilis*. While Gay contains the subtext within an account of a routine fire, the allusion nonetheless introduces into a climactic moment an impression of fire both as a threat capable of destroying the urban order realized in the public ways of London and as a force born in the narrow alleys of a working-class neighborhood unknown to the polite Walker. Dryden writes that the Fire spread from "source unknown" (865) yet specifies that it "in mean buildings first obscurely bred / From thence did soon to open streets aspire" (858–59). While Dryden figuratively overdetermines the Great Fire – in political terms it is associated with Cromwell – it represents the destruction of an established order. Gay's allusion to Dryden introduces the threat of popular insurrection even as recasting the fire as ordinary attempts to contain that threat. The fire and the crowd share figurative movements; they flow and rise: "The spiry Flames now lift aloft their Heads, / Through the burst Sash a blazing Deluge pours" (3.358–59). The glow of the fire makes it appear "The Heav'ns are all a-blaze" (3.375), burning the seats atop the hierarchy and the hierarchy itself, and giving "dire Presage of mighty *Cæsar*'s Doom" (3.378). Having presented and taught with confidence his understanding of the order of the city and the rules of its streets to establish and preserve an agreement between the gentry and the urban commercial class, Gay turns in the final image to an elemental force that has the potential to subvert all that he has said. The use of an allusion to displace the image of a popular movement indicates Gay's inability to present it within the terms of *Trivia*; it is finally a force that flows from what lies beyond his understanding – he can confront only obliquely the mysterious, obscure, and unmanageable potential for insurrection within the crowd.

"London Ingulphs Them All": Cowper's Overwhelming Urban Experience

During the eighteenth century new strains of urban ideology emerged as an interest in advancing specifically middle-class values and models of subjectivity evolved out of the project of gentrifying the urban and urbanizing the gentry. The terms of this shift appear in Habermas's history of the transformation of conceptions of publicity and privacy. Habermas links the formation of the liberal concept of the private individual acting autonomously within a public market to the cultivation of an intimate, domestic sphere as a world supposedly separate from the public world, as a domain of "private autonomy denying its economic origins."[45] This assertion of a private autonomy apart from the busy public world corresponds to an epistemological affirmation of a relative autonomy of the mind or soul apart from an apparently externally determined chain of perceptions. These currents combine to produce a model of a subject deeply invested in the public world of the market but preserving affective and intellectual autonomy and independence.

In his poetry and especially *The Task*, William Cowper fuses this cultivation of domestic and intellectual autonomy into a new historical form of an urban mentality. Cowper had suffered a mental breakdown and attempted suicide during his time in London, and for the rest of his life he associated the public bustle of London with psychological distraction and disorder. In *The Task*, his fluent blank verse represents the scenes of the city as too busy, imposing, and absorbing to permit proper reflection and cognition. For the evangelical Cowper, this overwhelming flow of images obscures the presence of God in the world. The poem contrasts the disorder, immorality, and secularism of urban life against the mental, moral, and spiritual virtues of an idealized rural retirement. In terms of literary kinds, the urban newspaper reproduces as it remediates urban chaos while poetry belongs to retirement. Composing poetry is spiritual and mental work that reflects the divine presence and order within the mind and the world. Cowper's celebration of personal autonomy and rural retirement, as critics have noted, masks the inexorable implication of retirement within the wider world of politics and trade. Leonore Davidoff and Catherine Hall remark that Cowper's celebration of the domestic scene of the "cosy fire, the close fitting shutters" attempts to shut out "the social disorder of the 1780s and 1790s." His decision to idealize "a quiet domestic rural life rather than the frenetic and anxiety ridden world of town and commerce" appeals to his middle-class readers' desire for a private retreat from urban life, even if the closest they could come to such a sanctuary would be a "suburban garden."[46] Cowper's idyll of a spiritual retirement serves in practice as an ideological support of suburbanization, domesticity, and social reform through moral and spiritual reform; as such it depends on and cooperates with the world of urban commerce it explicitly rejects.

The Task shares the tactics and values of the composite locodescriptive and georgic mode commonly used to represent social geography in eighteenth-century poetry. This composite mode pulls back from the particular detail and street-level perspective of *Trivia* to a distant prospect and abstract reflection. The level of abstraction allows such poetry to name or represent the benefits of urban civilization, such as a profusion of commodities and polite sociability, while simultaneously chastening corruption and masking material relations: the mode's figural repertoire for representing the city contains a set of scenes that split productivity from the sites of production and urbanity from urban life. In *Windsor Forest*, for example, Pope presents London as the distant, glittering "Augusta," an ideal but abstract engine of production that converts the trees of Windsor forest into the merchant and military ships that sustain the glory of the empire. In *The Seasons* (1726–30, 1746), James Thomson first views the city at a distance and then zooms in on emblematic scenes: England's "crouded Ports, / Where rising Masts an endless Prospect yield, / With Labour burn," and "Trade and Joy, in every busy Street, / Mingling are heard." The image of urban labor is abstract, emblematic, and so pleasant that "even Drudgery himself . . . looks gay."[47] Williams unearths the rhizomatic connection between this mode's sanitized representation of urban labor and "the familiar idyll of retirement," in which one enjoys the benefits of urban commerce but suffers none of the inconveniences of urban life. This combination, Williams writes, gives the composite mode "a distinctly suburban air."[48]

Cowper adapts the composite mode to valorize specifically middle-class intellectual work. Dustin Griffin argues that in *The Task* Cowper "reaffirms, though he significantly modifies, the traditional georgic values of steady dedication to a homely and unspectacular task" by "redefining labor . . . as a virtually spiritual activity." By substituting spiritual work for manual labor, "Cowper's redefined idea of georgic almost conceals the economic base that makes possible the life of retired leisure/labor that he celebrates."[49] Griffin overstates the novelty of Cowper's position because he focuses specifically on the georgic tradition: the composite mode already emphasizes the intellectual work of the poet and overlooks manual labor. Cowper emphasizes that his work is specifically spiritual, but in practice this spiritual work consists of maintaining intellectual discipline in the act of composing poetry. Thomas Pfau argues that the cultivation of picturesque landscapes in eighteenth-century poetry and painting emphasized the value not of the land itself but of the aesthetic skill of the professional observer and participated in a broader sociocultural strategy for the urban middle class to unify itself around a common esteem for mobile, rootless intellectual work.[50] The most influential mid-century poets – Thomson,

Gray, Collins, Young, and Goldsmith – similarly wrote poems that turned from urban life, celebrated retirement, cultivated an inward turn, and focused on techniques of observation and the pleasures of thought.

In his poetry, Cowper projects the spectrum of development, from urban to rural, as a figure for and correlative of a spectrum of spiritual and mental attitudes. In broad terms, the city absorbs the mind in the distractions of the temporal world, while rural retirement allows autonomous intellectual and spiritual work. In the famous sentiment from *The Task*, "God made the country, and man made the town,"[51] Cowper's attempt to coordinate the geographical and spiritual dimensions creates a logical tension: in terms of the town-country opposition, retirement stands for spiritual autonomy, but in terms of the world-spirit opposition, rural retirement remains within the temporal world. Cowper mitigates the tension by consistently qualifying the contrast in the course of his alternation between exaggerated rhetorical postures, and he ultimately places retirement and the city within a single spectrum of social geography, acknowledging that retirement requires the resources provided by the urban world, even if the work of supplying those resources generates sin and corruption. The immoral ways of London seep into the country – "The town has tinged the country" (4.553) – but so do its commodities. When Cowper considers that pure seclusion would require hard toil to procure bread and water, he resolves, "If solitude make scant the means of life, / Society for me!" (1.248–49). On the other side of the spectrum, however grudgingly, Cowper briefly praises London as the seat of the arts, philosophy, and commerce, conceding that in her "I see / Much that I love, and more that I admire, / And all that I abhor" (3.837–39); she is as a "freckled fair / That pleases and yet shocks me" (3.839–40). Martin Priestman observes that, after playing a prominent role in the first books of the poem, "the town-country contrast progressively evaporates" without ever disappearing.[52] The poem concludes with a reconciliation of the city and the country in the spiritual plane with a vision of "Salem . . . the labour of a God! / Bright as a sun the sacred city shines" (6.799–800). The divine city is more like the country than the town: God made it and it is bright as the sun while the plumes of smoke from earthly "Metropolitan volcano's" produce an "eclipse" (3.736–37). On the temporal plane, the reconciliation of limited domestic autonomy with urban activity appears specifically suburban.

Where Gay instructs the gentry in urban life, Cowper instructs the gentry in country living; Cowper's version of the urban ideology allows for the suburbanization of the gentry. Cowper takes up the myth that the ills of rural society arise from the gentry heading to London for the winter and that national order and prosperity would be assured if only the gentry would stay at their country estates year round. In his letters, Cowper says of *The Task*, "the whole has one tendency. To discountenance the modern enthusiasm after a London Life, and to recommend rural ease and leisure as friendly to the cause of piety and virtue," and again, that he wishes "to combat that predilection in favor of a Metropolis that beggars and exhausts the Country by evacuating it of all its principal Inhabitants."[53] In *The Task* London can "at the sound of Winter's hoary wing, / Unpeople all our counties" (3.830–31). As Williams notes, this myth overlooks how the gentry bring their vices to the city and act as aggressive capitalists in the country.[54] But Cowper goes further toward a specifically suburban ideology: he casts some level of involvement in urban commercial civilization as necessary and even invigorating and recommends middle-class social strategies for enjoying its benefits while avoiding its costs.

One of these strategies is a form of mental and spiritual discipline that Cowper defines in part through contrast with an urban mentality. Cowper's version of the urban mentality more closely resembles Simmel's than Gay's does; he criticizes this mentality in the midst of a passage that putatively praises London:

> Where finds philosophy her eagle eye
> With which she gazes at yon burning disk
> Undazzled, and detects and counts his spots?
> In London; where her implements exact
> With which she calculates computes and scans
> All distance, motion, magnitude, and now
> Measures an atom, and now girds a world?
> In London; where has commerce such a mart,
> So rich, so throng'd, so drain'd, and so supplied
> As London, opulent, enlarged, and still
> Increasing London? Babylon of old
> Not more the glory of the earth, than she
> A more accomplish'd world's chief glory now. (1.712–24)

Cowper associates city life with secular disenchantment, quantitative calculation, and commercial self-interest. London not only is where most scientific apparatuses, including telescopes, were made, it also instructs the eye in a bold, critical, disillusioned gaze that, like Apollonius unweaving the rainbow, focuses on the spots of the sun without wondering at its glory. The Londoner relentlessly calculates, computes, and measures all things, running a tape measure around the world. Cowper's attention to the quantitative mindset flows seamlessly into his remarks about the commercial market, which is at once overstocked and empty. For Cowper this insistently worldly mentality is specifically idolatrous. Whereas retirement will lead the mind to intimations of divine creation, the urban scene, like a prison, will "Propense his heart to idols, he is held / In silly dotage on created things / Careless of their Creator" (5.585–87). Substituting the artificial for the divine, people in cities "Prefer to the performance of a God / Th' inferior wonders of an artist's hand" (1.418–19); consumers in "gain-devoted cities" (1.682) worship "Profusion" (2.674) in the idol of the luxury commodity and serve as "A priesthood such as Baal's was of old" (2.678). London surpasses Babylon in opulence and, correspondingly, in profanity. Cowper faintly associates this diversion from thinking about God to the distracting tempo of urban life, as the accelerating repetition of "London" suggests a quickening pulse of activity and thought.

Cowper contributes a lively representation of the myth that the urban environment overwhelms the mind with sensations and reduces it to a state of incoherent distraction. He grounds his theory in empirical epistemological discourse. He echoes and alludes to Locke's *Essay Concerning Human Understanding*, and his overarching interest in associationism and specific response to Hume's skepticism testifies to the influence of James Beattie's *Essay on the Nature and Immutability of Truth* (1771).[55] Cowper derives from Beattie a sense that thought arises mechanically from the promptings of sensation and from the chain of associations between thoughts and a belief that God provides dynamic stability in both the physical universe and the mind that allows for the apprehension of truth. By obscuring the divine presence, the urban environment raises the dangerous possibility of physical and mental chaos. Indeed, Cowper appears to think of madness in terms set by Hume's atheistic and chaotic account of human cognition.[56] In the *Treatise of Human Nature*, Hume denies the possibility of demonstrating the existence of a coherent self apart from the flux of perception.

> I never can catch *myself* at any time without a perception, and never can observe any thing but the perception. . . . I may venture to affirm of the rest of mankind, that they are nothing but a bundle or collection of different perceptions, which succeed each other with an inconceivable rapidity, and are in a perpetual flux and movement.[57]

Hume can find no "single power of the soul, which remains unalterably the same, perhaps for one moment."[58] Hume skeptically denies any evidence of a transcendental subject apart from the flux the subject experiences, of a divine order within the flux, and of a perfect schematic relation between impressions and ideas. Seeking an example that demonstrates, contra

Locke, that complex ideas can be inadequate reproductions of sensory impressions, Hume turns to the city. "I have seen *Paris*," Hume says, "but shall I affirm I can form such an idea of that city, as will perfectly represent all its streets and houses in their real and just proportions? I perceive, therefore, that tho' there is in general a great resemblance betwixt our *complex* impressions and ideas, yet the rule is not universally true, that they are exact copies of each other."[59] Although Hume does not explicitly relate sensory overload to the rapidity and variety of impressions in the urban environment, he nonetheless provides the philosophical bridge between Locke's empirical confidence and familiar modern descriptions of the overwhelming experience of the city, which appear in Kant and Nietzsche before Simmel.[60]

Cowper recommends retirement as a figure for and situation conducive to a mode of reflectiveness capable of preserving mental stability. Retirement makes it possible to compose poetry, and Cowper's letters suggest that he wrote *The Task* in part as a form of therapy to ward off a relapse of madness.[61] Cowper remarks that "*In the year when I wrote the Task*, (for it occupied me about a year,) *I was very often supremely unhappy*, and am under God indebted in good part to that work for not having been much worse."[62] Writing helps Cowper exercise his capacity for concentration, his control over his shifts of attention, and his retention and comprehension of what he perceives. Readers since Coleridge have observed that the poem's digressive structure and fluent blank verse help represent the movement of consciousness through the convolutions of thought and zigzags of association.[63] Marshall Brown, for one, observes, "the formal disorganization of the poem is a mimetic representation of the problems of mental coherence and personal identity."[64] A poet, Cowper says, strives

> T'arrest the fleeting images that fill
> The mirror of the mind, and hold them fast,
> And force them sit, 'till he has pencil'd off
> A faithful likeness of the forms he views. (2.290–93)

Cowper here refers to Locke's description of images or ideas passing through the mind without a trace: "they disappear and vanish, and there remain no footsteps of them; the Looking-glass is never the better for such *Ideas*, nor the Soul for such Thoughts"; such images are "Characters drawn on Dust, that the first breath of wind effaces; or Impressions made on a heap of Atoms."[65] The impression seems to take time to set: if the images pass too rapidly they escape comprehension and reduce the mind and the poem to a disordered flux. The effect can arise from the mind's inability to focus on any single object in a various scene: in a letter to Unwin written from his "favorite recess, the Greenhouse," Cowper says, "you may suppose I have no interruption to complain of, and that my thoughts are perfectly at my command. But the beauties of the spot are themselves an interruption; my attention is continually called upon by those very myrtles, by a double row of Grass pinks just beginning to blossom, and by a bed of Beans already in bloom."[66] Or the rapidity can arise from the movement of the scene: "'tis not easy," Cowper remarks in "Retirement" (1782) of those who live in cities, "in a world where . . . The roving eye misleads the careless heart, / To limit thought" (123–27). The work of composing poetry requires the mental discipline to retain an impression long enough to reproduce it.

In his personal writings, Cowper represents London as a threat to the limitation and discipline that preserve a sense of mental integrity and autonomy. Toward the end of his *Memoir*, he resolves, "by the Lord's leave, to see London, the scene of my former abominations, no more."[67] A few years later, he remarks, "My Peace of Mind is of so delicate a Constitution, that the Air of London will not agree with it."[68] And as late as 1780, more than fifteen years after his breakdown, Cowper was still declining invitations to visit friends in London, telling Joseph Hill that "The Thought of it [a visit to London] distresses me, the Sight of it would Craze me."[69] In *The Task*, Cowper keeps his distance from the city: he never directly sees it just as he never directly refers to his madness. But Cowper's thoroughgoing contrast between retirement and the city associates the city with distraction; his model of an urban subjectivity anticipates Wirth's "schizoid" character, combining "personal disorganization, mental breakdown, [and] suicide," and Fredric Jameson's description of postmodern "schizophrenia," in which the "present suddenly engulfs the subject with undescribable vividness, a materiality of perception properly overwhelming."[70]

Cowper uses the same figures of being overwhelmed and engulfed to describe the condition of being caught up in the mental distractions of the city. Vincent Newey observes that "storm imagery was his characteristic means of emblematizing personal distress," and Byrd notes, "More than once in his poetry, in fact, Cowper uses the word 'overwhelmed' to describe his madness."[71] In epistemological terms, this sense of being overwhelmed represents the surplus of impressions over ideas, that is, the presence of unschematized perceptions, and it is this surplus that indicates the inherent implication of the subject within the temporal, material world. Paolo Virno describes just this relation by imagining a person standing on the shore of the sea, hearing but not aware of the sound of the waves: in this condition of perception without apperception, "the person standing there absorbed is one with the surrounding environment."[72] In her insightful reading of *The Task*, Kevis Goodman focuses on the moment in retirement that doubles and contrasts with this experience. She argues of the "indolent vacuity of thought" (4.297) that follows Cowper's perusal of the newspaper that "this lapse in Lockean ideation and identity, this interstitial moment of unthinking consciousness . . . is the *condition* for the entry of ongoing history's absent but immanent force."[73] But Cowper's indolent vacuity of thought uses the failure of Lockean ideation to assert against Hume the persistence of a soul distinguishable from the flux of perceptions and thought. The vacuities of thought in retirement aspire to register the spiritual rather than the historical world: the failure of ideation in the city does the opposite and testifies to the embeddedness of consciousness within the temporal world.

When Cowper confronts London, he interposes poetic tradition and the newspaper to organize the chaos of urban life. Cowper's account of London life is largely conventional, though it subtly suggests the threat of urban distraction. The country gentry head to town, and

> London ingulphs them all. The shark is there
> And the shark's prey. The spendthrift and the leech
> That sucks him. There the sycophant and he
> That with bare-headed and obsequious bows
> Begs a warm office, doom'd to a cold jail
> And groat per diem if his patron frown.
> The levee swarms as if in golden pomp
> Were character'd on ev'ry statesman's door,
> 'BATTER'D AND BANKRUPT FORTUNES MENDED HERE.' (3.816–24)

Organizing the syntax of a description of an urban scene on an anaphora of deictics is a convention extending in English back through Johnson's "London" and ultimately to Juvenal's third satire.[74] Cowper, however, insists on his distance from the city by repeating "there" rather than the more common "here" or a mix of the two. Cowper's rolling blank verse and slightly twisting syntax add a hint of swimming perception, and a persistent if submerged conceit compares the city to a sea that engulfs the nobility. Those who do not keep their distance are swallowed up by the city.

The newspaper belongs to and, as Goodman shows, represents the chaos of the city and must itself be remediated by poetic tradition before it will stand still in the mirror of the mind. If, as Julie Ellison argues, the newspaper offers Cowper a chance to maintain "a safe distance" that "tones down the cacophony of unmediated London voices all talking at once and shapes them into an intense but manageable composition," the newspaper itself needs to be remediated through poetic convention and translated into the imagery of rural retirement to be assimilated into Cowper's verse.[75]

> What is it but a map of busy life
> Its fluctuations and its vast concerns?
> Here runs the mountainous and craggy ridge . . .
> Here rills of oily eloquence in soft
> Mæanders lubricate the course they take . . .
> There forests of no-meaning spread the page
> In which all comprehension wanders lost. (4.55–57, 64–65, 74–75)

Cowper's description of the arrangement of print and information in the newspaper recalls his Juvenalian account of London, except that now he uses "here" as well as "there." While the poet draws nearer to the newspaper than he does to the city, he still applies the techniques that the professional observer uses to view the natural landscape, converting the newspaper into a map of a picturesque or sublime landscape. Poetry does not so much rival the newspaper as stand apart from and aestheticize it and its object.

Cowper provides a detailed, if negative, account of what an unmediated experience of the city would be like when he considers the effect of the newspaper as a medium. An unmediated encounter, he implies, would exactly overwhelm his senses and absorb him in the temporal world.

> 'Tis pleasant through the loop-holes of retreat
> To peep at such a world. To see the stir
> Of the great Babel and not feel the crowd.
> To hear the roar she sends through all her gates
> At a safe distance, where the dying sound
> Falls a soft murmur on th' uninjured ear.
> Thus sitting and surveying thus at ease
> The globe and its concerns, I seem advanced
> To some secure and more than mortal height,
> That lib'rates and exempts me from them all.
> It turns submitted to my view, turns round
> With all its generations; I behold
> The tumult and am still. (4.88–100)

London threatens to overload all the senses: he imagines feeling the press of the crowd, hearing a din so loud it hurts the ear, seeing a scene not in its totality but from a limited perspective immersed within it, and all as unintelligible as Babel. This surplus of unschematized perception would negate safety, security, ease, and stillness; the sense of absorption within the urban world would belie the impression of autonomy and liberty. As Goodman points out, Cowper here alludes to the opening of the second book of Lucretius's *De Rerum Natura*:

> How sweet it is, when whirlwinds roil great ocean,
> To watch, from land, the danger of another,
> Not that to see some other person suffer
> Brings great enjoyment, but the sweetness lies
> In watching evils you yourself are free from.[76]

The newspaper allows Cowper to watch from a suburban shore as London engulfs, overwhelms, drowns its inhabitants in its restless sea. The pleasure of autonomy depends on the sublime image of the wreck and on the reflexive feeling of distance from it. The newspaper allows Cowper to extract the pleasures of urban life without thinking himself involved in it.

Cowper criticizes the distractions of the urban scene and the venality of the commercial mentality, but he neither takes responsibility for participating in urban commerce nor seeks to reform it. The suburban bias of this ideology neutralizes its oppositional charge by displacing the call for reform into a spiritual dimension: even the criticism of urban society serves as a loyal opposition that supports the historical form of urbanization by recommending strategies for relieving the tensions it produces at the level of the private individual while leaving unaddressed the tensions created at the public and systemic planes.

The affiliation between this form of urban ideology and middle-class sociocultural interests appears in the celebration of intellectual labor and aesthetic technique, in the recommendation of a private and moral solution to a public problem, and in the specific recommendation of suburban retirement and domesticity. If this project invites the gentry to suburbanize, it excludes the lower orders. In Cowper's work, laborers appear naturally adapted to their hard lot. The postman who carries the newspaper on a frosty morning fortunately has, in Richard Feingold's phrase, "that low metabolism whose chief blessing is insensibility."[77] Cowper can confront the lower orders on a personal scale. Individual laborers or beggars may inspire the private virtues of "compassion" (4.375) and charity. But Cowper shows little concern for lower classes as classes, and he keeps his distance from places where working-class people gather.

Where Gay figures the dissolution of urban order as a fire and associates that fire with the unknown world of the urban working classes, Cowper never imagines the breakdown of urban order in *The Task* but elsewhere associates the breakdown with that antithesis of rural retirement, the crowd in the public streets. The crowd is a sea that becomes perilous in a storm. Cowper refers to the Gordon Riots of 1780 in his letters and occasional verse in terms that reappear in his representation of London in *The Task*. He worries about his correspondents' proximity to the riot, writing to John Newton anxious to hear of his safety, "situated as you were, apparently within the reach of so much danger." Upon hearing that Newton was safe, Cowper refers back to his friend's prophetic "reflections upon the state of London, the sins and enormities of that great city, while you had a distant view of it from Greenwich."[78] Cowper wishes his friends and family to stay distant from intellectual and sensory disturbance as well as from physical violence: he writes to Mrs. Cowper, "Remote as your Dwelling is from the late Scene of Riot and Confusion, I hope that though you could not but hear the Report of it, you heard no more, and that the Roarings of the mad Multitude did not reach you."[79] The resounding noise of the riot spreads like the cries of madmen. In *Table Talk*, Cowper calls for "active laws" to preserve liberty – which for Cowper is nearly synonymous with order – from "riot" and "wild excess" (314–16).

> When tumult lately burst his prison door,
> And set Plebeian thousands in a roar . . .
> When the rude rabble's watch-word was, destroy,
> And blazing London seem'd a second Troy,
> Liberty blush'd and hung her drooping head . . .
> She loses in such storms her very name,
> And fierce licentiousness should bear the blame.
>
> (318–19, 322–24, 328–29)

The plebeian crowd roars like madmen or like a conflagration as it breaks out of its prison; to Cowper this fierce rushing is a stain upon British liberty. The surging disorder takes the form of a fire and a storm.

Faced with the prospect of revolution, Cowper accepts the need for political reforms: he writes in a letter from 1792, "God grant that we may have no revolution here, but unless we have a Reform we certainly shall."[80] In *The Task*, however, the corrupt, distracting, and destructive nature of urban life constitutes a stage in a divinely ordered history that can be accepted or avoided but not altered. London is doomed to beget its own decline from decadence to ruin. Newey argues, "Cowper's sense of a horrifyingly amoral and monstrously voracious economic system is one with his sense of a wider activity, a headlong progress into ruin and chaos."[81] Speaking of the towns buried or burned in a Sicilian earthquake, Cowper warns that God retains the right and power to punish sin with cataclysmic force. "Has not God / Still wrought by means since first he made the world, / And did he not of old employ his means / To drown it?" (2.197–200). Urbanization is the sin that calls down divine justice and the flood that will overwhelm England.

"I Hear": Blake's Urban Community

In his *Life of William Blake*, Alexander Gilchrist recounts that Blake long remembered his "involuntary" participation in the Gordon Riots. In Gilchrist's retelling, the poet was out for a walk when he happened to encounter "the advancing wave of triumphant Blackguardism, and was forced (for from such a great surging mob there is no disentanglement) to go along in the very front rank, and witness the storm and burning of the fortress-like prison [of Newgate], and release of its three hundred inmates."[82] Jacob Bronowski rejects Gilchrist's telling as an apologetic softening of what more likely happened. "Blake," Bronowski bluntly declares, "did not grow afraid of the crowd, then or later."[83] David V. Erdman adds the crucial detail that "Blake was in the streets during the fifth day [of the riots] and at the center of the action," a day when, from the perspective of respectable society, the crowd grew out of control.[84] Known more for passionate intensity than detached neutrality, Blake was twenty-two, professionally insecure, and politically radical: Gilchrist's passive imagery of his being forced or swept along by a wave could be a metaphorical mistranslation of casting off self-discipline and getting carried away in a crowd. In the world of his poetry, Blake would not so neatly distinguish between internal and external surges. He might have remembered the event not because it was frightening but because it was thrilling. Whatever happened, these commentators all agree that the event lodged in Blake's imagination. The engraving Rossetti called "Glad Day" – of a giant man, naked, stretching his arms wide, and stepping forward in front of a rising sun – presents an image of Albion arising "from where he labourd at the Mill with Slaves / Giving himself for the Nations he danc'd the dance of Eternal Death": it is an image of the people arisen and united.[85]

As the difference between their responses to the Gordon Riots indicates, Blake's view of urban society was radically different from Cowper's: the two poets belonged to different classes, shared in different discourses, and wrote in different styles and modes. As an artisan engraver, Blake experienced firsthand the social transformations naturalized by mythical narratives of urban development, and his poetry protests the refinement of the division of labor, the deskilling of crafts, the standardization of production, and the separation of mental and physical labor. Blake recognizes in the world around him the correlation between the state of society and the mentality projected by the dominant urban ideology; his craft and the London social world was being transformed by the tendency to reduce qualities to quantities, to reduce social relations to monetary relations, and to disorder the mind by deifying rational intellection. In his poetry, Blake accepts the premise that specific mentalities correspond to specific urban forms, but he denies that the present urban form and mentality are natural or necessary and distinguishes the present state of London from the urban environment per se. As such, Blake participates in the loosely coherent, emergent alternative discourse on urbanization in Romantic-period culture.

Yet Blake stands apart from the main line of this emergent discourse in the specific nature of his imaginative vision of an alternative urban mentality and society. As Jon Mee and E. P. Thompson have demonstrated, Blake's major works draw on an eclectic mix of intellectual sources, discourses, and genres circulating through radical political circles and religious sects in London in the 1790s. Some elements of his response to urban ideology resonate with the discourse of polite radicalism and rational Dissent associated with the social circle gathered around Joseph Johnson's print shop, and this discursive resonance accounts for Blake's poetical affinities, remarked by critics of literary representations of the city, with Wordsworth or, *mutatis mutandis*, with Coleridge, Shelley, and Barbauld.[86] Other elements of Blake's reworking of urban ideology, however, depart from this discourse and derive from his participation in a radical antinomian tradition transmitted through the social institutions of London's artisan milieu, including chapels, periodicals, and ties of kinship and friendship. Blake's radical concept of the possibilities of urban community and his adoption of a prophetic style derive in part from his participation in a culture that supported the work of Richard Brothers (a prophet and self-proclaimed nephew of God), Thomas Spence (who called for communal ownership of the land), Garnet Terry (a fellow engraver and bookseller who reprinted works of seventeenth-century radicals), and others too radical to be considered reputable in polite culture.[87] Mee persuasively argues that in fusing discourses increasingly differentiated in class terms, Blake alienated his potential audiences: his "vulgar enthusiasm" was not respectable enough for a bourgeois public sphere intent on separating itself from plebeian culture, while his attempts to find a polite audience for his work diverted him from cultivating a possibly receptive plebeian audience.[88]

Blake's earliest writings show him still writing within the dominant urban ideology. In a manuscript fragment probably from the early 1780s known as "then She bore Pale desire," Blake writes, "hate Controlls all the Gods. at will. Policy brought forth Guile & fraud. these Gods last namd live in the Smoke of Cities. on Dusky wing breathing forth Clamour & Destruction. alas in Cities wheres the man whose face is not a mask unto his heart" (E 448). As David Punter notes of this passage, "what is significant is Blake's conventional attribution of the specific vices of 'Guile' and 'Fraud' to the urban environment"; one could add that Blake also attributes to the city a complex of dissembling, superficiality, alienation, and a masking of affect.[89] But when Blake returns to publishing his poetry during the period of revolutionary enthusiasm in the early 1790s, he breaks from convention, and in "London" he outlines a vision of various forms of urban life. He develops this outline in *Jerusalem*, which elaborates and reinterprets the imagery, illumination, and perspective of the earlier poem.

Blake's response to the dominant urban ideology in "London" and *Jerusalem* participates in his broader critique of the dominant model of subjectivity and the social processes and philosophical assumptions that construct and rely on it. Saree Makdisi compellingly argues that Blake opposes the Lockean "micropolitics of subjectivity" that informed the polite, even hegemonic, radicalism of Thomas Paine, John Thelwall, Mary Wollstonecraft, and others.[90] Blake disputes Locke's theory of mind not only for casting the mind as a passive product of the impressions of the senses but also for conceiving of the individual as an autonomous entity endowed with rights such as the right to property. This theory of the subject tends to view society as an aggregation of individuals related through the pursuit of self-interest, however tempered, in formations such as the bourgeois public sphere or the cash nexus. Drawing instead on the antinomian conceptions of the human community as the collective body of Christ, Blake conceives of the subject as part of the divine creative imagination, which is distributed through all people. In an unfallen state, the subject is inherently communal and united to its fellows by love, collaboration, and creative exchange. On Blake's terms, the notion that the urban environment determines specific mentalities depends on the

Lockean notion that the subject is formed *ab extra* by the nature of its impressions, redefining man not as the creator but as the product of something he created. Blake sees man's works and spaces in this absurd situation, "Ceasing to be His Emanations, Life to Themselves assuming!" (*J*90:2, E 249). Instead, turning the arrow the other way, the city is an environment that manifests the construction of the relation between the subject and the world. Commenting on this correspondence in *The Four Zoas*, Kenneth Johnston notes that "the cities the Zoas build are literally the form of their being";[91] or, as Blake writes, "Cities / Are Men" (*J*34:46–47, E 180). Indeed, a single city may exist in several forms simultaneously, corresponding to the different natures of its residents.

In "London" and *Jerusalem*, Blake represents the dominant urban form of contemporary London as the urban manifestation of this construct of the subject and its correspondence with the world of commerce and its social and political institutions. In "London," Blake refers to specific institutions that shape the subject's mores and behaviors – the church, the palace, certain trades that directly convert people into commodities – but he emphasizes that these disciplinary mechanisms coordinate at the urban level.

I wander thro' each charter'd street,
Near where the charter'd Thames does flow.
And mark in every face I meet
Marks of weakness, marks of woe.

In every cry of every Man,
In every Infants cry of fear,
In every voice: in every ban,
The mind-forg'd manacles I hear

How the Chimney-sweepers cry
Every blackning Church appalls,
And the hapless Soldiers sigh
Runs in blood down Palace walls

But most thro' midnight streets I hear
How the youthful Harlots curse
Blasts the new-born Infants tear
And blights with plagues the Marriage hearse. (1–16)

Williams argues that Blake's revision of "dirty streets" and "dirty Thames" (E 796) in his drafts into "charter'd" signals a dramatic change in perspective. "Suddenly, within this, he sees the capital in a new way: not the riot, the noise or the monstrous wen of earlier and contemporary observation; but an organisation, a systematic state of mind. . . . What he then sees, dramatically, are the submerged connections of this capital system."[92] Gavin Edwards checks the critical impulse to supply "the missing links in an argument only partly visible in 'London'" and proposes instead that Blake writes "in a way that suggests the active exclusion of chains of cause and effect."[93] Yet Williams's observation still holds: the obscurity of social relations within the urban order is one of the symptoms of its disorder, and mystification has a vital role in the capital system. The novelty of the representation of the city in the poem lies not in its disclosure of an urban system coordinated with a mentality – the same is true of Cowper's *The Task* – but in the suggestion, registered in the speaker's attitude of troubled wonder, that the city has fallen into an arbitrary and destructive system and could and should be otherwise.

This system, from its micropolitics, to its institutional formations, to its vision of social relations, is specifically that of Romantic-era capitalist modernization. Makdisi convincingly argues that Blake's imaginative mapping of London situates the city as ground zero for national and global modernization and the formation of a "Universal Empire." London becomes the space of modernization; to live in London is "To live and experience this modernization."[94] On these terms, Blake "must be seen to be tinkering with the basic conceptual and ideological building blocks of modernization, in effect rewriting the conceptual language of modernization for alternative political and aesthetic purposes."[95] Blake, that is, imagines urban forms based on noncapitalist social relations and imagines urbanization without modernization.

Blake's diagnosis of the modern urban mentality closely anticipates Simmel's account of the metropolitan mentality, turning conventional figures of urban mentalities against the contemporary urban order. Not coincidentally, the resemblance is strongest where Simmel links alienation, intellection, and general indifference to human uniqueness specifically with the money economy.

> But [the] money economy and the domination of the intellect stand in the closest relationship to one another. They have in common a purely matter-of-fact attitude in the treatment of persons and things in which a formal justice is often combined with an unrelenting hardness. . . . Money is concerned only with what is common to all, i.e., with the exchange value which reduces all quality and individuality to a purely quantitative level. All emotional relationships between persons rest on their individuality, whereas intellectual relationships deal with persons as with numbers, that is, as with

> elements which, in themselves, are indifferent, but which are of interest only insofar as they offer something objectively perceivable.[96]

As an engraver, Blake experienced the structural and individual consequences of the development of the money economy. Makdisi demonstrates that Blake felt the pressures of the growing tendency toward reducing the skilled craft of engraving to unskilled labor, a shift that tends toward a perception of the product and of the producer as standard, with labor valued at the common abstract exchange value of the wage or piece rate. E. P. Thompson's classic reading of "London" draws out the poem's deep concern with "the buying and selling of human values," a concern embodied by the practitioners of three occupations, typical of a London scene in 1794, that reduce humans to interchangeable and disposable commodities: the chimney sweeper, soldier, and harlot.[97] In his unpublished "Public Address," Blake connects the commercial system with the devaluing of individual genius: "Commerce Cannot endure Individual Merit its insatiable Maw must be fed by What all can do Equally well" (E 574). In a complex compression, the emanation Jerusalem, subjected to Albion's minute moral scrutiny, asks, "Why wilt thou number every little fibre of my Soul" (*J*22:20, E 167), questioning at once the motive for his destructive behavior and the premise that such analytical and abstracting assessment has any purchase on the state of a soul. The famous image of "dark Satanic Mills" (*M*1:8, E 95) similarly coordinates a mechanistic materialist view of a universe bound in revolving motions with a relentlessly repetitive labor that not only grinds corn or separates the fibers of cotton or wool but equally grinds down laborers into indifferent units of labor power and into small, hard, and distinct units, like the grains of sand that represent the condition of a subject in the state of Ulro. Under the commercial system, the expansive, communal subject has been torn apart, and the pervasive failure of self-recognition constitutes a mental disorder or "schizoid" mentality. Blake's major prophecies, including *The Four Zoas* and *Jerusalem*, tell of the struggle to recover from this fragmented condition.

Blake's novel sense that the urban mentality is disordered but capable of being restored informs the innovative form of "London." As Williams argues, in the poem the city appears systemically organized, but what is more striking is the speaker's complex relationship to that system: he is at once immersed within it and yet remains free from the symptoms of its influence. When Thompson notes that Blake's "treatment of the city departs from a strong literary convention" by presenting "the city as a unitary experience and not as a theatre of discrete episodes," he means in part that

Blake creates a weakly perceptible illusion of a consistent point of view. Blake does not narrate the experience of a single walk through the city the way Wordsworth does in stretches of Book 7 of *The Prelude*, but he declines the Juvenalian here-there structure and creates a sense of continuity of perspective by maintaining the present tense in "I wander," "I hear," and "I hear" and by echoing the wandering "thro'" each street in the first stanza in the speaker walking "thro' midnight streets" in the last stanza. Thompson refers this sense of immersion to the speaker's presumed social position: "Blake's 'London' . . . is seen, or suffered, from within, by a Londoner."[98] The speaker precisely is a Londoner, a subject of the city, and, in a sense, is London itself, the city as a man. But crucially the speaker is misaligned with his city, as if his mind were fitted to London and he found himself walking through London in its form as Babylon, as if he belongs to another urban order that survives hidden within the dominant order.

Related passages in *Jerusalem* suggest that part of what distinguishes Blake's wanderers from the victims of the dominant urban system is their willingness to communicate and sympathize with those around them. Los, Jerusalem, and London wander through familiar and yet strange versions of the metropolis. On plate 84, which bears an illumination that is the mirror image of the one to "London," Los announces, "I see London blind & age-bent begging thro the Streets / Of Babylon" (*J*84:11–12, E 243). The model of an alternative subject and urban form survives within the city but has been as diminished and disregarded as an old beggar. In Blake's most fully elaborated image of modern urban culture, Los descends from the hills in the suburbs of London through the narrow winding streets of the east end to the riverside and back north to Moorfields.

> He came down from Highgate thro Hackney & Holloway towards London
> Till he came to old Stratford & thence to Stepney & the Isle
> Of Leuthas Dogs, thence thro the narrows of the Rivers side
> And saw every minute particular, the jewels of Albion, running down
> The kennels of the streets & lanes as if they were abhorrd.
> Every Universal Form, was become barren mountains of Moral
> Virtue: and every Minute Particular hardend into grains of sand:
> And all the tendernesses of the soul cast forth as filth & mire,
> Among the winding places of deep contemplation intricate
> To where the Tower of London frownd dreadful over Jerusalem:
> A building of Luvah builded in Jerusalems eastern gate to be
> His secluded Court: thence to Bethlehem where was builded
> Dens of despair in the house of bread: enquiring in vain
> Of stones and rocks he took his way, for human form was none.
>
> (*J*45:14–27, E 194)

The form of the subject corresponds to the form of the disciplinary institutions in the built environment. The residents or minute particulars of London appear to Los as small, hard, and separate as grains of sand. Their interests do not extend beyond themselves, and they face a barren world with stony hardness. They form no affective bonds with others and flush tenderness away like so much excrement. Disciplinary institutions such as the gated Bethlehem asylum and the immured Tower of London image this hard carapace in the built environment. As the subject is meant for tenderness, so too, mythically, these structures are meant for social good: Bethlehem, now a den of despair, is Hebrew for house of bread; the Tower of London, now a political prison, was built by Luvah as a sanctuary for sexual pleasure. Blake's distrust of disciplinary institutions and mechanisms – prisons, asylums, law, watchmen, spies for the home office – cannot be restricted to a figure in an epistemological argument or in an abstract social philosophy; as Punter observes, "this is a matter of class perspective: to Johnson or to Wordsworth," one might add to Gay or to Cowper, "it might well look as though the law was not adequately doing its work[;] to Blake it seemed that it was performing all too well, repressing human potential and imposing violence on the city-dweller."[99]

For all the horrors Blake's wanderers see in the contemporary city, their ability to see these horrors as horrors indicates that a saving remnant of vision survives and that an alternative form of community persists within London. This alternative form of urban social order and community survives in the "winding places of deep contemplation intricate," in the thought and culture of working-class or poor neighborhoods of the city, like Smithfield, where roads are narrow and winding. In *Jerusalem*, when London sacrifices himself for Albion – taking on the specter form of Babylon and temporarily dedicating his spirit to worldly gain for the nation's sake – the unplanned, irrational, winding streets of the east end and the rookeries serve as "beautiful labyrinths" (*J* 83:27, E 241) that shelter the outcast Jerusalem, Albion's emanation and Blake's figure for an ideal community. "Improvement makes strait roads," Blake writes in the Proverbs of Hell, "but the crooked roads without Improvement, are roads of Genius" (*MHH* 10:66–67, E 38). These labyrinths are spaces of hope that protect the divine spirit precisely because they are beyond the reach of the disciplinary forces of rational improvement. Los preserves the divine vision throughout *Jerusalem* and declares, through Blake, "I write in South Molton Street, what I both see and hear / In regions of Humanity, in Londons opening streets" (*J* 34:42–43, E 180). What he sees is Jerusalem, the ideal city hiding within London, and *Jerusalem*, the text or emanation he produces. Where the streets in *Annus Mirabilis* open in the sense of growing broader as one moves westward, Blake's streets open like gates onto new worlds.

The fundamental turn from Babylon to Jerusalem requires overcoming selfhood and forging new social connections. In the case of "London," the contrast between a communal subject and a confined subject appears in the symmetrical contrast between the speaker of the poem and the Harlot in the last stanza, that is, as in *Jerusalem*, between London and Babylon. Heather Glen argues that the speaker of "London" "is decisively implicated in his society" and "is trapped within the world upon which he is trying to comment." Unable to achieve true critical distance from his object, "Blake releases a powerful imaginative sense of an unavoidable logic in the society that does not depend on him at all."[100] Such epistemological humility and resignation to social determination sounds foreign to Blake. If, as Michael Ferber argues, the speaker of the poem "has not arrived at the highest imaginative comprehension or spiritual liberty (it may be impossible before all or most of his fellows have joined him) . . . he is on his way."[101] The speaker, as a Londoner and as London, sees his alienated fellows around him and feels impoverished by their estrangement. His fellows sigh and cry and their lamentations break against the walls of the church or palace or vanish into background noise. They are physically, socially, and psychologically shut out and shut in, bound within a social system that casts them out. There are no exchanges of communication or of affection. The Harlot's curse, which critics generally gloss as venereal disease, may also be the vulgar oath "damn your eyes" spitefully cast at an infant crying as helplessly as all the others. The curse rebounds off the enclosed carriage or "marriage hearse." If so, then the Harlot's response to the suffering of innocents indicates the extent to which her affections have been severed and to which she has internalized the hardness that has been shown to her. In this context, the speaker's ability to "mark" the weakness and woe – however much he acknowledges his complicity in the social system by actively placing those marks – and his repeated affirmation "I hear," appear far more radical and significant than Glen would have them be. The poem's repetition of "hear" and the acrostic "HEAR" in the third stanza give the poem an ode-like quality: the speaker at once petitions for the divine humanity to hear – the first-person, present-tense verbs, stripped of their subject as in the acrostic, become imperative – and manifests that divinity by assuring those around him that their cries are heard.

Beside this act of sympathy, "London" does not provide a more detailed vision of what an alternative urban community would look like. For that critics turn elsewhere. Makdisi sees a positive social image of a non-empirical model of subjectivity in the revolutionary upheaval of *America*. The act of revolution, Makdisi sharply discerns, is not carried out by the posturing leaders of the revolution or by the revolutionary army but by the "fierce rushing of th'inhabitants together" (*A*14:12, E 56). "For the decisive scene in *America*," Makdisi writes, "is this collective action of a crowd of angry citizens surging through city streets," precisely the scene the hegemonic radicals wished to avoid in London in the 1790s.[102] The moment of breaking down the arbitrary subjective and social boundaries of Lockean epistemology and politics appears in the formation of a crowd. Blake refers several times to the "multitudes without / Number! the voices of the innumerable multitudes" (*J*31:3–4, E 177). The crowd inherently defies those who rule by dividing and by counting: the multitude is innumerable not only because it is immensely large but also because it is a collective unit.

But the fierce rushing of the crowd is only a revolutionary release, not a full image of a renewed urban society. Blake presents that image in the city of Golgonooza. Golgonooza is at once a storehouse of human acts and an image of the human body, built around the central sexual Gate of Luban and looms of Cathedron where Los stands and erects his Palace (*J*13:24–25, E 157). In its most contracted form, Golgonooza figures a single human body. Los's furnaces "howl loud; living: self-moving" (*J*73:2, E 228), as if the furnaces were the heart and lungs of the body. The work of building Golgonooza is an unalienated mode of self-realization in creative exertion. Golgonooza possesses both the furnaces of Los and the looms of Cathedron; it provides a vivid image of William and Catherine Blake collaborating as one on the illuminated books. This collaborative unit expands to the scale of the household as the sons of Los join in his labor. As the revolutionary climax approaches, Los labors "With the innumerable multitudes of Golgonooza" (*J*73:6, E 228). As still more join together building Golgonooza, Golgonooza approaches Jerusalem. The fierce rushing of *America* and the building of Golgonooza, or of Jerusalem, are not single acts but processes. Steve Vine remarks that the building of Jerusalem is "more an act than an object, more verb than noun – a build*ing*."[103] Golgonooza is "continually building & continually decaying desolate!" (*J*53:19, E 203). Blake repeats that Los "builded Golgonooza" (*J*12:24, E 155) – perhaps substituting "builded" for "built" to supply a past imperfect verb distinct from the past perfect and to highlight the continuousness of the labor. The work of building Golgonooza is then defined by self-realization through work in that the work allows the full exertion of one's genius and allows the subject to devote itself through collaboration to a community and to a project: it is an alternative form of urban community that already exists and operates within London's Babylonian form.[104]

Golgonooza presents a model of urbanization without modernization: it is urban renewal not through gentrification but through community organization. Makdisi negatively clears space for a study of Blake's theory of urbanization without modernization when he notes Blake's opposition to "the rationalizing, alienating, mechanizing, quantifying, modernizing, and empire-building culture of the nineteenth century," that is, to everything Simmel associates with urbanization with the conspicuous exception of urbanization itself.[105] Ideally for Blake, urbanization consists of men creating space for their interactions, and Golgonooza redefines those interactions outside the terms of monetary relations. Alternative structures of urban relations already exist, albeit in small form, in ties of kinship, friendship, and collaboration, which all have economic as well as affective dimensions. Looking over a site of new construction, Blake asks, "What are those golden builders doing?" (*J*12:25, E 155). The builders are golden both in the sense of seeking enrichment and in the sense of building, even if unknowingly, the new Jerusalem. This is not the development of a suburban retreat from the city but an expansion of the urban community.

> The stones are pity, and the bricks, well wrought affections:
> Enameld with love & kindness, & the tiles engraven gold
> Labour of merciful hands: the beams and rafters are forgiveness:
> The mortar & cement of the work, tears of honesty: the nails,
> And the screws & iron braces, are well wrought blandishments,
> And well contrived words, firm fixing, never forgotten. (*J*12:30–35, E 155)

Sarah Haggarty refers to such passages as revealing the "affective architecture" of Blake's cities.[106] The expansion of London coincides with the growth of Jerusalem in the potential expansion of this affective community and with the composition of the "well contrived words" of *Jerusalem* itself. These new houses can be filled with "the furniture" prepared in Blake's "pitying looms" (*J*12:38, E 155) in Lambeth, extending the imagined community of his readership.

In its positive social form, Golgonooza is a space for and practice of communication, exchange, and collaboration. Nicholas Williams suggestively describes Blake's utopian impulse in terms of Habermas's theories of the public sphere and of communicative action, though Makdisi's argument demonstrates that the Habermasian public sphere's investment in Lockean subjectivity, rationality, and the assertion of private self-interests cannot be projected onto Blake's utopian image of men "convers[ing] together in Visionary forms dramatic" (*J* 98:28, E 257).[107] Such a public sphere manages the internal conflicts of Babylon rather than transforms the city into Jerusalem. Hand, Blake's figure for the liberal publisher and champion of the freedom of the press Leigh Hunt, joins with his fellow accusers to "build Babylon" (*J* 42:63, E 190); in Hand's energetic battling in the public sphere, he "labour[s] mightily / In the Wars of Babel & Shinar" (*J* 8:41–42, E 151), wars that constitute those cities rather than try to destroy them.[108] Print is an important urban agora for Blake: it is a forum for public intimacy. "When in Eternity Man converses with Man they enter / Into each others Bosom (which are Universes of delight) / In mutual interchange. and first their Emanations meet" (*J* 88:3–5, E 246); "Man is adjoind to Man by his Emanative portion" (*J* 39:38, E 187). Men come together first through their creations, their texts.

> When Jerusalem was thy hearts desire in times of youth & love.
> Thy Sons came to Jerusalem with gifts, she sent them away
> With blessings on their hands & on their feet, blessings of gold,
> And pearl & diamond: thy Daughters sang in her Courts:
> They came up to Jerusalem; they walked before Albion
> In the Exchanges of London every Nation walkd
> And London walkd in every Nation mutual in love & harmony.
>
> (*J* 24:37–43, E 170)

The agora or exchange lies at the heart of Blake's Jerusalem, but at the exchange people neither buy nor sell nor rationally debate. In Blake's agora, people walk, talk, and live together in mutual love and harmony. The interchange of affection occurs along the "Fibres of love" that reach "from man to man" (*J* 4:8, E 146). Haggarty has shown Blake's deep investment in the "gift relationship," a term she uses to signify a kind of exchange or transaction that entails free giving and reciprocal obligation, yet that differs pointedly from strictly economic exchange mediated by money. This economy of gifts presupposes and constitutes the affective connection and site of exchange not found at present in the London stock exchange but in Golgonooza.

To Blake urban ideology naturalizes an inverted vision of the relationship of the urban environment and the condition of the mind. Not only can the city and its corresponding mentality be other than it is in its current form, alternative forms of urban community based on affective connections, non-monetized exchange, and collaborative work already exist within the artisan and working-class districts of London. In direct opposition to Cowper's defensive withdrawal behind the loopholes of retreat, when Blake looks out from his workshop, he sees potential collaborators and feels swept up in their energy: "I behold them and their rushing fires overwhelm my Soul" (*J* 5:35, E 148).

"[T]he Leading Word a Bait / Which Cannot Be Resisted": Wordsworth Takes on Urban Ideology

In his account of a walk through the busy streets of London in Book 7 of *The Prelude*, Wordsworth pauses to note how ballads and advertisements press on his attention. "These bold in conscious merit; lower down / That, fronted with a most imposing word, / Is, peradventure, one in masquerade" (7.212–14). The printed word in London is "imposing": it impresses, compels, and, when it wears a mask, diverts and deceives. In a manuscript draft, Wordsworth lingers on the reader reading: "[Inviting] is the leading word a bait / Which cannot be resisted, at the close / The Simple reader if he laugh not looks / Blank as an April Fool."[109] The header or lead commands the attention of those who pass by. The simple reader – perhaps one unpracticed in critical suspicion or, as in "We Are Seven," one who does not observe ordinary distinctions – misses the conventions of the form and misses the wit or joke of the advertisement or ballad. To those who understand the genre, the reader's miscomprehension marks him as an outsider. But he "looks / Blank" because he appears confused, because the text does not leave an impression on him, and because this absence of response makes him a mystery to those who look at him. His blank look signals his exclusion from the circuit of the reproduction of discourse in commercial advertisements and London street ballads and metonymically his exclusion from the customs of urban life. From the perspective of those who know the conventions, he looks foolish; from his perspective, however, the discourse seems strange.

The scene captures a crucial moment in Wordsworth's representation of the process of reproducing urban ideology in Book 7. It shows an urban environment constructed to inculcate and exploit particular discourses, behaviors, and modes of attention and an urban society that imposes its terms through a system of recognition or disregard. In the draft of this passage, Wordsworth emphasizes how irresistible this instruction in discourse can be: the words "cannot be resisted" and "must & will be read."[110] But this is also one of several scenes in which Wordsworth sees the reproduction of the urban mentality interrupted or discloses something that that mentality masks or renders blank or invisible. For Wordsworth as for Blake, other models of urban experience are not only possible but present in the city.

In Book 7 of *The Prelude*, Wordsworth takes on urban ideology: he adopts the model of a supposedly urban mentality and opposes it. Writing in the autumn of 1804, Wordsworth represents his experience when he first moved to London in 1791, and as always in *The Prelude*, this double consciousness allows him to represent his former state of mind from a critical distance. He writes the generic tale of a naïve country boy feeling overwhelmed in the big city and in doing so extends the traditional model of urban experience familiar from Gay and Cowper. But he also examines the limits of this perspective both by presenting scenes that do not fit the model in Book 8 and by subtly intimating an alternative perspective in double-edged ironic phrasing, in the dissonance between coordinated images, and in the disposition of thoughts in the verse.

Wordsworth's complex resistance to the model of an urban mentality arises from the collision of the generic conventions of polite poetry with the discourse of polite or hegemonic radicalism. Responding to Raymond Williams's emphasis on Wordsworth's recognition in London of "a new kind of alienation" and "new kinds of possible order, new kinds of human unity," Heather Glen remarks that new ways of seeing do "not just suddenly appear" but develop through complex struggles with generic conventions.[111] In her reading, Book 7 of *The Prelude*, like Blake's "London," shows "what it means to be both at odds with and yet conditioned by one's cultural ethos ... Each [poet] sees himself as implicated in and defined by his society, implicated and defined in his very modes of conceiving it." Wordsworth breaks from the conventions of Gray and Goldsmith, Glen argues, by questioning the adequacy of poetic images of social types "as a way of dealing with social reality."[112] Glen's insights have not been pursued: more recent criticism tends to assimilate Wordsworth's representations of urban life into the tradition of Cowper and the mainline of urban ideology.[113] And while Wordsworth situates his representations of urban life in relation to this tradition, his critical response to it, including his suspicion of types, derives from his well-documented involvement in the milieu and discourse of polite or hegemonic radicalism.[114] He shares with John Thelwall, for example, an interest in setting aside the generic types and presenting putatively direct encounters with people in the lower orders. Gregory Claeys writes that Thelwall, "In order to demonstrate the depths to which the working classes had sunk ... had himself even gone from farm to farm ... gathering evidence ... to support his views against the pervasive prejudices of those who did not know the real character of the working population."[115] Wordsworth similarly considers the prejudices within the prevailing representations of the urban working orders and their consequences and seeks instead to disclose the common humanity beneath the determinations of class and environment. The people of London are always represented through some ideological perspective and as such are never adequately represented. Wordsworth presents the apprehension of the inadequacy of typical representations in moments of blankness. In seeking to apprehend and disclose the common humanity manifest in this invisible remainder, Wordsworth stands at the radical limit of middle-class ideology. He acknowledges the value and individuality of workers and his own implication in the dehumanizing urban system as Cowper never does, yet he does so while holding to the model of subjectivity and social relations that Blake rejects.

At the opening of Book 7, Wordsworth introduces the main themes and patterns for the representation of London that will follow: he associates the ideological structuring of expectations about urban experience with the medium of literature, indicates the book will largely copy that form of experience, and suggests that these expectations will lead him to blank failures. Wordsworth recalls that his early reading led him to think of London as more wondrous than cities "built / By Genii of Romance," or what "hath in grave / Authentic History been set forth of Rome, / Alcairo, Babylon, or Persepolis" (7.82–85). He sets up this illusion to dispel it. He is disappointed when a boy from his town, "a Cripple from the birth" (7.95), goes to London and returns unchanged. Wordsworth feels the strange absence of "beams of glory" (7.103) when he beholds "the same / Appearance, the same body" (7.101–2). The young Wordsworth quizzes the boy to draw out tales of wonder, but the boy's answers fall flat. Throughout Book 7, Wordsworth returns to such baffling confrontations with the unexpected presence of particular bodies that refuse to conform to expected images of the city. After this thematic disappointment, Wordsworth declares that for the rest of the book he will "give way, / Copying the impression of the memory, / (Though things remember'd idly do half seem / The work of Fancy)" (7.145–48); that is, he will describe his memory of how he experienced the city in 1791, even if that memory is as fanciful and his former experiences as misguided as his childish impressions of London. He recalls that his expectations were frustrated when he "look'd upon the real scene" (7.139), but he found "keen and lively pleasure, even there / Where disappointment was the strongest" (7.141–42).

Wordsworth's representation of his experience in London largely follows poetic conventions, but it differs in its mimetic presentation of the distracting, alienating, and disorienting effects of the urban environment. As Wordsworth enters London, as if a rustic seeing the city for the first time, he struggles to comprehend a rapid succession of various impressions. Where Gay signaled his mastery of the manners of the city by organizing discrete images around formal resemblances, Wordsworth signals his subjection to the movement of the city by presenting his impressions as if in the sequence in which they occurred. He creates an illusion of a single point of view moving through the city by combining the conventional Juvenalian spatial markers "Here" (7.176) and "There" (7.179) with the markers of temporal sequence "Meanwhile" (7.184), "till" (7.184), and "then" (7.200), and with verbs of continuing progress in the phrases "We take our way" (7.190) and "Conducted through" (7.201). He registers appearances without comprehending them. His rapid shifts of attention break his syntax into parataxis, stripping subjects of predicates: "midway in the Street / The Scavenger, that begs with hat in hand" (7.163–64). Wordsworth suspends the phrase presenting the image of the scavenger at the end of a line, but before a main verb can appear, the sentence turns into a list as another sight intrudes. Following Cowper, Wordsworth's highly enjambed blank verse represents Hume's "perpetual flux and movement" of sensory stimulations in the city.

This flux of images absorbs Wordsworth into an urban society and ideology that reduces people and things to mere appearances and that forces these appearances to compete for attention. Ross King reads Wordsworth's representation of London alongside Baudrillard's analysis of industrial capitalism, in which images and commodities converge and these images relate to each other in a manner comparable to the mutual differentiation of signifiers.[116] Wordsworth presents a series of characters who manage their images to compete for attention. The parliamentary "Orator" (7.532) "winds away his never-ending horn" (7.539) as "Words follow words, sense seems to follow sense" (7.540); the "comely Bachelor" (7.547) behind the pulpit, "Fresh from a toilette of two hours" (7.548), uses "the Crook of eloquence" (7.564), ornamented with the flowers of others, to lead "up and down his captivated Flock" (7.566). Both speakers attend more to the form and effect of the presentation than to the meaning, and in both cases the act of following correlates with thoughtlessness. These are but two examples among "ten thousand others" (7.568), each of whom, "rear'd on his own Pedestal, / Look[s] out for admiration" (7.571–72). These "Candidates for regard" (7.577) compete in a market for attention, a competition that extends from members of Parliament and priests down to beggars. Wordsworth implicates himself and his fellow poets in this system. The images of the orator and priest follow Cowper's generic satirical vignettes. And among the crowd of candidates for regard, Wordsworth singles out "An English Ballad-singer" (7.196), a figure who at once represents plebeian street culture and doubles for the polite poet of *Lyrical Ballads.*

The market of appearances cannot be escaped: it fosters attempts to break its types and assimilates those deviations within its field in the type of the urban eccentric. Wordsworth here anticipates Simmel, who observes that in a metropolitan environment, "the attention of the social world can . . . be won for oneself. This leads ultimately to the strangest eccentricities, to specifically metropolitan extravagances of self-distanciation, of caprice, of fastidiousness, the meaning of which is no longer to be found in the content of such activity itself but rather in its being a form of 'being different' – of making oneself noticeable."[117] Seen this way, all individuals embody positions within the field of appearances.

> Folly, vice,
> Extravagance in gesture, mien and dress,
> And all the strife of singularity,
> Lies to the ear, and lies to every sense,
> Of these, and of the living shapes they wear
> There is no end. (7.572–77)

The inhabitants of London appear merely as the "living shapes" worn by allegorical figures of "folly," "vice," and countless other abstractions. This strife of singularity has "no end"; it reproduces itself indefinitely and serves no valid purpose. In what seems like an interjection from the perspective of 1804, Wordsworth calls these types and the struggle of eccentricity "lies," as if the system of appearances within the conventional model of urban society overshadows another, true way of seeing it, one that attends to the individual rather than to his or her position in the market of appearances.

Since any representation will either reproduce or create a new generic type, Wordsworth registers differences between how urban society is and how it appears through ironic suggestion and effects of the verse. He adverts to this gap in a passage that, fittingly, proclaims the wondrous power of words. As a child, Wordsworth wondered how Londoners

> lived
> Even next-door neighbours, as we say, yet still
> Strangers, and knowing not each other's names.
>
> Oh, wondrous power of words, how sweet they are
> According to the meaning which they bring!

Vauxhall and Ranelagh! I then had heard
Of your green groves, and wilderness of lamps,
Your gorgeous ladies, fairy cataracts,
And pageant fire-works. (7.118–26)

The exclamation on the power of words ambiguously refers to two misuses of language: it points ahead to the verse paragraph just begun and back to the end of the preceding verse paragraph.[118] If read as introducing a new thought, it wonders at the power of words to create images that far exceed reality. Indirectly, it also remarks that words represent not things in themselves but abstractions, and that the abstraction within verbal representation allows for the substitution between two things that may be in one respect equivalent but in another respect radically different. Words make things interchangeable as the system of marketed images makes people interchangeable. Wordsworth emphasizes this power of words with ironic diction. The phrase "gorgeous ladies" refers equally to polite daytime visitors and the prostitutes who use the park at night. The "fairy cataracts," as Richard Altick notes, were part of a larger spectacle of a rural landscape with a mill, and "evidently [were] produced by strips of tin shimmering in the light of concealed lamps. The other moving parts were faithful adaptations of components of the old clockwork theatre."[119] An image contrived by a mechanical system substitutes for the particular thing. If read as a retrospective reflection on the preceding verse paragraph, however, "wondrous power of words" refers to the absence of words among neighbors who do not know each other's names and remain strangers. The dominant sense of the passage is that neighborhood involves a personal relation and not mere proximity; Londoners appear to have neither the word for nor the relation of "next-door neighbours." But the passage leaves open the possibility that Londoners live in the familiar relation of neighbors with each other even while remaining strangers. This living relation exists independent of the exchange of names or representation in words. In one direction the exclamation remarks the power of words to mask what exists, and in the other direction it remarks that what exists does so independent of words. The passage reproduces an ideological image of urban life, but it also registers the limits of its representations. It registers that limit in a conceptual enjambment in the blank space on the page.

Wordsworth entertains different figures for the role of the individual in this system of appearances in his account of Bartholomew's Fair. The various prodigies Wordsworth lists – "The Horse of Knowledge, and the learned Pig, / The Stone-eater, the Man that swallows fire"

(7.682–83) – were not unique performers but roles reprised over hundreds of years. The most extreme and purest instance of the predominance of a role or image over the individual is "the Invisible Girl" (7.684). Timothy Webb describes the illusion of the invisible girl as an "extraordinary contrivance" in which a series of tubes fed into a closed room and, by channeling sound into the room, made it appear as if there were a girl in the room capable of speaking, answering questions, and playing the piano.[120] The invisible girl is an image of a human reduced to a function of a mechanism and renders literal the way individuals disappear into roles and commodified images. She belongs with the other mechanical humans: "The Bust that speaks, and moves its goggling eyes" (7.685), the "Puppet-shows" (7.687), and the advertisements that present "allegoric shapes, female or male, / Or physiognomies of real men" (7.179–80). In the manuscript drafts, Wordsworth refers to plural "invisible girls," extending the spectacle into a type.[121]

The invisible girl is another blank that registers the presence of something missed. Everyone knows her invisibility is an illusion, but they pretend not to see her anyway. The illusion of her invisibility relies on the same willing suspension of disbelief that allows Jack the Giant-killer to stalk about the stage dressed in black with "the word / Invisible . . . upon his chest" (7.309–10): the actor stands before the crowd but conventions of representation preserve the fiction of his invisibility. At Sadler's Wells, Wordsworth watches the crowd to observe the "laws and progress of belief; / Though obstinate on this way, yet on that / How willingly we travel, and how far!" (7.299–301). Wordsworth compares social life and theatre throughout Book 7, and this passage signals not only his youthful disregard for popular entertainments but the ways in which the power of words and conventional ways of seeing and representing the city can render people and popular culture invisible.

These passages in Book 7 that reveal a gap between the system of representation and the actual conditions of people's lives imply what Wordsworth states more directly in Book 8: the habits of perception ideologically associated with the urban environment obscure an alternative impression of the nature of urban experience that is not hypothetical or possible but real and observable. Critics who argue that Wordsworth finds the city antagonistic to the sustained and focused attention required for the operation of his imagination take his representation of urban life in Book 7 for his position and read his direct statements to the contrary in Book 8 as minor qualifications and exceptions.[122] For all the distractions of Book 7, in Book 8 Wordsworth offers the counterexample of the "Artificer" (8.854) who concentrates on the face of his child and looks upon it with strong paternal love. He remarks that he finds London, the "vast Abiding-place / Of human Creatures, turn where'er we may, / Profusely sown with individual sights / Of courage, and integrity, and truth" (8.837–40). Hugh Sykes Davies cites a version of these lines to show Wordsworth's interest in the way attention focuses on single objects.[123] An individual sight is also a sight of an individual, an apprehension not of a representation but of the truth, the truth that each individual shares fundamentally common humanity. Defined against the poetic conventions for representing urban life, Wordsworth's recognition of the individual humanity of members of the lower orders appears radical; yet compared to Blake, Wordsworth's investment in the individual remains bourgeois.

By taking on urban ideology, Wordsworth acknowledges that he is bound up in the urban world and in the perspective it putatively constructs. He confronts his implication in urban ideology in his account of his encounter with the blind beggar. He prefaces the scene by remarking that "one feeling was there which belong'd / To this great City by exclusive right" (7.593–94):

> How often in the overflowing Streets
> Have I gone forwards with the Crowd, and said
> Unto myself, the face of every one
> That passes by me is a mystery!
> Thus have I look'd, nor ceas'd to look, oppress'd
> By thoughts of what, and whither, when and how,
> Until the shapes before my eyes became
> A second-sight procession, such as glides
> Over still mountains, or appears in dreams;
> And all the ballast of familiar life,
> The present, and the past; hope, fear; all stays,
> All laws of acting, thinking, speaking man
> Went from me, neither knowing me nor known.
> And once, far travell'd in such mood, beyond
> The reach of common indications, lost
> Amid the moving pageant, 'twas my chance
> Abruptly to be smitten with the view
> Of a blind Beggar, who, with upright face,
> Stood propp'd against a Wall; upon his Chest
> Wearing a written paper, to explain
> The Story of the Man, and who he was;
> My mind did at this spectacle turn round
> As with the might of waters, and it seem'd
> To me that in this Label was a type,

Or emblem, of the utmost that we know,
Both of ourselves and of the universe;
And on the shape of this unmoving Man,
His fixed face, and sightless eyes, I look'd
As if admonish'd from another world. (7.595–623)

Wordsworth's feeling of alienation and of being lost in an unfamiliar flux signals his involvement in a conventional mode of urban experience. Like Cowper, he seeks security in disengagement: detached from the scene, his mind stands fixed as a mountain as the shadowy procession of modernity passes over it. Yet for Wordsworth the disruption of this mood is equally typical of the city. Wordsworth is stunned as the beggar comes into his view and, paradoxically, as he feels himself exposed to the view of the blind man. The grammatical ambiguity of who views whom suggests the two men double each other and compares the poet's conventional perspective to blindness, a comparison supported by the contrast between his blindness to the faces that pass by him and the sudden fixing of his eye on the face of the beggar.[124] At the sight, his mind recoils: "My mind did at this spectacle turn round / As with the might of waters." The reversal reveals to Wordsworth that his supposed detachment from the crowd was illusory; the figure of turning round inverts the perspective, as if he sees himself from the blind man's point of view and recognizes that he too is part of the crowd. His mind turns round "As with the might of waters," as if it were a ship overpowered by an eddy or as if it were the eddy itself. Wordsworth has already felt the loss of his "ballast" and the snapping of the "stays" of his mind, and without these means of maintaining stability he seems in danger of foundering at sea. Wordsworth alludes to *The Task*, borrowing Cowper's enjambment after "turns round," but he does not stand like Cowper and Lucretius safe on the shore but on (or as) the storm-wracked ship. Working this reversal through an allusion implies that the poetic convention alluded to is itself involved in the busy world, a constituent of an ideology that reproduces this mode of experience. If Wordsworth is in the position of the ship, then the blind beggar is in the position of the detached observer; poetry that assumes this detached perspective suffers from a kind of blindness.

In the verse paragraph that follows this passage, Wordsworth considers how the material world resists the application of the mental forms, whether of urban ideology or, more generally, of language or of Coleridgean idealism. The encounter with the blind beggar demonstrates the shock that results when the mind senses the instability of "such structures as the mind / Builds for itself" (7.625–26) even when they are "rear'd upon the base of outward things" (7.624). Wordsworth feels admonished or reprimanded for adopting a perspective that misrepresents the real; the admonition comes "as if" from another world because that part of the base of outward things upon which ideological representations are projected either does not appear within that representation or appears within it as nothing. In this sense, the blind beggar is the obverse of the invisible girl, an individual sight of the unknown particular being of the man. On a social level, the admonition warns of the consequences of continuing to overlook the foundation of common humanity beneath the supposed divisions of urban society. On a poetic level, it warns, in the words of Wordsworth's fragmentary and unpublished *Essay on Morals* (1798), against "fitting things to words" and calls instead for "fitting words to things."[125]

In taking on urban ideology, Wordsworth does not directly attempt the radical change in representation that would accompany fitting words to things, but he nonetheless ironically implicates within conventional images a sense of how the urban world would appear from this inverted perspective. The comparison between fine ladies and prostitutes in the ambiguity of the reference to the "gorgeous ladies" of Vauxhall is a generic satire of the luxurious pretentions and sordid vices of urban life; but it also adverts, in use of a common sign, to the common humanity of the high and the low. In Book 8, Wordsworth insists that when he was in London in 1791, he was not "ignorant that high things / Were round me" (8.688–89). In the lines that immediately follow, he supports this claim with an account of his first entry into London, when

> On the Roof
> Of an itinerant Vehicle I sate
> With vulgar men about me, vulgar forms
> Of houses, pavement, streets, of men and things,
> Mean shapes on every side. (8.693–97)

As Wordsworth enters the city, he assumes the urban mentality and the men around him lose their distinctiveness and fade into interchangeable forms and shapes as if on their way to invisibility. Yet by immediately following the assertion that "high things / Were round me" with a description of the "vulgar men" and "vulgar forms" and "Mean shapes" that were "about me" and "on every side," Wordsworth forces the comparison, if not identification, of the "high things" with the "vulgar men," "vulgar forms," and "Mean shapes."

Such inversions recast the city not as a producer of types but as a product of men, not as a spectacular market of regard but as a material space shaped by a long history of everyday life and labor. When Wordsworth crosses the threshold on the itinerant vehicle, he feels a "weight of Ages . . . descend / Upon my heart" (8.703–04). A few lines later, he confesses he never took much delight in the high histories of Greece and Rome, which have come down to us "Stript of their humanizing soul, the life / Of manners and familiar incidents" (8.775–76). On entering London, however, "a sense / Of what had been here done, and suffer'd here / Through ages, and was doing, suffering still, / Weigh'd with me" (8.781–84). Wordsworth is not inspired by the memory of the grand events in London's past; instead, he feels awed by an impression of how many people and over how many centuries people have lived their ordinary lives in this place. This impression does not diminish the city's grandeur. Upon entering the city, Wordsworth felt "a blank sense of greatness pass'd away" (8.744). He had an indefinite feeling of the grand history of the place; his former sense of what constituted greatness appeared blank and went from him; and he felt a different kind of greatness, a greatness that has passed away without its history being written. The gaps between these perspectives appear in a moment of blankness. This change in perspective does not change the urban world of commodified images, but it emphasizes that these images cannot be separated from the base of ordinary people and things; the people are not, as they may appear, the vessels through which the city and urban ideology reproduce themselves; rather, the city and urban ideology are products of their ordinary lives.

As evidence that the people produce the city rather than the other way around, Wordsworth offers his account of Bartholomew's Fair. He presents this alternative perspective in the ironic complications of an ambiguous scene, and he is left not with assured conviction but with a blank. The scene emphasizes both the degree to which urban ideology shapes urban society and the irreducible potential for the plebeian London crowd to break its forms. Wordsworth prefaces his account of the Fair by offering it as an instance of those scenes that come to the mind "Full-form'd" and "take with small internal help / Possession of the faculties" (7.627–28). The Fair, Wordsworth claims, seizes control of the mind and belongs among common scenes that are internal to the urban order and that yet reveal its fragility, such as "when half the City shall break out / Full of one passion, vengeance, rage, or fear, / To executions, to a Street on fire, / Mobs, riots, or rejoicings" (7.646–49). Behind these routine crises are still greater ones: the Great Fire, the Gordon Riots, and the French Revolution.

Wordsworth announces in advance that his account of Bartholomew's Fair will follow poetic conventions. Before he begins to describe the Fair, he calls for "the Muse's help" (7.656) to lift him "Above the press and danger of the Crowd / Upon some Show-man's Platform" (7.658–59). Wordsworth ascends the showman's platform from an impulse to survey the Fair from a safe distance, but in doing so he remains within the spectacle and compares himself to other showmen. As in the episode of the blind beggar, Wordsworth's allusions here to Spenser, Jonson, Milton, and Pope place himself within the tradition of polite poetry and associate that tradition with his position and perspective. He explicitly states that he wishes to avoid the "press" of the crowd, to separate himself from the crowd's literary culture, but he has already undermined the distinction between polite and plebeian culture by positioning himself on the showman's platform as a prominent participant in the spectacle.

The Fair appears as a mechanism that reproduces urban ideology. Wordsworth's long description of the Fair focuses almost exclusively on the performers rather than the crowd and presents a plebeian double of the market for attention. The people in the crowd are assimilated into the scene. They are "slaves unrespited of low pursuits, / Living amid the same perpetual flow / Of trivial objects" (7.701–03). Seen from above, "Tents and Booths, / Meanwhile, as if the whole were one vast Mill, / Are vomiting, receiving, on all sides, / Men, Women, three years Children, Babes in arms" (7.692–95). The mill revolves and processes its raw materials, here people, in bulk. The whole scene, as critics have noted, recalls Spenser's Error, her "vomit full of bookes and papers" and her "fruitfull cursed spawne of serpents small, / Deformed monsters, fowle, and blacke as inke."[126] Figured within literary convention, the crowd at the Fair appears as the offspring, excrement, and food of the monster, a cycle thoroughly mediated through text. Having implicated himself in the scene, Wordsworth recognizes that, as in the Spenserian allegory, the error here is at once an objective monster and a projected image of a misdirected mind.

The image of the Fair includes possible figures for how this cycle may be interrupted. These range from anarchic revolution to a change in literary representations. At one extreme, the account of the Fair anticipates the descriptions of revolutionary Paris. The bestial diction and images of whirling rounds accompany more directly political references to "Promethean thoughts / Of man" (7.689–90), "This Parliament of Monsters" (7.692), and an "anarchy" (7.660) of apparently disembodied "heads" (7.665). Read this way, the scene of the Fair is a conventional warning against the anarchic potential of urban popular democracy. The dense allusiveness of the passage suggests that the Fair is the social order's image of what lies beyond itself, and the prominent focus on roles and flows instead of on the experience of people within the crowd suggests that the chaos of the carnival is internal to the reproduction of the social order. Wordsworth also entertains the possibility that a change in literary representations of the city may contribute to a change in the urban order. He concludes Book 7 with a remark that suggests the possibility of reform.

> The Soul of Beauty and enduring life
> Was present as a habit; and diffused,
> Through meager lines and colours, and the press
> Of self-destroying, transitory things,
> Composure and ennobling harmony. (7.737–41)

In one sense, Wordsworth asserts his rustic power to remain unmoved among the threatening flux of the milling crowd. But "through" means not only deeply behind but also embodied in and by means of. Through meager lines and images of verse and through the press, whether polite or plebeian, this spirit of beauty and life can disseminate a sense of "composure" and "harmony." The allusion to Error, a monster devoured by her inky spawn, raises the possibility that the literary mediations that reproduce the figures and habits of urban ideology may turn round and devour it.

In Bartholomew's Fair, Wordsworth confronts both the ideological representation of the London crowd and the crowd itself: the scene is both a culmination and a refusal of urban ideology. The Fair, he claims, is "A work that's finish'd to our hands" (7.653) and that "lays . . . The whole creative powers of man asleep" (7.653–55). Either the scene has been so thoroughly written into an image that the imagination has no new work to do or the scene is so impressive that it stuns the imagination out of its habitual activity. Wordsworth writes it is "By nature an unmanageable sight" (7.709), a phenomenon that cannot be controlled or disciplined. But it "is not wholly so" to one who has "among least things / An under sense of greatest" (7.711–12). On the one hand, Wordsworth reasserts the imaginative power he received from his peculiar education among the mountains. But, on the other hand, the under-sense of greatness while among least things directly anticipates the scene of his entry into London with vulgar men and things about him. Bartholomew's Fair may seem terrible not because he is too close to it but because he is too distant from it. Once again, Wordsworth refers to the effect of this suspension between his absorption within urban ideology and an apprehension of an alternative mode of urban experience as a blank: the Fair is a "blank confusion! and a type not false / Of what the mighty City is itself" (7.696–97). It is a meaningless jumble. It is a temporary carnival inversion. But it is also a figure for the unrecognized mutual implication or fusing together of polite and low culture and an image indifferent to such distinctions. This blank confusion of the Fair is one way in which "the unity of man" was "Affectingly set forth" (8.826–27) in London.

Wordsworth stresses throughout Book 7 and Book 8 the power of literature to shape how people perceive and experience urban society. In this he agrees with Blake's identification of the process of building Jerusalem with the act of creating and reading *Jerusalem*. Both offer in their poetry sharp critiques of the present state of urban ideology and counter the assumption that the urban environment determines a particular mentality and pattern of social experience. They differ in their vision of an alternative model of urban experience, but both assert the agency of the people in the city to determine the nature of their own social relations. Despite the present state of urban life, the possibility of rewriting urban ideology leaves both guardedly optimistic about the future of urbanization. London inspires in Wordsworth

> elevating thoughts
> Of human nature. Neither guilt nor vice,
> Debasement of the body, or the mind,
> Nor all the misery forced upon my sight
> Which was not lightly pass'd, but often scann'd
> Most feelingly, could overthrow my trust
> In what we may become. (8.801–07)

2

Coleridge and the Civilization of Cultivation

In the course of tracing the evolution of urban ideology within representations of London in eighteenth-century and Romantic-period poetry, the previous chapter also caught poets reflecting on the relationship between these ideological forces and the conditions of poetic production, circulation, and consumption. To shift attention from how poets represented urban experience to how poets understood the place of poetry in an urbanizing society – as revealed in the representations of their poetry and in their practical negotiations of the literary field – is to raise the broader question of their senses of the relation between culture and society. The conception and analysis of the former relation depends on the conception and analysis of the latter.

In *Culture and Society, 1780–1950*, Raymond Williams demonstrates that the modern form of this broader critical inquiry began with the works of Romantic-period authors, especially poets, and preserves vestiges of Romantic-period thought. Williams focuses specifically on how the "social and economic change" of "the Industrial Revolution" motivated the canonical poets' new definitions "of art, of the artist, and of their place in society." With the emergence of a literary marketplace, Williams posits, "the production of art was coming to be regarded as one of a number of specialized kinds of production, subject to much the same conditions as general production,"[1] and the canonical poets reacted against this change of circumstances by asserting their independence from the financial and ideological determinations of the market and by proclaiming their superiority to the corrupt tastes of the common public. For Williams, the most influential expression of this position appears in the works of Coleridge. In his chapter "Mill on Bentham and Coleridge," Williams examines the Victorian appropriation of Coleridge's vision of culture. Mill reads Coleridge as offering culture as a means of personal cultivation through which a solitary artist awakens and educates the mental and spiritual faculties of a cloistered reader, faculties that would otherwise atrophy in the pursuit of market interests or in utilitarian calculation. Williams notes that this vision of culture does not oppose mechanical utilitarianism so much as facilitate its operation by relieving its stresses with salutary doses of spirituality and feeling. Williams argues that such a reading misrepresents Coleridge's idea of culture's role as an independent force operating within society. "This idea of Cultivation, or Culture, was affirmed, by Coleridge, as a *social* idea."[2] Far from focusing on solitary and private cultural production and consumption, Coleridge calls for an autonomous cultural establishment filling the place of a national church and opposing the relentless expansion of the market and its ideology.

In the decades since the appearance of *Culture and Society*, critics have further explicated the practical and theoretical ties between cultivation and civilization in Coleridge's professional life and work. The cumulative effect of this scholarship has been to resituate Coleridge within the context of the broader culture industry. Several critics have studied Coleridge's responsiveness to the state of the literary public and his tendentious constructions of reading audiences. Other critics have linked his work back to specific social and intellectual milieux.[3] The image of Coleridge that emerges is no longer that of the Romantic poet as a solitary genius free from the stain of commercial calculation, however much Coleridge may have cultivated that image. Instead, recent scholarship casts Coleridge as a canny manager of a personal brand flexibly adapting to an evolving cultural marketplace. Since *Culture and Society*, critics have attended less to the opposition within the dialectic of cultivation and civilization than to the moments of their coordination.

Even setting aside his influence on later ways of thinking about culture, Coleridge is an especially revealing case for an inquiry into the specific relation between urbanization and poetry: the incongruity between his activity in the literary field and his representations of his activity exposes both the evolution of the effects of urbanization on the literary field and the evolution of the ideologically inflected cultural response to those effects across the Romantic period. I aim to define how urbanization structured Coleridge's experience and representation of the place of poetry in society. I reposition critical formations such as the literary field and the construction of publics or audiences as mediations between the broad social process of urbanization and the individual cultural producer. Such a remediation can draw on the work of critics such as Jon Klancher, Peter Manning, and Kevin Gilmartin, who place Coleridge within urban cultural contexts but who do not explicitly attempt to relate his practice to the social processes that transform the cities.[4] It also affords a standpoint from which to assess

Coleridge's diverse attempts to theorize the relation. More generally, I rely on and try to substantiate two potentially tendentious claims about Coleridge. First, I find that Coleridge's representations of the city and of urbanization change in response to his experience with the spatial logic of the literary field. Second, I see a tendency for elements from earlier works framed in one set of terms to reappear as heterogeneous matter in later works that use different terms. In this respect, I follow Seamus Perry in preferring to consider the divisions or overdeterminations of Coleridge's thought rather than in straining to assert strict coherence beneath his apparent eclecticism.[5]

This chapter follows the evolution of Coleridge's experience and construction of the relation between urbanization and poetry throughout his career. It begins with an examination of the terms of Coleridge's Pantisocratic opposition to urban commerce in his Bristol lectures, traces the emergence of a more skeptical attempt to imagine a place for poetry in an urbanizing society during his retirement in Clevedon and Nether Stowey, and concludes by explicating the finer distinctions between urban habitus and cultural practices in the later prose. Through all these phases, Coleridge attempts to imagine ways to free culture from the determination of urbanization while he also asserts that urbanization may dialectically assist in the autonomization of literature. Coleridge's images of escapes from the historical process of progressive accumulation resemble his images for the end of the historical process: transcending and overcoming the process lead to the same end. Coleridge comes to recognize the constructive potential of urbanization largely in terms of the effects of structural urbanization, that is, in terms of the increasing coordination of economic and social activities in and through urban areas. He sees structural urbanization increasing the density of social connections, expanding and tightening literary and political publics, and expediting the dissemination of knowledge and culture. If Coleridge comes to praise these aspects of urbanization associated in Enlightenment moral philosophy with commercial expansion, in his later works he focuses less on cities as a whole than on the distinctions between different kinds of cultural production consumed by different audiences in the cities. In his view, the polite literary field shows the pervasive influence of the commercial spirit: the press aims not to cultivate its audiences but to make money, and under such conditions material impulses determine intellectual activity rather than the other way around. To Coleridge popular culture appears hopeless, and the working orders have no active role in his dialectics of progress. Only ideal works of genius transcend the determinations of geography and commerce. If true poetry influences urbanization indirectly and does not oppose the process per se so much as correct its imbalances and stabilize it, Coleridge nonetheless conjures the ideal of poetry free from the determinations of urbanization in part to show the extent to which at present urbanization defines the possibilities of poetry.

The Structural Formation of the Literary Field in Bristol, 1795–1796

In January 1795, Robert Southey traveled down to London to spirit Coleridge away from the convivial nightlife of its inns and drag him back to Bristol and to Sara Fricker. By this time, Coleridge had published poetry in a variety of venues. He had placed a handful of poems in London's *Morning Chronicle.* His *Monody on the Death of Chatterton* had appeared in a Bristol edition of Chatterton's *Poems.* Benjamin Flower in Cambridge had printed *The Fall of Robespierre* and had run a few of Coleridge's poems in the *Cambridge Intelligencer.* Coleridge had some practical experience with a number of different urban print markets and with the social networks linking producers across those markets. Nonetheless, as Daniel E. White, Peter Kitson, and Mike Jay have demonstrated, the two years Coleridge spent in Bristol had a formative influence on his early career and thought.[6] I use Coleridge's time in Bristol as a case study for an examination of how social geography defines the rough boundaries between literary markets. Coleridge's experience in Bristol instructed him in the correspondence between the city's economic role as a regional commercial center and its cultural position as a peripheral literary market. The literary market, heavily influenced by Bristol's Dissenters, fostered Coleridge's adoption of certain discourses. I reconstruct the attitudes toward social geography entailed in these discourses and argue that Coleridge emphasizes their anti-urban bias to define his relation to other positions in the field and to criticize the commercial spirit of his urban audience. In his early years Coleridge adapts these discourses in a manner consistent with the alternative discourse on urbanization. But Coleridge's use of anti-urban rhetoric in an urban milieu also reveals an apparent contradiction between his own theory and practice. His experience with the Bristol public unsettles rather than confirms his understanding of the relation between culture and social geography, undermining the utopian premises of Pantisocracy and driving him toward new speculations. Poetry in particular does not factor prominently at this stage of the argument, but the frames of thought and the analysis of situations put in play here are necessary preliminaries for the analysis of Coleridge's poetry in the next section.

The condition of Coleridge's Bristol can be understood by placing it in the context of the history of structural urbanization in Britain. From the sixteenth century onward, the growth of London had created such enormous demand for goods and services that it drove the integration of the national economy and encouraged regional specialization to maximize local competitive advantages.[7] This integration and coordination of the economy requires what Jan de Vries calls structural urbanization. "Structural urbanization," de Vries writes, "refers to the organizational innovations that increase the range of urban activities and increase the need for co-ordination and communications."[8] Structural urbanization does not describe a change in the distribution of the population or in behavior. It refers instead to the tightening coordination of economic and governmental activities. This coordination is necessary to organize regional specialization for efficient productivity, to rationalize the division of labor in preindustrial modes of production, and to realize the benefits of integrated markets by buying goods in the cheapest markets and selling them in the dearest markets. Two aspects of structural urbanization are especially important to Coleridge's Bristol. First, the increasing coordination of economic activities encourages investment in infrastructure as a technology of communication and as a means of decreasing the cost of transportation. In the eighteenth century, bankers channeled surplus capital into canals and turnpikes, which appeared to be secure investments capable of producing relatively high returns for their wealthy clients, while city corporations invested in improving ports and docks.[9] Along with reforms to the postal service by Ralph Allen and John Palmer, these improvements helped expedite communication between cities and regions: people, letters, news, and information could pass more quickly from one place to another. These improvements also decreased the friction of distance in commercial exchange and are a historical form of capitalist modernity's pursuit of the annihilation of space by time.[10] Second, structural urbanization tends to broaden and strengthen the control of an urban administrative hierarchy. This hierarchy has several tiers. Decisions made in London's government offices or in meetings in its coffeehouses influence the economic activity of the whole nation, including in regional centers such as Bristol. Decisions made in Bristol's offices, in turn, similarly coordinate the activities of its region.

In the 1790s, Bristol had long benefited from progressive structural urbanization but was beginning to be overshadowed by the rapid growth of Liverpool. Throughout the eighteenth century, Bristol had grown with progressive structural urbanization. Its population increased from about 20,000 in 1700 to about 64,000 in 1801.[11] For most of the century, Bristol was England's greatest western port. It was the main port for counties to its south and west and drew exports from throughout the nation.[12] Much of its industry related to the Atlantic slave trade: its brass works and ironworks produced materials for ships; its glassworks made bottles for rum; its distilleries and sugarhouses processed imported sugar.[13] Its economy relied on commerce, and it grew as the volume and speed of trade increased. But the integration of the national market also increased interurban competition. Bristol attempted with limited success to draw business for its hot wells from the steady flow of visitors to Bath. It was still less successful in responding to the boom of Midlands industry. In the early nineteenth century, Bristol continued to increase the tonnage and value of goods leaving its port, but it lost ground relative to Liverpool. Liverpool was linked to Manchester by a canal, and its city corporation invested in improving its port and docks. Liverpool quickly became the leading port in the west. Its population surged from 22,000 in 1750 to 83,000 in 1801.[14] In *The Friend*, Coleridge would remark, "Bristol has, doubtless, been injured by the rapid prosperity of Liverpool and its superior spirit of Enterprize."[15] At the end of the eighteenth century, structural urbanization enabled the unprecedented metastasis of urbanization; cities developed according to local advantages, such as the price of coal and access to transport. As a commercial city, Bristol facilitated the rapid movement of goods and capital that would enable industrialization and channel capital through other ports.

Structural urbanization changes the contours of print markets. It permits a wider geographic distribution of the audience by allowing print materials to travel more quickly and more cheaply. It also tightens the social, professional, and intellectual ties between audiences in different cities. As the markets in and around provincial cities expand, they become capable of supporting newspapers and booksellers who target their wares to regional interests. Several social and political factors mediate the relation between economic activity and the formation of regional literary markets, including the government's attitude toward freedom of the press, the presence or absence of a university, and the habitus associated with the major industries or demographics of a provincial city. But in general structural urbanization facilitates the emergence of provincial markets and helps to define the balance of the relation between the provincial markets and the national market. Once a city demonstrates it can support a regional press, among the more important indexes that define the nature of that public are the volume of its trade with the metropolis relative to the size of the provincial market, which indicates the degree of its participation in the national market, and the balance of trade with the metropolis, which describes the hierarchy between the two markets.[16] As structural urbanization produces a fractal of hierarchical administration, the structure of a regional literary market is determined from above by its relation to the national order and from below by the peculiar constitution of the local order. In the 1790s, Bristol had vibrant markets for newspapers and books produced locally and elsewhere. Its public participated actively in national discourse, yet it retained a significant degree of local peculiarity and independence. Jon Klancher contrasts the presence of regional publics in Britain against the absence of any such publics in France. "Where London forms the circulatory heart but not the absolute center of British writing and reading," Klancher observes, "Paris tells the provinces what and how to read. There are no Edinburghs, Sheffields, Bristols, Manchesters, or Norwiches that prevent the capital's domination of discourse."[17] Regional publics and markets may have been most independent at the point of their first emergence during either the eighteenth-century urban renaissance of provincial towns or during the Romantic-period boom of manufacturing towns. Progressive structural urbanization tends to tighten the national market.[18]

The boundaries and relations between print markets appear most clearly in the newspaper trade. Provincial towns began running their own newspapers at the beginning of the eighteenth century. Norwich, Bristol, Exeter, Shrewsbury, Yarmouth, and Worcester all started printing their own newspapers between 1700 and 1710. By the late 1740s, Bristol had three newspapers.[19] Provincial newspapers competed with London papers arriving by mail and were often largely pieced together from information printed in the London papers. Some provincial papers were sold in London. Richard Wilson notes of the second half of the eighteenth century, "There was an exchange of newspapers between the metropolis and provinces, with the balance of trade very much in favor of the former."[20] The reach of Bristol's newspapers indicates it was the center of a robust regional public. Jeremy Black suggests that the influence of Bristol's press over its region "can be measured by the delay in establishing newspapers in South Wales." The *Bristol Gazette* solicited advertisements from across the region, reaching as far north as Liverpool. But the *Bristol Gazette* had only a limited presence in the metropolis. Black records that in "December 1767 the *Bristol Gazette* named three London coffee-houses where it could be seen and included London in the list of places where advertisements were taken in."[21] The imbalance of trade indicates the gradient of influence. Bristol's publics read both Bristol and London papers; London's publics had relatively little interest in or access to the Bristol papers. Bristol imported metropolitan discourse but retained a degree of peculiar independence.

A similar balance appears in the book trade. Coleridge's publisher Joseph Cottle and his partner Nathaniel Biggs specialized in printing and selling the works of local authors. His list included the poetry and prose of Coleridge and Southey, the reports and proposals of Thomas Beddoes, and the sermons of local Dissenting ministers. When Cottle sought wider distribution, he often coordinated with a small set of ideologically congenial publishers in London, including Longman, Rees, and Button, G. G. and J. Robinson, and Joseph Johnson. Cottle printed for a local market and, by routing works through the hub of London, for the national network of Dissenting communities.

Publishing his poems in various Dissenting newspapers gave Coleridge early experience with interurban print networks, but his experience with the Bristol Dissenting public, especially in founding his journal *The Watchman*, gave him a deeper sense of the geographical divisions between literary markets. Coleridge pitched *The Watchman* in several different markets. The journal offered original literature to cities already saturated with news and provided news to cities that could use it. The hedge failed. Coleridge wrote to Thomas Poole, "In London, & Bristol the Watchman is read for it's [*sic*] original matter, & the News & Debates barely tolerated: the people [at] Liverpool, Manchester, Birmingham, &c take [it only] as a Newspaper, & regard the Essays & Poems [as int]ruders unwished for & unwelcome."[22] Each city had a separate literary field. When canvassing for subscriptions, Coleridge avoided encroaching on the markets of ideologically congenial journals such as Flower's *Cambridge Intelligencer* and James Montgomery's *Sheffield Iris*.[23] For Coleridge this separation has positive and negative aspects. Coleridge values the links between local print markets that unite communities. The itinerary of his canvassing traces a relatively coherent network of Dissenters served by the *Morning Chronicle* in London and by local papers. In a lecture later printed as *The Plot Discovered*, he warns that the Two Bills would cut off the circulation of the vital fluid of argument and inquiry that animates the press and constitutes the collective voice of the people. The "almost winged communication of the Press" converts "the whole nation" into "one grand Senate"; but where despotism cuts the lines of communication, "Every town is insulated: the vast conductors are destroyed by which the electric fluid of truth was conveyed from man to man."[24] This insulation may impede the flow of truth, but it may also afford a layer of protection. The government reaction against radicals in London may have been held back in Bristol by its active and powerful Dissenting community and by the partial insulation provided by its distance from the metropolis.

If the economic and geographical situation of Bristol shapes the boundaries of its literary market, the same factors also influence, although through a different set of mediations, the ideological structure of its literary field. Coleridge scholars have noted that the predominant habitus of Coleridge's Bristol public was characterized by an intersection of religious Dissent, oppositional politics, and commercial interests.[25] This habitus is not unique to Bristol. It resembles and shares social ties with other urban circles of Dissenters. At Cambridge, Coleridge had supported the group of radicals gathered around William Frend. Frend left Cambridge for London and found another lively Dissenting public that included William Godwin, Richard Price, and authors affiliated with Joseph Johnson's print shop.[26] The public associated Bristol's Dissenters specifically with the commercial spirit. White remarks, "the associations between Bristol's commercial and Dissenting class were inescapable." He cites an essay in the *Monthly Magazine* from June 1799 that indicates that Bristol's "inhabitants have been stigmatized with a want of taste, and described as the sordid devotees of Pluto." The essay associates this stigma with the perception that "no place contains, in proportion to its inhabitants so many dissenters."[27] Coleridge and the Pantisocrats share many of the religious and political positions of the Bristol Dissenters. Cottle remarks that "Few attended Mr. C[oleridge's] lectures but those whose political views were similar to his own."[28] Yet the Pantisocrats turn against the Bristol Dissenters by deriding their absorption in commerce. In *Bristolia, A Poem* (1794), local poetaster Romaine Joseph Thorn celebrates Bristol's "happy port," which "Prolific COMMERCE makes its lov'd resort" and observes its diverse residents all "Absorb'd in *Trade*." Pantisocrat Robert Lovell retorts in *Bristol: A Satire* (1794), "Trade, mighty trade, here holds resistless sway, / And drives the nobler cares of *mind* away."[29] Southey grumbles to a friend, "This city is peopled with rich fools."[30]

The pressures of the literary field encouraged Coleridge to use discourses prevalent in Bristol's Dissenting public. When he attempts to support himself by lecturing on politics and religion, he assumes the obligation of addressing local concerns, reading what his audience has read, and speaking their language, if not adopting all their positions. His lectures show that he borrowed liberally from "popular Whig sourcebook[s]" such as James Burgh's *Political Disquisitions* and Moses Lowman's *Dissertation on Civil Government*.[31] More directly still, in *The Watchman*, Coleridge draws his materials from specifically Bristolian sources, responding to works locally published and disseminating works of his local Dissenting associates.[32] In his Bristol writings, Coleridge's comments on social geography rely on conceptual frameworks circulating among his audience, including Hartley's associationism, Country Party ideology, and an Enlightenment stadial theory of historical progress. In each case, Coleridge refers to the framework in a manner that highlights the contradiction between the Dissenting public's discourse and its practical absorption in the spirit of urban commerce.

Coleridge builds his case against urban life in part on Hartley's associationism. Hartley argues that consciousness operates mechanically: ideas arise from the physical transmissions of associations between nerves, whether the effective excitation comes from the senses or from another idea. While Hartley remained an Anglican, Joseph Priestley saw an affinity between the implicit monism of Hartleyan associationism and Unitarianism and helped to introduce the theory into the mainstream of Dissenting culture.[33] Hartley only glances at the differences between city and country environs. He prefers natural environments because they build up the networks of pleasant associations that produce benevolence. "To these [pleasant associations with nature] we may add, the Opposition between the Offensiveness, Dangers, and Corruption of populous Cities, and the Health, Tranquility, and Innocence, which the actual View, or the mental Contemplation of rural Scenes introduces."[34] Coleridge elaborates the contrast. As he explains in a letter to George Dyer, "The pleasures, which we receive from rural beauties, are of little Consequence compared with the Moral Effect of these pleasures – beholding constantly the Best possible we at last become ourselves the best possible."[35] In a related passage in a lecture, Coleridge declares, "In the country, the Love and Power of the great Invisible are everywhere perspicuous, and by degrees we become partakers of that which we are accustomed to contemplate."[36] Hartley allows Coleridge to correlate the beautiful and the good – a correlation that informs his early speculations about the moral value of poetry. Cities, however, have the opposite effect. They form unpleasant associations and corrupt morals. "It is melancholy to think, that the best of us are liable to be shaped & coloured by surrounding Objects – and a demonstrative proof, that Man was not made to live in

Great Cities!"[37] In the city man partakes of the hideous consequences of human industry: "in Cities God is everywhere removed from our Sight and Man obtruded upon us" and "squallid [*sic*] wretchedness meets us till at last we have doubts of providential Benevolence."[38] A resident of suburban Clifton might fancy his lifestyle was being praised, if he bracketed the fact that he heard the lecture within the city limits. Coleridge's contrast between environments, however, is implicitly highly polarized and elides suburban middle spaces; the remark likely implicates Clifton's residents in the commerce of the city that begets wretchedness.

Coleridge takes up the discourse of the Commonwealthmen and the Country Party, which the Dissenters had adapted to their political purposes, to comment on the greed and corruption of cities. John Morrow refers to the works of Lowman and Burgh, two of Coleridge's main sources for his lectures, as compendia of "views from Commonwealth and Country Party sources."[39] Country Party ideology, a reworking of civic humanist discourse, associates commerce with corruption. It does not oppose commerce in the sense of trade in general; rather, it opposes a kind of commerce typical of early eighteenth-century party politics in which the government borrowed money from City interests to buy political loyalties by granting sinecures or awarding lucrative contracts.[40] This commerce occurs almost exclusively in London, and Bristolians could use the discourse to adopt a posture of virtuous independence from metropolitan corruption. The presence of an anti-commercial ideology among the commercial classes of Bristol therefore was not a contradiction. Bristol's Dissenters also appropriated elements of the discourse of the Commonwealthmen. As Daniel Malachuk notes, while the seventeenth-century republican Commonwealthmen had associated the republican civic virtues of social and political independence with rural life, the Enlightenment political economists redefined these virtues and associated them with urban tradesmen.[41] Bristol's Dissenters transplanted agrarian republicanism to their commercial hub.

In his lectures, Coleridge discards this distinction between kinds of commerce and associates corruption with all urban development rather than with the political brokering of the metropolis. For Coleridge the root of social immorality and evil lies in private property and the inequality it produces. In a letter to John Thelwall, Coleridge declares, "The real source of inconstancy, depravity, & prostitution, is *Property*, which mixes with & poisons every thing good – & is beyond doubt the Origin of all Evil."[42] In his lectures, he associates the institution of the "right of landed Property" with the rise of "Towns and Cities" and with the origin of the "accumulative system."[43] Cities appear only with the emergence of an economic system that siphons off the surplus value and goods produced by agricultural labor. Cities manifest the cumulative dispossessions of the accumulative system, and the self-reproduction of the accumulative system generates "more enormous Inequality with its accompanying Vices and miseries."[44] Commerce burdens laborers with "improportionable toil" to pay for the "unnatural Luxuries" of the wealthy. "Commerce," Coleridge continues, "is useless except to continue Imposture and oppression." This systemic inequality ensures that one cannot "walk the Streets of a City" without seeing "Drunkenness, Prostitution, Rapine, Beggary and Diseases."[45] Coleridge recognizes that at present the accumulative system also governs agricultural activity. But while property and inequality are necessary conditions of the existence of cities, rural communities may be equal or exist without property. He recommends Lowman's account of Moses's agricultural society, which regularly equalized the distribution of lands and forgave debts. A truly equal republic, Coleridge implies in his lectures, must be agrarian. His critique of Bristol negatively defines Pantisocracy: the Pantisocrats design their plan to reap the benefits of rural beauty and agrarian equality by escaping from the accumulative system and the urbanizing social geography it creates. The geographical correlative of the principle of "aspheterism" – Coleridge's invented term for the denial of the institution of private property – is utopia; the "experiment in human Perfectibility" must take place outside the bounds of the geography of capital.[46]

Coleridge presents Pantisocracy not as a nostalgic return to an outdated mode of society but as a leap forward anticipating a new form of society. He sees Pantisocracy as the culmination of the stadial model of history made current by Enlightenment historiography and political economy. Throughout his Bristol period, his letters and lectures consistently assume a historical narrative in which societies naturally progress from savage hunting to pastoral husbandry to communal agriculture to private property and the development of urban commerce.[47] Pantisocracy preserves historical advances in culture and religion and leaves behind the historical evils of property and self-interest. Pantisocracy would be a remarkably urbane agrarian commune. Southey imagined easy, authentic labor in America: "When Coleridge and I are sawing down a tree we shall discuss metaphysics; criticise poetry when hunting a buffalo, and write sonnets whilst following the plough. Our society will be of the most polishd order."[48] Like Cowper's retirement, Pantisocracy seeks urbanity without urbanization; it isolates desirable attributes of urban commercial life from the broader processes that produced them. By placing Pantisocracy as the next stage of human perfectibility, Coleridge implies that it can be reached either by escaping from the commercial world or by driving the progress of that world from within.

Also like Cowper's cultivation of retirement, the Pantisocrats' utopianism masks their practical involvement in the accumulative system and its geography. Critics have questioned whether Pantisocracy was free from accumulative impulses. Nicholas Roe suggests Southey may have thought of emigration, in the words of Adam Smith, as "'the most direct road to . . . fortune.'"[49] Coleridge reported to Southey a rumor that "literary Characters make *money*" in America.[50] In theory, urban commerce is a source of vice; in practice, it offers a source of income. As George Whalley remarks, "Pantisocracy needed money: this need threw them upon their only resource – their pens."[51] In one perspective, in practice and in theory, the path to Pantisocracy ran through the urban market. In another perspective, Pantisocracy existed only as a claim to territory in the urban market.

Coleridge's lectures demonstrate the influence that the social and ideological constitution of the Bristol literary field had in shaping the positions he took during and after his Pantisocratic phase. His practice of delivering lectures and publishing his poetry and pamphlets instructed him in the coercive force and the professionally enabling and socially constructive potential of urban literary fields. After the collapse of the Pantisocratic scheme during the winter of 1795, Coleridge reconsidered the relation between culture and social geography. In abandoning Pantisocracy, he accepts that the social geography of capital has become, in part through the means of commercial hubs such as Bristol, global and inescapable. Autonomous retirement no longer seems possible and appears as a mere posture. In rethinking the relations between the accumulative system, its geography, and cultural production, Coleridge participates in the wider emergence of the alternative discourse on urbanization. He imagines and skeptically considers ways of overcoming, transcending, or otherwise escaping the determination of the social geography of capital.

The Literary Field and the Ends of Retirement

For Coleridge, the collapse of Pantisocracy was part of a larger personal and professional crisis. In June 1795, his series of lectures ended. In October, he married Sara Fricker, moved to Clevedon, and for the first time became financially responsible for a household of dependents. In November, the

Two Bills were proposed and threatened to suppress the seditious gatherings and oppositional press that had provided Coleridge's main sources of income. Coleridge launched back into public life to oppose the Two Bills. He revised and published his first two Bristol lectures as *Conciones ad Populum*. He delivered and printed a speech against the Two Bills. He moved back from Clevedon to Bristol to start work on *The Watchman*. Coleridge considers the significance of his pivotal decision to return from Clevedon to Bristol in "Reflections on Having Left a Place of Retirement." In "Reflections," he weighs the relative benefits of rural retirement and urban activity. He would face similar choices for much of his career, regularly debating whether to stay in the country (whether Clevedon, Nether Stowey, or Keswick) or to return to the city (whether Bristol or London). The choice forces him to reexamine the relation between social geography and the literary field, and these deliberations inform his poetry written in and around Bristol in 1795–97.

In the previous section, I distinguished between Coleridge's ideal of Pantisocracy as an escape from the geography of the accumulative system and a practical interpretation of Pantisocracy as an oppositional position situated within Bristol's cultural field. In this section, I claim that, in contrast to his representation of Pantisocracy, Coleridge recognizes that his residence in retirement remains within the bounds of the accumulative system. Distinguishing between Coleridge's representations of Pantisocracy and retirement constitutes a small but significant departure from a critical consensus. The main line of criticism assumes Coleridge's views on social geography remain consistent between his Pantisocratic lectures and the poetry of his *annus mirabilis* in 1797. Nigel Leask suggests that "In the years between 1795 and 1801 Coleridge persistently attempted to put his dream of Pantisocracy and agrarian communism into a practical form." As the product of rural collaboration, Leask writes, Coleridge's poetry appears as paradoxical "'aspheterized' property" and retirement represents "an idealization of culture severed from history and society."[52] Tim Fulford also reads Coleridge's retirement poetry as an extension of the radical moral philosophy of the Bristol lectures. For Fulford, Coleridge follows Cowper by seizing the "moral high ground," figured in his poetry by elevated rural prospects, and by asserting "The pernicious effects of city life and the restorative power of rural beauties upon the morals of society."[53] Critics tend to associate retirement with poetry and the commercial city with journalism and the more heteronomous positions of the literary field. Richard Holmes remarks that Coleridge's early years appear to present a "tension between a poetic existence in the provinces, and a journalistic one in the metropolis."[54] I contend that Coleridge's experience in Bristol had instructed him in the inescapability of the social geography of the accumulative system and that his dream of complete literary autonomy vanished with the demise of Pantisocracy. In his retirement poetry, rural retirement and absorption in urban commerce appear as poles within a single plane of social space, each offering a different balance of cultural, economic, and social opportunities and costs. Coleridge treats the topos of retirement critically, disputing its ideological representation of the independence of rural life from the corruptions of commerce. For Coleridge, retirement remains within the accumulative system and minimizes his ability to defend social liberties and to make money with his pen. Retirement is not autonomous enough and too autonomous.

Considering the geographical implications of Bourdieu's literary field offers a more nuanced insight into the determinations of the geography of Coleridge's cultural production than the vague association of poetry with the country and journalism with the city. Bourdieu's model of the literary field "takes account of the major oppositions among genres, but also the more subtle differences observed inside the same genre."[55] At the level of oppositions among genres, different kinds of literary production correlate more or less strongly with different kinds of space. Some literary kinds have practical and financial incentives to being produced and consumed in urban areas; other kinds appear to be relatively independent of spatial determinations. The strength of the correlation depends on the modes of production, consumption, and remuneration. Some forms of theater, professional lecturing, and periodical writing have economic and practical incentives to concentrate their production and consumption in urban areas. Theaters and lecture halls require large investments of fixed capital and require proximity to a large potential audience.[56] A playwright or lecturer benefits from living near the site of performance while preparing for and during production. Coleridge lived in London when he lectured on literature and the history of philosophy and when he saw *Remorse* and *Zapolya* through production.[57] For periodicals, especially newspapers, cities provide the means to maintain short production cycles. In cities, editors can communicate quickly with authors and printers; cities offer direct access to markets for supplies such as paper; they serve as hubs for networks of information passing through coffeehouses, government offices, and other newspapers; and they offer ready access to means of distribution such as the post office. When publishing *The Friend* from Penrith, Coleridge lacked all these advantages and only managed to produce a weekly journal without news with the help of Daniel Stuart in

London. As early as 1795, Coleridge acknowledged the necessity of rapid communication with London to a professional author. Thinking about moving Pantisocracy to Wales, Coleridge wishes "to be employed in some department of Literature which does not require my Residence in Town ... In short, we wish and mean to live (in all the severity of Economy) in Wales – near some Town, where there is a speedy Communication with London."[58] Steady literary jobs that do not require him to be in the mighty heart of the metropolis still require him to be near a main artery.

Except for the poetry editors of newspapers, writing poetry was not a steady literary job in the 1790s. Southey held such a post for Daniel Stuart's *Morning Post* in the late 1790s, and Coleridge recoiled from the heteronomous conditions of production imposed upon a poet.[59] For Coleridge, to write poetry that had a chance of enduring took time and was tenable only at the slower rate of production and consumption seen in volumes, in which an edition might be composed and sell out its first run over a year or more. But conditions conducive to producing poetry were not conducive to supporting even a frugal rural household without other sources of income. The tight circumstances of Wordsworth at Racedown and Coleridge in Nether Stowey prove the point. Since a poet could not expect to live by poetry alone, the correlation between poetry and social geography is weak and indirect from the perspective of practical incentives of production. Coleridge's association of poetry with the country is overdetermined by his inheritance of eighteenth-century attitudes toward social geography and by his imitation and admiration of Cowper and Bowles. In the city or in retirement, the poet remains subject to the coercive pressures of the accumulative system and the literary field.

The divisions within the literary field along the lines of habitus allow more specific correlations between positions in the literary field and positions in space. Bourdieu argues that the "process of differentiation [within] each genre is accompanied by a process of unification of the whole set of genres, that is, of the literary field, which tends more and more to organize itself around common oppositions"; that is, "the opposed sectors of each subfield" tend to align with similar divisions in other subfields and split the field into two layers. For Bourdieu, the literary field splits between the autonomous "pole of pure production" and the heteronomous "pole of large-scale production, subordinated to the expectations of a wide audience."[60] The central fault line corresponds to a division between the class identities of the respective audiences. In Romantic-period Britain, the structure might be thought to split in three, albeit with considerable complications, between the polite and the popular and, within the polite, between the heteronomous and autonomous, a split in poetry, say, between newspaper verse and volumes published by relatively adventurous presses run by sociable publishers, such as Cottle and Biggs. Each layer of the field roughly corresponds with a habitus, and these habitus may concentrate in specific parts of town. These connections play a larger role in Coleridge's prose, and I will address them in the next section. In his early poetry, Coleridge focuses primarily on the more general correlations between kinds of literature and urban or rural space.

In "Reflections," Coleridge casts Bristol and Clevedon as poles within a single plane of social geography. He emphasizes both the generic seclusion of the Clevedon cottage and its practical proximity to Bristol. The cottage lies within a *locus amoenus* with "Thick Jasmins twin'd" about its porch and with myrtles blossoming in the smokeless "open air."[61] This "little landscape" (6) was "a spot, which you might aptly call / The VALLEY of SECLUSION" (9). The intimate confines of a prelapsarian or Hartleyan domestic idyll suggest Pantisocratic utopian detachment from the social world. But Coleridge insists that the cottage lies within the wider social world. He hears "The Sea's faint murmur" (4), the distant sound of the busy Bristol Channel, "At silent noon, and eve, and early morn" (3). He may hear the sea all day. More importantly, through this valley of seclusion, perhaps not so aptly called, strolls a man on a Sabbath constitutional from Bristol: "Once I saw / (Hallowing his Sabbath-day by quietness) / A wealthy son of Commerce saunter by, / Bristowa's citizen" (9–12). The citizen might happen by incidentally, or he might, as Coleridge supposes, seek the serenity the scene provides. The citizen walks from Bristol to Clevedon while the poem's title announces Coleridge's contrary movement from Clevedon to Bristol. Coleridge raises the conventional poetic opposition between retirement and urban life but immediately subverts it by showing Bristol and Clevedon to be within comfortable walking distance of each other.

In Coleridge's polar opposition of city and country, each position appears inadequate. The disadvantages of one situation correspond to the advantages of the other. In each situation his interests in one field – say, his personal finances – interfere with his interests in another – say, his poetry. Nicola Trott notes that the movement of the poem arises not from the attraction of the city or the pull of retirement but from "a division of feeling itself, about the relative merits and claims of both stances."[62] Bristol offers opportunities to earn a living while advancing the cause of liberty. As White shows, the title "Bristowa's citizen" identifies the man with the

Bristol Dissenters' characteristic republican sympathies while his "thirst of idle gold" (13) associates him with Bristol's devotees of Pluto. In his account of his decision to come out of retirement, Coleridge looks to the more positive image of benevolent employment of prison reformer John Howard. Howard "works . . . good" (51). Coleridge imagines his own work in terms that call to mind his goal for *The Watchman*. He resolves to "go, and join head, heart, and hand, / Active and firm, to fight the bloodless fight / Of Science, Freedom, and the Truth in CHRIST" (60–62). Writing joins head, heart, and hand, and the coordination of knowledge, liberty, and Christ echoes in the motto for *The Watchman*, taken from the Gospel, "THAT ALL MAY KNOW THE TRUTH; AND THAT THE TRUTH MAY MAKE US FREE!"[63] I will return to consider the important asymmetry that Howard's work is not specifically urban. But Coleridge's departure for Bristol associates the opportunity to work good with the city as opposed to retirement and with prose as opposed to poetry.

In "Reflections," Coleridge criticizes a specific kind of sentimental retirement poetry that masks its involvement and complicity in the accumulative system behind its posture of autonomy and its decorous but idle expressions of social concern. "Sensibility," Coleridge asserts in an essay written during the composition of "Reflections," "is not Benevolence."[64] In a later version of the poem, Coleridge scorns "Pity's vision-weaving Tribe! / Who sigh for Wretchedness, yet shun the Wretched" (56–57). In contrast to retired poets, whom Coleridge sees "Nursing" their smug sentiments of social concern "in some delicious solitude" (58), Howard appears physically and compassionately nursing the wretched. The attitude of sighing for abstract wretchedness covers for a failure to act on behalf of the wretched. Similarly, the posture of independent retirement masks the involvement of the poet and poetry in the accumulative system. All poetry, even Coleridge's own, participates in the luxury economy arising from the inequalities of the accumulative system. Coleridge writes the division between the readers and writers of poetry and the working classes into "Reflections." He refers to the working classes as his "unnumber'd Brethren" (45); they are "unnumber'd" because they are numerous, uncounted, and unenfranchised and because they are unversed in poetic numbers. What can be "scann[ed]," according to versions of the poem published after 1828, are the textual suspirations of Pity's vision-weaving Tribe.[65] These poets can afford "pamp'ring" (47) and "slothful[ness]" (59). Coleridge notes that only the wealthy can achieve Harringtonian independence or Cowperian retirement. In leaving Clevedon, Coleridge acknowledges he cannot pretend to afford such independence for long. At the end of the mountaintop vision at the middle of the poem, he exclaims, "Blest hour! It was a Luxury—to be!" (42). The line supports several readings. In one reading, the dash lingers on the notion that this vision is itself a luxury or that luxury is a precondition of such a vision. As J. C. C. Mays notes, the motto of the poem, *sermoni propriora*, may indicate Coleridge "was joining himself with Horace in disclaiming the title of poet so far as this and other poems are concerned."[66] In one sense, the motto announces Coleridge's critical distance from the conventional attitude of retirement poetry.

Coleridge hints that the inescapable pressures of the accumulative system and the limited financial rewards of poetry draw him out of retirement. After his mountain-top vision, Coleridge exclaims, "Ah quiet Dell! dear Cot! and Mount sublime! / I was constrain'd to quit you" (43–44). He does not say what constrained him. While the movement of the poem implies his social conscience applied the constraint, his letters and surge of publications after leaving Clevedon suggest the constraint came from a want of money. Before moving to Clevedon he had planned to support himself by writing poetry. "Cottle has entered into an engagement to give me a guinea & a half for every hundred Lines of Poetry, I write – which will be perfectly sufficient for my maintenance."[67] Little came of the impractical engagement, and as he worked on "Reflections" and *The Watchman* back in Bristol, he expressed greater interest in practical literary profits, "Marriage having taught me the wonderful uses of that vulgar article, yclept BREAD –. My wife, my wife's Mother, & little Brother, & George Burnet – five mouths opening & shutting as I pull the string!"[68] Coleridge sees that a poet may conceal but cannot escape his implication in the commercial world.

Coleridge reacts against his impression of the inescapability of the geography of the accumulative system and imagines ways in which it might be overcome or transcended. As was the case in his Pantisocratic phase, his imagined moments of transcendence appear as anticipations of the self-overcoming of the current stage of history. He no longer expresses his utopian impulse by seeking a displacement in space: he turns instead to displacements in history or in mind. The poem's clear structural opposition between Clevedon and Bristol has led critics to look for a dialectical reconciliation between the two spaces and, incidentally, to discuss Coleridge's view of urbanization. Paul Magnuson sees Coleridge hoping for a synthesis but not finding one. "The reconciliation, the full unity of Clevedon and Bristol, is not in the poem except in the prayer for the coming of the millennium."[69] Jon Mee also looks for an image of reconciliation and finds it wanting. The "dialectic of retirement and [urban] sociability becomes stalled," Mee claims, and the poet surrenders to the "attractions of the isolated state of harmony."[70] Such dialectical readings hinge on the last lines of the poem, in which the millennium appears to give every man his English cottage. "[S]weet Abode! / Ah—had none greater! And that all had such! / It might be so —but the time is not yet. / Speed it, O FATHER! Let thy Kingdom come!" (68–71). This egalitarian millennium appears to resolve the geographical polarity in favor of Clevedon, though perhaps "such" also entails Clevedon's proximity to a city. Coleridge offers a vision of this kind of reconciliation in an article reproduced from *The English Review* in *The Watchman.* The article includes "A Sketch of the History of Canals" and projects that the growth of canals may reduce the friction of distance to the extent that the development concentrated in cities could be scattered across the country in a network of villages.[71] In this vision, structural urbanization overcomes other modes of urbanization, and Bristol's commercial civilization helps spread Clevedon's moral cultivation. The accumulative system appears to resolve the historical problem of the limits of urban and rural life.

If Bristol's civilization generates the impulse of progress, then the moral vision of Clevedon's culture steers society toward its proper end. In "Reflections," Coleridge entertains the possibility that his poetry may have a role in overcoming the accumulative system. His poetry participates in society in its dual role as a luxury good and as a medium for the cultivation of moral benevolence. Coleridge does not address his poem to his unnumbered brethren; he aims instead to influence his wealthier readers. During his time in Clevedon, Coleridge revised the *Conciones* to specify that reformers should "plead *for* the Oppressed, not *to* them."[72] He imagines culture diverting the attention of the wealthy away from the drive for accumulation. In his first lecture on revealed religion, Coleridge argues that "by the magic power of association" people can be seduced from the pursuit of a given end to the pursuit of the means to that end.[73] In *Religious Musings,* Coleridge specifically sketches how such short circuits occur in the seduction from progressive accumulation to intellectual cultivation. The drive to increase the power of production or to defeat rivals militarily leads to investment in human knowledge: "From Avarice thus, from Luxury and War / Sprang heavenly Science; and from Science Freedom" (224–25). Art and philosophy are by-products of progressive accumulation that become ends in themselves. He imagines the redemptive potential of

The timbrel, and arch'd dome and costly feast,
With all th' inventive arts, that nurs'd the soul
To forms of beauty, and by sensual wants
Unsensualiz'd the mind, which in the means
Learnt to forget the grossness of the end,
Best pleasur'd with its own activity. (207–12)

Poetry entices the wealthy with the promise of sensual gratification but distracts them from their sensual drives toward an appreciation of mental activity itself. Poetry's complex status as a luxury commodity and artwork allows it to appeal to those who purchase it as a form of cultural capital and to redirect their minds to activities that supersede such selfishness. The beauty of poetry forms networks of positive associations and cultivates moral benevolence. In "Reflections," when the wealthy son of commerce gazes on the conventionally poetic cottage, the sight calms his thirst for idle gold and he poetically "muse[s]" with wiser feelings. Lucy Newlyn observes that, "In undergoing a transformation from misreader to ideal reader, the visitor from Bristol performatively underwrites the poet's authority."[74] By circulating his poetry through the city, Coleridge may propagate such suspensions. The urban world of luxury commerce enables social progress by supporting the producers of culture and by distributing their products. Cultural products in turn may temper the avaricious impulses of Bristowa's citizens and help bring forth a more cultured and more equal society. Another reading of the line "It was a Luxury—to be!" could stress the tenses of the verbs: the luxury temporarily "was" within history but is "to be" in the millennial infinitive of the egalitarian future in which all have such.

Coleridge's vision of historical progress and of the millennium in "Reflections" derives largely from his Unitarian theology. At the same time that he was writing "Reflections," he was reexamining the principles of Unitarianism for the final revision of *Religious Musings*, the poetic summa of his Bristol period.[75] Following Priestley, Coleridge believes in a unitary God who was the first cause and who remains the universal efficient cause in a universe governed by Necessity. God's inherent benevolence guarantees historical progress and justifies optimism. What appears temporarily as evil arises out of the disjunction between the individual mind and the divine mind. With the progress of knowledge, the human mind and the divine mind draw into closer communion, and evil, always the product of ignorance, gradually vanishes. The advance of science or divine truth thus serves as an index of social progress. Individuals, however, may receive divine revelation in moments of epiphany. Such moments are necessarily only temporary.[76] Coleridge's Unitarianism informs both of the ways he imagines overcoming or transcending the determinations of the social geography of the accumulative system. The son of commerce plays the role of Satan, an unwitting agent of the dialectical progress of history as the accumulative system works through evil toward ultimate good. And Coleridge allows moments of anticipatory perception of divine truth in epiphanies of an omnipresent deity. Since God is everywhere, these epiphanies can occur anywhere. Divine omnipresence offers Coleridge a way to transcend the polarity of city and country.

Two such epiphanies occur in "Reflections," and Coleridge pairs them in a way that suggests that they transcend the determinations of space. First, as noted earlier in this chapter, Coleridge imagines that gazing on the "blessed place" calms Bristowa's citizen's thirst for idle gold. Second, Coleridge himself repeats and inverts the citizen's experience in the next verse paragraph. He hikes up a mountain to view a sweeping prospect that encompasses "the Wood, / And Cots, and Hamlets, and faint City-spire" (34–35) and the Channel. To Coleridge, the whole "seem'd like Omnipresence" (38). After the vision Coleridge resolves to return to active life. The juxtaposition of the two scenes confirms that both country and city life are limited. The juxtaposition also shows that both the citizen and the retired poet can experience such epiphanies and that the epiphanies lead both men back from extreme positions toward some common ideal. Crucially, Coleridge's epiphany culminates in an impression of "Omnipresence" that includes both the rural hills and the "faint city-spire" in one divine whole.[77] "Reflections" suggests science and benevolence may be indifferent to space. The structure of the poem loosely correlates Howard's work as an author and a witness before Parliament with urban activity, but Coleridge's set piece presents Howard working good anywhere there is a prison. Similarly, while Coleridge associates the vision-weaving tribe with some "delicious solitude," sighing for wretchedness and shunning the wretched are not exclusively occupations of retirement. Coleridge makes space for the transcendent perspective by limiting the correlation between morality and geography. Like Howard, the relatively autonomous poet works in no specific place. In both of the poem's titles – first "Reflections on Entering into Active Life" then "Reflections on Having Left a Place of Retirement" – the poet remains in transition: he is entering or he has left, but he has not arrived. The verbs consistently orient the poet in motion toward the city, but the noun "Reflections" shows him also looking back to the country. The poet's position relates to both places but belongs to neither. Coleridge strips Cowper's moral high ground and Harringtonian retirement of their geographic components and projects authority onto an epistemological and theological plane.

Coleridge returns to the question of the relations between social geography, commerce, and poetry within a framework of Unitarian optimism in "This Lime-Tree Bower My Prison." Lucy Newlyn reads the poem as part of a friendly debate between Coleridge and Wordsworth on one side and inveterate Londoner Charles Lamb on the other over the influence of urban space on the mind. In a reading that assumes that Coleridge's attitudes on geography remain the same between the Bristol lectures and the summer of 1797, Newlyn argues, "The city of 'This Lime Tree Bower' represents all that is at enmity with human virtue; but it is also an emotional state, poetic shorthand for the suffering that Lamb has gone through, with his sister's madness and the appalling disasters of 1796."[78] Coleridge's goal in the poem, as William Ulmer demonstrates, is to convert Lamb into a "Berkeleyan Unitarian" and to instruct him in the experience of feeling himself a part of divine omnipresence.[79] As in "Reflections," Coleridge qualifies his cultivation of retirement as a privileged locus of poetry and theological insight. He allows the imagination to flourish in the city and sees the city as an engine of historical progress. Once again, Coleridge's ideal condition can be reached both by transcending space in an epiphany and by continuing the pursuit of urban commerce.

Coleridge invokes the conventional poetic image of a city dweller venturing into the country for refreshment in order to test it. In "This Lime-Tree Bower," Charles Lamb plays the role of Bristowa's citizen, a man of commerce who benefits from a redemptive epiphany amid rustic beauty. Coleridge, confined to his bower by an accident, imagines Lamb and the Wordsworths wandering on

> In gladness all; but thou, methinks, most glad,
> My gentle-hearted Charles! for thou hast pined
> And hunger'd after Nature, many a year,
> In the great City pent, winning thy way
> With sad yet patient soul, through evil and pain
> And strange calamity! (27–32)

The line "In the great City pent" alludes to Milton's epic simile for Satan's reaction to seeing Eve after his escape from hell in *Paradise Lost*. The allusion compares London to hell and implies that Londoners may carry their hell within them into the country. But the allusion also associates Lamb with the dialectical historical energy of Satan and

Bristowa's citizen. By alluding to Milton, Coleridge emphasizes the poetic conventions that shape his description of Lamb's experience; at the same time, he knows his description is misleading. Just a year before, Lamb had written to Coleridge wishing that fortune would bring his old friend back to London. "*London*," Lamb declares, "is the only fostering soil for *Genius*."[80] Coleridge would have known Lamb never felt any such hunger for nature, and the misrepresentation may signal his doubts about the retirement tradition.

The structure of "This Lime-Tree Bower" leaves in doubt whether or not Coleridge has any special vision to impart to Lamb. Throughout the poem Coleridge seems split between his doubles. On the one hand, he adopts a Wordsworthian posture as a poet in independent retirement with insight into the divine life of the mind; on the other hand, he compares his circumstances in the bower to his friend from Christ's Hospital's life in the city. Coleridge has long expected his friends' visit; Lamb has "pined . . . many a year." Coleridge has had an "accident"; Charles has suffered through a "strange calamity."[81] Coleridge refers to the bower as a prison comparable to the city in which Lamb has been penned. The walkers' journey out of the dell to the wide prospect and Lamb's journey out of the city into the country map externally Coleridge's internal development within his lime-tree bower. Coleridge reiterates this journey into vision so many times that it becomes difficult to establish valued relations within the matrix of comparisons and contrasts. The equivalence of experiences suggests nature may have no special power to heal Lamb.

Lamb may not need either nature's or Coleridge's help. In "The Dungeon," a poem Coleridge had reworked earlier in the summer of 1797, Coleridge contrasts the damaging influence of a prison with the benevolent influence of nature. Nature heals the prisoner, who gradually "wins back his way" (28).[82] Lamb is already "winning [his] way" in the city. If this phrase primarily refers to Lamb's fortitude weathering personal tragedy, it also refers to his work earning a living. When the poem was first published in Southey's *Annual Anthology*, it carried the subtitle, "A Poem Addressed to CHARLES LAMB, of the India-House, London."[83] The subtitle identifies Lamb not by his tragedy but by his place of business, where he was, in Carl Woodring's colorful phrase, "daily chained to a clerical stool."[84] Lamb's work at the India-House, not the strange calamity, informs the phrases "many a year" and "sad yet patient soul." Lamb switches from filling the place of Satan to filling the place of man, enduring evil and earning his bread by the sweat of his brow.

Like Bristowa's citizen, Lamb leads Coleridge to imagine the progressive qualities of urbanization. Coleridge wonders whether his work as a poet in retirement, his feet lamed and his visions perhaps superfluous, qualifies as winning his way. His description of the bower includes a meditation on work: "though now the Bat / Wheels silent by, and not a Swallow twitters, / Yet still the solitary humble Bee / Sings in the bean-flower!" (57–60). The only being making noise is the solitary bee, who "sings" like a lyric poet. The solitary bee may represent the solitary Coleridge, working productively and sweetly humming while temporarily isolated. But in poetry, bees are notable for sociable industry. In political economy, they figure the productive power of a division of labor. A solitary bee must return to the hive on which its survival depends. Moreover, the bee buzzes while it works; buzzing is not its work. In this respect, the bee represents Lamb better than it does Coleridge. Lamb maintains his literary life while working as a clerk in the city. A pun hovers over "pent," or "penned," as if representing Lamb as suffering urbanite were merely penning a literary commonplace, or, perhaps, as if Lamb were armed with a pen. Lamb reconciles the commercial activity of Bristowa's citizen – actively advancing the historical dialectic through the global diffusion of commercial social ties in the India-House – with the possibility of literary creation and Unitarian consolation independent of the determinations of social geography. Coleridge's inability to console Lamb offers some consolation to Coleridge. If Lamb can win his way in the city and sing like the bee in the midst of his labor, then perhaps the power of the imagination to perceive divine truth can transcend geographical determinations. Perhaps Coleridge can distance himself from the haunting ego-ideal embodied in Wordsworth, the poet free from the burden of writing for profit and firmly rooted in rural life.

Coleridge's Genius in the Urban Culture Industry

From his sketch of Pantisocracy through *On the Constitution of the Church and State* (1834), Coleridge returns to the question of the relation between poetry and a modernizing, urbanizing society. His responses change over time, but a common tension or division persists throughout. When Coleridge discusses the literary marketplace, he sounds like a cultural materialist. He recognizes what scholars including James Raven and Nicholas Mason have shown to be revolutionary developments in advertising, branding, and retailing literature and discerns the deep penetration of market forces and ideologies into the production, distribution, and consumption of literature.[85] But when he considers his own literary production or imagines what he might have done, he tends to look for loopholes in the heteronomy of the marketplace and to reach for ideals of autonomy. In his early lectures, he assails the Bristol Dissenters for their absorption in matters of property and for the immoral environment they inhabit and create while he associates his own perspective with a utopian scheme of social relations. From a materialist perspective, an ironic tension appears in charging admission to a series of lectures in Bristol that blast the commercial practices of Bristolians. The posture of escaping the determinations of the structure and discourse of the local cultural field signals instead a negatively defined and branded position within that field. With the collapse of Pantisocracy, Coleridge abandons the attempt to escape social geography by moving in space or by reinventing social relations and imagines ways in which its influence may be transcended or overcome. In "Reflections" and "This Lime-Tree Bower," his new sense of the inescapability of the accumulative system prompts him to question the conventional association of retirement with poetic autonomy. All too aware of the coercive power of the need for money, Coleridge sees retirement not as a position of virtuous independence but as a position of luxury that masks its involvement in the accumulative system. Coleridge recasts autonomy as an epistemological or theological quality: revelation can occur anywhere and transcends all other determinations. One may live in the city, hold a job, and still write and read poetry. But his ideal of intellectual autonomy remains in tension with the recognition implicit in the inaccessibility of poetic luxuries to his "unnumber'd brethren" and with his doubts about the moral integrity of his own vision. Behind the rotating frames of thought, Coleridge's impulse to defend poetic autonomy consistently opposes his experience with and insight into the material determination of culture.

Coleridge's desire for poetry, as a synecdoche for literary writing, to have the moral authority of autonomy persists throughout his later prose writings, though he continues to tinker with the terms and frames of his conceptions. His tinkering has a general tendency to refine his organizing distinctions. He distinguishes not only between country and city and poetry and prose but between audiences associated with different spaces and habitus within the city and between different kinds of poetry within the literary field. Coleridge remains ambivalent about urbanization, and the structure and balance of his ambivalence changes with the refinement of his analytical distinctions. On the one hand, he thinks the present mode of urbanization tends to foster the subordination of culture to the commercial spirit. That is, urbanization tends to develop the heteronomous areas of the literary field such as newspapers and to subject more of the literary field, including the emerging category of literature, to commercial pressures. The unchecked spirit of commerce drives the business of urban culture as a river drives a mill. On the other hand, Coleridge claims urbanization itself has no direct influence on the poetry of genius, which can circulate within the commercial literary field without submitting to its logic and which remains free from the determinations of the social geography of the accumulative system.

Coleridge's late work thus reiterates the tension inherent in the Pantisocratic lectures of bringing to market cultural products that argue against markets. By defining the autonomy of poetry in terms of the mysterious literary and epistemological quality of genius rather than in terms of its relation to the market or to society, Coleridge emphasizes the oblique influence of poetry on society over the countervailing influence of society on the work of genius. True poetry helps to stabilize the dialectic of social progress but remains removed from it; it rebalances urbanization but does not seek directly to resist or reimagine it. Coleridge makes this argument in part in a series of urban lectures that he artfully promoted with unabashedly commercial purpose. Both by positioning culture as a counterbalance to ensure the continued and steady development of commerce and by joining in the business of culture, as Jon Klancher notes, Coleridge inscribes within his conservative polemics "a modernizing vision."[86]

Coleridge's thought on the relation between urbanization and poetry evolves throughout his later prose. While at any point he may mix innovations with atavisms, he generally tends to revise his analytical categories as he recognizes the inadequacy of his former categories and as the exigencies of circumstance force reappraisals. In his later prose, he presents the influence of commerce on literature as historically contingent. The expansion of commerce facilitates the dissemination of literature and thought but potentially inculcates the habit of self-interested calculation systematized by utilitarian political economy. Coleridge posits certain correlations. Too little trade or too much interest in trade stunts culture. Coleridge claims that by restraining trade, Napoleon's continental system threatens to return the continent to an uncultured state of "barbarism."[87] Too little culture ruins a nation and sinks trade with it, and, as an end in itself, culture can never be excessive. In the "Essay on Method," added to the 1818 *rifacciamento* of *The Friend*, Coleridge claims that "under the ascendancy of the mental and moral character the *commercial* relations may thrive to the utmost *desirable* point," while an overbalance of the commercial character "is ruinous to both, and sooner or later effectuates the fall or debasement of the country itself."[88] Coleridge states these correlations as if they were empirical observations of cause and effect: he does not analyze the mechanisms that ensure the correlations. He describes the relation between trade and literature in a set of coordinated distinctions that similarly leave the nature of the connections undefined.

> As there are two wants connatural to man, so are there two main directions of human activity, pervading in modern times the whole civilized world ... Trade and Literature. ... As the one hath for its object the wants of the body, real or artificial, the desires for which are for the greater part, nay, as far as respects the *origination* of trade and commerce, *altogether* excited from without; so the other has for its origin, as well as for its object, the wants of the mind, the gratification of which is a natural and necessary condition of *its* growth and sanity.[89]

Trade and literature, standing in for civilization and cultivation, provide respectively for man's bodily and mental wants. He may use the distinction between body and mind to emphasize the power of the mind to determine the proper ends for the body. By defining the two wants in terms of origins and ends, Coleridge declines to address the matter of means. His silence is ambiguous. It might mask the complicated connections that muddle the neat distinction. In the present cultural market, considering the means of satisfying intellectual wants would reveal the metamorphosis of literature into a commodity form at its moment of production, its assimilation into the world of trade, and its reappearance in the domain of literature only at the moment of consumption. In this sense, Coleridge preserves his idealism by evading the mediation of cultural production by the market. But his silence might also signal a desire to leave the question of means open rather than to naturalize the mediation of literary production and consumption by trade.

In his late prose, Coleridge argues that the transformations of social geography only change the means and magnitude of the circulation of literature and the dissemination of its ideas; they do not change its inherent quality. During the recent flourishing of commerce during the Napoleonic Wars, Coleridge notes, the nation saw "Every where roads, rail-ways, docks, canals, made, making and projected. Villages swelling into towns: while the metropolis was surrounding itself (and became, as it were, *set*) with new cities."[90] These connections have "rendered Great Britain ... a BODY POLITIC, our Roads, Rivers, and Canals being so truly the veins, arteries, and nerves, of the state; that every pulse in the metropolis produces a correspondent pulsation in the remotest village on its extreme shores!"[91] The structural urbanization generated by commerce unfolds the circulatory and nervous systems of an integrated national organism.

Positive as this sounds, commerce remains associated with the body as distinct from the mind, and the circulatory system of commercial print culture can spread disease as well as nutriment. In *The Friend*, Coleridge imagines a man who stands over an anthill and watches "the effect of a sudden and momentary flash of sunshine on all the countless little animals within his view, aware too that the self-same influence was darted co-instantaneously over all their swarming cities as far as his eye could reach." Coleridge notes the powerful "shock of feeling in seeing myriads of myriads of living and sentient beings united at the same moment in one gay sensation, one joyous activity."[92] In context, the image develops into a figure for the spread of revolutionary enthusiasm in Paris and especially in London. The united sentiment of the sentient but not rational ants anticipates Coleridge's disparagement of the thoughtless susceptibility of the lower orders of London to the texts of enthusiastic religions and the ubiquitous advertisements of quacks, to "the Animal Magnetists; the proselytes of Brothers, and of Joanna Southcot"; and the "infamous Empirics, whose advertisements pollute and disgrace all our Newspapers, and almost *paper* the walls of our cities," all "vending . . . poisons."[93] The true danger, however, comes not from poisoning the body but from subordinating the mind to the body. Coleridge is troubled when he sees the same unanimity "in a multitude of rational beings, our fellow-men, in whom too the effect is produced not so much by the external occasion as from the active quality of their own thoughts."[94] Coleridge accepts that the thoughtless crowd will yield mechanically to external influences, but the active subordination of active intellect to external influences seems to him a perverse betrayal, an almost Blakean inversion and idolatry, and evidence that the French, and implicitly the British, had become an "overcivilized" nation.[95]

Coleridge sees the early symptoms of a similar disease in Britain in the overbalance of the commercial spirit. The commercial spirit – the attitude and values structured by the accumulative system – values all things as objects of trade, deals exclusively in externals, and as such overlooks the value of literature, which lies in a different dimension.

> We are – and, till its good purposes, which are many, have been all atchieved and we can become something better, long may we continue

> such! – a busy, enterprising, and commercial nation. The habits attached to this character must, if there exists no adequate counterpoise, inevitably lead us, under the specious names of utility, practical knowledge, and so forth, to look at all things thro' the medium of the market, and to estimate the Worth of all pursuits and attainments by their marketable value. In this does the Spirit of Trade consist.[96]

A vestige of the dialectical history imagined in "Reflections" reappears in the thought that the preeminence of commerce may continue until it accomplishes its ends and gives rise to something better. Coleridge laments the incursion of market logic into the domain of culture. The passage permits a distinction between trade and literature within the domain of literary production. Bourdieu describes this fissure as the split between heteronomous and autonomous modes of production. "Each of the genres," Bourdieu writes, "tends to cleave into a research sector and a commercial sector, two markets between which one must be wary of establishing a clear boundary, since they are merely two poles, defined in and by their antagonistic relationship, of the same space."[97] For Bourdieu, the autonomous sector remains bound by the logic of the field by answering the social determinants of the pursuit of symbolic or cultural capital. For Coleridge, the autonomous sector doubles as an area within the literary field bound by the market and as an approximation of an ideal of intellectual independence.

In the *Biographia Literaria*, Coleridge represents the logic of a kind of literary production subject to market interests through a figure that interrelates historical social conditions, technological modes of production, and the form and style of literature. When authors write to gratify the demands of the audience, production defaults to reproduction, reception sinks to consumption, and the ready rearrangement of tried formulae fills the place of thought.

> But now, partly by the labours of successive poets, and in part by the more artificial state of society and social intercourse, language, mechanized as it were into a barrel-organ, supplies at once both instrument and tune. ... I have attempted to illustrate the present state of our language, in its relation to literature, by a press-room of larger and smaller stereotype pieces, which, in the present anglo-gallican fashion of unconnected, epigrammatic periods, it requires but an ordinary portion of ingenuity to vary indefinitely, and yet still produce something, which, if *not* sense, will be so like it, as to do as well. ... Hence of all trades, literature at present demands the least talent or information; and, of all modes of literature, the manufacturing of poems. The difference indeed between these and the works of genius, is not less than between an egg, and an egg-shell; yet at a distance they both look alike.[98]

The logic of the central figures of the stereotype press and barrel organ seems straight out of Walter Benjamin: it posits an evocative but undefined set of correspondences between literature, capitalism, and technology and, as an organ grinder resembles a rag-picker, deflates middle-class cultural pretensions by revealing the logical condensation of their culture to be a marginal character. When mediated by the market, the literary field is absorbed by trade: the producer's mind drops out, the effect on the consumer's mind drops out, and what remains is automatic circulation without end. Jerome Christensen argues that Coleridge imagines the professional "man of letters" absorbed in and identified with the language he uses; in terms of the literary field, Coleridge imagines the author in heteronomous sectors absorbed in the self-reproduction of the market.[99] The determinations of this scheme of cultural manufacturing, however, do not influence the works of genius. Genius remains autonomous. To the superficial eye, works of genius look the same as mechanical works and can be printed and can circulate alongside them. The difference appears only when one tries to crack the shell and finds the latter hollow or when, in time, the former hatches and new life emerges.

Coleridge sees the press propagating the ideologies of the commercial classes. In *Church and State*, Coleridge posits the operation of "two antagonist powers or opposite interests of the state, under which all other state interests are comprised, are those of PERMANENCE and of PROGRESSION."[100] The landed property holders profess the interests of permanence, while the interests of progression find champions among the "members of the manufacturing, mercantile, distributive, and professional classes" located in the "ports, towns, and cities."[101] In the *Lay Sermons*, Coleridge retails a political history of Britain in which "the rising importance of the commercial and manufacturing class" swept away "old feudal privileges and prescriptions" and brought with it "the predominance of a presumptuous and irreligious philosophy." He suggests an analogy between the emphasis on appearances in Lockean empiricism and the emphasis on external wants in trade. Casting a critical glance back at Bristol's Dissenters, Coleridge finds "in our cities and great manufacturing and commercial towns, among Lawyers and such of the Tradesfolk as are the ruling members in Book-clubs," a disturbing fashion for "Socinianism."[102] The infection of the press by the commercial spirit corresponds historically with the growth of cities.

The connection between urbanization and the subordination of thought to commerce is historically contingent rather than necessary. In his second *Lay Sermon*, Coleridge declares, "There is surely no inconsistency in yielding all due honor to the spirit of Trade, and yet charging sundry evils, that weaken or reverse its blessings" when it is mistaken "as the paramount principle of action in the Nation at large." The evils of the commercial and manufacturing systems are not "*necessary* consequences of our extended Commerce."[103] As Blake and Wordsworth argue that the model of urban consciousness is a product of ideology rather than natural necessity in order to envision the possibility of an alternative urban culture, so too Coleridge separates urbanization from the dangerous preeminence of the commercial spirit in order to leave open the possibility of a prosperous, cultivated urban society receptive to the works of genius. The dialectics of permanence and progression and of cultivation and civilization project a society in which modernization is a product of the means of the pursuit of cultivation rather than an end. Present distresses arise from an "OVERBALANCE OF THE COMMERCIAL SPIRIT IN CONSEQUENCE OF THE ABSENCE OR WEAKNESS OF THE COUNTER-WEIGHTS."[104] In this dialectic, imbalance, not commerce, is overcome. If anything, strengthening the counterweights would assure more stable progress.

Coleridge presents religion as the primary counterbalance to the commercial spirit, but he commonly notes that religion entails the best effects of poetry or describes of the effects of religion in terms he previously used to describe the operation of poetry.[105] Sometimes Coleridge uses "poetry" to signify a kind of literature within the field; sometimes he uses "poetry" to signify works of genius beyond the determination of the field. If anglo-gallican poetry is an instance of the former, he treats poetry of genius as the latter when he claims, "Poetry tends to render its devotees careless of money and outward appearances."[106] In *Church and State*, poets in the latter sense form part of the clerisy. The clerisy stands at the point of "relative rest" within the dynamic conflict of interests and helps maintain the proper balances in social life.[107] Members of the clerisy transcend social geography; they can be recruited from anywhere in the nation and are to be "planted throughout the realm."[108] Coleridge insists of the poet, "how remote, both from his own intentions and from the nature and purposes of poetry itself, is any *direct* influence on the actions of men."[109] Anticipating Arnold's disinterested critic, the Coleridgean poet derives his authority from his independence from external interests.

John Stuart Mill observes Coleridge's model of a national church "pronounced the severest satire on what in fact it is"; Coleridge's ideal of autonomous poetry equally pronounces a satire on what poetry in fact is.[110] As Williams argued, independence for Coleridge is always a "*social* idea": for the poet to be truly careless of money and outward appearances, he must have his living assured outside the market. Coleridge recognized that Harringtonian and Cowperian autonomy depended on private luxury. In "This Lime-Tree Bower," he wonders if Lamb has the right idea in working a day job: the idea returns in *The Friend* when Coleridge tellingly assigns the position of being "the true balance of society" not to a clerisy but to the "*middle class*."[111] In *Church and State*, Coleridge proposes instead that a national establishment should have been created to free men of letters from the coercions of the market. Coleridge's vision of the autonomous poetic genius represents an ideal of his potential and of the circumstances that would have fostered it. He laments the absence of circumstances that would have freed him from the determinations of circumstances.

In Coleridge's later period, the tension between his ideal of autonomy and his necessarily heteronomous practice appears most sharply in his lectures on literature. In these lectures, Coleridge follows Schlegel by repeatedly emphasizing the universality and autonomy of the poet. "One character attaches to all true Poets," Coleridge is reported to have said; "they write from a principle within, independent of everything without. … It is natural that he [the Poet] should conform to the circumstances of his day; but a true genius will stand independent of these circumstances."[112] The taste of the reading public, however, has been corrupted by habits associated with a cultural market oriented toward consumption and thoughtless gratification, including a "passion of public Speaking" and the spread of "Magazines, Selections – These with Newspapers & *Novels*."[113] Peter Manning suggests that in his lectures Coleridge cultivates the image of the autonomous Romantic poet as a brand identity within the cultural market and as a way to retail the aura of his performances. Manning observes that "the fame of Coleridge's lectures grew by exploiting the conditions of the city – new audiences and institutions, newspapers, the entire mechanism of publicity and reproduction" even as Coleridge deprecates such conditions in the lectures.[114] Sarah Zimmerman adds, "the mantle of the poet effectively cloaked the public performer," and reveals the care Coleridge took to choose venues for his lectures that his aristocratic clientele would agree to visit: "I begin very much to doubt, whether my scheme will answer, for few if any of my Friends at the West End of the Town will condescend to attend a Lecture in the City."[115] But Coleridge does not so much perform the role of independent poet as the role of wasted genius. Henry Crabb Robinson remarked that Coleridge's self-referential remarks on the character of

Hamlet were not a satire on himself but an elegy.[116] The disparity between the image of the independent poet and the commercial lecturer suggests Coleridge directs the satire against the audience and the market: his ruin is the measure of their submission to the spirit of commerce.

Within the sphere of polite culture, Coleridge distinguishes between heteronomous works and independent works of genius; within the whole literary field, however, Coleridge further divided polite culture as a whole from popular culture. As early as the *Conciones*, Coleridge posits an unbridgeable gap between the two classes of culture. Truth, he argues in the *Conciones*, cannot "by a gradual descent . . . reach the lowest order . . . [B]etween the Parlour and the Kitchen, the Tap and the Coffee-Room – there is a gulph that may not be passed."[117] Coleridge divides popular culture from polite culture in terms of class, space, and cultural habits. As Gilmartin demonstrates, Coleridge condenses the correspondences of popular literary culture in the figure of the alehouse. Gilmartin focuses specifically on a letter Coleridge wrote after the assassination of Prime Minister Spencer Perceval. Coleridge, having left the offices of *The Courier*, ducked "into the Tap room of a large Public House frequented about 1 o/ clock by the lower Orders" and found the crowd exulting and drinking healths to the radical leader Sir Francis Burdett. In his letter, Coleridge urges Southey to write to alert the nation to the urgent danger of "the sinking down of Jacobinism below the middle & tolerably educated Classes into the Readers & all-swallowing Auditors in Tap-rooms."[118] Coleridge presents the popular public space of the alehouse as a scene of thoughtless, bodily absorption; the lower orders swallow and soak up radical discourse because it intoxicates, and demagoguery spreads through the crowd like animal magnetism. Coleridge promised to write three lay sermons – one to the clerks, one to the higher and middle orders, and one to the masses – but never wrote the third, indicating his inability to bridge the gulf between his publics and the popular public.

Coleridge hews to an ideal of culture that transcends the social geography of the accumulative system, but his ideal reacts against and comments on his practical failure to attain such transcendence. Poetic genius may be universal, but literary fields are local. Coleridge's sense of the magnitude of the influence of urbanization on poetry corresponds to the gap between his ideal and his practice, and he repeatedly returns to the city for its markets, its means of production, and its networks of distribution. His desire for an alternative vision of culture persists in what may appear both as idealistic evasions of material conditions and as skeptical questionings of the necessity of the submission of cultural production to the logic of the market.

Works of genius, perhaps including his lectures, may already circulate in the world of polite culture as eggs among eggshells, or perhaps they might have circulated if an establishment had existed capable of supporting them. Whether anticipated in practice or solely prospective, Coleridge's ideals of poetic genius and clerisy appear intellectually free from the determinations of social geography. Cultivation ideally relies on civilization only as a means, while civilization depends on cultivation for its ends and direction. Cultivation does not oppose urbanization so much as indirectly regulate its form. Coleridge does not provide a positive image of the effects of balanced urbanization, but he gives no indications that he expects to resolve the social divisions urbanization has widened between audiences, habitus, and classes. If, as Klancher claims, Coleridge places the clerisy "[b]eyond classification and beyond ideology," Coleridge also places the working orders outside the dialectics of permanence and progression and cultivation and civilization.[119] The working class has no place in Coleridge's vision of a healthy literary field, because a gulf lies between the alehouse and the coffeehouse that he cannot cross. In the next chapter, I examine Wordsworth's confrontation with this gulf between polite and popular urban cultures.

3

Wordsworth and the Affects of Urbanization

While William Wordsworth was visiting friends in London from late April to early June 1812, the atmosphere around him was charged with class tension. His friends Sir George and Lady Beaumont were troubled by Luddite disturbances in Nottinghamshire. They debated whether or not to return to their country estate that summer.[1] The whole city was tense after John Bellingham assassinated Prime Minister Spencer Perceval on the evening of May 11. Bellingham was hanged a week later. Wordsworth, who had heard Perceval speak at the House of Commons ten days before the murder, planned to "see the Execution without risk or danger," that is, safe from the potentially tumultuous crowd, by viewing it from the "top of Westminster Abbey."[2] In the event, the execution took place not in Palace Yard, as Wordsworth expected, but before Newgate. Peter Linebaugh argues that public executions in eighteenth- and early nineteenth-century London "were the central event in the urban contention between the classes, and indeed were meant to be so."[3] Hangings were at once an occasion for the ruling class to display the power of its laws to the crowd and an opportunity for the lower orders to express their opinion of such laws. In the letters Wordsworth wrote to family and friends in the days after the assassination, he looks down on London's lower orders with uncharacteristic revulsion. His tone resembles that of Coleridge's account of his descent into a working-class taproom on the night of the murder. In one letter, Wordsworth recounts overhearing a woman hawking "the life of Bellingham" in the streets conclude her pitch by praising the "good deed he [Bellingham] did." Aghast, Wordsworth writes, "Nothing can be more deplorably ferocious and savage than the lowest orders in London."[4] He comments on the spread of this depravity among the urban poor in language that recalls and sharpens the language in the Preface to *Lyrical Ballads* regarding the effects of the "encreasing accumulation of men in cities":[5]

> the lower orders have been for upwards of thirty years accumulating in pestilential masses of ignorant population; the effects now begin to show themselves, and unthinking people cry out that the national character has been changed all at once, in fact the change has been silently going on ever since the time we were born; the disease has been growing, and now breaks out in all its danger and deformity.[6]

Urbanization has gradually warped the characteristic temperament of the English people. Detached from rural community and cast into the vicious competitive urban world, the lower orders pursue a shortsighted self-interest with antagonistic resentment toward the upper classes. Recalling the excesses of Jacobin enthusiasm, Wordsworth fears class antipathy has overwhelmed compassion for Perceval and for members of the superior classes as individuals. In his disdain for the lower orders and in his fearful retreat to the top of Westminster Abbey, however, Wordsworth expresses a structure of feeling typical of the upper ranks equally shaped by the historical form of urbanization. At this critical moment, Wordsworth tellingly focuses not directly on political or economic matters but on the affective charge of the relation between London's classes.

Wordsworth here draws on the commonplace conceptual framework that informs urban ideology and ramifies into various discourses ranging from civic humanism to pastoral poetry. This framework associates rural life with unmediated feeling, with unalienated labor, and with community united by strong emotional ties; it associates urban life with social affectation, the indolence of luxury or dullness of tedious unskilled labor, and, with the absence of communal feeling, the aggressive pursuit of private self-interest. Within this framework, the history of urbanization appears as a transformation from one kind of society to another. These attitudes and assumptions inhabited structures of feeling that shaped how people felt and how they were thought to have felt about their work, their culture, and each other. Often deeply held, these attitudes surface in apparently spontaneous affective responses, such as Wordsworth's reaction to the woman marketing Bellingham's life.

In this chapter, I focus on Wordsworth's response during his golden decade from 1798 to 1807 to these commonplace understandings of the transformations in structures of feeling associated with urbanization and on his sense of the relation between these supposed transformations and the reconfiguration of relations between classes and genres in the literary field. I find that Wordsworth takes on this framework in much the same way that he takes on urban ideology. In the first chapter, I argued that in Books 7 and 8 of *The Prelude*, Wordsworth tests ideologically tendentious constructions of the influence of the urban environment on the mentalities and behaviors of its residents from within; in doing so, he criticizes ways of representing the city that confirm and perpetuate this ideology and seeks to uncover other, unacknowledged kinds of experience that can and do exist in the city. In a similar fashion, Wordsworth evokes the commonplace framework of the affective consequences of urbanization but does so to define the limits of the determination of structures of feeling and modes of affect and to disclose the persistence of affects inconsistent with those produced and reproduced by that framework. In setting these limits, Wordsworth reasserts the possibility that poetry could appeal to supposedly uprooted receptive and sympathetic affects still circulating among potential urban and working-class audiences. For Wordsworth, poetry has a peculiar power to reveal dissonant affects by jarring readers out of their socially determined structures of feeling, and his poetry seeks to produce in his urban readers the affective responsiveness it claims they possess.

I develop this argument in four sections. In a reading of the Preface to *Lyrical Ballads*, I argue first that Wordsworth posits and subverts the traditional contrast between the conditions conducive to strong and healthy feeling in rural life and the artificial affectations and corrupting selfishness in urban life. Wordsworth instead treats "rural" and "urban" as heuristic metonymies for regimes of affect not strictly tied to specific forms of social geography. In loosening these customary associations, Wordsworth suggests that the increasing mediation of social relations through competitive markets has limited the opportunities to develop mature affective ties to place, work, or community and fostered antagonism within and between classes in both the country and the city. In the second section, still working with the Preface, I argue that Wordsworth presents urban polite and plebeian cultures, for all their differences, as equally subject to the competitive logic and affective disposition of the market mentality. Wordsworth defines his poetic project against both audience formations and against the uniformity supposed by audience formations as such. He posits that an individual never wholly belongs to an audience or a class, and this unresolvable dissonance, the product and premise of his poetics, signals the limits of any generalization about the determination of feeling. In the third section, I argue that Wordsworth tests the trope of the "rural" in *Michael*. In *Michael*, Wordsworth shows that supposedly "urban" mentalities appear already present within a conventional image of traditional rural life while entertaining the possibility that "rural" affects can survive the translation into an urban commercial world. In the final section, I study Wordsworth's representations of the split in urban culture along class lines in a series of lyrics from his 1807 *Poems, in Two Volumes,* "Composed upon Westminster Bridge, Sept. 3, 1802," "Stray Pleasures," "Star Gazers," and "Power of Music." In these lyrics, Wordsworth stages polite speakers observing plebeian gatherings and inquires into the nature and consequences of the affective distance between the ranks. Within the poems' ambiguities lie images of existing and possible ties between classes but also images of the political and social dangers of the present mutual disregard and antipathy.

Feeling Displaced

In the Preface to *Lyrical Ballads,* Wordsworth draws on commonplace understandings of the effects of urbanization and, more specifically, on the discourse of Enlightenment political economy. But he undermines the prevailing generalizations that identify kinds of space with kinds of feeling by pointing to other factors that determine possible structures of feeling. These factors include a broad social and cultural shift toward abstract understandings of time and space and the tendency to simplify complex, skilled labor into repetitive, time-disciplined tasks capable of being performed by unskilled labor. Wordsworth questions the determining influence of these factors in turn, finally qualifying any theory that represents a group as wholly determined in what and how it feels.

Wordsworth's sense of the transformation in the national character reflects a general conception of the change in behaviors, values, and manners coincident with urbanization. In his *Customs in Common,* E. P. Thompson studies this tectonic shift in the national character and frames his analysis not in terms of rural and urban types but in terms of the "conflict between customary and innovative ('market') *mentalités.*" Thompson proposes that "custom in the singular" exists "as ambience, *mentalité,* and as a whole vocabulary of discourse, of legitimation and of expectation."[7] The changes constituting the shift from customary to market mentalities include an increasing reference to clock time, signaled by an expanded market for clocks and watches and the eventual standardization of time zones, and by the spread of the wage relation and the tightening of work discipline. This new attitude toward time reset the terms of class relations: "propaganda of time-thrift continued to be directed at the working people" and spread the expectation that "all time must be consumed, marketed, put to *use*; it is offensive for the labour force merely to 'pass the time.'"[8] In *The London Hanged,* Peter Linebaugh studies the use of capital punishment to enforce the reduction of compensation strictly to wages and the criminalization of workers' customary entitlement to keep scraps of the materials they worked with: "the monetary abstracting of human labour as wages presupposed criminalizing customary appropriation."[9] Both Thompson and Linebaugh see this transition develop over centuries but place the pivotal consolidation of wage relations in the Romantic period.[10] While Thompson crucially does not locate this broad cultural transition specifically in cities, urbanization nonetheless helps produce the effects he analyzes by minimizing labor's dependence on natural temporal rhythms and emphasizing the need for temporal coordination in modes of production with highly refined divisions of labor.

In his construction of a market mentality, Thompson points to a general tendency toward abstraction and alienation. Time, space, and labor come to be valued and experienced through abstract standards that facilitate their conversion into monetary value instead of being valued and experienced in reference to their peculiar intrinsic or sentimental qualities or to comparable experiences. The wage relation directly measures particular labor as abstract labor power and denies the laborer's claim to property in the materials he works with.[11] Borrowing terms from Deleuze and Guattari, Lawrence Manley proposes that, in the early modern period, "the function of London's growth [was] to deterritorialize peasants from the land and reterritorialize them as wage-laborers."[12] Henri Lefebvre correlates the ascendency of wage labor with the production of "abstract space" or the "space of accumulation," that is, with a way of conceiving of space in terms of its value in capital circuits. In abstract space, life is not "'lived' for lived experience is crushed, vanquished"; "affectivity ... cannot accede to abstract space."[13] These changes – the increasing mobility of labor, the changing relations within labor, the conception of time as an increment of profit – all coincide with Romantic-period urbanization and have become identifying signs of modernization. Anthony Giddens, for example, defines modernization by its tendency to produce "'empty' dimensions" abstracted from "the particularities of contexts and presence."[14] To identify this complex of abstraction and alienation with urbanization, however, would be to subscribe to urban ideology: Lefebvre insists urban space is not necessarily abstract space; Deleuze and Guattari conceive of deterritorialization and reterritorialization as "always connected, caught up in one another," with the wage laborer fixed to the loom and the capitalized land shifting beneath the peasant's roots; Thompson follows market mentalities as they spread through town and country.[15]

The shift from customary to market mentalities and the change in social relations it enables and reflects also entails a reconfiguration of the potential structures and qualities of affective relations. This occurs at a level of greater generality than particular structures of feeling. By "structure of feeling," Raymond Williams means the "affective elements of consciousness and relationships: not feeling against thought, but thought as felt and feeling as thought." Structures of feeling comprise "meanings and values" as they are "actively lived and felt."[16] These structures circulate as objective dispositions within cultural and social discourses and appear subjectively in conditioned and apparently spontaneous affective responses. Since they are inseparable from thought, structures of feeling carry ideological charges; they are what Sianne Ngai calls "affective ideologemes."[17] The broad infiltration of market logic into relations toward space, time, and labor replaces particular, sentimental, or interested attachments not with the rational absence of feeling but with the competitive, envious, self-interested, antagonistic disposition integral to the operation of markets. Paolo Virno's discussion of the "*immediate coincidence*" between "the revolution of labor processes and the revolution of sentiments" in the late twentieth century applies, *mutatis mutandis*, to a comparable coincidence at the beginning of the nineteenth century: these structured sentiments "*enter into production.*" The shift toward a market affect sets the terms for the formation of structures of feeling. Virno calls this more general field of determination the "*emotional situation*," a mode "of being and feeling so pervasive as to be common to the most diverse contexts of experience," including the work and leisure of different classes.[18] To emphasize the coincidence of the emotional situation with a historical regime of accumulation, I refer to this general field as the regime of affect.

Eighteenth-century and Romantic-period moral philosophy recognized the influence of geographical and social circumstances on affective dispositions. In the discourse of sensibility, the effect of urbanization on sensibility was thought to vary by class. G. J. Barker-Benfield notes that David Hume "specified how the creation of cities, with consequent increase in human contact, organization, knowledge, and pleasure, produced 'an increase of humanity,' that is, humanitarianism." But Hume also remarked that urbanization does not have the same effect on workers: as the "skin, pores, muscles and nerves of a day labourer are different from those of a man of quality, so are his sentiments, actions and manners."[19] Other critics have discussed eighteenth-century theories of the effeminizing and weakening effects of urban environments on the nerves.[20]

In the Preface to *Lyrical Ballads*, Wordsworth assumes that he writes during a change in regimes of affect, and he associates, rather than identifies, this change with urbanization. The Preface repeatedly evokes commonplace contrasts between rustic and urban life. In a reading that treats the Preface as a pragmatic essay rich in figurative and rhetorical tactics, Thomas Pfau argues that Wordsworth uses the "rural" as "a master trope" for an original and healthy regime of affect prior to "the progressive alienation that allows Wordsworth to characterize present urban culture as in need of redemptive meanings." Wordsworth, Pfau claims, "deploys the very concept of 'rustic life' as a metaphor for 'passion.'"[21] The history of urbanization provides Wordsworth with an accessible vehicle for an argument about the history of feelings. Wordsworth chooses "Low and rustic life" because it offers a clearer prospect of feeling in action, "because in that situation our elementary feelings exist in a state of greater simplicity and consequently may be more accurately contemplated and more forcibly communicated" (*PrW* 124). By treating the "rural" as a metonymy for a regime of affect, Pfau recasts Wordsworth's sense of the relation between social geography and emotional situations not as causal but as rhetorical.

Pfau uses this decoupling of feeling from place to argue that Wordsworth presents "the affective" as an essential and universal attribute of humanity. For Pfau's Wordsworth, the essential passions evident in rural life persist "unconstrained by the shifting economies of time and place" and rely on and provide an "idea of a human essence preexisting the historicity that permits its definition." By recovering and representing these passions during a period of urbanization, Wordsworth is "restoring the 'human' to an order of authenticity now besieged by historical contingency" and "restoring 'homogeneity' to an entire culture."[22] The trope of the "rural" masks a fundamentally middle-class and urban project of cultural regeneration through the managed recuperation of feeling. In Pfau's reading, Wordsworth seeks to repair the damage urbanization has inflicted on the affective well-being of the very middle classes who have driven urbanization.

As the frame of a transition from rural to urban society implies, however, Wordsworth presents affect not as a subjective absolute but as a quality of relations conditioned by historical circumstances. The poet, Wordsworth claims,

> considers man and the objects that surround him as acting and re-acting upon each other, so as to produce an infinite complexity of pain and pleasure; ... he considers him as looking upon this complex scene of ideas and sensations, and finding every where objects that immediately excite in

> him sympathies which, from the necessities of his nature, are accompanied by an overbalance of enjoyment. (*PrW* 140)

For Wordsworth, affect is not subjective but exists as a quality of the relation between subject and object. Affect, that is, has an extra-subjective, historical existence. Adela Pinch shows how Wordsworth represents emotion as having an extravagant life of its own and passing infectiously from one individual to another, while Rowan Boyson similarly observes that Wordsworth represents pleasure as "inherently communal rather than private or solipsistic" and arising from "a feeling of collective dependence and interaction."[23] When Wordsworth refers to "essential" human passions, he refers not to any permanent set of passions but to the persistence of affective relations through and evolving with historical changes. Structures of feeling are as historically contingent as habits of thought: "For our continued influxes of feeling are modified and directed by our thoughts, which are indeed the representatives of all our past feelings" (*PrW* 126). Feeling prompts thought, and thought structures feeling. This close conjunction implies that whatever shapes thought – whether ideology, discourse, or a broader mentality – also structures feeling. In order to show Wordsworth treating affect as indifferent to history, Pfau associates the "rural" with all feeling and leaves the emotional or intellectual significance of the "urban" undefined, perhaps implicitly identifying it with unfeeling instrumental rationality. But Wordsworth's rhetorical use of the "rural" as a trope coheres with his fluid and historical concept of affect only if the "rural" represents not all feeling but a particular residual regime of affect in contrast with the emergent "urban" regime. Reading the terms "rural" and "urban" as tropes severs the connection between space and feeling that they posit when read literally; it also allows the possibility that "rural" passions may survive in urban spaces and "urban" passions may tinge the country.

Wordsworth loosens the spatial determination of feeling to allow for factors such as class to influence the formation of structures of feeling. He describes "Low and rustic life" with undefined comparatives: in low and rustic life, essential passions find a "better soil" to mature, speak a "plainer and more emphatic language," "exist in a state of greater simplicity," and "are more durable" (*PrW* 124). The comparatives implicitly contrast this world against the urban world but also against the patrician rustic world – which, due to the London season, is inseparable from the patrician urban world. Low and rustic life putatively allows affective structures to unfold more organically from experiences less powerfully mediated by social norms. By contrast, patricians learn how to feel as the contingent and mutable fashions of socially recognized affects dictate they should feel. When Wordsworth describes the effects of urbanization, however, he refers primarily to the demographic urbanization of the lower orders.

> For a multitude of causes unknown to former times are now acting with a combined force to blunt the discriminating powers of the mind, and unfitting it for all voluntary exertion to reduce it to a state of almost savage torpor. The most effective of these causes are the great national events which are daily taking place, and the encreasing accumulation of men in cities, where the uniformity of their occupations produces a craving for extraordinary incident which the rapid communication of intelligence hourly gratifies. To this tendency of life and manners the literature and theatrical exhibitions of the country have conformed themselves. The invaluable works of our elder writers, I had almost said the works of Shakespear and Milton, are driven into neglect by frantic novels, sickly and stupid German Tragedies, and deluges of idle and extravagant stories in verse. (*PrW* 128)

In the next section, I will consider the treatment of class and culture in this passage. For now, I will focus on Wordsworth's critical use of Enlightenment political economy in his account of how urbanization influences the expression of the regime of affect among the urban lower orders. In this passage, Wordsworth refers to a passage in Adam Smith's *Wealth of Nations*. Smith argues, "The man whose whole life is spent in performing a few simple operations ... has no occasion to exert his understanding. ... He naturally loses, therefore, the habit of such exertion, and generally becomes as stupid and ignorant as it is possible for a human creature to become. The torpor of his mind renders him not only incapable ... [of] rational conversation, but of conceiving any generous, noble, or tender sentiment."[24] These occupations stunt the growth of thought and obstruct the formation of benevolent feelings. Smith ties the intellectual torpor and affective corruption to highly refined division of labor practicable only in cities.

More specifically, Smith refers to highly divided and unskilled labor. David Simpson sees Wordsworth basing his "psycho-sociological" argument against urbanization and in favor of small rural communities in part on this analysis of the division of labor in eighteenth-century moral philosophy.[25] For Adam Ferguson, the division of labor multiplies the number of skilled crafts, and "Every craft may ingross the whole of man's attention, and has a mystery which must be studied or learned by a regular apprenticeship." The division between crafts produces the division between minds: "Every profession has its point of honour, and its system of manners."[26] In *The Theory of Moral Sentiments*, Smith remarks, "The objects with which men in different professions . . . are conversant, being very different, and habituating them to very different passions, naturally form in them very different characters and manners."[27] In Simpson's reading, Wordsworth sees the division of labor breaking society into groups of specialists. This specialization impairs people's ability to understand each other and impedes the imagination's task of reconciling "the many and the one."[28] Wordsworth, however, refers to a passage in Smith that presents a different effect of the division of labor. Smith describes the intellectual and affective consequences of reducing complex, varied, and skilled work to a series of simple, monotonous, and unskilled tasks. Wordsworth points specifically to the "uniformity of occupations" in unskilled and time-disciplined work.[29] Wordsworth does not attribute the distortion of urban working-class affect to the division of labor itself. The division of labor is not "unknown to former times," and Ferguson's workers maintain their craft mysteries and their interest in their work. Wordsworth attributes the torpor instead to an emerging kind of labor that strips work of the joy in skill.

Looking into the class and labor grounds of Wordsworth's account of the effects of the increasing accumulation of men in cities qualifies Wordsworth's supposed opposition to urbanization. As a trope for a regime of affect, the "urban" is not necessarily characteristic of or limited to urban spaces. It could refer to the monotonous time discipline imposed in agricultural wage labor such as threshing or in rural domestic spinning. Conversely, those who live in cities, perhaps even the laborers Ferguson and Smith describe, could still have "rural" feelings. In his study of Wordsworth's relationship to Enlightenment moral philosophy, Alan Bewell argues that Wordsworth tends "to write within and at the same time to displace, submerge, or repress the very paradigm that had initially authorized" his perspective, and this relationship holds for Wordsworth's relation to the period's political economy.[30] For Wordsworth to hold the possibility of finding "rural" feelings among urban workers would require him to subvert both the figurative contrast between "rural" and "urban" and the association of urbanization with the abstraction and alienation of affective investments involved in the transition between customary and market mentalities. In the Preface, Wordsworth frames an inquiry rather than stating a general theory. In his description of his poetic project, Wordsworth rejects the notion that urbanization precludes such capabilities of feeling and seeks out the limits of the conditioning power of the "urban" regime of feeling.

Composing a Dissonant Heart

In the Romantic period, a transition between regimes of affect accompanied the shift between customary and market mentalities and the shift toward time discipline and wages in labor relations. A regime of affect belongs to the social and cultural logic of a regime of accumulation and takes shape in the negotiation of the terms of class conflict. Structures of feeling realize this negotiation at a less abstract level, inhabiting particular discourses, ideologies, and literary kinds and genres; they arise from and help constitute class-specific attitudes and dispositions. In the Preface to *Lyrical Ballads*, Wordsworth sees the "urban" regime of affect corrupting the cultural practices of audiences of all classes. He criticizes the arbitrary and exclusive pretensions of high patrician culture, the thoughtless gratifications of mainstream polite culture, and the compulsive thirst for violent stimulation of plebeian culture. The sole preserve of healthy culture appears to be the vanishing "low and rustic" life. By using "urban" and "rural" as tropes for regimes of affect, Wordsworth loosens the connection between kinds of feeling and kinds of social geography and posits a "rural" audience outside the determinations of class-specific attitudes within the "urban" regime of affect.

The main lines of criticism on Wordsworth's construction of his audience divide over his treatment of place and class. Critics see Wordsworth either retreating into a nostalgic vision of low and rustic life or using it as a rhetorical figure in a calculated appeal to his urban middle-class audience; Wordsworth either censures the urban middle class or speaks to and for them. Jon Klancher organizes his influential analysis of Wordsworth's audiences around a series of coordinated contrasts between rural and urban life. In Klancher's reading, Wordsworth associates cultural decline with urbanization, a "vast social transformation that since Wordsworth's birth had been turning one (full) culture into another (empty) culture." Wordsworth links the natural, healthy cultural habit of "reception" with rural life and links the contingent, debased cultural habit of "consumption" with the urban middle class. "Reception" here refers to a mode of thoughtful and reflective reading that treats the text as a symbolic gift; "consumption" refers to the thoughtless amusement that treats the text as a commodity. With *Lyrical Ballads*, Wordsworth "attempts to transform commodified textual relations into an older relation of symbolic exchange."[31] Klancher analyzes this attempt primarily in terms of Wordsworth's claim to use "the real language of men" (*PrW* 118) in his poetry. Referring to Bakhtin, Klancher holds that readers identify themselves with an audience or class in part by identifying with a particular social language or sociolect and its affiliated hermeneutic habits. This identification depends on differential, heteroglossic encounters with other sociolects. Klancher sees Wordsworth torn between contrary impulses. In this reading, Wordsworth aspires to "bridge and erase" the differences between rural and urban and between lower, middling, and upper ranks with a commonly intelligible language, yet he also fears that urbanization has left poetry "as a discourse without social audiences."[32] David Simpson and Lucy Newlyn emphasize Wordsworth's anxious doubts about his chance of finding urban readers capable of enjoying his poetry. For Simpson, Wordsworth belongs to the tradition of "eighteenth-century ruralists, of the likes of Goldsmith, Cowper and Smollett," trapped in an urbanizing world that offers "no place either for a poet or for an audience for poetry."[33] Lucy Newlyn sees Wordsworth cultivating "small interpretative communities" in despair of reaching the "benighted souls whose restless urban existence numbs their capacity for deep Wordsworthian feeling."[34] John Guillory recasts Wordsworth's contrary claim to universality as part of an attempt to seize the terrain of poetry from the aristocracy for the middle class: his Wordsworth tries to replace aristocratic poetic diction with the "language of an ordinary, educated, middle-class person" or "language of educated Londoners," which he naturalizes as the pure essence of low and rustic speech.[35] Like Pfau after him, Guillory reads "low and rustic life" as a rhetorical figure and a stalking horse for Wordsworth and the eighteenth-century ruralists to advance the logic of their role as cultural producers of and for a new urban middle class.

In the Preface to *Lyrical Ballads*, Wordsworth criticizes the cultural practices typical of classes, but in doing so he emphasizes the limits of thinking about cultural practices in class terms. Rather than offering his reader a heteroglossic encounter between sociolects, Wordsworth concentrates on the dissonance between individual experience and any sociolect. As Williams observes, there are "experiences to which the fixed forms do not speak at all, which indeed they do not recognize."[36] Simpson observes a similar disparity at the center of Wordsworth's poetry: "at the most specific level there is *no totally common* cultural slot," and Wordsworth consistently engages in the "problematization" of models of "subjectivity, or perception, and of expression."[37] Wordsworth wants his readers to recognize the difference between feeling and structures of feeling, between the full range and complexity of their affective responses and their culturally conditioned habits of affect, and his poetry represents and seeks to reproduce this dissonance. His strictures on the cultural practices of different classes entail a suspicion of any cultural practices determined by class. This suspicion of class reconfigures the distinction of "consumption" and "reception" as a difference in the cultural practices not between readers of different classes but between readers who consume texts within the hermeneutic bounds of their class and readers who receive the text with less narrowly determined affective responses. Wordsworth sees the transition from "rural" to "urban" regimes of affect creating a dangerous antipathy between classes and potentially heading toward a revolutionary crisis. Any attempt to counteract or redirect the course of the evolution of the regime of affect must appeal to feelings beyond its determination. Simpson argues that Wordsworth encourages his readers to break down received patterns of thought without providing them with a definitive alternative: the same could be said his treatment of structures of feeling, though each new feeling must be received through sympathy and carried into the heart by pleasure.[38]

In his account of the adverse cultural effects of urbanization, Wordsworth misaligns causes and effects. He associates the causes of corruption primarily with working-class conditions. While some causes – such as the frantic pace of newspaper production and consumption offering a stream of accounts of military violence – influence culture across all classes, the uniformity of occupations specifically describes the urban working class. Yet Wordsworth presents the effects of corruption largely through examples from polite culture. According to William St. Clair, the audience for the "frantic novels" Wordsworth refers to, likely the "gothic 'German' romances" published by the Minerva Press, "never widened beyond the aristocratic, professional, and business classes."[39] The "sickly and stupid German tragedies," foremost among them the plays of August von Kotzebue, which enjoyed a rush of fashion from 1798 to 1800, were performed with great success at the licensed theatres at Drury Lane, Covent Garden, and Haymarket, not in plebeian venues such as Sadler's Wells.[40] Simpson catches this disparity and suggests that Wordsworth implies that "the world-view or ideology that emerges from and goes along with the manufacturing economy will corrupt many of those who live within it, and at all social levels."[41] More generally, both the causes and effects are "urban"; they are moments in the systemic and coherent transformation of the terms of the relation between classes and the cultural habits of each class.

The misalignment between cause and effect forces a comparison between the cultural habits of polite and plebeian audiences. The upper as well as the lower ranks have cultivated habits of commodified cultural consumption that serve to facilitate the reproduction of the social order. Low and rustic life serves as the figure for a contrary mode of reception. But Wordsworth's comparatives – the "essential passions of the heart . . . are less under restraint," "exist in a state of greater simplicity," and are expressed "less under the action of social vanity" (*PrW* 124) – indicate that this situation offers only relative freedom from the impulses that in greater magnitudes determine and constitute the "urban" regime of affect, specifically, the desire for money and status. Wordsworth remarks the influence of poverty on humble rustics' affective dispositions throughout the period of *Lyrical Ballads*, especially in fragments drafted in Goslar and for *Michael*. In "There is a law severe of penury," single-minded concern with procuring the means of subsistence renders a poor "cottage boy," in language resembling the Preface, "Dull, to the joy of its own motions dead . . . Scarce carrying to the brain a torpid sense / Of what there is delightful in the breeze."[42] In a related fragment, "For let the impediment be what it may," a father pressed to provide for his family feels that any act that has not "this single tendency" appears "trivial or redundant" (Butler and Green 311). Pressed by poverty, rural workers resemble the urban workers described in Enlightenment moral philosophy. Among the "many circumstances, especially in populous cities, [that] tend to corrupt the lowest orders of men," Ferguson observes that among the worst, worse than ignorance, are "a principle of envy" when regarding the rich and "a habit of acting perpetually with a view to profit."[43] Those who impose the uniformity of occupations or improve the production on their estates act as much out of a view to profit as the poor do: the logic encompasses all classes. Wordsworth does not think all profit-seeking is malicious; he appears to define it as "urban" only at the point it eclipses or precludes finer, "rural" feelings.

Wordsworth defines the novelty of his poetics in part as a rejection of the sociolect of polite poetic diction and its structures of feeling. According to the mythical history Wordsworth entertains, poets originally spoke high language from strong feeling but then conventions of poetic diction turned poetry into a privileged and specialized sociolect. Poets "became proud of modes of expression which they themselves had invented, and which were uttered only by themselves." The reflexive gratification of participating in an exclusive sociolect overshadowed the pleasures derived from "common life" (*PrW* 161), "thrusting out of sight the plain humanities of nature" and substituting "a motley masquerade of tricks, quaintnesses, hieroglyphics, and enigmas" (*PrW* 161–62). Poets "separate themselves from the sympathies of men" as they "indulge in arbitrary and capricious habits of expression in order to furnish food for fickle tastes and fickle appetites of their own creation" (*PrW* 124) and organize structures of feeling to suit class-determined habits of consumption. Wordsworth insists that, before judging the *Lyrical Ballads*, his reader should set aside "pre-established codes of decision" (*PrW* 116) and "decide by his own feelings genuinely, and not by reflection upon what will probably be the judgment of others" (*PrW* 154). He asks his reader to acknowledge the difference between what he feels when he reads the poems and what current structures of feeling suggest he should feel. In a letter to John Wilson, Wordsworth thanks Wilson for saying that he (Wordsworth) has "reflected faithfully in my poems the feelings of human nature." Wordsworth refines the point by insisting the poet should not attempt merely to reflect but "ought to a certain degree to rectify men's feelings, to give them new compositions of feeling, to render their feelings more sane pure and permanent, in short, more consonant to nature, that is, to eternal nature, and the great moving spirit of things."[44] A "composition of feeling" neatly describes a concept akin to a structure of feeling with a specifically literary existence. The negative meaning of "consonant to nature" may be more definite than its positive meaning: positively, it means something vaguely similar to the qualities of "low and rustic life," while negatively, it specifically signals dissonance from prevailing compositions of feeling. Breaking down the pride and caprice entrenched in established codes allows for the rapprochement of the sympathies of men with the plain humanities of nature.

Wordsworth places the "sympathies of men" that constitute the proper object of poetry outside the boundaries of class-bound language or feeling. The poet should address himself to the "knowledge which all men carry about with them, and to these sympathies in which, without any other discipline than that of our daily life, we are fitted to take delight" (*PrW* 140). The poet writes "under one restriction only, namely, the necessity of giving immediate pleasure to a human Being possessed of that information which may be expected from him, not as a lawyer, a physician, a mariner, an astronomer, or a natural philosopher, but as a Man" (*PrW* 139). This notional distinction between man and his class, profession, or other discipline acknowledges the limits of the social determination of mentalities. It is in this sense that a poet is a "man speaking to men" (*PrW* 138): the poet writes, to the extent possible, from outside any particular sociolect to please his reader without reference to any more particular situation. When poetry nods into poetic diction, it becomes another professional idiom. When written according to Wordsworth's poetic principles, poetry could, in theory, please an individual who otherwise participates in any particular audience. Borrowing Wilson's term, Wordsworth expresses a wish for his poetry to please "human nature." He laments that "People in our rank" regularly make the mistake of "supposing that human nature and the persons they associate with are one and the same thing." To have a fairer view of human nature, the poet must extend his regard beyond the world of professionals and gentlemen and "descend lower among cottages and fields and among children . . . I have done this myself habitually."[45] He remarks to Francis Wrangham that "some of the Poems which I have published were composed not without a hope" that they might "circulate among other good things" that find their way into humble cottages.[46] Wordsworth neither overlooks the practical divisions between the cultures of the classes nor simplifies them into absolutes. Klancher shows that most of Wordsworth's audience belonged to the polite urban classes; while Wordsworth acknowledges this, he aims to minimize the obstacles that would prevent his poetry from being enjoyed by people of any situation.

In place of the hieroglyphic abstractions of poetic diction complicit with class differences, Wordsworth prefers to offer images of particular objects and particular people in order to redefine and strengthen the feelings produced by poetry. In *Essay on Morals*, Wordsworth contrasts the impotence of any "book or system of moral philosophy" to "melt into our affections[? s], to incorporate itself with the blood & vital juices of our minds." Only an arresting "picture of human life" "can convey . . . feeling" (*PrW* 103) deep enough to change a reader's habits. Wordsworth scatters a similar claim across three paragraphs in the Preface. Immediately after his account of the multitude of causes reducing the mind to almost savage torpor, Wordsworth says he finds grounds for hope in his "deep impression of certain inherent and indestructible qualities of the human mind, and likewise of certain powers in the great and permanent objects that act upon it which are equally inherent and indestructible" (*PrW* 130). While he never defines what these qualities, objects, and powers are, he implies that they allow people to escape prevailing structures of feeling; they are the social equivalent of the poetic resources he employs in place of artificial language. In the following paragraph, Wordsworth explains that he avoids arbitrary personifications and abstractions in order "to keep my Reader in the company of flesh and blood, persuaded that by so doing I shall interest him" (*PrW* 130). Wordsworth commits to the belief that vivid images of particular people will awaken the sympathetic powers and stimulate the affective interest of his reader. Flesh and blood, then, may be those great and permanent objects on which Wordsworth depends. Wordsworth's poetry opposes the tendency of the "urban" regime of affect to allow class-bound generalizations or abstractions to obstruct the formation of sympathetic feeling between members of different classes. His poetry often arises out of encounters that defy expectations and tries to reproduce the uncertain feeling of bewilderment.

Sympathetic structures of feeling can survive within the "urban" regime of affect, but they tend to exist within social groups and to amplify the wider conflict of social groups. In a letter to John Taylor, Wordsworth entertains his correspondent's distinction between the "pathos of humanity," which Wordsworth says, "is the very excellence at which I aimed," and "jacobinical pathos." Wordsworth identifies the latter as characteristic of "writers who seem to estimate their power of exciting sorrow for suffering humanity, by the quantity of hatred and revenge which they are able to pour in to the hearts of their Readers."[47] The Jacobin writer advances his political interests at the expense of corrupting his and his readers' habits of feeling. Similar in kind but less severe in degree, the generic images of poverty and structures of feeling of eighteenth-century sentimental verse gratify the polite audience's sense of its own refined sensibility rather than disturb its complacency; as Coleridge remarks in "Reflections," these poets sigh for abstract wretchedness yet shun the particular wretched. Robert Mayo demonstrates the extent to which *Lyrical Ballads* resembles the sentimental verse common in the periodical press of the 1790s: the volume shares with the other verse sympathetic representations of poor or marginal figures, verse forms, and a plain style. The *Lyrical Ballads* differs from similar verse, Mayo claims, primarily in "that they were much better."[48] Mayo's sense of quality likely entails the formal, conceptual, and affective complexity and nuance capable of producing dissonance from generic structures of feeling.

Wordsworth's interest in affective dissonance makes it difficult to identify his project wholly with the cultural logic of any particular class. It shares certain qualities with Romantic middle-class ideology: it entertains the universality of middle-class feeling, invests in personal improvement through cultural reception, employs polite poetic forms, relies on middle-class channels of publication, and seeks to alleviate class antagonism without explicitly trying to change the terms of class formation. But identifying his poetics with middle-class ideology would obscure their unsettling social charge. Pfau, for example, reads Wordsworth's cultivation of slow, rural feeling as providing "constitutively alienated middle-class urban consciousness" with a "journey of affective self-recovery," the kind of journey that John Stuart Mill took in his spiritual crisis.[49] As the personification of middle-class utilitarianism, Mill uses Wordsworth's poetry to nourish the private feelings without which he could no longer survive. The bourgeois qualities of this use of Wordsworth lie in the subordination of feeling to the purposes of utility and in the conception of feeling as private, subjective, and psychological rather than social and relational. In this reading, Wordsworth's poetry does not blank out the structures of feeling that condition Mill's encounters with others, and in that respect, it does not accomplish its object.

Wordsworth, however, frames his project of composing affective dissonance in public and social terms, tying regimes of affect to regimes of accumulation and structures of feeling to particular classes and audiences. Dissonance is a negative concept, and Wordsworth declines to offer a strong didactic statement about how to reconcile the incursion of market pressures into all social relations with a more receptive and richer regime of affect. He distinguishes between social geography and regimes of affect, but he appears only to assert the possibility and define some of the conditions of possibility for preserving the "rural" in the urban. By comparing the cultural habits of polite and plebeian urban culture, Wordsworth indicates that this possibility is, with the possible exception of most extreme poverty, not bound by class position. Indeed, a healthy disposition consists in part in being willing to acknowledge feelings that the structures of feeling entailed within one's class perspective cannot recognize. In theoretically decoupling the distinctions between classes from the distinction between reception and consumption, Wordsworth defines the relation to the text in terms of the kind of pleasure the text produces. Consumption involves the gratification of belonging to a particular sociolect, while reception involves the pleasure of sympathetic encounters with particular people or with representations of flesh and blood that sociolects would mask behind generalizations. In this sense, Wordsworth cultivates the receptive disposition and spontaneous energy of social interchange realized in conversation. In the Advertisement to the first edition of *Lyrical Ballads*, Wordsworth says that the poems were written to see "how far the language of conversation in the middle and lower classes of society is adapted to the purposes of poetic pleasure" (*PrW* 116). His emphasis falls as much on "conversation" as on the specification of classes. To converse can be to take turns, to make verses together, and, perhaps, to share poetic pleasures. Such poetic exchanges constitute, however briefly, a reconfiguration of social relations.

Turning Steps from the Public Way

While Wordsworth sets the poems of the first volume of *Lyrical Ballads* in locations scattered across England and America, the settings of the poems of the second volume huddle closely together in and around the Lake District. The second volume appears to bind an ideal life rich in pleasure, feeling, and community to the particular sheltered rural spaces of the Lake District. Several poems claim to represent inscriptions. Several more describe the naming of places and consecrate sites charged with memories of loved ones as sacred landmarks of a communal life. In "To Joanna," one of the "Poems on the Naming of Places," however, Wordsworth considers the limits of this project. In the poem, a local vicar asks the poet, "for what cause, / Reviving obsolete Idolatry" (26–27), the poet carved Joanna's name into a rock. The poet deflects the vicar's question with a digression and tells of a walk he took with Joanna. On the walk, the poet caught sight of the tall face of a rock before him and stopped to admire the scene. Joanna, raised "Amid the smoke of cities" (1) and uninitiated in Wordsworthian habits of seeing, "looking in my eyes, beheld / That ravishment of mine, and laugh'd aloud" (52–53). Her affectionate derision checks the poet's adoration of the landscape and reworks the vicar's warning about idolatry. For the priest, the inscription might appear idolatrous in serving as a textual icon to preserve the memory of a relationship with a person whose absence the icon signals and supplements. For Joanna, the idolatry might appear as pantheistic or pagan rather than catholic worship. Alert to the idolatrous potential within opaque mediating images, Wordsworth appends a note that several local inscriptions "had been mistaken for Runic" but are "without doubt Roman" (Butler and Green 246), permitting a wandering chain of metonymies to allow the ancient Roman occupation of Britain to conjure Catholic superstition. Wordsworth internalizes and resists idolatrous overinvestment in particular places: he invents the walk with Joanna, which could not have happened as described in the poem, and Joanna was not, in fact, raised in the city. And, as Hilary Zaid observes, the "Poems on the Naming of Places" imply the need for poems to copy, circulate, and supplant the inscriptions.[50]

In "To Joanna," Wordsworth stages without decisively valuing a failure of communication across the gap between the "rural" regime of affect rooted in particular spaces and the "urban" regime of affect that compensates for its shifting ground with the endless regression and reproduction of signs. The priest's and Joanna's quizzing of the poet focuses on the structure of affect within his writing and seeing, and each character in the poem bristles when confronted with a different perspective or sociolect.[51] When the mountains echo and redouble Joanna's laughter, she recoils in "fear" (76), conforming to the generic morphology of sublime experience; the poet, perhaps moved by equally typical poetic "visionary impulses" (71), hears the mountains share an unsettling laugh. The mountains in turn "belong to the same Cluster" (Butler and Green 246), and their echoes of the city girl's derision voice their own sociolect, which resembles and reproduces the sound of arbitrary fashionable judgments of the polite urban public. Wordsworth extends his inquiry into sociolects down to the smallest level. The poet struggles to establish affective consonance with either his future sister-in-law or his beloved mountains. If Joanna appears not to belong to the little rural community, it may be because Wordsworth questions the possibility of belonging as such. When Wordsworth calls himself and his friends "transgressors of this kind" (9), Zaid argues, he is "suggesting not only that he is one of a group of transgressors, but also that he may be transgressing his group/kind."[52] Wordsworth says, "The poem then concludes in a strain of deep tenderness" (Butler and Green 398): the recognition of a strain or dissonance gives depth to the tenderness.

I dwell on "To Joanna" because the poem raises concerns that Wordsworth continues to consider in *Michael* – the poem that directly follows the "Poems on the Naming of Places" – that might be seen but noticed not when reading *Michael* alone. In *Michael*, the only poem in the second volume written after the Preface, Wordsworth considers whether the connection between rural life and an idealized mode of social relations and regime of affect reflects ideological and literary conventions rather than an actual and vanishing historical mode of experience. In her influential reading of the poem, Marjorie Levinson sees Wordsworth subscribing to the contrast between traditional rural life – characterized by "unalienated" and "nonspecialized" labor, investment in use values, subsistence economy, and "Jewish" theology of direct covenant – and modern urban life – characterized by wage labor, preoccupation with exchange value and "money," surplus accumulation, and "Christian" theology entailing mediation.[53] "If the 'affections' – that all-important anchor of thought, feeling, and community – are to survive[,]" Levinson claims, "they must maintain contact with the real places and objects of their origin." In this reading, Wordsworth's "'hard' primitivism" is part of an attempt to "revive the social and existential values associated with the pastoral, organic community."[54] Mark Jones challenges this reading by emphasizing Wordsworth's adaptation of the dialogic form of pastoral into a "double perspective": Wordsworth evokes pastoral "rural" ideals but in ambivalent or parodic moments also exposes the difficulty of reconciling these ideals with material circumstances.[55] Unlike Levinson, Jones treats the speaker of the poem as a dramatic persona. Simpson describes Wordsworth's persistent yet subtle "dramatic method" as one of the "formal manifestations of Wordsworth's ideological openness or insecurity" and as a way "to invite a critical response without quite demanding it."[56] Acknowledging Wordsworth's dramatic method means reading the poem not as an endorsement but as a critical examination of the commonplace understanding of urbanization. In *Michael*, I will argue, Wordsworth parses the trope of the "rural," reassigning some of its virtues to the influence of other determinants, questioning its adequacy as a representation of rural life, and considering the weaknesses of the "rural" ideal on its own terms. Wordsworth imagines the possibility that the "rural" regime can survive or can already be found within the commercial city. Uprooting the "rural" comes at the expense of the concept and figure of rootedness: paradise is lost either way, whether through the forced exile from Eden or through the disillusioned revelation that Eden was always already a nostalgic figurative ideal.

Wordsworth calls into question public impressions of rural life shaped by pastoral conventions. In the poem's induction, the speaker challenges the reader to adopt a different perspective:

> If from the public way you turn your steps
> Up the tumultuous brook of Green-head Gill,
> You will suppose that with an upright path
> Your feet must struggle; in such bold ascent
> The pastoral Mountains front you, face to face.
> But, courage! for beside that boisterous Brook
> The Mountains have all open'd out themselves,
> And made a hidden valley of their own. (1–8)

From the public way the brook appears tumultuous, the ascent imposing, and the course hard; but once you leave that path and follow the natural course of the stream, the brook seems sportive, the mountains open up, and an Edenic valley, hidden from the road, appears. The "way" is a path and a manner of seeing, feeling, and reading. The speaker rejects the public view of "pastoral," which makes the mountains and the rural life they contain appear distant, imposing, and exclusive; the mountains appear as the physical manifestations of the mode of address implied in poetic diction.[57] The speaker proposes instead that you "turn your steps" and make and read verses that need not "struggle." If freed from the arbitrary and oppositional attitude of poetic conventions, the encounter between a presumably urban reader and rural life could be one of mutual openness and welcome.

Wordsworth signals a similar suspicion of generic expectations in his representation of Michael. The full title of the poem, *Michael, A Pastoral Poem*, suggests that the character Michael embodies the genre, and, like pastoral life, how he appears depends on the reader's expectations. In a draft fragment, Wordsworth remarks that if you were to ask Michael directly about his thoughts and feelings, he would respond in generic terms: "if you in terms direct had ask'd / Whether he lov'd the mountains," Michael "might have stared at you and said that they / Were frightful to behold." But talk with Michael "in more particular sort / Of his own business," and in his response you will see "That in his thoughts there were obscurities / Wonders and admirations." If Michael happened "to converse / With any who could talk of common things / In an unusual way and give to them / Unusual aspects," then he looked at "the man with whom he so convers'd . . . as with a Poet's eye" (Butler and Green 330). Poetry emerges from "converse" over defamiliarized particulars, as Michael and his interlocutor exchange the role of poet and interested listener. To converse with Michael, one must not approach him with an address that assumes his otherness but with common and sympathetic interest.

By leaving this passage out of the printed version of the poem, however, Wordsworth suspends Michael between the poles of an individual with a dissonant heart and a generic construct come to life. Michael's life appears as a text written and read within conventional representations of rural life. He has deep affective and physical ties to the land and identifies with it. The fields "were his living Being even more / Than his own Blood" (75–76), and they "had lay'd / Strong hold on his Affections, were to him / A pleasurable feeling of blind love, / The pleasure which there is in life itself" (76–79). Wordsworth nonetheless figures this deep identification as textually mediated.

> [T]he hills, which he so oft
> Had climb'd with vigorous steps; which had impress'd
> So many incidents upon his mind
> Of hardship, skill or courage, joy or fear;
> Which like a book preserv'd the memory
> Of the dumb animals, whom he had sav'd,
> Had fed or shelter'd, linking to such acts,
> So grateful in themselves, the certainty
> Of honorable gains. (66–74)

The land leaves its textual impress on his mind and appears in turn as the printed record of his memories. Michael's land is his book of account, his curriculum vitae, and his autobiography. This passage introduces the gradual transfiguration of Michael into a text. As Lore Metzger observes, the shepherd and his family become literary tropes among their neighbors: his household serves "as a proverb in the vale / For endless industry" (96–97) and their lantern stands as a "public Symbol" (137) of their life.[58] The residents of the valley assimilate Michael's story into their sociolect and convert it into a "Tale" (27). But the process begins with Michael himself writing and reading the record of his life through generic expectations. When Michael tells his history to Luke, he refers to "the family mold" (380), a phrase that signifies at once the family soil, character, form of life, and graveyard; it is the form to which Michael has fitted his life. Michael thus becomes the first to translate his life into a portable ideological parable about urbanization in which he functions as a generic figure for the loss of customary rural life. Every representation refers to a prior representation, and Michael tells his tale in the public way.

Wordsworth subtly but persistently subverts the contrast between the rural world he describes and the "urban" regime of affect, distinguishing the practices of Michael's rural life from the ideal it evokes. Wordsworth entertains commonplace contrasts between rural and urban temporality, relations to place, and modes of labor but recasts them as distinguished in degree rather than in kind. Mark Schoenfield notes the contrast between the "slow-paced continuity" of Michael's natural temporality and the "time of business" regulated by the clock, which requires Michael to send Luke to his urban kinsman "forthwith" (320).[59] Michael compares his diligence to that of the "sun" (243) and the villagers, remarking the regular lighting of his lantern, call his cottage "The Evening Star" (146). But as Simpson observes, according to later local testimony, the cottage of the family Wordsworth based his tale on was known as the "Village Clock."[60] The name change preserves and subverts the contrast in temporalities. The poem fictively addresses a "few natural hearts" (36), perhaps including those who would recognize the substitution. A sense of time-disciplined labor resonates even without the substitution: the house was proverbial for its "endless industry" and the "constant light" was exceptionally "regular" (143). Michael has always needed putatively "urban" discipline to preserve his rural way of life.

Michael's intimate connection with his land seems qualitatively different from the abstract space of commerce. After Luke "slacken[s] in his duty" (452), he escapes in "ignominy" (454) to a "hiding-place beyond the seas" (456). In contrast to Michael, who knows his land and whose land appears to know him, Luke goes where he has no name or reputation.

The successful tradesman Richard Bateman grew wondrously rich "Beyond the seas" (277) and sent a marble for the floor of a local chapel from "foreign Lands" (280). The marble does not fit with local geology, and the spaces of global commerce are specifically foreign and unfamiliar.[61] After Isabel's death, the family estate was sold "into a Stranger's hand" (484): the owner was unknown by the neighbors or, implicitly, by the land. But Michael's relation to the land is nonetheless insistently economic. In a draft passage, Wordsworth imagines Michael selling his land for the right price:

> if you had asked if he
> For other pastures would exchange the same
> And dwell elsewhere, I will not say indeed
> What wonders might have been perform'd by bribes
> And by temptations, but you then had seen
> At once what Spirit of Love was in his heart. (Butler and Green 330)

Michael would have at least deeply considered such an offer. By omitting this passage, Wordsworth allows Michael to remain absolutely and ideally invested in his land. Wordsworth qualifies the relation by questioning the land's investment in Michael. Michael ironically uses idioms for the transfer of property that imagine the land in fluid motion. He would not rest if "these fields of ours / Should pass into a Stranger's hand" (240–41) and resolves "the land / Shall not go from us" (254–55). In each case, Michael expresses his refusal to leave the land, but his words express a desire to restrain the lands from leaving him. Like Luke, the land is always somewhat foreign and restless to depart. The poem celebrates small landed property as capable of inspiring strong affections but, by showing the land in motion, also compares it in kind with the circulating capital and moveable property of the urban commercial classes.

The poem similarly evokes commonplaces about rural and urban labor and directs attention specifically toward the laborer's relation to the means of production. Asserting the family's self-sufficient economy, Levinson refers to Michael's labor as "unspecialized." His work is unspecialized insofar as it is varied, but Michael significantly takes pride in his "skill" (69). Schoenfield gives a number of examples of Michael's household participating in the wider market: Isabel buys Luke's clothes, takes in flax to spin, and serves oaten cakes from her market basket.[62] Michael's labor is not clearly qualitatively different from that of an independent London artisan. Luke, in contrast, likely goes to the city to perform unskilled wage labor: he has no relevant marketable skills and if he "quickly will repair the loss" (262) he will not have time to serve an apprenticeship in a craft. In his letter to Charles James Fox, Wordsworth refers to the "power" of the "affections" that small landowners derive from their land and connect with their "domestic feelings." These feelings are "inconceivable" to "hired labourers, [tenant] farmers, and the manufacturing Poor."[63] The operative distinction is not between urban and rural work but between owning and not owning the means of production. Though, since Isabel sells her labor power spinning flax, even this distinction may be qualified.

By loosening the identification of Michael's way of life with the rural ideal, Wordsworth shows that Michael's strong affects can survive with some participation in supposedly urban and commercial social relations. "Rural" feeling can endure a measure of time discipline, looser ties to place, and participation in the money economy; it can be sustained in work that preserves the laborer's property in skill and in the means of production and, perhaps, in small doses of uniform wage labor. The difference between rural and urban life appears quantitative rather than qualitative.

Wordsworth also suggests that the rural ideal of rooted feeling may not be ideal on its own terms. Writing of *Michael*, Pfau remarks that Wordsworth's "characters appear increasingly restless . . . within the manifestly closed system of . . . 'low and rustic life,' 'slow feelings,' and 'simple and unelaborated expressions.'"[64] This restlessness derives both from what might be considered as the incursion of "urban" attitudes and from Michael's deep investment in his particular surroundings. Michael's traditional concept of time and anchored ties to the land limit his understanding of the world. Michael

> had learn'd the meaning of all winds,
> Of blasts of every tone, and often-times
> When others heeded not, He heard the South
> Make subterraneous music, like the noise
> Of Bagpipers on distant Highland Hills. (48–52)

Schoenfield notes that the separation between "winds" and "South" "allows the latter, a metonym for 'South Wind,' to suggest the direction of London and the industrial cities."[65] But to Michael, the tectonic rumble of urbanization in the south sounds like bagpipers in the Scottish Highland Hills to the north. As Penny Fielding has shown, the Highlands were thought to preserve the last remnants of ancient traditional cultures untouched by the modern world.[66] Bound in a universe of endless repetition, Michael fails to distinguish past and future – an error repeated in the speaker's claim to retell Michael's tale "for the sake / Of youthful Poets, who among these Hills / Will be my second Self when I am gone" (37–39). Michael regularly acts in an untimely fashion, having Luke late in life, rushing Luke to work "prematurely" (197), and then deciding, at first, to send the boy off "at such short notice" (329) that important things "Would surely be forgotten" (330). Michael struggles with finite, linear time and with forms of transmission other than unvarying reproduction.

Michael's limited, narrow perspective informs the poem's equivocal fixation on particulars and aversion to abstraction. In revising *Michael,* Wordsworth tests the principles of the Preface by rigorously cancelling passages of abstract commentary. He cuts fragments that sound like *The Prelude* or *The Excursion* and in retrospect seem out of keeping with the final poem:

> In many a walk . . .
> Have we to Nature and her impulses
> Of our whole being made free gift . . .
> Look'd inward on ourselves, and learn'd perhaps
> Something of what we are. (Butler and Green 324)

> in such regions, by the sovereignty
> Of forms still paramount to every change . . .
> Our feelings are indissolubly bound
> Together. (Butler and Green 328)

Wordsworth's cuts include passages of general commentary later incorporated into Book 13 of *The Prelude.* People who "think that strong affection" requires for its growth the privileges of "Retirement, leisure, language purified / By manners thoughtful and elabourate," unfairly think such affections can rarely develop in "men of low estates." This is, however, a "true inference" about men who live "In cities, where the human heart is sick / And the eye feeds it not and cannot feed" (Butler and Green 332). Within the context of *Michael,* even if these lines express a latent prejudicial structure of feeling, it would be consistent with the rest of Wordsworth's revisions if he excluded them precisely because they express a prejudice. Wordsworth erases these generalizations, but they leave a trace in the final poem in the significance afforded to particular objects and in the representation of how characters think.

When prompted to think beyond the horizon of his fields, Michael refers back to his limited particular experience and relies on generic attitudes and ideological narratives. Wordsworth allows Michael only two ways to pay his nephew's debts: either sell or mortgage the land or send Luke to work in the city. Wordsworth does not record Michael's deliberations. Wordsworth shows Michael announce his decision, and then, in a unique shift in narrative to indirect speech, transcribes Isabel's thoughts. She remembers the tale of Richard Bateman. The parish collected money and sent Bateman, a charity boy, with "A Basket" full of "Pedlar's wares" (272) to London. The boy

> found a Master there
> Who out of many chose the trusty Boy
> To go and overlook his merchandise
> Beyond the seas, where he grew wondrous rich,
> And left estates and monies to the poor,
> And at his birth-place built a Chapel, floor'd
> With marble which he sent from foreign Lands.
> These thoughts and many others of like sort
> Pass'd quickly through the mind of Isabel
> And her face brighten'd. The Old Man was glad. (274–83)

Wordsworth shows Isabel thinking what Michael likely thought but could not be shown to have thought. She understands Michael's proposal through the generic legends of country boys striking it rich in the city, in which credulous awe fills in the voids left by a lack of specific information. Isabel focuses with envious avarice on the marble floor of the chapel. Wordsworth compares her diversion from her affective ties to Luke to envying the riches of Bateman to a diversion from spiritual concerns to worldly wealth. Wordsworth alludes to Milton's Mammon: "ev'n in Heav'n his [Mammon's] looks and thoughts / Were always downward bent, admiring more / The riches of Heav'n's pavement . . . Than aught divine."[67] The allusion places avarice within the traditional rural community and raises the specter of idolatry. Mammon prefers the material of the symbolic space to what it represents; public and urban viewers see "pastoral Mountains" in place of rural life; Isabel sees streets of gold in lieu of urban life.

Michael's attention to particulars may afford him occasional poetic power, but his failure to think beyond his particular fields or beyond unvarying reproduction leaves him open to charges of trying to revive obsolete idolatry. Michael brings Luke to a place where he had gathered a heap of stones, and asks Luke to "lay one stone . . . for me" (396–97) as the cornerstone of a sheepfold that will be "a covenant . . . between us" (424–25). Michael's sheepfold is an antithesis of Bateman's marble floor: both are condensations of a way of life and memorial stones. With the sheepfold, Michael reifies a relation that to this point has been invisibly "bound ... Only by links of love" (411–12). The sheepfold is a poor memento and serves as a physical reminder only to Michael, who already has the text of his life always before him. Michael risks substituting the sheepfold for the relation it represents. While Luke "Wrote loving letters" (442), Michael, whom Wordsworth never explicitly says wrote back, "Wrought" (451) at the sheepfold. Michael cannot detach his affection from the medium of his land. In marking his love for Luke on the land he makes himself his only audience and – as fit punishment for his failure to transmit his tradition – his own second self. He tells Luke, "I will begin again / With many tasks that were resigned to thee" (402–03), the enjambment momentarily suspending an image of Michael reborn and starting over. The sheepfold should be Luke's "anchor" (418), symbolically keeping him fixed to the place against the tides of urban life. Instead, it appears like a millstone around Michael's neck: "many and many a day he thither went / And never lifted up a single stone" (474–75).

Wordsworth elaborates the logical fault of the covenant through an allusion to Adam's fallen reaction to his impending expulsion from Paradise in *Paradise Lost.* Adam laments to the angel Michael that in contrast to Eden, the one place "Familiar to our eyes, all places else / Inhospitable appear and desolate, / Nor knowing us nor known" (11.305–07). He wishes to remain among the places where God appeared to him:

> here I could frequent,
> With worship, place by place where he voutsaf'd
> Presence Divine, and to my Sons relate;
> On this Mount he appear'd, under this Tree
> Stood visible ...
> So many grateful Altars I would rear
> Of grassy Turf, and pile up every Stone
> Of lustre from the brook, in memory,
> Or monument to Ages ...
> In yonder nether World where shall I seek
> His bright appearances, or footstep trace?
>
> (11.317–21, 323–26, 328–29)

Like the sheepfold, the stone altars and the trace of a footstep serve as icons to preserve a memory at the same time that they mark the absence for which the memory tries to compensate. As in "To Joanna," writing emerges from and signals this tension. Milton's Michael reproves Adam for his superstitious attachment to the incidentals of his relation to the divine: "his Omnipresence fills / Land, Sea, and Air" (11.336–37); "surmise not then / His presence to these narrow bounds confin'd" (11.340–41).

In "Reflections," Coleridge uses similar language when considering his departure from idyllic Clevedon. Wordsworth drafted *Michael* in part in a copy of Coleridge's *Poems on Various Subjects* (1796) and would have had "Reflections" in hand while working on the poem.[68] Michael, however, cannot separate his affections from the rural land and fixes on the land rather than the regime of affect it putatively supports and represents.

While *Michael* is undoubtedly what Marshall Berman, discussing Goethe's rewriting of the Philemon and Baucis myth in *Faust, Part Two*, refers to as a "tragedy of development," seen from another angle, the poem appears circumspect about the virtue of staying fixed in place.[69] By loosening the correlations between regimes of affect and domains of social geography, Wordsworth focuses specifically on affective relations and speculates whether the best qualities of the traditional regime can be translated into an urban world. Michael sends Luke to "Another kinsman" (258), and while this kinsman does not stop Luke from falling into dissolute courses, he nonetheless has several "rural" virtues. He takes on Michael's burden as Michael took on his nephew's; he maintains the claims of kinship despite distance; he is "prosperous" (259), a word etymologically derived from the Latin verb for "to hope." Luke, Wordsworth emphasizes, is Michael's "hope" (216). The kinsman supports this hope without projecting a second self.

The case of the kinsman merely suggests that sympathetic and familial feeling can survive in urban life. His feeling, however, might be a privilege of his prosperity. Wordsworth's representation of the urban laboring class in *Michael* pointedly restates generic *rus in urbe* commonplaces and appears only in flashes of the lives of Luke and Bateman. But in the letter to Fox, Wordsworth says he wrote *Michael* "with a view to shew that men who do not wear fine cloaths can feel deeply." He hopes his poems "may excite profitable sympathies" and show "that our best qualities are possessed by men whom we are too apt to consider, not with reference to the points in which they resemble us, but to those in which they manifestly differ from us."[70] Looking to turn his reader from the public way, Wordsworth presents a sympathetic image of a man from the vanishing rural middle class, who has seen his second self migrate to the city to perform unskilled labor. In *Michael*, Wordsworth proposes a different strain of tenderness, stretching the reader's receptive interest to encompass the rural middle classes and their apparent historical successors in the rural or urban laboring classes.

Questioning Distance

Wordsworth's most direct poetic representations of the effects of urbanization on the affective life of the lower orders in London appear in poems written during visits to London in 1802 and 1806 and published in his 1807 collection, *Poems, in Two Volumes*. In this section, I discuss poems that Wordsworth thought of publishing in sequence: "Composed Upon Westminster Bridge, Sept. 3, 1802," "Stray Pleasures," "Star Gazers," and "Power of Music."[71] Wordsworth remarked to Lady Beaumont that, read individually, the short poems of the volume may appear "very trifling," but, "taken collectively," they "fix the attention upon a subject eminently poetical."[72] This sequence fixes the attention on the affective relation between the polite and lower orders. Wordsworth has his polite speakers speculate about the feelings and attitudes of the lower ranks, while posing the speakers and the relation between classes they depict and exemplify as objects for examination in turn. Wordsworth dramatically adopts and undermines the privileged and abstracted viewpoint of a polite culture invested in Enlightenment moral philosophy. In these poems, as Bewell observes more generally, Wordsworth "assumes . . . a more elevated moral vantage point than the less privileged people he describes . . . [and if] we frequently feel uneasiness when reading his poems, this discomfort is part of their meaning."[73] Simpson notes that when Wordsworth "speaks of life in towns and cities, he speaks from a distance that is certainly falsifiable or questionable" and lacks the "sort of physical proximity or conversational event" typical of his rural poems.[74] Wordsworth's urban lyrics question this affective distance. These speculative, bewildering lyrics neither deny the gulf between classes nor pretend to patch it over. Focusing on the Preface, Klancher sees Wordsworth undertaking a "high humanist effort to bridge social and cultural difference in a powerful act of cultural transmission" that ultimately "founders against the deepening division of social audiences themselves."[75] In these lyrics, Wordsworth appears less interested in uniting classes or audiences than in analyzing the antipathy and suspicion growing between them, an analysis that entails an interest in reforming the regime of affect and its corresponding regime of accumulation.

The least apparently dramatic of the poems of the series, the "Westminster Bridge" sonnet nonetheless employs recognizable, generic techniques of observing the city associated with polite culture and only more subtly reveals the unremarkable presence of another way of experiencing the city associated with the urban working class. As critics have noted, Wordsworth presents a picturesque cityscape and panoramic vista. Pfau demonstrates that the picturesque was part and product of the middle classes' attempt to constitute themselves as imagined communities and to extend their social principles into aesthetic terms. Picturesque values the abstract aesthetic form of the landscape over the physical land itself and as such participates in the middle classes' investment in mobile and virtual forms of capital against the landed capital of the aristocracy. For Pfau, the emphasis the picturesque places on disciplined technique pointedly contrasts with both the amateurish taste of the aristocracy and the tasteless cravings of the lower orders.[76] Reading "Westminster Bridge" in terms of the picturesque suggests that Wordsworth evokes or participates in the demographic unconscious of the middle classes.

> Earth has not any thing to shew more fair:
> Dull would he be of soul who could pass by
> A sight so touching in it's majesty:
> This City now doth like a garment wear
> The beauty of the morning; silent, bare,
> Ships, towers, domes, theatres, and temples lie
> Open unto the fields, and to the sky;
> All bright and glittering in the smokeless air.
> Never did sun more beautifully steep
> In his first splendor valley, rock, or hill;
> Ne'er saw I, never felt, a calm so deep!
> The river glideth at his own sweet will:
> Dear God! the very houses seem asleep;
> And all that mighty heart is lying still! (1–14)

As in the picturesque, Wordsworth's speaker looks at a scene from a distant vantage point and aestheticizes the city as a "sight." He repeatedly separates the aesthetic quality of the city from the city itself: the city wears the beauty of the morning like a garment. The distinction between garment as form and body as content reappears in "touching *in* its majesty" and "steep / *In* . . . splendor." Wordsworth conspicuously uses the nouns "beauty," "majesty," and "splendor" rather than refer to the city as beautiful, majestic, or splendid. Read this way, Wordsworth focuses on the aesthetic appearance of the city rather than the city itself.

This construction of a picturesque perspective exists alongside an equally pronounced construction of a panoramic mode of presentation that extends yet interferes with the logic of the picturesque. The panorama completes the project of the picturesque by inventing professional techniques to produce a virtual world and transform the appearance of the city into a commercial spectacle. This spectacle had the blessing of polite tastemakers such as Sir Joshua Reynolds and Benjamin West.[77] Wordsworth, however, thinks panoramas substitute mechanical mimesis for aestheticization. In Book 7 of *The Prelude*, Wordsworth refers to the panorama as "Expressing, as in mirror, sea and land, / And what earth is, and what she hath to shew" (7.250–51). The picturesque city wears beauty like a garment, but the panorama shows the city "bare." The city looks like what it is: in Paul Fry's terms, Wordsworth's language tries to express an ontic disclosure of being and present the city as a formation of matter akin to "valley, rock, or hill."[78] Rather than abstracting the aesthetic form from the land, this reading suggests, Wordsworth immerses the city in elemental diction of "Earth," "fields," "sky," "air," "sun," "rock," and "river." The sonnet glimpses what the city *is*, outside of historical temporality and in the *nunc stans* of a post-catastrophe geological timescale. Curiously, Fry finds support in Williams, who sees Wordsworth projecting "a permanent way of seeing any historical city."[79] Both Fry and Alan Liu note that the poem refuses to supply the specific description it seems to promise: the list "ships, towers, domes, theatres, and temples" cannot be aligned with a single turn of the head and the plural "domes" conspicuously flouts St. Paul's singular preeminence in the skyline from Westminster Bridge.[80] In Book 7, Wordsworth criticizes the panorama's distant and merely technical perspective as presumptuous and ultimately misleading.

While Wordsworth presents the city through the middle-class techniques of picturesque and panorama – the one clothed, the other bare; the one abstract, the other concrete; the one regarding form, the other content – he also includes within the poem a vision of the city that does not share the common middle-class assumptions of these perspectives. Wordsworth inscribes within the sonnet's suppressed imagery of movement an unacknowledged perspective of the urban working class. The largely negative presence of this perspective, like the rural hidden behind the pastoral in *Michael*, enacts its eclipse by current polite perspectives. The inclusion of this dissonant perspective indicates that Wordsworth does not simply identify with the cultural unconscious of the middle class: although he criticizes Michael's excessive and idolatrous investment in his particular land, he does not devalue the power of labor to create affective investments, however temporary, in place. If the sonnet constructs a bridge between these perspectives, between polite Westminster and working-class Lambeth, it does so not in the sense of reconciling them but in the sense of posing their practical relation and affording the poet and reader a vantage from which to observe them both from without.[81]

Wordsworth contrasts these distant and unusual views of the still city against the experience of the city of those who work to sustain its daily bustle. The appearance of the city corresponds with how the poet sees and feels: "Ne'er saw I, never felt, a calm so deep." A similar correspondence completes the contrast between a cityscape "all bright and glittering," an implicitly bright poetic eye, and the assertion that he who could pass by such a sight would be "Dull of soul." In context, this dullness sounds like the dullness of a torpid worker, "Dull, to the joy of its own motions dead," absorbed in the drab, smoky city. This opposition is unstable: the traveler who halts on the bridge to read the dead image of the city shares in that dead stillness himself, his soul as calm and dull as a rock. The charge of dullness itself evokes the abstract generalizations of eighteenth-century moral philosophy that Wordsworth's poetic practice and theory rejects. In this sense, the accusation of dullness recoils on the speaker, whose preference for an inanimate image of the city over feeling invested in its activity signals a suspension of the poet's mighty heart.

Suspending the generic perception of the dullness of the worker's soul, Wordsworth allows for the possibility that the worker may appear deeply moved. The perspective of the urban worker informs the peculiar temporality of the scene in which the city is apparently still and outside time and yet moves. At this moment, "The river glideth at his own sweet will." The river's flow is "sweet" in that it is freshwater: at London the Thames is estuarial and saltwater flows in and out with the tide. The port depends on this tidal flux and reflux, which is the systole and diastole of the city's commercial heart. The unseen beating heart figures the natural, productive, daily life of the shipping trade. When a class of schoolboys was asked to gloss this line with the poet before them, Edward Quillinan reports, "One boy said there were no boats—that was the nearest. Poet explained."[82] Since "Ships" appear in the poem, Wordsworth likely refers to the absence of boats used for unlading ships anchored in the river. Wordsworth defines the temporal situation of the city's image in relation to the temporality of urban working life. In a draft of "The sun has long been set," written in the summer of 1802 and published in 1807, Wordsworth sets a similar scene at the beginning of night:

> The Labourer wont to rise at break of day
> Has closed his door, & from the public way
> The sound of hoof or wheel is heard no more
> One boat there was, but it has touched the shore. (Curtis 327)

At the end of the working day, the laborer has time to himself, and the public way falls blank and silent. The "Westminster Bridge" sonnet illuminates this hidden temporality that is neither on nor off the clock but for an instant apparently free from the cycle of expending or reproducing labor power. As Charles Molesworth observes, the poem represents a rare moment "Free of anxiety about temporal processes."[83]

The poem extends the diurnal rhythm of labor into a vision of historical tradition; in this sense, the poem sketches the outline of an urban answer to *Michael* in which London fills the place of the laborer's fields as the collective realization of interested labor. The city appears as the product of ages of human life, built up by labor and worn down by time and use. In Book 8 of *The Prelude*, Wordsworth refers to "that vast Metropolis" (8.746) as "Chronicle at once / And Burial-place of passions" (8.749–50), an inscription of affective investments as deep and pervasive as Michael's power to trace throughout his property "vestiges of human hands, some steps / Of human passion" (Butler and Green 326). On his first entry into London, Wordsworth records

> a sense
> Of what had been here done, and suffer'd here
> Through ages, and was doing, suffering still,
> Weigh'd with me, could support the test of thought,
> Was like the enduring majesty and power
> Of independent nature. (8.781–86)

Returning to the figure of "Westminster Bridge," Wordsworth ties the weighty impression of the city to its appearance as a memorial of the labor mixed with affect, whether of interested craft or suffering. The mighty heart lies or misleads if it sees the still image of the city instead of a living record of affective investments.

Wordsworth suspends several perspectives – entertaining the picturesque, the panoramic, and a perspective sympathetic to the working life of the city – in order to explore the blind spots of distant observers. Between 1802 and 1807, Wordsworth wrote his most sustained lyric appraisals of urban life and culture, and the perspectival problems of the encounter with the Blind Beggar and of confronting the alterity of London's lower orders persist through the lyrics written during and after his trip to London in 1806. When Wordsworth left for London, he said he wanted "to crowd as much people and sight seeing as I can into one month."[84] Seeing people is the central concern of "Stray Pleasures," "Star Gazers," and "Power of Music." The sequence examines from different angles the affective qualities of the urban working class and of the polite cultural observers who generalize about the crowd. In each case, Wordsworth's focus remains on the affective quality of the relation between polite and popular classes.

Wordsworth strikes the keynote of the sequence in the opening line of "Star Gazers": "What crowd is this? what have we here! we must not pass it by" (1). He defines the lower orders as his object of inquiry. The speaker observes a crowd of people "Poor in estate, of manners base" (22) gathered in Leicester Square for a chance to look through a showman's telescope. The majority of the poem consists of a series of questions the speaker asks as he wonders why each star gazer comes away from the telescope, as revealed in the poem's final line, "as if dissatisfied" (32). Lucy Newlyn reads the poem as an allegory of poetic reception. The stars, she argues, represent "poetic genius," and the speaker's questions voice Wordsworth's doubts about the crowd's ability to appreciate his poetry.[85] But the opening question compares the crowd's technologically mediated view of the stars to the distant and socially mediated perspective of the speaker. Like the crowd, the speaker senses an opportunity for an insight and, like the crowd, he comes away confused and without a definitive revelation. After five stanzas of questions, the poet can only say that the people "Seem" (30) dissatisfied. The speaker's social distance from the crowd doubles the physical distance of the crowd from the stars, and his ideology doubles their telescope. Indeed, the heavens the lower classes observe appear like London's haut ton: the "resplendent Vault" (12) is full of "pomp" (13) and the "silver Moon" has hills of "mightiest fame" (15). If the speaker focuses on the crowd, Wordsworth focuses on the split between the perspectives and sociolects of polite and popular culture. At his most generous moment, the speaker shifts from speculating about the crowd, the aggregate "they" (20), to wondering about an individual if not a specific "him" (26). He wonders if perhaps "a deep and earnest thought" employs the "blissful mind" (25) but "admits no outward sign, / Because not of this noisy world" (27–28). The joy may not "admit" an outward sign in the sense of not reveal one. The noisy world has no sign in its language for this insight: the bliss of deep thought among the lower orders can be apprehended by this speaker only as an illegible blank. Wordsworth's ambiguous language associates the star gazer's bliss with a similar blank perception: he "admits" no outward sign from the noisy world; he reveals nothing but also takes nothing in. Wordsworth associates the deep pleasure with dissonance from the sociolects and structures of feeling of the noisy world. The speaker experiences what Ngai calls "affective disorientation in general . . . a meta-feeling in which one feels confused about *what* one is feeling. This is 'confusion' in the affective sense of bewilderment."[86] This bewilderment is an affective realization of a dissonant heart.

In "Stray Pleasures," Wordsworth develops the possibility, merely hinted at in the parallels of "Star Gazers," that affect can be shared across class lines. The speaker of the poem describes a scene of a "Miller with two Dames" (4) dancing to overheard music by a "floating Mill" (1) in the Thames. Wordsworth saw the scene while walking with Charles Lamb, whom Wordsworth calls in his Fenwick note to the poem "an idolatrous Londoner" (Curtis 421). The dancers do not pay money for the music but enjoy it and possess it anyway. So too, the poet enjoys the sight of the dancers: "They dance not for me, / Yet mine is their glee!" (25–26). Wordsworth correlates this diffusion of affect with an image of an economic system stripped of competitive antagonism and abstracted exchanges. Simon Jarvis reads the poem as Wordsworth's statement against the logics of either commercial or gift exchange. These pleasures, Jarvis notes, "can be claimed by whoever finds them, who will owe no recompense or even gratitude to the disseminators."[87] Abundance arises from the nature of pleasure and the pleasure of nature, and the joy there is in life itself diffuses without division.

By referring to the floating mill, however, Wordsworth ties his poem to a specific field of urban class conflict very much within the horizon of commerce. On his way to London in April, Wordsworth had ridden with Robert Southey from the Lake District to Alconbury.[88] In his *Letters from England by Don Manuel Espriella*, first published in 1807, Southey refers to the floating mill and frames his reference to it by describing the "ruins of . . . the Albion Mills," the first steam-powered mills in London, which were built to secure "a certain supply of flour" and prevent "the inevitable miseries" and riot that would have followed high bread prices. Displeased with this threat to their trade, millers protested.

> The Albion Mills took fire; whether by accident or not is doubtful: but the mob . . . stood by now as willing spectators of the conflagration; and before the engines had ceased to play upon the smoking ruins, ballads of rejoicing were printed and sung upon the spot. The fire broke out during the night, a strong breeze was blowing from the east, and the parched corn fell in a black shower above a league distant. . . . There is a floating mill upon the river thus constructed: a gun boat is moored head and stern, with a house built on it, and a wheel on each side which works with the tide.[89]

For Southey, the burning of the mills is a form of frame breaking: tradesmen destroyed industrial machines to protect the value of their labor. The burnt grain carried by the wind from the slums to the east suggests the possibility of a conflagration of working-class discontent. Behind the floating mill of "Stray Pleasures" lies the traditional class conflict over flour prices, bread production, wages, and the transition from small to industrial production.

As in the "Westminster Bridge" sonnet, the scene of the poem appears in a tense suspension of the daily milling of urban labor. The floating mill "lies dead and still" (2), and the "breast" (4, 18) of the Thames is still and "calm" (18). In this interval, the confined space of the mill feels expansive and welcoming: "The Platform is small, but there's room for them all" (5). The dancers feel no hurry, no bound to their energy, and cry out as if to the musicians, "'Long as ye please!'" (24). For a moment "all" appears indifferent to class divisions, and the polite speaker and the laborers share a common pleasure across cultures: they enjoy polite music, he enjoys their humble dance. Wordsworth acknowledges the rarity of such moments and the difficulty of generalizing this economy of redundant natural generosity by consistently using language of appropriation. The dancers "take" (11) the music, which is "a prey which they seize" (21), and pleasure, while ample, must "be claim'd" (28). Wordsworth suggests that freedom and shared pleasure are not incompatible with commerce and scarcity but that their possibility depends on negotiation over the nature of the working day. The negative image of the burnt ruins of the Albion Mills warns that reconfiguring the regime of accumulation also reconfigures the regime of affect and potentially replaces shared pleasures with destructive enmity.

In "Power of Music," Wordsworth considers the social and cultural consequences of the gulf between classes seen in "Star Gazers" and of the time-disciplined labor shadowing "Stray Pleasures." Wordsworth's polite speaker observes as a blind street fiddler entices passing workers to stop and listen. The speaker adopts the perspective of employers and notices the loss of productivity. "That errand-bound 'Prentice was passing in haste – / What matter! he's caught – and his time runs to waste" (17–18), the hurrying "News-man is stopped" (19), and the busy "half-breathless Lamp-lighter" (20) pauses. As in "Westminster Bridge" and "Stray Pleasures," on the one hand, the interruption of urban temporality allows workers to feel what their work does not allow them. "The weary have life, and the hungry have bliss; / The mourner is cheared, and the anxious have rest; / And the guilt-burthened Soul is no longer opprest" (10–12). The fiddler is an

"Orpheus" (1), using music to draw the people out of the infernal logic of the noisy world. In this sense, urban popular culture appears as a temporary release. On the other hand, Wordsworth implies the fiddler extends the logic of the world from which he supposedly delivers people and, like Orpheus, does not draw them all the way out. Wordsworth insists the fiddler plays for money. He shows the "boons" (26) dropped in his hat and associates the performance with a pickpocketing scheme in which "a Thief ... might pilfer at ease" (23). The apprentice was bound on an errand, but the "Mother" listening to the music finds her "Spirit in fetters is bound" (39). As in the Preface, popular culture appears determined by and absorbed within the regime of production; carefully dosed relief and joy enter into production. Wordsworth's terse Fenwick note – "Taken from life" (Curtis 421) – equivocally refers to people who have escaped the dreariness of urban labor and who have been separated from the joy there is in life itself.

In the last stanza of "Power of Music," Wordsworth associates the condition of being "taken from life" with the cultural and social separation between urban classes. The scene is self-enclosed and isolated from the rest of the city. The crowd stands in a semi-circle with their backs to the street. The fiddler stands with his back to the wall. A "Lass" (22) "sees the Musician, 'tis all that she sees!" (24). The fiddler sways his captive audience like a populist demagogue. The music animates a Leviathan-like "tall Man, a Giant in bulk" (33) "like wind through a tree" (36). Polite culture's handwringing about popular culture murmurs by unheeded:

> Now, Coaches and Chariots, roar on like a stream;
> Here are twenty souls happy as Souls in a dream:
> They are deaf to your murmurs – they care not for you,
> Nor what ye are flying, or what ye pursue! (41–44)

The polite appear to the lower orders only through the metonymy of their vehicles. The "roar" of the wheels drowns out the "murmurs" of concern. The lower orders, when constituted as an audience, "care not for you." The separation of cultures corresponds to either a literal expression of apathy or an idiomatic expression of antipathy. Both "Power of Music" and "Stray Pleasures" associate the separation with veiled images of destructive revolution. In "Power of Music," Wordsworth implicitly compares the state to a "Cripple" who "leans on his Crutch; like a Tower / That long has lean'd forward" (37–38). In "Stray Pleasures," the dancers dance "In sight of the Spires / All alive with the fires / Of the Sun going down" (13–15). The enjambment allows the flash of an image of the overseeing metropolitan churches in flames. The cry "Long as ye please" sounds a minatory note: we will dance as long as you please us.

While Wordsworth primarily analyzes and speculates in the lyrical sequence, the last stanza of "Stray Pleasures" offers a positive image of a stable and desirable urban regime of affect.

> If the Wind do but stir for his proper delight,
> Each Leaf, that and this, his neighbour will kiss,
> Each Wave, one and t'other, speeds after his Brother;
> They are happy, for that is their right! (33–36)

Jarvis argues that "the wind is not imagined as engaging in a mutually beneficial exchange with the leaves, as it might be in some horrible physico-theological extension of the logic of providential economism to winds, leaves and birds, but as pursuing his own pleasure alone: 'his proper delight.'"[90] To deny an economistic reading of these lines begs the poem's central question of the relation between the redundant generosity of nature and the commercial competition for scarce resources. The wind figures the circulation of the commercial system rather than a participant within it. The stakes of this vision are high. The language of "neighbour," "Brother," and the emphatic "right" conjure a "rural" regime of affect in the commercial urban world. The passage hinges on the meaning of "proper." It could mean private or pertaining to property, in which case the stanza would present a laissez-faire utopia in which the market breeds public good from private interests. But it could also mean appropriate or within social bounds. The wind spreads pleasure if it blows mildly and does "but stir," perhaps at a temperate pace rather than violently tossing like a tempest. Wordsworth defines the "proper" wind, the proper pace of commerce and labor, as one that enables neighborhood and brotherhood. The wind also figures the communication of cultural pleasure as well as the spirit of commerce. The wind turns leaves as a reader turns pages in a book, specifically the very pages Wordsworth refers to as "that and this." As in the Preface to *Lyrical Ballads*, the reader will receive and scatter pleasure if he attends to his proper delight while reading rather than submit to preestablished codes of decision. Equally, the wind may figure the inspiration of the poet, writing what brings him delight, even if it is no more remarkable than common workers dancing by a floating mill. The transmission of pleasure through culture remains inseparable from the economic and political valences of the same lines: the cultural, political, economic, and affective regimes depend on each other and to change one regime produces changes in each other.

Wordsworth inherits a conceptual framework that casts urbanization as a transition between the customary ways of life characterized by rich potential for affective relations to mature and the modern ways of life characterized by displacement, alienation, time discipline, and sharpened, polarized class conflict. He discerns how this framework conditions affects by representing them and serves the self-reproduction of a particular social regime. He attempts to jar his readers, whether urban or rural, out of their ideologically tendentious structures of feeling and cultivate their bewildered and bewildering dissonant hearts. In doing so, he argues positively for organizing social relations in a fashion that protects the preconditions of receptive affective dispositions across class lines. He does not seek to restore the old regime of affect or to supplant the emerging one with a new and equally hegemonic ideal. Instead, he insists on exerting the poet's peculiar power and prerogative to encourage the constant reappraisal and reinvention of affective regimes and to foster the apprehension of those moments in which the unity of man can be seen affectingly set forth.

4

Shelley and the Political Representation of Urbanization

While the chapters in this book analyze different poets and different sets of concerns about urbanization, each poet's reflections touch on each set of concerns and reveal the contours of a common alternative discourse on urbanization. Blake, Coleridge, and Barbauld recognize and resist urban ideology and the emerging regime of affect, and Wordsworth and Robinson reflect on urbanization's influence on the literary field. Shelley shares these concerns as well, and the works examined in this chapter – *The Mask of Anarchy, A Philosophical View of Reform*, and *Peter Bell the Third* – could serve as exhibits in arguments about changes in urban ideology, the literary field, and regimes of affect. But in these works and others Shelley provides a particularly searching analysis of how urbanization reflects and shapes the conditions of political representation and of the relation between those conditions and poetry. Shelley's sense of the political dimensions of the relation between urbanization and the production, circulation, and consumption of poetry appears in his representations and negotiations of the changing conditions in the public sphere and of the conditions of publicity.[1]

Shelley associates urbanization with a change in the distribution of the means of political representation. Over the past few centuries, Shelley observes, urbanization has distorted the representative quality of Parliament and increased the political establishment's control over the conditions of publicity. Demographic urbanization increased the disparity between the distribution of population and the distribution of parliamentary representation, while the polarization of class divisions set the interests of those with access to political representation against the interests of those without. Shelley sees this disproportionate political power of the establishment expressed in and sustained by its control over the public sphere, where it disproportionately sets the terms for what can be published. At the same time, however, Shelley sees in urbanization a dialectical counterforce increasing the possibilities for political action beyond the control of the establishment. The population in manufacturing districts had outgrown the customary parish and aristocratic institutions for maintaining order, and the expansion of the public sphere and refinement of radical networks had increased the potential for revolutionary energy to cascade across the nation. It is in this ambiguous situation that Shelley imagines his poetry and poetry in general intervening.

The effects of urbanization on the distribution of the means of political representation appear to fall in between the critical formations of urban theory.[2] Raymond Williams's concept of a "metropolitan" social organization has the strongest purchase on the connection between the configurations of social space and political authority. Williams uses the term to describe imperial relations in which a "metropolitan" or "advanced" society directs the activities and shapes the culture of "underdeveloped" or "under-industrialized" nations as "an extension to the whole world of that division of functions which in the nineteenth century was a division of functions within a single state."[3] The metropolitan organization indicates a hierarchical pattern of relations within an integrated political and economic system. In the case of early nineteenth-century Britain, it represents the emergence and consolidation of the asymmetrical influence of London as metropolitan center over regional centers and, repeating the form like the iterations of a fractal, of regional centers over the surrounding towns, and of those towns over the rural periphery. The asymmetry is at once administrative, economic, political, and cultural. The structure of metropolitan organization allows for hierarchical distinctions within the urban network and, given its fractal-like structure, for comparisons across levels of the hierarchy. The metropolitan pattern serves as an ideal pattern through and against which the evolution and particular forms of the reorganization of the means of political representation can be analyzed.

The emergence of the metropolitan pattern appears in Shelley's thought not as an object of inquiry but as a factor shaping the conditions of publics. Where Coleridge emphasizes the influence of structural urbanization and the uneven integration of the national market on the literary field, Shelley emphasizes the influence of similar circumstances on the public sphere and on publicity more generally. On the one hand, Shelley sees the Romantic-era public sphere as an index and engine of historical progress, with broader participation and more rapid communication over greater distances than any other public in history. On the other hand, Shelley sees the function and operation of the public sphere determined by the economic and political forces that produce and preserve the unequal distribution of authority that characterizes the metropolitan pattern. Referring to

Shelley's remarks in the preface to *The Cenci* and epistolary comments on Tasso, James Chandler argues that Shelley contrasts "the limits of manuscript culture" with "the public sphere of print culture in the late eighteenth and nineteenth centuries in England." Beatrice Cenci and Tasso "appear to have been hopeless because of both the absence of a literary public and the means to reach it." Chandler concludes, however, that Shelley, alert to the limits of the Regency public sphere, thinks that developed public spheres are necessary but not "*sufficient* grounds for radical social transformation."[4] The public sphere is not a sufficient ground because the conditions of publicity entail economic, political, and social factors interested in preserving the uneven distribution of power and because these same factors influence discourse and reading practices.

I argue that Shelley sees urbanization influencing the distribution of parliamentary representation and of opportunities to participate in political acts of representation, whether in the form of a print pamphlet, a popular protest, or any other way of appearing in public. The argument unfolds in four sections. While I refer to texts from throughout Shelley's career, I focus primarily on those written soon after the Peterloo Massacre, when concerns about the historical form of urbanization and political representation were for Shelley most clearly interrelated. In the first section, I relate Shelley's specific history of Britain after the Restoration to his broader history of civilization. Cities and the civilizations they represent rise and fall on the basis of the quality of their political representation. Shelley scatters images of ruin throughout his poetry as warnings to the metropolitan public of what will happen to their city and nation without reform. The logic of the warning indicates that Shelley sees the extent of urbanization as an index of historical progress, though whether urbanization advances or falls to ruin depends on its form. In the second section, I show how Shelley's radical Humean skepticism informs his conception of the revolutionary possibilities within urban life. Shelley uses Hume's skeptical disjunction between cause and effect to assert the inherent and continuous possibility of interrupting the customary, stereotyped self-reproduction of the metropolitan public and its conditions. Shelley grounds this opportunity in the intrinsic peculiarity of every reader and of every reading. Out of these conjunctions some new, unforeseeable, and irresistible event may emerge to reconfigure the public. This revolutionary event may be either apocalyptic – a total and instantaneous transformation – or part of an incremental utopian project sustained by continual creative acts of clearing away old representations and creating new ones. In the third section, I focus specifically on Shelley's representation of the metropolitan public as an unrepresentative imposture comparable to the unreformed Parliament. He sees the metropolitan public – including print culture, the political scene, and the physical city itself – as structured to serve the interests of the establishment. For Shelley, a sufficient reform would have to encompass all these dimensions of publicity. In the final section, I argue that Shelley's revolutionary moral philosophy allows him to profess the possibility of changing history by interpreting it. *The Mask of Anarchy* represents Shelley's attempt to shape the metropolitan public's response to Peterloo and yet includes his reflections on the institutional obstacles to his success. The poem skeptically entertains the possibility of its power to spark the reformation of the public and of the conditions of publicity. Poetry, Shelley believes, has the power to reform the process of urbanization, and the reshaping of the form of urbanization, by definition, must be a work of poetry.

The History of Urbanization and the Unrepresented Multitude

Shelley writes a history of urbanization both at the general level of the history of civilizations and at the particular level of recent British history. He represents the general level most thoroughly in *Queen Mab*. Queen Mab points to "'Palymra's ruined palaces'" as emblematic remnants of a prosperous civilization ruined by "Monarchs and conquerors" who "Proud o'er prostrate millions trod."[5] Anne Janowitz notes the tie between the image and the "democratic theme" of C. F. Volney's *Ruins*: cities prosper under free and democratic institutions and fall under tyranny and oppression.[6] Queen Mab suggests that this cycle has repeated throughout the infinite reach of human history, occurring so often and so pervasively that "Thou canst not find one spot / Whereon no city stood" (2.223–24). Alan Bewell observes that in Shelley's social climatology, the fall of cities creates the wilderness or desert around their ruins. Shelley, Bewell argues, "sees the physical environment itself as a social product," and "thus inverts the traditional understanding of the relation between the city and the wilderness by claiming that *cities come first.*" On these terms, if urbanization were to break free from the cycle of rise and fall, if freedom were to dwell and flourish rather than abandon the nation to tyranny, Shelley would hail the resulting extension of man's mastery over his environment "as the recovery" – or, more precisely, as the progressive realization – "of the human face of nature."[7] At the general level, urbanization indicates historical progress. This view of the history of urbanization persists throughout Shelley's career, and it implicitly frames his more detailed analyses of recent British history. Palmyra serves as "An awful warning" (2.118) to London. In *A Philosophical View of Reform*, Shelley represents urbanization as a dialectical process that simultaneously indicates the political and economic progress of the nation and, by distorting the scheme of political representation, strengthens the tyrannical impostures that threaten to reduce the nation to ruin.

In *A Philosophical View of Reform* Shelley aims to provide an accessible analysis of the historical roots of Peterloo and to sketch the reforms that seem to him necessary and immediately practicable. He does not attempt a full, direct statement of his political and economic opinions; instead, he proposes a few reforms in a manner rhetorically calculated to join in the most robust political debates of the London public. In the *View*, Shelley represents Peterloo as a pivotal moment in British history. Urbanization has been an effect and instrument of historical progress for more than a century, but it has also distorted the scheme of political representation and concentrated economic, political, and discursive power into the hands of a few people in the metropolitan center. Shelley does not focus on the accomplished form of the metropolitan distribution of authority but on the imbalances and opportunities created during its emergence. The consolidation of the metropolitan pattern of organization coincides with the polarization of class relations and the opposition of class interests. The greater the opposition of class interests, the more completely the working class is excluded from political representation. In the *View*, urbanization appears to render the multitudes invisible in the public but also to increase their potential to seize the means of publicity for themselves. The dialectical logic of the *View* carries over to the logic of Shelley's poetical figures of cities.

In his analysis of British economic history, Shelley represents urbanization and the expansion of commerce as concomitant processes that are morally neutral in themselves but that increase the potential for happiness. With an elliptical swiftness that assumes the reader's familiarity with the outline of the argument, Shelley asserts that after the Restoration "the nation advanced rapidly towards the acquirement of the elements of national prosperity" with the institution of freer market conditions – the obliteration of "Feudal manners and institutions," the abolition of "monopolies," and the securing of property.[8] The "Population increased," and "towns arose where villages had been" (*Works* 22). Shelley pointedly specifies that urbanization has brought the elements of national prosperity rather than prosperity itself, a distinction that indicates Shelley's concern with the distribution as well as the absolute magnitude of the nation's wealth. Despite their potential to spread the resources of happiness across the nation, the growth of the productive capacity and the facilitation of commercial exchange have worsened the living conditions of the multitude:

> Commerce was pursued with a perpetually increasing vigour. . . . The benefit of this increase of the powers of man became, in consequence of the inartificial forms into which society came to be distributed, an instrument of his additional evil. The capabilities of happiness were increased, and applied to the augmentation of misery. (*Works* 10)

Advances in the social power to generate wealth have outpaced advances in the principles of just social organization. The tools capable of increasing the happiness of all have been used to immiserate the many to supply the luxuries of a few. Shelley remarks an unequal progress between the "principle of Utility as the substance, and liberty and equality as the forms according to which the concerns of human life ought to be administered" (*Works* 10). He returns to this point in the *Defence of Poetry* when he asks why "all invention for abridging and combining labour" have led "to the exasperation of the inequality of mankind," and why "the discoveries which should have lightened, have added a weight to the curse imposed on Adam?"[9] The rationalization of production, circulation, and exchange in the name of extracting profit has degraded rather than improved the condition of those who earn their bread by the sweat of their brows.

Shelley joins with other radicals in pointing to the financial system of the metropolis as a major factor responsible for the inartificial form of society. More than some of his sources, however, Shelley sees the use of government financial instruments as means of private accumulation not as the disease itself but as a symptom of a systemic malady. In this sense, Shelley diagnoses a metropolitan organization of wealth extraction, with local exploitation hierarchically reiterated at the national level through the metropolitan financial instruments of taxation and the national debt. In the *View*, Shelley claims this financial system has produced a "double aristocracy" (*Works* 30). He follows William Cobbett in concentrating his polemical fire on the new aristocracy, on those who employ their "money to take advantage of the necessity of the starvation of their fellow-citizens for their profit" (*Works* 37). Among this "set of pelting wretches," he lists the "government pensioners, usurers, stock jobbers" (*Works* 28), and above all the issuers and holders of the national debt (*Works* 34–36). The national debt allows London financiers to siphon money out of the working class through regressive taxation. Like the fund holders, pensioners use the government as a means of private accumulation, while usurers and stock jobbers similarly use debt and fraud for private gain. In *Peter Bell the Third*, Shelley rattles off what makes Hell so closely resemble London: Hell has "a public debt" (166), "Taxes" (177) on basic commodities, and, in a telling rhyme, "robbers" (189) and "stock-jobbers" (190). Cobbett denounces the holders of debt as "the omnium-eaters; all the innumerable swarm of locusts, who, without stirring ten miles from the capital, devour three-fourths of the produce of the whole land."[10] Financial chicanery is a London institution.

The "inartificial form of society" refers to the pattern of the distribution of wealth rather than to urbanization as a geographical organization of society. Shelley's focus on London corruption does not imply that his economic principles are intentionally or effectively anti-urban. His comment on the wealth of some requiring the starvation of others shares in what Kevin Gilmartin calls a "radical view of political economy as a zero-sum game" that entails "a relentless calculus of deprivation."[11] The logic of the zero-sum game informs Shelley's general sense of class conflict and extends his critique of political economy beyond London to all modes of accumulation that aggravate inequality of property, whether agricultural, industrial, or commercial. Donald Reiman provocatively suggests that Shelley "never quite outgrew his predisposition to think of social, economic, and moral questions from the viewpoint of a landed aristocrat" and "opposed laws and programs that favored monetary, commercial, and industrial expansion."[12] While Shelley adopts Cobbett's critique of the national debt, his belief in historical progress refuses Cobbett's nostalgic idylls of rural Old England. In the *View*, Shelley scorns the landed aristocracy that arose from and reaps the profits of "usurpation, or imposture, or violence" (*Works* 38) and entertains its eventual abolition. Shelley's strictures on metropolitan financial practices do not signal an opposition to economic expansion. They signal instead his opposition to systematic accumulation by dispossession and, here in line with Wordsworth, to the brazen selfishness that drives the overheated and self-destructive pursuit of profit. When Shelley touches on economic expansion, on the component of political economy that is not strictly a zero-sum game, he praises the formal increase of the powers of man for increasing the capabilities of happiness.

Shelley's economic principles are not anti-urban, but he follows other radicals by recognizing the zero-sum calculus realized in the physical conditions of the great towns and the metropolis, where rich suburbs arise around squalid slums. In an article in *The Examiner* in the weeks following Peterloo, Leigh Hunt imagines that every aspect of the social and physical environment of Manchester must remind the weavers of their exploitation: "Every hostile look, – every face of sneering or threatening assumption, – every spot in which they had slaved to little purpose . . . must have reminded them of all they had borne and suffered."[13] "Their wretchedness seems to madden them against the rich, who," Hunt notes with irony in another article, "they dangerously imagine engross the fruits of their labour, without having any sympathy for their wants." Every "second or third house" in a particular neighborhood of Manchester, Hunt observes, "is a pawnbroker's shop, with scarcely any other articles than the property thus wrung from distress and misery, to award [*sic*] off famine." The same article compares conditions in Manchester to those in London, saying of Manchester's Irish Town that it "may be called the St. Giles's of Manchester. Indeed, no part of the metropolis presents scenes of more squalid wretchedness."[14] The slums of Manchester resemble the slums of London, and both are products of the same system of accumulation by dispossession. Engels's classic account of the divisions of great towns into working-class slums and wealthy neighborhoods describes the same conditions and derives in part from the same discourse.[15] In a zero-sum game, the slums are negative images of the wealthy neighborhoods. Riding by London, William Cobbett sees the wealth of the nation built into the new suburban houses protruding from London and asks, "how is this Wen to be *dispersed*?"[16]

The settling of the metropolitan organization of the economic system coincided with the strengthening of a metropolitan structure in both the political establishment and the reform movement. The need for national political organizations administered from London derived from political circumstances destabilized by urbanization. Urbanization forced both the government and the extraparliamentary opposition to rethink and reconfigure the form, scope, and nature of their political institutions and the ideological visions of society upon which those institutions were premised. In his history of the Regency period, R. J. White emphasizes the challenge urbanization posed both to the institutions of local administration and the beliefs behind them. "[T]he little towns of the older England," White writes, "needed to grow very little in order to present urgent problems of administration for the primitive governmental machinery of the early nineteenth century."[17] The manufacturing cities were getting too large for their local governments, and the mass protest meetings, such as in Spa Fields and in Manchester, threatened to exceed administrative control. In response to the menacing scale of these protests, Prime Minister Robert

Banks Jenkinson, Lord Liverpool, proposed to limit meetings "to those held 'under known constituted authorities,'" reasoning that "'In most cases . . . the gentlemen who live in the parish would have influence enough to check those with whom they are so intimately connected'." Seeing the quaint anachronism of Liverpool's idea, Lord Grenville questioned whether this would suffice for "'the metropolis and the great towns which are at present the chief seat of this evil?'"[18] A local gentleman's personal influence could no longer control discontent in the great towns. Changes in the structure and scale of reform organizations enabled by urbanization demanded changes in the structure of administration and policing that signaled new concepts of the nature of political authority.[19]

Building on the experience of the 1790s, during the Regency the organization of the extraparliamentary opposition became more national and metropolitan; the government responded with similar attempts to reinforce and coordinate peripheral administration through the Home Office in London. The government had prohibited national political organizations such as the London Corresponding Society in the Seditious Societies Act of 1799, and, in the early days of the Regency, E. P. Thompson writes, "pockets of parliamentary reformers throughout the country had been without a national leadership or strategy." The Luddites, for example, "knew of no national leadership which they could trust, no national policy with which they could identify their own agitation."[20] Reform groups maintained casual ties with neighboring groups and collectively formed an irregular underground network. This informal, local coordination prepared conditions for the emergence of more unified national organizations coordinated from the metropolis. Veteran London reformer Major Cartwright toured the country in 1811, 1813, and 1815, founding Hampden Clubs and encouraging local reform groups to join a national network. This network blossomed in 1816 and held a convention of deputies in London in 1817.[21] Metropolitan reformers shaped peripheral publics. William Cobbett's *Political Register*, by far the most widely read periodical among the working class, was, as White puts it, "flung down from the London coach as it dashed through northern towns and villages."[22] London-based orator Henry Hunt traveled throughout the country presiding over mass assemblies; he organized the gatherings that would become notorious for the Spa Fields Riots and the Peterloo Massacre. These ties did not establish the hegemony of London in the reform movement; they established a metropolitan structure within a network that negotiated provincial differences and increased the power of regional centers by organizing them. At the convention of Hampden Clubs at the Crown and Anchor Tavern, the delegates from the midlands and north overruled the platform proposed by the London organizers. Reform organizations centered in the metropolis, but most reformers focused their attention on the midlands and manufacturing towns: only the Spenceans appear to have thought that London would serve as the epicenter of revolutionary action.[23] Shelley felt the draw of London as the political hub of the nation. Shelley's attempts to distribute his satire *The Devil's Walk* (1812) in Lynmouth, Steven Jones remarks, "reminds us of just how badly Shelley wanted to bridge that distance, to project his local activities in Devon into national events at the center of society."[24]

While Lord Liverpool continued to think local authorities could manage the popular reform movement, Robert Stewart, Viscount Sidmouth looked to disciplinary institutions and networks coordinated through the government in London. Sidmouth sought, and in 1818 received, a million pounds from Parliament to build new churches in London and manufacturing towns. Reverend Thomas Chalmers remarked the crucial role of Christian churches in curbing urban political unrest. The subtext of his sermon "On the Day of the Funeral of Princess Charlotte" – a subtext explicit in Shelley's pamphlet on the same occasion – is the execution of the leaders of the abortive Pentridge Rising of 1817. In the sermon, Chalmers declares, "if it be true that towns are the great instruments of political revolution . . . if we learn, from the history of the past, that they are the favourite and frequented rallying-places for all the brooding violence of the land – who does not see that the pleading earnestness of the christian minister is at one with the soundest maxims of political wisdom." Only the "the artillery of the pulpit," he proclaims, can extinguish the "foul and feverish depravity . . . in our overgrown cities."[25] Sidmouth also responded to calls from manufacturers for stronger protection of their property by building barracks to station the returning army around manufacturing towns.[26] Looking to move out of Cumberland in 1811, Shelley writes that he does not wish to live "near any *populous manufacturing dissipated* town. – We do not covet either a propinquity to *Barracks*."[27] Finally, Sidmouth organized a network of spies to report on reformers to the Home Office. The spy and agent provocateur Oliver circulated among Nottingham reform groups in the guise of an itinerant delegate from a reform club in London. Shelley highlights the perfidy of Oliver in his *Address to the People on the Death of the Princess Charlotte* and in *Peter Bell the Third* refers to both Oliver (671) and "Castles" (152), the agent who provoked the Spa Fields Riots.

The formation of these coordinated networks depended on a preceding expansion of the scope and scale of publics. As seen in Chapter 2, eighteenth-century structural urbanization fostered the development of print markets in provincial towns, allowing regional presses to emerge and survive, while at the same time extending the reach of the national, London-based press. Periodicals, Thompson remarks, "radiated Radicalism out from London to the provinces," creating a national network of radical "editors, publishers, booksellers, hawkers, and even bill-stickers."[28] As the manufacturing towns grew, they founded their own presses. By the time of Peterloo, Manchester had several daily newspapers, and the *Manchester Observer* had a circulation approaching that of Wooler's *Black Dwarf*.[29] The maturation of regional print publics not only enables the metropolitan organization of the reform movement but also crucially helps turn print audiences into physical gatherings. Kenneth Neill Cameron notes that during the 1790s, "a large meeting consisted of 500, but in the stormy days following the end of the war in 1815, of 30,000 or more."[30] The scale of the meeting at St. Peter's Field was possible in part because the newspapers publicized it. The meeting renders visible and palpable the numerical and physical disproportion between the ranks of the discontented multitude and the limited resources of the eighteenth-century parish authorities highlighted in Grenville's response to Liverpool. Urbanization increased the size of the popular urban publics, improved the means of their coordination, and facilitated the embodiment of those publics on unprecedented scale in mass meetings.

The emergence of a metropolitan organization of both the reform network and the government's efforts to repress reform lies in the background, persistent but implicit, of Shelley's treatment of urbanization; in the *View*, he focuses more directly on how urbanization has deformed parliamentary representation. The growth of the population has diluted the representation while internal migration has distorted it. Shelley calculates that the proportion of those who could vote to those who could not rapidly fell from one to eight in 1641, to one to twenty in 1688, to "one to many hundreds in the interval between 1688 and 1819." The changing ratio signals the further consolidation of the influence of a wealthy and powerful few: "The number therefore of those who have influence on the government, even if numerically the same as at the former period, was relatively different." Since the dissolution of the Long Parliament, Shelley recounts, villages "which sent no members to Parliament became great cities" and "towns which had been considerable enough to send members dwindled from local circumstances into villages." The redistribution of population without a reallocation of parliamentary representation "no doubt contributed to the general effect of rendering the Commons' House a less complete representation of the people" (*Works* 23). Shelley bases his analysis on a common proposal to transfer representatives from rotten boroughs to more populous districts.[31]

For Shelley, the emergence of the "double aristocracy" refutes any notion that Parliament functions as "a virtual Representation of the People" (*Works* 23). Defenders of the principle of virtual representation argued that, while individuals may not vote in elections, the elected representatives nonetheless represented their "interests." Interests were generally thought of in terms of economic sectors – such as agriculture, commerce, or industry – sometimes in particular regional forms.[32] Virtual representation depends on the assumption that the common interests of individuals within a sector outweigh the opposition of interests within that sector, such as the opposition between owners and laborers. The zero-sum-game logic of his economic commentary implies that Shelley finds the principle of virtual representation untenable due to the opposition of economic interests along class lines. But Shelley's direct argument against virtual representation relies on a discussion of shifting political alliances between classes after the Glorious Revolution. Before 1688, he says, the whole nation shared a political interest in restricting the power of the monarchy. The concessions won from the monarchy in the Revolution transferred despotic power to the double aristocracy and in doing so left the multitude without allies. "At this period began that despotism of the oligarchy of party, and under the colour of administering the executive power lodged in the king, represented in truth the interests of the rich" (*Works* 24); members of Commons now "actually represent that which is a distortion and a shadow" and "virtually represent none but the powerful and the rich."[33] "The name and office of king," meanwhile, has become "merely the mask of this power, and is a kind of stalking-horse ... Monarchy is only the string which ties the robber's bundle" (*Works* 25). No longer needed for the political purposes of the double aristocracy, the multitude lost any claim to political representation. "[T]he nation universally became multiplied into a denomination which had no constitutional presence in the state. This denomination had not existed before, or had existed only to a degree in which its interests were sensibly interwoven with that of those who enjoyed a constitutional presence." "A fourth class therefore appeared in the nation, the unrepresented multitude" (*Works* 23). The wealthy exploit the distortion of representation created by the migration of population and by the sharpening antagonism of class interests, and they arrogate political representation for themselves at the expense of the unrepresented multitude. Among the consequences of this "false representation," Shelley lists "captivity, confiscation, infamy and ruin" (*Works* 11). The ruin he predicts is not merely figurative.

The figures Shelley uses when representing cities in his poetry reflect his sense of the costs and progressive potentials of the political, economic, and ideological dimensions of the current historical form of urbanization. Images of ruined cities sound awful warnings about the consequences of the unequal distributions of wealth and political representation. In a related image, Shelley presents cities as tombs or graves for the multitude, for those invisible in the scheme of political representation and oppressed in the economic system. Shelley sees some dialectical hope in both ruins and tombs. The spirit haunting the ruins of Palmyra offers guidance to the onlooker. Tombs are portals to the unknown and sites for hopeful vigils. Shelley often represents the multitude as buried in order to imagine it rising from the grave. In a cancelled stanza of *The Mask of Anarchy*, Shelley imagines cities emptying in response to his call, "Let a great Assembly be" (262):

> ~~in from~~ caves
> From the cities, [where], ~~[?lean] Famine~~
> ~~Faint at Lux~~
> Like the dead from putrid graves
> ~~Pale Gliding thro the yellow air~~
> ~~Of the smoky atmosphere~~
> Hosts of starvelings gliding come
> Tenants of a living tomb.[34]

Shelley likely first thought of the zero-sum game: "Lux," likely luxury, leaves workers starving, faint, and lean. The yellow, sooty atmosphere of an industrializing town resembles a torch-lit tomb or a Platonic cavern. But in their infernal expanse, the downtrodden have found an opportunity to organize themselves into disciplined "Hosts," perhaps recalling accounts of the demonstrators' orderly march into St. Peter's Field.[35] Shelley uses a similar figure of the revolutionary potential dialectically hidden in the city in his Esdaile notebook poem, "On Leaving London for Wales." He calls London a

> . . . miserable city! where the gloom
> Of penury mingles with the tyrant's pride,
> And virtue bends in sorrow o'er the tomb
> Where Freedom's hope and Truth's high Courage died. (1–4)

Poverty follows from luxury, but burial seems a prelude to disinterment. Freedom's hope and Truth's Courage died in a tomb, as if they had been buried alive. The figure of death-in-life opens the possibility of life-in-death. Moreover, Freedom and Truth did not die; only their attributes "hope" and "Courage" died. Virtue, for Shelley, consists of keeping watch over the spirits buried in London and quickening their resurrection.

The Moral Philosophy of Revolutionary Representation

Shelley returns repeatedly to images of ancient cities in ruin in an attempt to read the past in service of writing a different future. Steven Goldsmith argues that Shelley has a habit of representing apocalypses that clear out or annihilate cities to make room for his ideal or utopian visions. Shelley's use of the topos of "the scene of annihilation," Goldsmith argues, "manifests a utopian impulse; the urban environment that seemed nearly permanent can be thought away ... This utopian desire ... exercises a blind, directionless blow to the contemporary, creating a relatively blank future that is better than a complicated and burdensome present." Shelley's ruined cities prepare a "utopian blank slate."[36] Goldsmith's broader interest in apocalypse leads him to see in Shelley sudden and total upheavals that wipe out earthly cities and open space for the appearance of New Jerusalem. But Shelley's apocalyptic impulse is only a specific case of his skeptical view of the process of social change that equally allows for progressive gradualism.[37] Shelley tempers his gradualism with images of volcanic eruptions, and he tempers his apocalyptic imagery with a sense of the slow process of utopian progress. Fredric Jameson's analysis of utopia as method offers the gradualist obverse of Goldsmith's apocalypticism. Utopian imagery, Jameson argues, is "calculated to disclose the limits of our own imagination of the future, the lines beyond which we do not seem able to go in imagining changes in our own society and world." These images force

> violent ruptures with what is, breaks that destabilize our stereotypes of a future that is the same as our own present, interventions that interrupt the reproductions of the system in habit and in ideological consent and institute that fissure, however minimal and initially little more than a hairline fracture, through which another picture of the future ... might emerge.[38]

These fractures or openings are the same as Goldsmith's blank slates, but Jameson imagines them as part of an endless process: the fractures are local rather than total, interruptions rather than annihilations, and endlessly reiterated rather than singular. Ever skeptical, Shelley leaves the nature of the blank unknowable in advance; its nature appears only retroactively through the nature of its effects. Shelley's philosophy of history thus turns Hume's critique of causality against Hume's historiography of probabilistic repetition.[39] Shelley seizes on the theoretical unknowability and idiosyncrasy of all historical circumstances to assert the possibility of writing or creating the historical significance of what has already happened by actively determining its consequences. Thinking in terms of urbanization instead of the city registers Shelley's tendency to think in terms of processes; and if urbanization appears to make the routines of daily life that reproduce the social order with the regularity of a stereotype, Shelley turns to urban life to show that this apparent regularity masks the continuous possibility of a revolutionary rupture.

In his fragmentary essay *Speculations on Morals*, Shelley uses an image of everyday life in the metropolis to demonstrate that what appears as the regular customary operation of society is an inherently unstable series of unpredictable conjunctions between unique agents. Shelley uses the idiosyncrasy of personal experience as part of a counterargument against Enlightenment universal history. Shelley may have learned this maneuver from Godwin, who uses a similar tactic in his essay "Of History and Romance." Jon Klancher argues that Godwin's essay is "an attempt to rethink the genre of historiography as an enquiry into the private, secretive, and politically formative moments of individual lives." Godwin turns to the contingency of individuality and of romance specifically to reject the universal historians' "ineluctable logic of 'probability,' the 'dull repetition' of a general history," and "cancellation of possible, unrealized futures."[40] The image of urban life, Shelley proposes, displays "two classes of agency, common in a degree to every human being" (*Works* 82), that is, the customary and the peculiar:

> To attain an apprehension of the importance of this distinction, let us visit, in imagination, the proceedings of some metropolis. Consider the multitude of human beings who inhabit it, and survey in thought the actions of the several classes into which they are divided. Their obvious actions are apparently uniform: the stability of human society seems to be maintained sufficiently by the uniformity of the conduct of its members[.] ... The labourer arises at a certain hour, and applies himself to the task enjoined him. The functionaries of government and law are regularly employed in their offices and courts. ... The domestic actions of men are, for the most part, undistinguishable one from the other, at a superficial glance. (*Works* 81)

Looked at from a distance, urban life appears mechanically regular and determined by custom. The working lives, social relations, and domestic lives of both the privileged and laboring classes appear knowable and predictable. "The external features of their conduct," Shelley observes, "indeed, can no more escape it, than the clouds can escape from the stream of the wind" (*Works* 82–83). Shelley ordinarily uses the wind to figure Necessity. Using it here to figure custom is a subtle catachresis, an error that anticipates Shelley's turn against Hume's characteristic promotion of a social institution to fill the place of a natural power.[41] The apparent regularity of Humean custom, Shelley claims, is only superficial. Individual experiences within the city remain inherently peculiar, inexpressible in terms of probability, and unpredictable.

> But, if we would see the truth of things, they must be stripped of this fallacious appearance of uniformity. In truth, no one action has, when considered in its whole extent, an essential resemblance with any other. Each individual, who composing the vast multitude which we have been contemplating, has a peculiar frame of mind, which, while the features of the great mass of his actions remain uniform, impresses the minuter lineaments with its peculiar hues. Thus, whilst his life, as a whole, is like the lives of other men, in detail, it is most unlike. (*Works* 81–82)

Moral inquiry, like Godwin's romance, should not focus on abstract laws or tendencies but search out the irreducible particularity of each action that bears the signature of the actor's mind. This peculiarity constitutes an inherent source of unpredictability in the reproduction of the social order: because the minds of individual agents cannot be known, how a person will interpret and react to any event is as unknowable as the link between cause and effect in Hume. Shelley describes this inherent peculiarity of the mind with a figure from his poetry: "[The] deepest abyss of this vast and multitudinous cavern, it is necessary that we should visit" (*Works* 82). The image represents the mind as a Platonic cavern, but it also echoes the initial invitation to visit the metropolis and its multitudes. The city appears as a place haunted by shadowy appearances, as a figure for the inaccessible depths of the mind, and as a mysterious abyss out of which a new spirit may arise. As Goldsmith remarks, Shelley offers an image of "negative freedom that, like Demogorgon, resides beneath our everyday existence and only awaits our discovery of it." *Speculations on Morals* indicates that the revolutionary vent of Demogorgon's mighty portal does not presuppose, as Goldsmith suggests, "a freedom from people" but remains always open amid the metropolitan crowd.[42]

For Shelley, individuals and the city shape each other through dialectical interchange, and as such the city appears as a medium capable of enforcing custom or of recording and preserving the effects of its interruptions. In his essay *On Christianity*, Shelley notes, "Every human mind has, what Lord Bacon calls its *idola specus*, peculiar images which reside in the inner cave of thought. These constitute the essential and distinctive character of every human being, to which every action and every word bears intimate relation."[43] Bacon defines the *idola specus* – the "*Idols of the cave*" – as distortions of perspective peculiar to each individual; these distortions arise from "the individual nature of each man's mind and body; and also in his education, way of life and chance events."[44] What for Bacon is a source of error and a limit on the standardization of interpretation is for Shelley also a source of individuation and a limit to custom. The *eidola* are, as Shelley translates, images: they are representations of that part of the world that the individual has experienced. The mind reflects and refracts images rendered from the ostensibly outer world. In return, individuals' words and actions at a collective level construct the appearances of that outer world. In this relation, one never leaves a domain of representations: the self and world share a dialectical relation of mutual reflection and transformation in which there is no beginning and no stability. Custom creates a degree of apparent uniformity, but, as in the *Speculations*, the dialectic of the *idola specus* shows that the reproduction of the social order remains continuously susceptible to interruption by unforeseeable events.

This dialectic largely accords with readings that analyze the decentered, sourceless, dynamic logic of Shelley's thought and poetry, but it places greater emphasis on the relation between (fluid) personal identity and the (fluid) appearances of the practical and material world. Critics such as Jerrold Hogle and Stuart Curran have directed analysis of this process specifically toward questions about Shelley's treatment of the ideological content of language. Curran voices a consensus when he argues, "Shelley has located the source of the power of ideologies and the problem of dispelling them: words. ... The distrust of language ... to me seems rooted in the poet's obsession with signs as the instruments of ideology."[45] While contests over language are central to Shelley's model of political action, they are not by themselves sufficient. For Shelley, ideology sets the form of urbanization and shapes the built environment. The material conditions of the age represent an image of the collective mind and vice versa. Social power distorts the scheme of representation, and the double aristocracy has far greater influence over social geography than the unrepresented multitude has. Cities, like Parliament, represent the interests of the portion of the population with power over the means of representation. On these terms, revolution or reform must be total. Mere words do not suffice. Trelawny records Shelley remarking that "men herding in great cities might differ widely in theory, but all of them did the same things in their daily life, and though they denounced abuses and clamored for reform, any changes that interrupted their habits they would have abhorred; they exhausted their strength in words."[46] Shelley emphasizes not the regularity of the city demystified in *Speculations on Morals* but the insufficiency of words alone. A change in the collective mind must be accompanied by changes in the scheme of representation and in the practices and material organization of daily life.

Shelley approaches urban form with the same historicist perspective and impulse to creative reconfiguration evident in his remarks on literature. The spirit of a civilization's political institutions is legible in its urban forms. In *Queen Mab* "The ghost of Freedom stalks" through "The long and lonely colonnades" (2.168) of the ruins of the states of "Athens, Rome, and Sparta" (2.162). In a letter to Hunt written a month after Peterloo, Shelley notes, "I have not yet seen Florence, except as one sees the outside of the streets, but its *phisiognomy* [*sic*] indicates it to be a city, which though the ghost of a republic, yet possesses most amiable qualities."[47] The form of the republic survives like a ghost in the worn yet lovely face of the city. The urban figure of the republic has outlived the republic itself. The streets and buildings have kept alive the image of the republic for centuries, and Shelley points to them because they have the potential to fracture complacent assumptions about the historical form of urbanization and to offer a basis for imagining the possible form for a future republican city.

The Mask of the Metropolitan Public

In *The Mask of Anarchy* and *Peter Bell the Third*, both written soon after Shelley first heard of the Peterloo Massacre, Shelley critically analyzes how the structure of the metropolitan public manages the possibilities of expression and perpetuates interested misrepresentations of the social order. In her study of Shelley's relation to his reviewers and prospective readers, Kim Wheatley argues that Shelley saw the radical writer in a bind in which "establishment writers . . . dictate the terms of public debate" and drive each opponent, as God drives Satan, into "the stance of a defiant rebel [that] tends to uphold the orthodoxy that it purports to challenge."[48] James Chandler shrewdly distinguishes between Shelley's sense of the historical progress in the resources and scales of publics and his sense of the institutional constraints on what can become public. "Print culture made it possible . . . to achieve both a publicity of facts and opinions," Chandler argues, but what was published was limited by the uniform adoption of unimaginative utilitarian discourse and by narrow disputes over "what Shelley despairingly calls sad realities and enforceable dogmas."[49] Both Wheatley and Chandler read Shelley as identifying the limit of the Regency public in its confinement to a single discourse, whether that of establishment journalism or of utilitarianism. In both *The Mask of Anarchy* and *Peter Bell the Third*, Shelley focuses not only on discourse but also on the institutions that set the terms of discourse and control the means of publicity.

Shelley relates the metropolitan public's political and social function to the conditions of its formation. How publics can be constituted determines what those publics can do. Michael Warner relates the "making of a public" to "conditions . . . such as the organization of media, ideologies of reading, institutions of circulation, text genres." Every appeal to a public signals a relation to these conditions, and, Warner argues, "when people address publics, they engage in struggles . . . over the conditions that bring them together as a public."[50] A change in conditions of publicity produces a change in the function of the public sphere. Writing of the post-Romantic period in Britain, Habermas argues that "the press itself became manipulable to the extent that it became commercialized." Rather than critically exposing "political domination," "publicity now adds up the reactions of an uncommitted friendly disposition."[51] As Wheatley suggests, Shelley recognizes this function of the public in the Regency as a mechanism for internalizing and neutralizing opposition. Shelley figures the conditions of publicity as structured in a way that serves the political and financial interests of the double aristocracy. Like Habermas, Shelley sees the conditions of publicity subject to the coercive pressures of the market. As E. P. Thompson notes, a "main business of the Radicals was to increase their sales," and the radical publicity network had an interest, predominant or not, in preserving the conditions of their business.[52] The Regent and the establishment also applied political pressures to manipulate the press, sponsoring loyal publishers, imprisoning or prosecuting publishers they considered seditious, and cultivating a reign of alarm that silenced radical dissidents or drove them underground. Shelley shares Warner's sense that each entry into the public reproduces or recreates the conditions of its appearance. Jon Klancher argues that Shelley tends to think of society in terms of institutions and to present these institutions as sustained by a process of continuous, active reestablishment. Shelley, Klancher observes, uses "the active or verbal sense of *institution*" in balance with "the nominal or structural sense of *institution*."[53] The historical form of these institutions evolves with the evolution of commercial markets and the restructuring of establishment power; through these mediations, the conditions of publicity are influenced by urbanization. Shelley figures the present form of the public, like Parliament, as an imposition that pretends to serve as a virtual representation of popular interests but actually represents the interests of the double aristocracy.

In *Peter Bell the Third*, Shelley negatively defines the outlines of a radical publicity against his analysis of the prevailing regime of publicity. Michael Henry Scrivener reads the poem as organized around a polar contrast between the "creative imagination and the cash nexus," with the hellish "London governed solely by isolated egos pursuing personal gain."[54] This distinction does not align with distinctions between opposition and establishment or between radical and non-radical. At the beginning of his list of what there is in Hell that makes it resemble London, Shelley includes "A Cobbett" (153). Richard Cronin explains that Shelley represents "Cobbett and the 'vulgar agitators' as if they were in league with the perpetrators of the Peterloo massacre and the ministry that had congratulated them on their staunchness."[55] At least, Cobbett's vehement, violent rhetoric plays into the establishment's image of the bloodthirsty radicals. Shelley laments that the poor take up "Cobbett's snuff, revenge" (239), a form of violence only capable of reproducing tyrannical oppression. In his letters, Shelley regrets that in Cobbett "so powerful a genius should be combined with the most odious moral qualities" and find expression in "the sanguinary commonplaces of his creed."[56] By referring first to "A Cobbett," Shelley refers not to a man but to the social role and function he performs within the literary and political fields. Given the poem's general critique of the London public, Shelley implies that Cobbett may be selling radicalism in pursuit of selfish fame and profit, a charge not without grounds. Thompson notes that "In default of democratic political organisation, Radical politics were personalized" with each radical leader having his own "London following," a situation that brought out Cobbett's vanity.[57] A Cobbett might be a radical institution that affirms the self-interested logic of the London public and that loudly denounces abuses it tacitly supports in practice. "There is great talk of Revolution –" Shelley notes in an ironic juxtaposition – "And a great chance of Despotism" (172–73). Regardless of Cobbett's genius or his platform, his cooperation with the conditions of publicity reduces him to a placeholder, a mask, a false and empty appearance. In contrast, the sacred few, who "believe their minds are given / To make this ugly Hell a Heaven" (244–45), refuse the terms and traps of internalized opposition. Shelley skeptically considers the possibility that their refusal to "ap[e] fashion" (129) might mean that their publications would appear as nothing. As the coal of his imagination faded, Peter "was no Whig, he was no Tory . . . He got so subtle, that to be / Nothing, was all his glory" (565–68). To elude partisan publicity is either to become an impotent nullity or to refuse the selfhood of "A Cobbett" and construct and enact, like Demogorgon, the blank opening for the making of a new public.

Shelley's concept of publicity extends beyond print culture. Metropolitan spectacles such as masks, triumphs, or pageants appear often in his poetry from 1819 onward, usually as a way to figure the customary reproduction of the public order and to imagine its potential interruption. Paula Backscheider argues that from the Restoration through the early nineteenth century, the establishment used political spectacles to manufacture popular support for its rule, awing the public and performing its special privilege to rule. In their appeal to popular consent, such spectacles both acknowledge and attempt to discipline the effective sovereignty of the people.[58] In *The Mask of Anarchy*, the scene of the metropolitan spectacle represents several modes of publicity at once, including political spectacle, print culture, social roles and routines, and the physical and symbolic values of the built environment of the metropolis. The mask, that is, figures the metropolitan public.

In *The Mask of Anarchy*, Shelley generalizes the spectacle of the Peterloo Massacre in a way that emphasizes the emergence of a metropolitan pattern of administration and its influence over modes of publicity. Although the poem is "*Written on the Occasion of the Massacre at Manchester*," the central catastrophe of the *Mask* takes place "in London town" (53). The reasons for the move are so obvious – London is the seat of government and represents concentrated political power – that the implications of transferring to the capital an event potentially associated with the specific problems of the manufacturing towns have passed largely without critical comment. Shifting the scene to London highlights the spread of urbanization across the landscape and the privilege of London as the metropolitan center. Anarchy and the Destructions pass "Over English land" (39) and trample the whole nation as the Manchester yeomanry trampled the crowd at St. Peter's Field. The move compares circumstances in Manchester to circumstances in London and throughout the country: what happened in Manchester could have happened, and implicitly does happen in a different mode, in London or in any other urban area. In generalizing the event, Shelley also generalizes the agents of repression. The characters in the triumph represent individual members of the government, their posts, and, more generally, "Murder" (5), "Fraud" (14), "Hypocrisy" (24), and other facets of the inartificial form of society. The procession represents the public, customary daily life that protects the interests of the double aristocracy; it figures the superficially regular and autonomous reproduction of the social order imagined in the view of the metropolis in *Speculations on Morals*. By moving the spectacle to London, Shelley also emphasizes London's unique status as the national metropolis. The historical roots of Peterloo lie not only in the conditions of Manchester slums or factories but in the government offices and financial houses of London that helped determine those conditions.

London hosts the mask and is a part of it. The institutions and built environment of the metropolis participate in the spectacle. Shelley juxtaposes Anarchy's control over the arbitrary signs of authority – such as the regal "scepter, crown, and globe" (80) – with his call for his lackeys "To seize upon the Bank and Tower" (83) and to convene his "pensioned Parliament" (85). The financial, disciplinary, and legislative institutions of the nation claim and rely on the same kind of symbolic power as the crown and globe. Shelley includes the built environment in the same spectacle. He refers to Sidmouth, "Clothed with the Bible" (22), and his scheme for building churches and barracks. But more telling is the verb "to seize," which belongs to the discourse of physical force. It might apply to the cavalry at Peterloo trying to arrest Henry Hunt or to the misadventure of the Spa Fields Riots of 1816, in which a small faction of Spenceans, under the influence of the spy Castles, abortively tried to seize the Tower. Shelley leaves open the possibility that their error was not that they chose violent insurrection but that they carried out the establishment's orders. Shelley pairs Anarchy's call to take the Tower with the image of the growth of the revolutionary "Shape" (110) that defends Hope and rejects Anarchy. The Shape arises "as clouds grow on the blast, / Like tower-crowned giants striding fast" (106–07). Shelley imagines the Tower playing sharply different roles in a possible revolutionary event. The image might represent the spread of the words of reformers who, in place of a coronation, have had their symbolic authority confirmed through literal or figurative imprisonment in the Tower, perhaps recalling the radical victory of the Treason Trials of 1794. In this reading, the growth of the Shape would represent the mustering of radical thought in the public mind. But the image of clouds growing on the blast may also represent a cloud of smoke rising after an explosion. G. M. Matthews explains that Shelley uses imagery of volcanic eruptions to figure revolutionary convulsions, and the cloud here is one of Matthews's volcanic plumes.[59] The tower-crowned giants would then be Titans imprisoned underground, rising to renew war with heaven. When placed in London and colored by memories of the Spa Field Riots, the image of the blast suggests an explosive demolition, perhaps reminiscent of the Gunpowder Plot.[60] In Act 3 of *Prometheus Unbound*, The Spirit of the Hour declares that after the revolution, the "Thrones, altars, judgement-seats and prisons" (3.4.164) decay from neglect, and "Stand, not o'erthrown, but unregarded now" (3.4.179). In *The Mask of Anarchy* the process of reshaping the city to represent the interests of the people, of clearing out the physical signs of tyranny for urban renewal, may involve more active and abrupt kinds of demolition.

In *The Mask of Anarchy*, the source of metropolitan power lies with the people, and Anarchy depends on the administration that extracts consent from the people in their daily lives. As in Warner's discussion of the formation of publics and Backscheider's discussion of political spectacles, the pageant of Anarchy depends continuously on the reproduction of popular submission to the conditions of speech and practice. Anarchy's pageant relies on and wins the support of the urban disciplinary apparatuses: a crowd of "hired Murderers" (60) – the standing army stationed in newly constructed barracks – join in chorus with the "Lawyers and priests" (66), and

> all cried with one accord;
> 'Thou art King, and God, and Lord;
> Anarchy, to Thee we bow,
> Be thy name made holy now!' (70–73)

Those who bow before Anarchy declare by fiat that his name will be "made holy now." This is an illocutionary act: the name becomes holy when the people, in this case in unison with the embodiments of the local establishment, declare it holy. Anarchy's logos depend on the prior logos of the people who confer power on him in the act of deferring to his symbolic trappings. Anarchy's power is realized in its distribution across the metropolitan order. He is both the leader of the procession and the procession itself. In social terms, he is the merely nominal head of the administration and therefore nothing but the administration. In terms of the metropolitan public, he represents both the prevailing conditions of publicity and their collective product. Shelley blends Anarchy into the process that supports him by linking him with his horse: "he rode / On a white horse, splashed with blood; / He was pale even to the lips" (30–32). The syntax leaves ambiguous whether horse or rider is splashed with blood and pale. Indeed, Anarchy's name suggests he may be little more than a stalking horse. The compulsive but varying repetition of "Thou art King, and God, and Lord" constitutes the effective act of the metropolitan public and is necessary to sustain the mask. The emphatic, line- and stanza-terminal "now" suggests that the process of affirming and reproducing the conditions of publicity is necessarily continuous. The need for continuous affirmation implies that the potential for the interruption or overthrow of the spectacle is equally continuous.

As in the *Speculations*, the potential to disrupt the pageant lies in the skeptical gap between how people appear in their public roles and how they are in their irreducible particularity. Shelley introduces this gap in his famously ambiguous similes for the governmental officials: "I met Murder on the way – / He had a mask like Castlereagh" (5–6). In one sense, Murder transcends Castlereagh, who is only his mask and counter in an abstract system of misrule. In another sense – if Murder had a mask in the way Castlereagh had a mask – Castlereagh is a man who chooses to take up and realize the function of Murder and wears it as his mask. Thomas Edwards incidentally provides an astute analysis of the importance of dissimilitude within the similes by collapsing them into identity: "there is no value to distinguishing the man from the function he performs ... Castlereagh *is* Murder." To identify Castlereagh and Murder, Edwards argues, "would be to see politics as an absurd pageant ... Shelley, in short, seems on the verge of acknowledging a radical disillusionment with politics."[61] To identify the man with his public role in government would be to reduce politics to an autonomous and mechanical spectacle, with popular authority consulted only while the government rotates its masks. The similes as similes indicate that the public order cannot completely determine particular individuals, and the self-reproduction of publicity can never achieve complete autonomy and overcome its reliance on affirmation in the public acts of the people. Although "she looked more like Despair" (88), Hope recognizes her peculiarity and her dissatisfaction with the role she occupies. Her actions represent the interruption of the customary procession in different modes: she pronounces her own name against her role, she "cried out" (89) against the echoing affirmations, and she "lay down" (98), an act with poetic connotations, in the street to block the physical progress of the horses.

Shelley thinks of publicity in broad terms, but he figures it primarily in terms of the press. In the act of writing the poem and sending it to Leigh

Hunt for publication in *The Examiner*, Shelley takes a positive stance on the restriction of access to publicity by the reign of alarm. Susan J. Wolfson argues that Shelley suspected the poem was "unpublishable." In Wolfson's argument, Shelley was aware of "the indictment of Richard Carlile for having published Paine's *Age of Reason*" and would not have expected Hunt, who had already been imprisoned for sedition, to print the *Mask*.[62] Wolfson reads the signs within the poem that Shelley was aware of its status as an ineffectual visionary and dreamy performance of political oratory. Wolfson's vigorously skeptical reading of the poem checks a particular kind of enthusiastic gushing over the poem's political commitment and agency. But the reading implies that Shelley concedes in advance to the repressive conditions of publicity and accepts that the function of the public is to cheer at triumphs. If Shelley had reason to doubt Hunt's willingness to publish the poem, he had equally strong reason to believe in it. While holding back the *Mask*, Hunt scoffed at Shelley's publisher, Charles Ollier, for his lack of political nerve. In December 1819, Hunt wrote to Shelley regarding his "political songs & pamphlets, which we must publish without Ollier, as he gets more timid & pale every day."[63] And while Shelley appreciated the risks Hunt undertook in publishing *The Examiner*, he both wrote a poem that self-consciously reuses the language and tactics of representations of Peterloo already published in the journal and recognized the difference between Carlile, a popular bookseller vending cheap, pirate editions of a notorious radical pamphleteer, and Hunt, the editor of a polite newspaper. In his draft letter to *The Examiner* on the Carlile affair, Shelley insists specifically on the different treatment of polite and popular letters.[64] Shelley concludes the letter with an attempt to rally Hunt to his task of publishing *The Examiner* against the will of tyrants and outside the bounds of a friendly opposition:

> Whatever you may imagine to be our differences in political theory, I trust that I shall be ab{le} to prove that they are less than you imagine, by {agr} eeing, as from my soul I do, with your principles {of} political practice. . . . I leave you to your task of opposing the great & various resources of your accomplished mind to the de{} tyrants & impostors who surround you.[65]

Shelley asserts that he agrees with Hunt on the principles of political action, which includes employing their minds and *The Examiner* as a vehicle in which to oppose tyrants, impostors, and their power to discipline the public. The idea of reform has to appear in public, even if the voice that speaks it appears distant, despairing, dreamy, or buried. The speech that makes up the final two-thirds of *The Mask of Anarchy* "arose / As if" from the "Earth" (138–39), erupting from Demogorgon's secret lair with an earthquake for birth pangs, breaking forth from obscure caverns of the metropolis and shaking it to its foundations.

Shelley views the metropolitan public the way he views the commerce that helps to condition it: its development has an absolute value apart from its historical disposition and operation. Chandler observes this logic in Shelley's sense of the historical advance from the manuscript culture of Tasso to the public of the Regency. The expansion and integration of the public correlative with the metastasis of urbanization consolidates the conditions that obstruct the appearance of a radical intervention but also allows for a more efficient chain reaction to send representations and interpretations of such an intervention cascading across the nation. For any such transformation to succeed, it cannot by definition occur solely within a public that obeys its operative rules of publicity but must entail a transformation of the conditions of publicity. This transformation would not remove the mask of the metropolitan public but transform that mask, the public and the metropolis, into a true representation of the people.

The Poetics of Urbanization

Shelley's earliest surviving response to the Peterloo Massacre indicates his keen interest in hearing how the people will interpret the event: "I wait anxiously [to] hear how the Country will express its sense of this bloody murderous oppression of its destroyers."[66] Shelley appears concerned with how the people understand Peterloo and what means they use to express their response. By setting the procession of *The Mask of Anarchy* in London, Shelley presents an image not of Peterloo itself but of the reception of the news of Peterloo by the metropolitan public. He sent the *Mask* to Hunt in an attempt to help shape that interpretation. In a sharp reading of Shelley's sonnet "England in 1819," Chandler considers the poem's imagining of its own textuality as a way of testing "the limits of the poem's performative self-consciousness about historical representation – of its apparent commitment to the notion of changing history *by* interpreting it."[67] In the *Mask*, Shelley links the movement of history to the practice of textual production and reception. Jameson does something similar when he calls for us to abandon "our stereotypes of a future that is the same as our own present." Shelley figures the reproduction of custom in specifically textual terms, including the historically conditioned institutions that determine the possibilities of publishing, distributing, and reading texts. The deeply ambiguous imagery in *The Mask of Anarchy* suspends a range of possible interpretations of the power of the press and of the poem itself. At one extreme, the poem imagines itself as the decisive Shape that interrupts the triumph of Anarchy. At the other extreme, the poem imagines that the conditions of the medium or of the readers may be such that the poem will fail to communicate its interpretation of Peterloo. The structure of the ambiguities suggests, however, that revolutionary action can only succeed in one of the ways outlined in the poem and that the triumph will reproduce itself until a successful course of action emerges. The necessary course of action requires the people to change the structure of the public that conditions their interpretations and the metropolis that corresponds with that structure.

In the *Mask*, the conflict over the conditions of publicity and in particular over the institutions of print determines the course of history. But Shelley's skeptical moral philosophy and philosophy of history prevent him from offering a detailed vision of how texts produce a radical change of the public mind. Since a cause can only be known by its effect, the nature of the cause cannot be known in advance. Shelley's refusal to determine how a text can destabilize the stereotype of custom has allowed critics to propose a number of viable possibilities.[68] Wolfson discloses the counterplot by which Shelley subverts the poem's apparent self-presentation as a rallying song for the crowd. Her argument should exclude reductive critical readings of how Shelley imagines the poem may influence its public, but it should not exclude the poem's self-presentation as an urgent rallying cry. Forest Pyle, following Wolfson, argues that while the poem's claim to immediate influence may have been "unrealizable in actuality" because the poem was "literally unpublishable," Shelley imagined the poem could eventually inspire protestors thanks to "its blank opening onto futurity."[69] Andrew Franta similarly argues that Shelley's political poetry "lies in wait, as it were, until the materialization of its proper audience"; read as an address to a future audience, the *Mask* "imagines a future that will see the present for what it was."[70] The poem supports these readings. But if Shelley did not assume the poem was unpublishable, the readings represent alternatives in case the poem's more urgent intervention fails. Shelley's immediate focus on how the country will respond to Peterloo suggests that the poem, rushed off to *The Examiner*, is his attempt to shape the practical interpretation of the event. Since the nature of the cause is determined at the event of the effect, the people have an opportunity to determine by their actions whether Peterloo was a revolutionary event that launched a major change in the course of history or merely another instance of continued systemic oppression. The opportunity to determine the nature of a past event never fully closes. The possibility of future agency Pyle and Franta detected is part of Shelley's claim that revolutionary change depends on a kind of intervention, whether it happens now or in the future. Shelley does not primarily address a future audience that will see the present for what it was but a present audience that might learn to see the recent past for what it might yet have been.

In both *The Mask of Anarchy* and *A Philosophical View of Reform*, Shelley entertains a number of different ways to pursue reform, and while he prefers the course of nonviolent, consensual reform mediated through print or protest, he reserves the right of popular insurrection. Shelley notes in the *View* that reformers "must not sh[rink]" from the prospect of "civil war" (*Works* 53). Other modes of opposition owe their efficacy in part to the threat of civil war. Shelley prefers a nonviolent course of protest and civil disobedience that aims to inundate the public with written arguments and to drown the administration in paperwork. He wishes to marshal "an overwhelming multitude of defendants before the courts of common law"; "Petitions . . . ought to load the tables of the House of Commons"; and the prominent "poets, philosophers and artists ought to remonstrate" (*Works* 51–52) in a series of memorials written for the papers. The "true patriot . . . will urge the necessity of exciting the people frequently to exercise their right of assembling, in such limited numbers as that all present may be actual parties to the proceedings of the day" (*Works* 48). These different methods of resistance and demonstration appear predominant at different points in *The Mask of Anarchy*, with the threat of violence always looming.[71] The different modes of protest signal the different components of a successful social reform: the press records a change in prevailing ideas; the protests represent and demonstrate the unity of the popular will; and the possibility of civil war warns of the scale of destruction involved in clearing out the material and practical forms of custom.

The appearance of the "Shape" overlays images of military violence, reading and writing, and popular protest; it is the undefined and overdetermined cause of which the overthrow of Anarchy is the effect. The Shape appears "arrayed in mail" (110), at once dressed in chainmail and organized through the post, whether letters or poems to the editor or newspapers, an ambiguous phrase that anticipates the "simple words" (299) that serve as "swords" (300) and "targes" (301) in the great assembly at the end of the poem. The Shape floats up on rainbow-like wings, with Venus on its "helm" (114), "And those plumes its light rained through / Like a shower of crimson dew" (116–17). The plumes are clouds rising from a volcano, translucent angel feathers, and quills. When read as quills, the plumes transmit light through the liquid medium or rain of ink. The light itself is overdetermined: "its" refers back to Venus or the Shape, and the light belongs to Love, to the public itself, and to the power of the poem to kindle the reader's imagination. Shelley puns that this light *reigns* through the quill. He wrests sovereignty from Anarchy and transfers it to the light for which print is the medium. This rain may fall like "crimson dew," an image predominantly of blood spilled in reactionary and then revolutionary violence; "the blood that must ensue" (338) rests on the tyrants who "have first shed blood."[72] Alternatively, the light may shower "with refreshing power or with gentle fall," a definition for "dew" that the *OED* supports with two citations from Shelley's poetry.

Shelley's account of the Shape emphasizes the perilous formal resemblance between the liberating revolutionary act and the deposition of one tyrant by another. The Shape and Anarchy both depend on and consist of particular conditions and acts of the public. One can always turn into or overthrow the other. The metrical procession of the Shape's "footstep" (122) or "step" (125) resembles the poet in the opening stanza being led forth "To walk in the visions of Poesy" (4) and serves as the obverse of the Destructions' "trampling" (43). Walking and trampling both leave traces, footprints, or imprints.

> With step as soft as wind it past
> O'er the heads of men – so fast
> That they knew the presence there,
> And looked, – but all was empty air. (118–21)

In Shelley's translation of Plato's *Symposium*, Agathon says Love "'treads on the softest of existing things . . . within the souls and inmost nature of Gods and men.'" When the Shape appears, the people look about and see nothing but "empty air": the Shape, as Love, is only the bond of their unity, a form inseparable from its content, an assembly in which all take part, and an image of democratic representation. Anarchy pretends to be a sovereign apart from the people, but the Shape presents nothing beyond the people. But then again, Agathon contrasts Love with Homer's description of Calamity, who, in contrast to Love, "'makes her path upon the heads of men.'"[73] In overthrowing Anarchy, the Shape may appear to trample the crowd and to be another copy of tyrannical history's one page; it may appear as the angel of a vengeful god destroying some but passing over others; or it may appear as a gentle spirit that picks its way by stepping over rather than upon the heads of a prostrate multitude.

Whether or not the Shape represents a leap out of the cycle of tyranny and ruin depends not or not only on the means of the overthrow, whether it occurs through violence, protests, or print, but on the animating motive of the people, whether they act out of love or take Cobbett's snuff, revenge.

But Shelley leaves equivocal whether or not the Shape's conditions of possibility, which are also the conditions of publicity, have been fulfilled. Shelley leaves ambiguous whether or not the metropolitan public will allow him to help shape the effective interpretation of Peterloo. Wolfson emphasizes that the speaker of the poem never explicitly wakes up and that, in a sense, the poem represents a dream of political oratory closed off from the world.[74] Scrivener and Jones, on the contrary, have demonstrated that the poem performs its active engagement with the metropolitan public and shown how Shelley loads the poem with references to images circulating in London culture at the time, including paintings, prints, and reports of Peterloo.[75] Chandler notes that the "voice" that comes "from over the Sea" (2) at the opening of the poem "must in one sense be simply the voice of Hunt's *Examiner*."[76] Shelley entertains a number of ways in which the poem could misfire. Hunt could cave to Anarchy and not publish. It could, like his other works, appear and then vanish without receiving much notice. Or the poem could be misunderstood. The relatively approachable, exoteric style of the *Mask* gestures at an attempt to appeal to elite radicals, middle-class reformers, and working-class protestors and to produce what Gilmartin refers to as "the elusive possibility of an integrated radical front."[77] Timothy Webb refers to the *Mask* as "directed at the people of England" and written under an uncongenial pressure "to simplify" his habits of expression for a broad audience.[78] Stephen Behrendt links the *Mask* to Shelley's proposal to write a series of "*popular songs*" intended for "the general public," though he acknowledges the *Mask* would be "different stylistically and aesthetically" from the other popular poems and the "longest and most complex."[79] Goldsmith attempts to define Shelley's constructed audience more precisely and claims that he adopts the language of apocalypse "to speak to an audience of working people who traditionally expressed their discontent and their struggles in the language of radical Protestant millenarianism."[80] For all his popularizing tactics, Shelley submits the *Mask* specifically to *The Examiner*. William St. Clair estimates that *The Examiner* had a circulation of around 7,000 to 8,000 per week, and Philip Harling describes its readership as "well-educated reform-minded members of the urban 'middling sort'."[81] *The Examiner* was a long way from Cobbett's tuppenny trash. Jones says Shelley's language in the *Mask* merely "*imitates*" simplicity; Cronin ventures that Shelley "patronises the popular style in which he writes."[82] Shelley recognizes but does not concede the misalignment between the audiences implied in the poem's projected venue of publication, popular rhetoric and range of cultural reference, and structures and figures as intricate as anything reserved for the select few who would appreciate *Prometheus Unbound.* He writes in a manner calculated to increase the likelihood of the poem being published, read, and influential, but he inscribes his doubts that the poem will be read or understood. "The system of society as it exists at present," Shelley remarks to Hunt, "must be overthrown from the foundations with all its superstructure of maxims & of forms before we shall find anything but disappointment in our intercourse with any but a few select spirits." Yet Shelley sees this remedy, while not "one of the easiest," nonetheless as an obligation of the reformers.[83] Anarchy and the Shape both depend on and consist of the conditions of publicity, and the emergence of the Shape as the public of the unified radical front presupposes and constitutes such an overthrow of foundations.

Shelley's power to influence the popular interpretation of Peterloo is limited by the reach of *The Examiner* and his power to communicate through print. In the *Mask*, the metropolitan public struggles with reading and interpretation. In the first third of the poem, the multitude adores the procession that destroys it. Children misread Fraud's tears for gems and, as the tears "Turned to mill-stones as they fell" (17), the children "Had their brains knocked out by them" (21). Goldsmith argues that the "stifling repetition" on "King, and God, and Lord" (71) implies that "words are limited in supply, belong to few, and can be combined only in prescribed, mechanical ways that endlessly reproduce the structure of power."[84] This is the effect of the repetition, but the variation within the repetitions suggests misreading. Anarchy has "I AM GOD, AND KING, AND LAW!" (37) marked on his brow. The groups that praise him repeat the phrase because they read his text aloud. They rearrange the phrase and never get it wholly right. Shelley implies that the act of reading and interpreting involves an inherent measure of interference – the product of Bacon's idols – that destabilizes the act of transcriptive reproduction. If misreading potentially subverts Anarchy's power, it also potentially limits the power of the Shape. The revolutionary voice that rises "as if" from the Earth and speaks the last two thirds of the poem turns "every drop of blood" (143) that has fallen "upon her brow" (141) into speech. The voice mirrors the act of reading affirmations off the brow of Anarchy, and its voice in turn remains subject to interpretation. Even if *The Mask of Anarchy* found its way into the hands of the people, perhaps they would misunderstand it or perhaps it would be too obscure and ineffectually pass "O'er the heads of men."

Shelley skeptically declines to specify the necessary means of reform or to say whether or not his poetry in particular will change much of anything, but he has a more definite sense of the role poetry, both as a general act of imagination and as a particular literary kind, must play in the reform. As a literary kind, poetry jars words out of their roles in customary discourse and in doing so awakens new, unstereotyped, imaginative thought. As Shelley puts it in the *Defence*, poets "create afresh the associations" (*SPP* 512) between words and thoughts. True poetry breaks the Humean chains of custom. The voice that rises as if from the Earth calls for an overhaul of political discourse and the conditions that it masks and that support it. Slavery, the voice says, is to be cold "When the winter winds are bleak" (170) and "to work and have such pay / As just keeps life from day to day" (160–61); Freedom is "bread . . . clothes, and fire, and food" for the laborer (217, 221). Words such as "Justice" (230), "Wisdom" (234), "Peace" (238), and "Love" (246) have been reduced to empty counters used alike by the establishment and opposition. Cronin reads this as an example of Shelley's "language of dissent," that is, of his attempt to strip words of their ideological freight and, in doing so, to reclaim them for radical purposes.[85] Shelley claims the political keywords for his purposes, but he does so in a way that lays bare the arbitrariness of such claims and highlights how conventional political discourse "disorganize[s]" (*SPP* 512) the relation between words and the practical resources, rights, and opportunities those words putatively signify. Supplanting the establishment discourse of "Freedom" with a radical discourse of "Freedom" might be constructive, but it would ultimately amount to preferring one mask to another. Shelley emphasizes the process of seeing through discourse to its relation to material conditions. As Shelley notes in his letter to Hunt as editor of the *Examiner*, "*We* cannot hesitate which party to embrace; and whatever revolutions are to occur, though oppression should change names & names cease to be oppressions, our party will be that of liberty & of the oppre{ss}ed."[86] As the revitalizers of language, the poets have the power to shape whether language represents or masks the conditions and interests of the oppressed.

For Shelley, the power and obligation to transform the social system – even beyond the domain of language – belongs to the poets. Critical debates in the last decades of the twentieth century about the relation between aesthetics and politics have obscured Shelley's sense of the potential social agency of poetry. Neither the frame nor the terms of the aesthetics and politics debate suits Shelley's thought particularly well. The "aesthetic" carries a Kantian association with disinterested and autonomous appraisal of art, and this supposed autonomy separates it from the world of politics. Kim Wheatley argues that Shelley turns "to aestheticism and aesthetic appreciation" as "an alternative to politics" and a way to avoid the frustrations of seeing his opposition serve the interests of the establishment press.[87] Robert Kaufman puts an Adornian twist on Kantian autonomy and argues that Shelley thinks poetry, as an aesthetic product, indirectly influences politics by exercising the reader's disinterested critical faculties.[88] Such readings misrepresent Shelley's thought by substituting politics for publicity and aesthetics for poetry both as a literary kind and as an act of imagination. Shelley's experience with the press gave him no reason to think written poetry was neutral terrain in the public sphere, and Habermas suggests that the public sphere organized its ideological image and discourse through aesthetic debates. To argue that Shelley locates the social agency of poetry in its ability to produce critical thought – which Kaufman aligns with Enlightenment rationalists – would be to align him with what Chandler identifies as the narrowly rationalistic, utilitarian consensus in public discourse.

Where Adorno separates art and politics and reconnects them through critical thought, Shelley sees art and politics as products of the same imaginative, poetic process. Poets in the general sense, in their capacity as "unacknowledged legislators" (*Works* 20), break down and reinvent social forms in the same way poets in the particular sense break down and renew the materials of discourse. In the *Defence*, Shelley claims "the true Poetry of Rome lived in its institutions; for whatsoever of beautiful, true and majestic they contained could have sprung only from the faculty which creates the order in which they consist" (*SPP* 523). "[C]ivil habits of action" are among the "instruments and materials of poetry; they may be called poetry by that figure of speech which considers the effect as a synonime [*sic*] of the cause" (*SPP* 513). In the act of publishing, poets transform the public both at the level of the individual and at the level of the institutions constructed by the conditions of publicity as effects produce their causes. The dialectic of the *idola specus* guarantees the former; the construction of publicity by each public utterance guarantees the latter. At the moment of its appearance, poetry transforms the animating spirit of the public; it displaces the antipathetic, selfish, cash-nexus driven by the Devil in *Peter Bell the Third* and manifest in Anarchy in *The Mask of Anarchy*, and it opens a clearing for the shaping of new thought under the star of Venus. In the metropolitan public, the difference between affirming the terms of publicity and poetically reconfiguring them within vital language is the difference between calamity and love. To change history by interpreting it also entails changing the methods of interpretation and the kind of relations and conditions that determine literary production and reception. Shelley defines poetry in the general sense as that which dissolves dead customs and reshapes the public and the conditions of publicity.

By definition, then, only poetry can interrupt the procession of Anarchy and the distortion of political representation and historical form of urbanization that it represents. Until poetry appears as the decisive Shape, the trampling will continue. In the third and final section of *The Mask of Anarchy*, the voice calls out, "Let a vast assembly be" (295). The assembly the voice conjures strongly resembles the gathering at St. Peter's Field; the voice appears to recommend the people respond to Peterloo by reenacting it. The multitude should gather again, and again the cavalry should "Slash, and stab, and maim, and hew" (342). There are differences between the vast assembly and Peterloo, but the differences are narrow enough that they would fall within the range of representations and interpretations of the event. The figure of the assembly seems forked: either interpret Peterloo as that vast assembly, as an event already accomplished, or find yourselves doomed to repeat it. Without some other change, more urban assemblies will result in more Peterloos. The chorus "Rise like lions after slumber" (368) echoes "again—again—again" (367), ringing out indefinitely until the multitude ceases to reproduce the terms of publicity that deny it the means of representation.

Shelley does not reject urbanization per se or retreat from it; instead, he calls for it to be reimagined in a form that represents the interests of multitude. His skepticism restrains him from imagining what a reformed city might look like. For Shelley, forming and reforming the social system is a continuous poetic process. The dream frame of the *Mask* shows the poet walking in visions of poesy, using his imagination to create a space (walking is one of the poem's metaphors for poetic activity) and inhabiting that creation (walking within a world transformed into poetry). If the frame does not close, it may be because the work of recreating social space is never done. In order to be fully realized, this process – initiated and maintained through the working of the metropolitan public – must change the form of metropolitan institutions and the daily life and built environment of the metropolis itself. The vast assembly includes within it a vision of the possibility of a new form of urbanization. The people stream out of "every hut, village and town" (272) and "the workhouse and the prison" (275) and gather "On some spot of English ground / Where the plains stretch wide around" (264–65) in the presence of "All that must eternal be" (268). This universal evacuation can only be conceptual. The great assembly represents, at least in one respect, an intellectual willingness to set aside old forms and start anew as if on fresh-cleared land and remove all bounds on the imagination other than the universal laws of physics. The "blue sky overhead" (266) that witnesses the event echoes the "empty air" of the formal presence of the Shape, and suggests that the assembly represents and includes the whole population as actual participants in the process of recreating social geography. The multitude, previously hidden in urban caves, creates a public and a city to render itself visible. Morton Paley notes that the poem's rewriting of Revelation raises the expectation of "the millennial descent of the New Jerusalem"; for the skeptical Shelley, the heavenly city appears not as a definite form – that, he acknowledges, lies beyond his imagining – but as a process of urbanization evolving through perpetual rebuilding.[89]

5

Robinson, Barbauld, and the Limits of Luxury

The preceding chapters focus on analytical formations that describe fields that mediate the mutual influence between urbanization and English Romantic poetry; collectively, these chapters trace in the poets' representations of and involvement in those fields the contours of an emergent alternative discourse on urbanization. While the histories of social and cultural discourses – including Enlightenment political economy and moral philosophy, civic humanism, artisan antinomianisms, and political radicalisms – have played prominent roles in each chapter, the poets' negotiations of the interactions between these discourses have not been the primary object of analysis. In this chapter, I turn to the history of discourse and consider Mary Darby Robinson's and Anna Letitia Barbauld's poetic negotiations of conflicting conceptions of urbanization in civic humanism and in an influential line of Enlightenment moral philosophy. I focus in particular on the concept of luxury, which lies at the crux of the disagreement between these two discourses. In each discourse, the concept of luxury participates in a broader moral and social philosophy that interrelates a theory of civilizational progress, the production of the surplus, urbanization, and constructions of gender.

This conflict of discourses sets the terms for Robinson's and Barbauld's poetic treatments of the relation between urbanization, gender roles, and the possibilities of historical progress. Drawing on both discourses, Robinson and Barbauld assess the extent to which the present regime of accumulation and the gender roles it has produced – in coordination with or opposition to the influence of sexual hierarchies – are consistent with the conditions of civilizational progress. They adopt the general outline of the model of progress in Enlightenment discourse: increasing the surplus and expanding the production and consumption of luxuries drives urbanization, increases the volume of commercial exchange, fosters sociability, and refines manners by increasing the social interaction between the sexes. They invoke the civic humanist concept of luxury to define and describe the limits of the Enlightenment model. Without adopting the civic humanist ideals of rural independence and austere masculinity, they leverage the residual moral force of the suspicion of luxury in civic humanist discourse in criticizing the costs of the unrestrained commercialism underwritten by Enlightenment discourse. Robinson and Barbauld link this highly commercialized mode of producing and distributing the surplus to the stark economic inequality in the metropolis and to the imposition of time discipline throughout culture and society. They regard historical progress as jeopardized by a luxury economy that supports cultural goods implicated in the logic of commerce, such as the newspaper, but that neglects elements of culture associated with progressive refinement, such as the sociability and writing of women and the production and consumption of relatively autonomous poetry. In attending to the condition of the lower orders, questioning the historical form of urbanization, and calling for reform, Robinson's and Barbauld's representations of the metropolis participate in the alternative discourse on urbanization; relative to the other poets discussed in this book, however, they attend more prominently to the relations between urbanization and gender and between urbanization and the positions of women and especially women writers.

Luxury: Genealogy, Gender, Genre

Through a complicated series of debates spanning the long eighteenth century, the emerging discourses of Enlightenment political economy and moral philosophy appropriated for the urban man of commerce the political virtues that the discourse of civic humanism assigned to the independent landowner.[1] In the course of this negotiation, as John Sekora and Christopher Berry show, Enlightenment discourse set aside the association in civic humanism of the concept of luxury with moral corruption and civil decline, and instead recast it as a category of economic activity linked with indicators of the progress of civilization, such as sociability, commercial activity, and cultural refinement.[2] This change involved a change in gender constructs: where civic humanism valued an ethos of masculine austerity, Enlightenment discourse promoted sociability that gave a prominent role to women. At the beginning of the Romantic period, the concept of luxury had two different sets of associations and connotative charges derived from these two different discourses. In each discourse, the concept also had a complex structure: it could refer both to a sphere of commercial consumption and cultural practice associated with the fashionable world of London and to the economic processes of producing and distributing the surplus. Robinson and Barbauld exploit this complex structure and critically reflect on the implication of women's roles in urban society within broader processes of modernization.

In the social philosophy of civic humanism, luxury is part of a structure of political, economic, military, and gender values that determines the historical course of civilizations. This tradition presents the ideal citizen of the virtuous republic as an independent landowner whose wealth allows him a disinterested devotion to the public good: he lives a modest or an austere life, which readies him for the hardships of military service; and he possesses the masculine virtues of hardiness and selfless courage. According to this tradition, as long as its citizens are virtuous, the polis flourishes and grows into an empire. The great dangers to the polis come from luxury and despotism. Luxury corrupts all of the citizen's virtues: it draws men out of the bracing life of the country and into the decadent world of the city; it makes them selfish and avaricious as they seek ever more exorbitant consumption; and it makes men soft, effeminate, and incapable of enduring the trials of war. Historians such as Sallust and Livy associate virtue and vice, as well as the security and vulnerability of the state, with the material austerity and self-indulgence, respectively, of Roman rulers and society. Out of these classical sources a historiographic tradition emerged in which the virtues of the early republic created Rome's great empire, and imperial conquests exposed Rome to the ruinous contagion of Asiatic luxury and despotism. The civic humanist concept of luxury, then, implies a paradigmatic parabolic historical trajectory in which prosperity generates the conditions of decline.[3]

In the long eighteenth century, Enlightenment social discourses disputed the link between luxury and vice and presented luxury instead as an indication of progressive commercial development. Berry argues that in the eighteenth century, the concept of luxury was de-moralized and recast as a neutral term for a category of economic activity.[4] David Hume's essays "Of Commerce" and "Of Luxury" (1752) are typical in this respect. Hume acknowledges that luxury "may be taken in a good as well as in a bad sense," but he tendentiously minimizes the bad sense, briefly noting at the end of the essay that luxury is vicious not in itself but only insofar as it interferes with one's ability to perform one's duties.[5] Otherwise, "Refinement on the pleasures and conveniencies of life has no natural tendency to beget venality and corruption."[6] In discussing the good sense of luxury, Hume focuses on surplus production. When agricultural laborers produce more food than they consume, the surplus allows others to "apply themselves to the finer arts, which are commonly denominated the arts of *luxury*," and these laborers in the finer arts "add to the happiness of the state."[7] Where civic humanism recommends investing the surplus in public goods and the military, Hume recommends reinvesting the surplus in the production of luxuries. For Hume, reinvesting the surplus in production is the condition of possibility of urbanization, and urbanization corresponds with an increase in the proportion of the population working to produce the things that are not merely necessary to life but that make life comfortable and pleasurable. Rejecting the notion that laborers must be kept poor in order to motivate them to work, Hume argues that if luxuries were affordable to laborers, the drive of emulative consumption would motivate them not only to work but to impose time discipline on their own labor, improve their productivity, and increase the surplus.[8] In Hume's argument, rather than depleting the wealth of the nation in a negative balance of trade, luxury consumption increases the wealth of the nation by increasing productivity; rather than indicating corrosive inequality, the consumption of luxuries redistributes the wealth of the richest and supports the livelihood of tradesmen.[9] According to Hume, in this ideal image of a commercial society, "where luxury nourishes commerce and industry, the peasants, by a proper cultivation of the land, become rich and independent."[10] For Hume and writers in his tradition, the concept of luxury participated in a historical narrative of a compounding commercial expansion that increases and broadly distributes the means of happiness.

More than de-moralizing the concept of luxury, Enlightenment discourse in fact re-moralized it, repurposing its association with civilizational change to underwrite a new morally charged narrative of historical progress. The surplus supports the pursuit of knowledge; refined arts of manufacture accompany refined taste and manners; and the busy enterprises of commerce expand the horizon of sociable relations:

> The more these refined arts advance, the more sociable men become[.] ... They flock into cities; love to receive and communicate knowledge; to show their wit or their breeding; their taste in conversation or living, in clothes or furniture. ... Both sexes meet in an easy and sociable manner; and the tempers of men, as well as their behaviour, refine apace.[11]

I cited this passage in the introduction as a mission statement for the investment in recreational facilities for polite culture that Borsay calls the English urban renaissance; as Maxine Berg writes, "Luxury was ... increasingly perceived as a sociable activity, generated by cities, and participated in by the middling as well as the upper classes."[12] Here I want to observe that, for Hume, private luxury consumption indicates the progressive refinement of collective culture and the advance of civilization and that his representation of civilizational progress refers to polite rather than plebeian culture.

In presenting the sociable interaction of the sexes in polite urban settings as an important mechanism for refining manners, Hume implicates changes in gender constructs and relations in the processes of urbanization and civilizational progress. His rethinking of gender roles participates in what E. J. Clery calls "the feminization debate," a dispute that ran throughout the eighteenth century over proper gender roles and that informed the gendering of the attributes of the man of commerce. From the perspective of civic humanism, which values masculine independence and fortitude, the man of commerce's self-interestedness, industriousness, sociability, taste for fashion, and manners refined by the company of women all appear effeminate; but Hume and other Enlightenment writers advanced a new model of masculinity that emphasized productivity and efficiency and acknowledged the moral authority of a refined sensibility.[13] In linking the refinement of men's sensibilities to sociable interactions with women, this line of thought also reflected and encouraged a greater role for polite women in the public culture of the metropolis. During the eighteenth century, polite women exerted increasing influence on social and cultural practices associated with luxury. Gillian Russell writes that upper-class "Women made their presence felt as participants, sponsors and sometimes subjects of a vibrant social scene" and shaped the public life of London through "dress, consumerism and developments in sociability and print culture – what contemporaries referred to as the 'fashionable world'."[14] "The woman of fashion," Harriet Guest remarks, began "to acquire significance not just as the embodiment of corruptions of commercial luxury, but as the sign of the polished politeness that is the fruit of commercial prosperity."[15] Writers in Hume's tradition represented the increasing sociable and public influence of women, including through the press, as an indication of historical advancement, creating what Clery describes as a "linkage of the progress of commercial society and the progress of women."[16]

As gender roles changed, so did the gendering of literary genres. During the eighteenth century, women writers exerted as profound an influence on certain genres of poetry as they did on the novel. Paula Backscheider notes that in the eighteenth century, "Of all literary forms, poetry was the most respectable for women to write."[17] Polite women were expected to be able to write occasional verse and *verse de société* as part of the culture of sociability. Over the course of the century more women published their verse and published more explicitly public and political verse. Nonetheless, women tended to write in poetic genres compatible with prevailing notions of femininity and gendered genres of experience, and publishers, reviewers, and the literary market enforced these tendencies. Stephen Behrendt notes, "It was expected that . . . women poets should confine themselves to the lyric and the sentimental modes," and he focuses his study of Romantic-period poetry by women on the sonnet, occasional verse, and the verse tale.[18] Women, that is, were welcome to write in genres invested in feeling, urban sociability, or idle entertainment. But as Backscheider observes, through the eighteenth century and into the Romantic period, "Women's poetry was associated with morality and moral issues." Such an association gave women license to speak as the moral conscience of the home and the nation.[19]

The concept of luxury offered a way for women poets to comment on the conventionally masculine debates about the production and distribution of the surplus and the course of history while writing on conventionally feminine topics related to the fashionable world and morals.[20] Backscheider remarks that women's poetry in the early Romantic period "often evaluates and attempts to direct 'progress'," and Clery hints that in the Romantic period feminist writers sought to break the coordination of the progress of women with the progress of commerce and sought ways to improve the condition of women "in critical relation to the capitalist status quo."[21] Breaking from the influential poetic precedent of Oliver Goldsmith's *The Deserted Village* – which uses the civic humanist concept of luxury to warn against urbanization as a prelude to ruin – Robinson and Barbauld use the civic humanist concept of luxury to criticize the historical form of urbanization for not sufficiently realizing the wide prosperity and influential roles of women promised in Enlightenment discourse and to direct urbanization toward a progressive course.

Robinson and the Refashioning of Urban Poetry

In her trailblazing study of Mary Robinson's public career, Judith Pascoe presents Robinson as a canny operator in the fashionable world of London, artfully adapting and marketing her public image to make a living in a commercialized cultural field. In Pascoe's reading, Robinson represents London "as a thriving marketplace offering considerable opportunities to a female writer," as a stage for spectacle and spectatorship that she finds "more inviting than alienating," and as "a place of amusement."[22] More like Charles Lamb than Wordsworth or Coleridge, Robinson writes about and participates in the commercial bustle of the metropolis with pleasure and excitement.[23] Following Pascoe's lead, Diego Saglia argues that in her posthumously published *Memoirs*, Robinson presents herself as an epitome of "good luxury."[24] But Robinson's representations of the commercialized cultural scene are far from uniformly celebratory. Jon Klancher argues that, while Robinson admires the cultural consumption in London, she expresses frustration with "the recent and drastic change in the conditions of its cultural producers" as "the tissue of recognitions that had sustained the older Republic of Letters" unraveled with the advance of commercialization.[25] Indeed, Robinson uses the civic humanist concept of luxury to signal her critical reflection on the conditions of production associated with the historical form of urbanization. She focuses in particular on the rigorous time discipline that permeates urban society from the demands of productivity imposed on the working class, to the revolving cycles of fashionable consumption and sociability in polite culture, to the strenuous regimen of serving as the primary poetic contributor for a newspaper. Always writing with an eye on the market, Robinson compares the vicissitudes of profitable poetic genres to those of fashion, both asserting her authority as a woman of fashion and lamenting the ephemerality of poetry written under such heteronomous conditions. Critical of the demands of commercial cultural production, Robinson proposes a variety of alternative ways of distributing the surplus – such as restoring patronage and creating cultural establishments – that would better support women writers.

During the mature phase of her poetic career, from when she first returned to London after four years on the continent in 1787 until her death in December 1800, Robinson sought out genres – as literary kinds and as modes of production, distribution, and consumption inseparable from social networks, venues of publication, and markets – that offered opportunities for a woman writer to make a living. She adapted to poetic fashions. On arriving in London, she wrote her way into the Della Cruscan circle of poets, attempting to share in the success of the highly erotic and overwrought verse exchanges, first published in the newspapers *The World* and *The Oracle*, that had become a sensation in the fashionable world. When opinion turned and Della Cruscan poetry became a common target of derision, Robinson wrote in different styles and published in different periodicals.[26] In 1799, she was appointed by Daniel Stuart to serve as the main poetry contributor for the *Morning Post*, a post previously held by Robert Southey, at a time when the paper was publishing poems from the first edition of *Lyrical Ballads* to encourage sales of the volume.[27] Along with the steady stream of occasional pieces she contributed to the paper in 1799 and 1800, Robinson also took up the genres of the *Lyrical Ballads*. Pitching the volume that would become *Lyrical Tales* (1800) to a prospective publisher, Robinson noted that several of the poems in the volume were written "on a variety of subjects in the manner of Wordsworth's Lyrical ballads."[28] The change in genre was part of a professional strategy. She recognized that the Lake Poets held a promising position in the field, and she sought to associate herself with them: they had professional connections that ensured their poetry could appear in important periodicals; the *Lyrical Ballads* had begun to get good reviews; and they benefited from the gendered system of mutual credentialing organized through universities, academies, and homosocial intellectual coteries from which she was excluded.[29] In this context her persistent assertions of her unappreciated individual merit and originality, like Coleridge's professions of his ruined genius, are claims of a vestige of autonomy, protests against the commercialized literary field, and part of a branding strategy.

In the several texts published during the 1790s, Robinson expresses her concern that the conditions of production in the commercialized literary field were not conducive to the production of poetry that would endure, a standard that poetry, more than other genres, conventionally sets for itself. Even before accepting the position at the *Morning Post*, Robinson associated these heteronomous conditions with writing newspaper verse, which had a poor reputation in the Romantic period.[30] In her role as Stuart's main poetic contributor, Robinson had to produce or otherwise supply a certain amount of poetry daily. The pace was relentless and exhausting. Even the notoriously prolific and disciplined Southey struggled to produce enough poetry on schedule.[31] To meet the demand, Robinson republished her earlier poetry, composed new occasional poems by drawing material out of the paper, and hastily composed imitative verse in fashionable genres. She was proud of her ability to write quickly, but she was also aware that what was written quickly tended to fade quickly. In the preface to her sonnet sequence *Sappho and Phaon* (1796), she distinguishes her sonnets, not previously published in the papers, from the "ephemera" that fill "the monthly and diurnal publications" (146). Although poems from *Lyrical Ballads* and *Lyrical Tales* both appeared in Stuart's newspapers, Wordsworth's and Coleridge's poems first appeared in their book while several of Robinson's poems were published first in the newspapers. Robinson's poems, that is, first appeared in less prestigious forms of publication, and she was more completely subjected to the time discipline of commercial production and to the emerging standardized chronological construction of time that James Chandler strikingly refers to as "an increasingly periodized (i.e., 'periodicalized')" time.[32]

For Robinson, commerce alone does not adequately support poetry. When she praises the support given to the arts, she invokes the Enlightenment concept of luxury; but when she criticizes the consequences of the excessive commercialization of cultural production, she invokes the civic humanist concept of luxury. In her essay on the "Present State of the Manners, Society, Etc. Etc. of the Metropolis of England," Robinson praises the embellishments and ornaments of London in the terms of the Enlightenment concept of luxury: "As London is the great emporium of commerce, it is also the centre of attraction for the full exercise of talents, and the liberal display of all that can embellish the arts and sciences."[33] The luxury economy has transformed the metropolis into a cultural scene that distributes "A certain species of refinement" through "the various classes of the community" (116). Robinson recognizes that print culture produces and is a product of this refinement. "London is the busy mart of literary traffick. Its public libraries, its multitudes of authors, its diurnal publications ... all contribute to the important task of enlarging and embellishing the world of letters" (108), and the profusion of "so many monthly and diurnal publications ... may in great measure, be attributed to the expansion of mind, which daily evinces itself among all classes of people" (118). The present state of literary traffic sustains a robust market for periodicals, but it leaves Robinson seeking the alternative relations to the means of production offered by patronage or by institutions that could support poets. "[P]atronage has been frigid; and the lot of the sons and daughters of the Muses has been too often marked by neglect or chequered by calamity" (108–09). Robinson turns to the civic humanist concept of luxury as she blames the failure of patronage on the dissipation of the aristocracy. Unlike their hardy ancestors, the "effeminized race of modern nobility" has degenerated into "plants of a fashionable hot-bed, where indolence begets vice, and vice becomes the parent of lassitude, apathy, disease, and death" (112). While current patterns of luxury consumption generally support what Enlightenment discourse casts as civilizational progress, for Robinson, they do not direct a sufficient portion of the surplus into the production of poetry.

Robinson's call for greater support for poetry is also a call to reconfigure the gendering of opportunities in the literary field. Like Coleridge, Robinson criticizes the commercialized literary field by imagining the formation of literary establishments, but where Coleridge's clerisy tacitly reproduces the gendered exclusions of the church and universities, Robinson's proposals seek to secure resources and regard for women writers. In her *Monody to the Memory of Marie Antoinette* (1793), Robinson presents the queen, as Harriet Guest observes, as "a figure of feminine literary and cultural authority" who encouraged female poets; for Robinson, the queen's death represented the "fragility if not the collapse of an idealized cultural regime."[34] This vision of prominent women acting as patrons of women artists is one of several ways Robinson imagines of providing greater opportunities for literary women: in *A Letter to the Women of England*, she calls for a "UNIVERSITY FOR WOMEN" and in the "Present State" essays she calls for strategic cooperation, "union of sentiment, and sympathy of feeling" (115), among women writers.[35] In default of organizing support for women writers in particular, Robinson repeatedly calls for an "Aristocracy of Genius," which Adriana Craciun interprets as ideally "meritocratic" and therefore ideally indifferent to gender.[36] In all of these proposals, Robinson seeks to rectify what she sees as the market denying literary women their due share of the surplus and the opportunity to move out of the heteronomous regions of the literary field.

In a move that challenges vindications of luxury such as Hume's, Robinson allows that luxury generates Enlightened refinement only to the extent that it provides people with the independence that such refinement requires. Robinson notices that peasants have not in fact become rich and independent, and, going beyond civic humanism into the political economy of 1790s radicalism, she associates the luxury of the few with the overwork and poverty of the many, including neglected writers, as if economic accumulation were a zero-sum game.[37] In a poem initially published in the *Monthly Magazine* as "The Italian Peasantry" and later incorporated into *The Progress of Liberty* (1801), Robinson observes that the fertility of the land provides a "pledge / Of future luxury" (17–18), and yet "LABOUR's sons" (34), like Goldsmith's peasants, can no longer "ON THEIR OWN cultur'd plains / Reap the full harvest" (38–39). Their toil supports the rich, who consume exotic delicacies (60–78) in "the marble PALACES OF PRIDE" (55), "By luxury unnerv'd!" (62). In the "Present State," Robinson similarly juxtaposes the luxurious indolence of the nobility with "the sons and daughters of genius and of labour . . . starving in the obscure abodes of industry or sorrow" (112). The comparison between writer and laborer emphasizes that the writer too is subject to exacting demands of productivity. In "The Poet's Garret," Robinson sympathizes with the comic figure of the starving poet and notes "his pen's hard labour" (39); in her Sylphid essays, Robinson observes "the genuine sons and daughters of the Muses, pining in obscure poverty, and labouring incessantly for a scanty pittance . . . no luxuries were seen on the board of weary toil."[38] Her references to incessant labor point to the lack of autonomy and to the time discipline imposed by the demands of the commercialized production.

For Robinson, the highly commercial mode of producing and distributing the surplus applies time pressure across all ranks of society, from agricultural laborers to polite women in urban society. The luxury economy imposes time pressure on polite women in the forms of the exacting social schedule of the season, the quick vicissitudes of fashion, and the depreciation of aging in the marriage market. Although published long before she depended on writing verse for newspapers, Robinson's "Letter to a Friend on Leaving Town" (1775) signals a discomfort with the tempo of urban society that would later find expression in reflections on the conditions of production at the *Morning Post*. Robinson adopts the conventional attitude of a poet retiring from the vicious bustle of urban luxury to the tranquil, reflective solitude of the country, but, as Saglia notes, she savors the luxurious activities she renounces.[39]

> Adieu, gay throng, luxurious vain parade . . .
> No more the Mall, can captivate my heart,
> No more can Ranelagh, one joy impart.
> Without regret I leave the splendid ball. (5, 7–9)

Robinson's rhetorical renunciations so strongly assert what they grammatically deny that they invert the generic preference for retreat and read like a lament for the rapid succession of pleasurable events: this is Robinson as the exponent of "good luxury." Robinson, however, directs her generic complaint not at luxury itself but at the time pressure imposed by the social life of the fashionable world. In the second verse paragraph she invites the reader to mark the women of fashion:

> Luxurious pleasures, all her days divide,
> And fashion taints, bright beauty's greatest pride . . .
> Beaux without number, daily round her swarm . . .
> Till, like the rose, which blooms but for an hour,
> Her face grown common, loses all its power. (29–30, 33, 35–36)

Pleasures not only punctuate her days; they shorten them. The season falls into a daily routine, and that daily routine seems to last a single hour, and that hour signifies a single moment of opportunity. The pressure to find a marriage partner subjects a woman to the coercive caprice of "reigning fashion" (44). She has no choice: this life is the only life there is, and the ephemerality of urban pleasures figures the fleetingness of life. For those who have exhausted their youth swept up in "the fashionable current" (54), the "sequester'd shade" (61) of retirement awaits like death. Given this inevitable end, Robinson says, it is no wonder "that I can leave, / Those transient pleasures, only born to grieve. / Those short liv'd shadows of a fleeting day" (67–69). The rhetorical comma and line ending draw the sense of the verse away from the grammatical meaning, identifying the "transient pleasures" with women like the speaker. The rapid tempo of the fashionable world reduces them to ephemeral shadows. This reflection resonates with Robinson's thoughts on the production and consumption of newspaper verse: the gratifications of luxuries such as poetry are worth savoring even if the compulsory and hurried routine inexorably renders them ephemeral.

In her renderings of urban life in her occasional verse for the *Morning Post*, Robinson develops a formal scheme for representing the compression of time that coordinates fashionable luxury with the conditions of the lower orders and the conditions of production of newspaper verse. These poems catch time in an unending present or hold it to a moment by moving through space. In "January, 1795," Robinson juxtaposes scenes of the city, often highlighting the disparity between rich and poor:

> Lofty Mansions, warm and spacious;
> Courtiers, cringing and voracious:
> Titled Gluttons, dainties carving;
> Genius, in a garret, starving! (5–8)

Timothy Webb writes that the running present tense captures "activities which have not been completed but which are still going on."[40] Robinson uses the same form for "Modern Female Fashions" (1799) and "Modern Male Fashions" (1800), a pair of gentle satires on the caprices of fashion, as if implying that the conditions of London and its authors are subject to the same fundamental determinants that drive fashion. In "January, 1795," Robinson draws on the civic humanist associations of luxury while juxtaposing wealth and poverty: she refers to the decay of masculine strength (27), military weakness (26, 39–40), and "Ruin hasten'd" (43). In the jumble of juxtapositions, the rapid cadence of the verse, and the minute partitioning of time, these poems adopt a presentational mode suited to the newspaper, and as such implicate the newspaper in the commercialized world of luxury the poems critique.

Robinson presents a limit to the determining power of this commercial world in "London's Summer Morning," which first appeared in the

Morning Post on August 23, 1800. She translates the temporality of urban experience into the structural rhetorical repetition of "Now," and she singles out the routine sounds of the daily work that reproduces city life. Robinson notes the cry of the "chimney-boy" (4), the rattling of the "milk-pail" (7), and the ring of the "dustman" (8). Much of the labor in the poem consists of cleaning, and, as in Gay's *Trivia*, the art of urban living revolves around taking care of one's clothes. "The ruddy housemaid twirls the busy mop, / Annoying the smart 'prentice" (18–19), who dodges or wipes off the grimy splatter. At the center of the poem Robinson describes storefronts full of "gay merchandize" (23):

> Now, spruce and trim,
> In shops (where beauty smiles with industry,)
> Sits the smart damsel; while the passenger
> Peeps thro' the window, watching ev'ry charm.
> Now pastry dainties catch the eye minute
> Of humming insects, while the limy snare
> Waits to enthral them. (23–29)

Robinson pairs the two scenes by juxtaposition and by structural parallels: each scene entertains a possible deflection of a desiring gaze. In the first scene, the presumably male passenger "peeps" through the window, though the object of his gaze could be the charms of either the merchandise or, more likely, the damsel. The twisted syntax compares the woman and the shop, linking "spruce and trim" to the "smart damsel" only by way of the "shops" and leaving the "beauty" that "smiles with industry" suspended between the "gay merchandize" and the damsel. In this sense, Robinson shows the woman absorbed like a commodity in the world of commerce. If the beauty that smiles is the young woman, then she either smiles with pleasure in her work or does work by smiling. In the second scene, flies gaze on pastries as flypaper waits to trap them. For a poet as sensitive to relationships of spectatorship as Robinson, the juxtaposition of gazes suggests a significant relation: the limy snares resemble the commodities in the shop as things disregarded, and the gaze of the fly perhaps resembles the gaze of the passenger as indifferent to the object's role as a commodity. Robinson, that is, implicates the well-dressed damsel in the world of commerce but also distinguishes her from the merchandise, as if she maintained some reserve of autonomy and was in some way more than what the daily routine of commerce has made her.

In "London's Summer Morning," Robinson offers an oblique comment on her role as a woman poet writing for a newspaper. Robinson involves the figure of the poet within the poem in the city's daily toil. The poem ends as "the poor poet wakes from busy dreams, / To paint the summer morning" (41–42), as if the poet wakes every morning to write the poem she has just completed. But Robinson also casts the smart damsel – who, like Robinson, is involved in the spectacle and spectatorship of the metropolitan scene – as a double for the poet within the poem. The crucial point lies in Robinson's association of newspaper verse with fashion. In her "All For-Lorn" (1800), published in the *Morning Post* four months before "London's Summer Morning," Robinson presents a series of scenes from London's fashionable world. The poem opens with the injunction, "LET FASHION and FANCY their beauties display, / And vaunt what they will for the hour, or the day" (1–2) and closes by bidding "adieu to the pleasures which FANCY can bring" (31), identifying the occasional poem as a fleeting product of fashion and of fancy and suggesting that all such products pass quickly away. In "London's Summer Morning," Robinson similarly associates newspaper verse with the transience of fashion, but she also signals her critical distance from the genre. The damsel at once masters the terms of the commodified domain of fashion – she is "spruce and trim" as well as "smart" – and, through the juxtaposition of scenes, remains in an undefined way removed from it. Robinson stands back from her genre and criticizes its commercial logic without breaking its conventions. Between the smart damsel and the poet appears the figure of "The old-clothes man" (33), who calls for business "In tone monotonous" (34) and purchases "pilfer'd treasure" (37) from thieving domestics. The pressure of need and the competitive consumption of fashion drive a sordid market that circulates secondhand clothes at a discount rate; the same forces drive the circulation and adoption of genres in heteronomous regions of the commercial literary field, generating "monotonous" rounds of derivative, ephemeral verse. While comparing poetry with fashion claims poetry as a domain of women's, and especially Robinson's, acknowledged expertise and influence, the comparison also reduces poetry to a field of commodity exchange.

Robinson adopts the general outline of the narrative of cultural refinement associated with the re-moralized Enlightenment concept of luxury, but she invokes the civic humanist concept of luxury to mark those aspects of urbanizing society that do not fit that narrative. She uses the civic humanist concept of luxury not to affirm the principles of civic humanism but to define specific moral and social problems related to the production and distribution of the surplus, such as the costs of unchecked commercialization, which she then examines through the discourse of 1790s radicalism. The present state of the luxury economy has turned the metropolis into a bustling cultural marketplace and engine of civilizational refinement, but that refinement is jeopardized by the failure of the commercial market to distribute its benefits widely and by the imposition across all ranks of a pressing time discipline. In terms of literary genres, the commercialization of the literary field has reduced the condition of writers in heteronomous sectors of the field, such as writing verse for a newspaper, to that of laborers starved into productivity and has reduced the noncommercial means of support for autonomous production, a change that subjects professional women writers to the vicissitudes of literary fashion. Robinson seeks instead a "good luxury," consistent with the alternative discourse on urbanization, that would distribute the surplus in a way that would temper the demands of time discipline and productivity, improve conditions in the poor areas of the metropolis, and afford writers, especially women writers, a degree of autonomy.

Barbauld and the Ends of Metropolitan Affection

When she wrote *Eighteen Hundred and Eleven* (1812), Anna Letitia Barbauld had a different relation to the metropolitan literary field than Robinson did when writing poetry for the *Morning Post* twelve years earlier: Barbauld had a separate source of income from her educational work; she published the poem as a book rather than in a periodical; and she had a reputation as a learned and respectable writer. But for all these differences, Barbauld, like Robinson, follows the model of progress associated with the concept of luxury in Enlightenment discourse and uses the civic humanist concept of luxury to mark how conditions fall short of that model. In negotiating the conflict of discourses in similar ways, Barbauld and Robinson share common themes in their representations of urbanization: both poets associate the historical form of urbanization with the excessive commercialization of social relations, a limit on the role of women in public culture, a widening gulf between classes, the emergence of periodicalized time, the imposition of time discipline throughout society, and the rise of the newspaper and relative disregard of poetry.

Several scholars have considered Barbauld's handling of the tension between these discourses.[41] Placing *Eighteen Hundred and Eleven* in the tradition of eighteenth-century landscape verse, Maggie Favretti argues that Barbauld claims for herself and for women writers more generally the masculine, "authoritative vantage point of 'disinterestedness'" associated in Harringtonian civic humanism with the independent landowner.[42] Jon

Mee follows Favretti's lead and argues that Barbauld put "less store in sympathetic power" and the transmission of affect than in the cool disinterest of "classical republicanism"; Mee supports the claim by citing contemporary reviews that reproached Barbauld for her unwomanly "privileging of speculative opinions and stoical disinterestedness over the ties of hearth and home."[43] If Barbauld writes from such a perspective, I argue, she focuses on the profound emotional and social costs of arriving at it. For Barbauld, the social fabric is held together by ties of benevolent affection that radiate from familial intimacy through the amiable sociability of the metropolis to the wider world: consistent with Enlightenment discourse, this expanding fabric coincides with increasing surpluses, growing cities, and the progress of the arts. But Barbauld invokes the civic humanist concept of luxury to suggest that this expansion generates forces that oppose it. As the social fabric expands, more of its ties become weaker and more distant until benevolence can no longer restrain avarice and tyranny and the progressive arc of history bends back into a parabolic rise and fall. In *Eighteen Hundred and Eleven*, Barbauld questions whether a woman and a poet – two roles associated with strong affective ties – can still sustain the affective connections between the intimate sphere of the hearth and the wide prospect of the modernizing metropolis. On these terms, distant disinterest would be a symptom of the ruin she imagines.

Barbauld's sense of the cohesive force of benevolence and of the potentially dissociative threat of luxury derives from a line of early Enlightenment thought. William McCarthy notes that Barbauld would have found in Francis Hutcheson, whose works were influential at the Warrington Academy, the Shaftesburian principle that benevolent affection moves outward from family through community to embrace "all mankind."[44] In his *Inquiry into the Original of Our Ideas of Beauty and Virtue* (1726), Hutcheson argues that this benevolence grows weaker over social distance: "This *universal Benevolence* toward all Men, we may compare to that Principle of *Gravitation*, which perhaps extends to all Bodys in the *Universe*; but, like the *Love* of *Benevolence, increases* as the Distance is diminish'd, and is *strongest* when Bodys come to *touch* each other." We feel stronger feelings, Hutcheson writes, the "more *nearly*" someone is "*attach'd* to us," and feel "colder general Sentiments" toward strangers.[45] In *A Short Introduction to Moral Philosophy* (1747), Hutcheson distinguishes between good and bad luxury on the basis of whether it interferes with benevolence. Luxury consumption has no ill effects on the rich, "if it be inconsistent with no duty of life" and if it accompanies "liberality, in raising the condition of indigent friends."[46] The sociable ties of commerce and the arts supplement the ties of the close-knit village and allow for the progressive expansion of a benevolent regime of affect to the metropolitan or universal scale. But "With the luxurious generally every thing is venal," that is, luxury becomes a moral problem when social relations reduce to economic relations and self-interest predominates over benevolence.[47] For Hutcheson, the distinction between harmless or potentially progressive commercial luxury and the civic humanist concept of luxury depends on a distinction between affects. Hutcheson does not consider the question of whether the expansion of the weakly benevolent ties of commercial interaction would eventually be counteracted and overpowered by the increasing proportion of interactions in urban environments with distant strangers.

Barbauld encountered such an increase in the scale of the sociable environment when she moved from Warrington to Hampstead, and, as Anne Janowitz argues, she changed her poetic style as she changed sociable contexts.[48] In relatively intimate Warrington, Barbauld's poetry cultivates what Mee calls the "poetics of amiable sociability," both representing and sharing in friendly conversations.[49] Her benevolent ties radiated outward, bridging the intimate and the public: her poetry circulated among friends, was read and recited more widely within the Warrington Academy, and, thanks in part to connections in the Dissenting community, was published by Joseph Johnson in London.[50] Although reviewers found the poems too cool and learned for a woman, Barbauld professes, as Deirdre Coleman notes, "a belief in the virtues ascribed to her sex, such as sympathy and affection, sociability and conversation, and innate delicacy of taste."[51] After moving to Hampstead, Janowitz writes, Barbauld encountered in the social circle around Johnson's print shop "a more urban and militant notion of sociability," defined by political rather than familial ties.[52] Barbauld's poetry turns increasingly toward public and political occasions. For example, in the sharp rhetoric of her *Epistle to William Wilberforce* (1791), she joins other women poets in moral opposition to the slave trade and tests the reviewers' sense of gendered decorum. The prevailing affect of such verse, Janowitz contends, has shifted from "amiability" to "ardour."[53] After she moved to Stoke Newington in 1802, Barbauld largely stopped publishing poetry, but her major work of the period, *Eighteen Hundred and Eleven*, written in the long shadow of grief cast by the suicide of her husband, examines the links between the intimate and public spheres. She condemns the nation's immoral war policy and mourns the loss of amiable sociability with a combination of public ardor and personal sadness.

In *Eighteen Hundred and Eleven*, the affects of the intimate and international spheres correspond, but rather than benevolent affection radiating from the home out to universal sociability, the dissociative force of social distance encroaches on and severs domestic ties. Throughout the poem, Barbauld associates distance – whether temporal, spatial, or social – with abstraction and unfeeling calculation. The opening line strikes the keynote: Britain hears the "death drum, thundering from afar."[54] Hearing the distant drum, Britain sends more troops, but the sound is too muffled by distance to raise a frisson at the horrors of war. Barbauld commented on this condition in her essay, *Sins of Government, Sins of the Nation* (1793):

> Of late years, indeed, we have known none of the calamities of war in our own country but the wasteful expence of it; and sitting aloof from those circumstances of personal provocation ... we have calmly voted slaughter and merchandized destruction – so much blood and tears for so many rupees, or dollars, or ingots. Our wars have been wars of cool calculating interest, as free from hatred as from love of mankind; the passions which stir the blood have had no share in them. (312)

The government's cool and venal support for the war is only possible because its members remain distant from it: their land is not destroyed, their family members are not killed, and they do not see the destruction for themselves. Between one verse paragraph evoking the horrors of the Napoleonic Wars and another warning that Britain will not long be able "to sit at ease" (39) and "sport in wars, while danger keeps aloof" (43), Barbauld imagines a mother and a young woman reading a newspaper for news from the war (24–38). The mother has lost her sons and the young woman has lost her prospective husband in the war. The vignette brings the global conflict home. For Barbauld, the affectionate, familial, feminine domestic sphere is connected to the global public conflicts both through the mediation of the newspaper and through a correspondence of affect: the severing of domestic ties coincides, the poem posits, with the failure of benevolence in international relations. Barbauld grounds her authority on the topic not on her stoic coolness but precisely on her domestic feelings, on her ability as a woman to feel the costs of a distant war at home and as a poet to communicate those feelings to the wider public.[55]

Barbauld turns to the metropolis when she represents the pivotal moment at which benevolent sociability ceases to expand and social distance begins to pull apart the social fabric, the moment at which the narrative of Enlightenment progressive history bends into the parabolic arc of rise and fall in civic humanist discourse. Mediating between the domestic and the global, the metropolis first appears between the vignette of women reading the newspaper and a vision of a future in which Britain lies in ruin:

> Nor distant is the hour, low murmurs spread,
> And whispered fears, creating what they dread;
> Ruin, as with an earthquake shock, is here,
> There, the heart-witherings of unuttered fear,
> And that sad death, whence most affection bleeds,
> Which sickness, only of the soul precedes. . . .
> No more on crowded mart or busy street
> Friends, meeting friends, with cheerful hurry greet;
> Sad, on the ground thy princely merchants bend
> Their altered looks, and evil days portend,
> And fold their arms, and watch with anxious breast
> The tempest blackening in the distant West. (47–52, 55–60)

The earthquake marks a change in the course of urbanization as an index of the progress of civilization. Barbauld does not explicitly identify the cause of the change. Later in the poem Barbauld imagines a "Spirit" (215) in whose presence civilizations follow the Enlightenment course of progress but with whose departure civilizations decline into ruin. Suvir Kaul wittily refers to this as one of Barbauld's "crash courses" in history.[56] Barbauld emphasizes that this Spirit is "capricious" (242) and "vagrant" (259); its arrival and departure cannot be predicted, though its presence or absence can be known through its effects. The poem's coordination among these effects of military failure, economic recession, and impending ruin suggests luxury as a cause. But, in Hutcheson's terms, luxury is only harmful when it interferes with moral duties; that is, corrosive luxury is a consequence, rather than a cause, of the absence of the spirit of benevolence. In the passage, the failure of sociability may precede the destructive course of ruin. Before the change, London was the image of benevolent and amiable sociability on a metropolitan scale. Friends met friends on crowded streets, and everyone took pleasure in the bustle of commercial life. But this open cheerfulness yields to closed-off postures of lowered eyes and folded arms; fears speed the ruin; and the withering of hearts leads to the decay of the city.

By invoking the civic humanist concept of luxury, Barbauld entertains the possibility that the expansion of sociability with urbanization produces the conditions of its own decline. The "sad death" or suicide of bankrupted financier Abraham Goldsmid captures this sense of self-unraveling. Marlon Ross observes that Barbauld presents Britain "falling to ruin *as a result* of its rise to empire."[57] In civic humanist discourse, Rome's success brought it in contact with the goods and customs of Asiatic luxury, and the importation and internalization of those foreign goods and customs led to its fall. For the modern metropolis, this appears as a dialectic in which the foreign is brought near and the near is made foreign. Barbauld notes that at its peak, London was a place where "the turban'd Moslem, bearded Jew, / And woolly Afric, met the brown Hindu" (165–66). The image represents commercial sociability on a cosmopolitan scale, and yet, in its focus on depersonalizing ethnic identifiers and on religious, cultural, and racial differences, it serves as an extreme instance of a more general sense of urban society as a gathering of distant strangers. In another ambiguous image, this contraction appears inherent within the expansion. During the period of its rapid growth London "by every road, / In floods of people poured itself abroad" (159–60). This is a precise image of London's extramural growth spilling out along the course of the roads at the high "tide of Commerce" (62). But it is also an image of the depopulation of the city, as in *The Deserted Village*, through mass emigration.

In *Eighteen Hundred and Eleven*, social distance derives in part from the transition, discussed in Chapter 3, to a regime of affect associated with the penetration of abstract conceptions of space, time, and labor into social relations. In "The Uses of History" (1826), a late essay that returns to several motifs of *Eighteen Hundred and Eleven*, Barbauld frames the contrast between personal and abstract conceptions of space and time as, in part, a matter of scale. On small scales, Barbauld notes, people treat time and space as dimensions of personal experience marked by strong affect. Major events in our lives "mark the annals of domestic life more readily and with greater clearness, so far as the real idea of time is concerned, than the year of our Lord, as long as these are all within the circle of our personal recollection."[58] Similarly, in terms of space, "To the unlettered peasant who has never left his native village, that village is his country, and consequently all of it he can love."[59] Beyond the horizon of personal familiarity, these ways of thinking about time and space lose their clarity and are less useful than abstract and universal chronology and spatial coordinates. In her essay on history, Barbauld emphasizes the capacity of historical writing to strengthen a person's affective ties with distant times and spaces. She asserts in Burkean language that the "Englishman conversant in history has been long acquainted with his country. He knew her in the infancy of her greatness."[60] But she acknowledges the limits of this familiarity by recommending her student read history with a chronology and map at hand.[61]

In *Eighteen Hundred and Eleven*, Barbauld is circumspect about the power of writing to counteract the attenuation of benevolent affect worked by distance and by abstract conceptions of time and space. In the scene in which the women read the newspaper, Barbauld associates the newspaper with the coolness of abstraction. Kaul regards the newspaper in the poem as a "powerful icon of modern temporality," an exponent of the pace of literary commerce and of abstract, universal, periodicalized time. In the newspaper, Kaul writes, the women "learn the precise coordinates – in space and time – of the ravages of war."[62]

> Frequent, some stream obscure, some uncouth name
> By deeds of blood is lifted into fame;
> Oft o'er the daily page some soft-one bends
> To learn the fate of husband, brothers, friends,
> Or the spread map with anxious eye explores,
> Its dotted boundaries and penciled shores,
> Asks *where* the spot that wrecked her bliss is found,
> And learns its name but to detest the sound.
>
> (31–38, Barbauld's emphasis)

In one sense the daily paper brings home the costs of the war and makes the names of distant places more familiar. But in another sense, the mediation preserves the distance, and the names of distant places signify foreignness. In asking "where" and referring to a map, the woman indicates that someone has moved beyond the horizon of her familiar experience. The removal of a loved one by death or by distance wrecks her bliss and produces grief, anxiety, and frustration. The newspaper forms urban sociable ties and yet incorporates distance into those ties. The scene faintly genders the abstract conception of time and space and the newspaper as masculine and the experiential conception of time and space and the touching closeness of a "soft-one" as feminine.

The genre associated with the experiential conception of time and space in the poem appears to be poetry. The poem itself, written by a woman, seeks to communicate the feelings of the women reading the newspaper and to carry out to the public the feelings of the hearth. But Barbauld also questions poetry's ability to convey feeling beyond the shrinking limits of amiable sociability in a periodicalizing metropolitan society. As Janowitz suggests, the poem is in part an elegy for the poet and for the sociable city she knew: "There is a poignant identification between Barbauld and the city; she is elegiac in her evocation of the fading city."[63] When Barbauld imagines a future American tourist visiting the ruins of Britain, she shows him lingering over the relics of Romantic-period culture and specifically over the memorials of Barbauld's world. She faces a time, perhaps already present, when the London she knew, and all sociable London, will pass out of familiar experience and into the distance of abstract history. If she writes from a vantage point of disinterestedness, she does so because she feels she has already lost her world and its interests.

Poetry preserves a trace of these fleeting intimate attachments, but it only does so by internalizing abstraction and converting feelings into generic tropes. Ties to particular places or persons quickly degrade into nostalgia. When the Spirit of civilization arrives in America, "by Missouri's rushing waters laid, / 'Old father Thames' shall be the Poet's theme" (92–93). The American poet alludes to Pope's *Windsor Forest* and Dryden's *Annus Mirabilis,* turning a phrase that once implied Burkean intimacy with an "Old father" into a nostalgic commonplace of purely literary geography comparable to "the vale of Tempe, or Ausonian plains" (260) and mediating direct experience through an abstract convention. Implicitly comparing her poem to the newspaper, Barbauld litters her verse with the uncouth names of distant places. While the poem's imagery of rivers, seas, and shores evokes a sense of global interconnection, Barbauld acknowledges the foreignness of the new world by selecting places with names derived from non-European languages. She refers to the Missouri River, "Apalachian hills" (83), "Niagara's fall" (96), "Ontario's lake" (130), "Chimborazo's summits" (325), and the mines of "Potosi" (330). "Niagara" must have been unfamiliar to Barbauld: according to the meter, she appears to pronounce it with four syllables and a misplaced accent.[64] The new world is not Barbauld's world. Barbauld's figures for falling out of touch in a periodicalized society with weak and distant ties of benevolence would ironically be confirmed by the harsh reviews of the poem.

For Barbauld, these weaker ties of benevolence have practical political and economic consequences. As in Hutcheson's definition of harmful luxury, failures of benevolence divert the surplus into channels that do not foster progress. Like Hutcheson and Hume, Barbauld associates historical progress with increasing surpluses. As an abstemious Dissenter, however, she does not consider increasing the production and consumption of luxury commodities as an end in itself. As Kathryn Ready argues, Barbauld thinks the Dissenters "avoid the negative effects of commerce upon virtue" by channeling the surplus into investments in "the realm of intellect."[65] In *Eighteen Hundred and Eleven*, Britain's greatest glory is its contribution "to Science and the Muse" (74) and its "full harvest of the mental year" (76). While Barbauld does not deny the possibility that urban expansion might contribute to the weakening of social ties, she avoids, contrary to Goldsmith, presenting urbanization per se as a misuse of the surplus, a threat to the "rural" regime of affect, or a threat to poetry. The muses arrive as urbanization begins (229, 235) and depart as it subsides. Instead, Barbauld associates the decline of Britain with the insinuation of social distance into politics, apparent foremost in Britain's investments of money and soldiers in the Napoleonic Wars, and with the imposition of abstract conceptions of time and space on the processes of production. The metaphor of a "full harvest of the mental year" participates in a larger thematic contrast between the plentiful surplus supplied by the rhythm of natural, feminine fertility and the waste created by interfering with this rhythm and misdirecting its produce. During the war, "Glad Nature" (12) appears "Bounteous in vain" (11), as "The sword, not sickle, reaps the harvest" (18). In social terms, the scene of the women reading the newspaper points to the depopulation produced by interrupting the rhythm of natural, sexual reproduction: the matron, "Fruitful in vain" (23, 27), has lost her sons; and as young men die in the war, for young women, "the rose withers on its virgin thorns" (30). Kaul notes that Barbauld writes "in the 'loss-of-rural-fecundity and innocence' vein popularized by *The Deserted Village*."[66] But the waste of fecundity is as much urban as rural. During good times, "spontaneous plenty" (167) flows through the metropolis, but "Commerce, like beauty, knows no second spring" (316). As Britain falls, natural fertility has been spoiled; its ruin leaves a waste behind. When the genius of civilization departs, "Even Nature's changed" (245) in the "wasted realms" (244).

By emphasizing the artificiality of the disturbances of natural profusion, Barbauld suggests that the limits of progress could be pushed back and decline postponed, perhaps indefinitely, by reforms that mitigate rather than increase the distances within the social fabric. The first priority for Barbauld is to end the war. She also seeks to mitigate the urban inequality intensified by the imposition of time discipline and the wage relation on labor. In his essay "On the Inequality of Conditions" (1794), Barbauld's brother John Aikin associates the different classes in the metropolis with different narratives of history. "Between the inhabitant of the splendid square, and the tenant of the gloomy alley," Aikin writes, "the apparent difference is such, that if we take our ideas of the nature and destination of man from the one, they seem no more applicable to the other, than if they were beings of different orders."[67] The condition of the polite orders provides evidence of historical progress while the condition of the poor suggests stagnant savagery. While staying clear of radicalism, Aikin implies that historical progress depends on improving the condition of the poor.

"Every good government," he notes, "contains in it a *levelling principle*" to mitigate the inequality and to prevent the interests of the lower orders from "being sacrificed to the avarice and ambition of the higher."[68] Barbauld shares her brother's concerns. William Keach remarks that "Barbauld is keenly in touch with heightened class division," and she presents a choice between "levelling principles" (348) in her "Thoughts on the Inequality of Conditions" (1807).[69] The essay is Barbauld's response to Patrick Colquhoun's *Treatise on the Police of the Metropolis* (1796), in which Colquhoun decried and sought to address the prevalence of petty thefts in the metropolis, focusing in particular on workers skimming goods while unloading ships. Linebaugh demonstrates Colquhoun's role in the consolidation of wage relations and time discipline in the Romantic period.[70] Barbauld argues that extraordinary inequality is possible because wealth "generates *power*," which "embanks and confines the riches which otherwise would disperse and flow back in various channels to the community at large" (347, Barbauld's emphasis). She acknowledges that, in conditions of severe privation and unnatural inequality, when the rich grow out of touch, theft and fraud become leveling strategies among the lower orders.

In *Eighteen Hundred and Eleven*, Barbauld associates the decline of Britain with its economic inequality. As in her essay, the extreme distance between the upper and lower ranks has fostered extralegal leveling: "With grandeur's growth the mass of misery grows" (320), and "Crime walks thy streets, Fraud earns her unblest bread" (317). Barbauld pairs the civic humanist concept of "Enfeebling Luxury" with "ghastly Want" (64), as if it were the gulf between the rich and poor within a zero-sum economy, rather than the condition of either class, that endangered progress. The wage relation and time discipline entail abstract conceptions of time and labor value, transgressing the natural rhythms of commercial fecundity and reducing social relations to abstract monetary relations. This venal turn meets Hutcheson's definition of harmful luxury and participates in the civic humanist historical narrative of a civilization's self-subversion. When anxiety grips the metropolis, "low murmurs spread" (47). As John Bugg shows, during the 1790s, "murmurs" referred to muffled expressions of sedition: these murmurs are low because they cannot be spoken directly and because they spread among the lower orders.[71] The final verse paragraph of *Eighteen Hundred and Eleven*, that is, seeks to bring home the conditions of the metropolitan poor. Without introducing leveling principles into the distribution of the surplus that could improve the conditions of the urban poor, Britain risks being leveled as a nation either through slow decline or with an earthquake shock from below.

Robinson and Barbauld follow the model of urbanization entailed in Hume's revaluation of the concept of luxury – urbanization increases the surplus, extends the ties of sociability, and refines culture, arts, and manners – but they invoke the civic humanist concept of luxury to describe conditions in the metropolis that do not conform to that model. More specifically, they use the civic humanist warning against the social and moral costs of excessive involvement in commerce and venality to point to ways in which the penetration of market relations into social relations threatens to subvert the progress that commerce has generated. Their critical view of urbanization participates in the alternative discourse on urbanization: they have no objection to urbanization per se, but seek to reform its historical form. Where they depart from the other poets considered in this book, however, is in their critical attention to the implication of gender roles within the process. Robinson and Barbauld argue that for the urban social and cultural world to sustain an arc of historical progress, it must offer greater support and recognition for women's sociable, cultural, and affective contributions to public culture.

CONCLUSION

English Romantic Poetry and Urbanization

In the introduction, I proposed that an alternative discourse on urbanization emerged during the Romantic period and that that discourse appears in the poetry of the period in departures from the conventional figural repertoires for representing the various interrelated dimensions of urbanization. The chapters that followed sketched elements of the dominant discourse on urbanization inherited from eighteenth-century moral philosophy and poetic conventions while outlining the manifestations of the emergent discourse in the poetry of William Blake, Samuel Taylor Coleridge, William Wordsworth, Percy Bysshe Shelley, Mary Darby Robinson, and Anna Letitia Barbauld. The argument focused on four fields mediating the relation between urbanization and poetry – urban ideology, the literary field, regimes of affect, and the configuration of political publics – and on the interactions between discourses. The alternative discourse on urbanization that links these representations consists of a set of loosely coherent perspectives: it distinguishes between the current historical form of urbanization and urbanization per se; it examines the costs of the present form, especially on the lower orders; and it considers possible projects of reform. In its articulation within the genre of poetry, it considers the role poetry may have in these reforms.

This alternative discourse on urbanization has a long history, and if the discourse of the Romantic period stands out, it is as a moment of unusual, if still limited, coherence and prevalence. Urbanization is a complex process, and various discourses, often overlapping and with hazy boundaries, address and interrelate several of its dimensions. Under certain conditions, combinations of these perspectives coalesce into relatively coherent discourses on urbanization. The previous chapter followed the discourses of civic humanism and Enlightenment moral philosophy, but other discourses also factor prominently in the Romantic period. The intellectual tradition of Dissent, for example, running from the seventeenth century through the Romantic period, strongly influences Coleridge, Wordsworth, Shelley, and Barbauld as well as Hazlitt, Godwin, Hunt, and Lamb. The tradition of Dissent associates urban life with the freedom of the press, with the diffusion of knowledge, and with sociability. If in the late eighteenth century these ideals were often combined, as in Cowper's *The Task*, with bourgeois ideals of domesticity and with a retreat from public engagement, at other times and in other contexts they merged with more radical views of the possibilities of public urban life. Shelley, Hazlitt, and Hunt, for example, associate the freedom of the press and urban sociability with radical urban politics.[1] Radical visions of community were also available in the political discourse of the Commonwealthmen and in antinomian religious traditions, and these models of community could be reimagined as specifically urban. Alternative perspectives on elements of urbanization, that is, are as old as the dominant urban ideology, and, like urban ideology, they evolve over time. In certain circumstances – especially when conditions in the cities appear related to a social crisis, such as when a major revolution occurs at the same time as an unprecedented metastasis of urbanization – these detached perspectives combine into loosely coherent alternative discourses on urbanization.

While this alternative discourse on urbanization appears in several different media and genres, it has an important relation to poetry, a genre that, according to its own conventions, has conditions of possibility that are jeopardized by urbanization. As in the Preface to *Lyrical Ballads*, from within the alternative discourse, the project of reforming poetry is inseparable from the project of reforming the historical form of urbanization. But in the Romantic period poetry was a genre so invested in conventions that the subtle departures from generic repertoires, figures, tropes, and styles that poets used to signal changes in attitude appeared illegible even to their contemporary readers. As the discursive context for those departures faded into historical distance and as canon formation trimmed the ties between the works of major authors and their culture, readers absorbed what were subtly circumspect treatments of a convention back into that convention. The poets considered here were quickly and effectively detached from an alternative discourse on urbanization, and the poetry of the Romantic period – largely reduced to Wordsworth, though more recently including Blake – has, since the end of the period, appeared complicit with the dominant discourse. The stakes of such a reabsorption have been high: over the past two hundred years, the literature from the Romantic period that has had the greatest influence on popular attitudes toward social geography has been its poetry.

With the connection between Romantic poetry and an alternative discourse on urbanization severed, Romantic poetry has been reduced to a fetish in contemporary discourse on social geography. Despite the tendency of the past thirty years of work in Romantic literary studies, urban studies and the popular imagination still associate Romantic poetry with a vague love of natural scenes and an aversion to city life. And that abstract association with nature makes the poetry available to support any number of attitudes toward social geography. Edward Glaeser, for example, writes that suburbanization represents a desire to follow the lifestyle of natural retreat recommended by "Thoreau and Wordsworth," and this "dream of garden living endorsed by Ruskin and Wordsworth" has become "an ecological nightmare."[2] Early works in Romantic ecocriticism would dispute that Wordsworth endorses suburban life but not that his work teaches people, as Jonathan Bate writes, "to look at and dwell in the natural world."[3] Glaeser and Bate both factor out the ideological, cultural, affective, economic, and political dimensions of Wordsworth's representations of social geography. Indeed, recovering the interconnections within the Romantic-period alternative discourse on urbanization raises the possibility of discovering resonances and misalignments between Romantic poetry and contemporary discourse. Gillen D'Arcy Wood, for example, reads Leigh Hunt's Hampstead poems as an early statement of the ideological association of the semi-natural environment of suburban life with good health.[4] The association of suburban life and health persists through two centuries, but it belongs to a different constellation of social values for Hunt than it does for the present middle class. Jeffrey Cox discerns a tension within the Hunt Circle between middle-class values, such as an investment in professionalism, and a radical sense of sociability as a "model for an alternative society" systematically opposed to the culture of "money-getting."[5] Hunt presents the Hampstead suburb as a place, commensurable with Barbauld's amiable metropolis but now unfamiliar, that fosters "Love for love's self, and ardour for a state / Of natural good, befitting such desires, / Towns without gain."[6]

Recovering the alternative discourse on urbanization within Romantic poetry raises the possibility of constructing a tradition of writers interested in reforming the process of urbanization, even if these writers are united less by a consistent discourse or set of perspectives than by their departures from the dominant conventions of their times. Such a set of alternative visions would provide a new set of representations for urban theory. Urban theorists readily acknowledge that they rely on literature for analyses of the relations between historical urban forms, sensibilities, affects, and mentalities. Chicago School urban sociologist Robert Ezra Park observes, "We are mainly indebted to writers of fiction for our more intimate knowledge of contemporary urban life."[7] David Harvey acknowledges that his "thinking on the urban process has been as much influenced by Dickens, Zola, Balzac, Gissing, Dreiser, Pynchon, and a host of others as it has been by urban historians."[8] Analyzing the history of the complex conjunctions of different perspectives on urbanization in relation to specific social and discursive contexts would qualify formal arguments such as Simmel's and recover a stock of past perspectives that could be reassembled into models of urban experience and discourses on urbanization as the conditions of social geography continue to evolve. Walter Benjamin sought to assemble one such past vision, stuffing the Konvoluts of his *Arcades Project* with clippings of literature, especially from Baudelaire; in one chain of echoes, Benjamin quotes Baudelaire expressing his pleasure in a print of Paris by translating a line from *The Excursion* that Wordsworth in turn drew from Coleridge.[9]

In a lyrical passage at the beginning of *The Country and the City*, Williams subtly ties his attempt to rethink the history of urbanization to the process of urbanization itself. He recalls feeling the wearying monotony and incessant rush of urban scenes. "I have stood in many cities and felt this pulse," Williams remarks, vaguely echoing Wordsworth's "mighty heart." And as in Wordsworth, exhausting as it is, this pulse enlivens: Williams feels animated by the city's "dynamic movement," its restless energy and relentless evolution. He feels the city around him – its office buildings, government edifices, and disciplined routines – built up and reshaped in the continuous fluid motion of urbanization. The image anticipates his later unmasking of rural manor houses as condensations and crystallizations of centuries of rural labor. This intuition of fluid motion within the apparently solid built environment leads Williams back to another author, and he paraphrases what "H. G. Wells once said, coming out of a political meeting where they had been discussing social change, that this great towering city was a measure of the obstacle, of how much must be moved if there was to be any change."[10] Immediately after reproducing Wells's image of the malleable city, Williams revises it, remarking the irresistible power of the skyline to inspire a humbling and exhilarating feeling of the immense scale of what is possible. Williams places himself in Wells's position, and, in doing so, he signals that he seeks not only to rethink the history of literary representations of urbanization but also, like Wells, to rethink the history of urbanization itself. For a similar image of the grandeur and the continuous motion of urbanization, Williams could have looked back past Wells to Wordsworth. Speculating on ever-growing London, Wordsworth feels a sense of what "had been here done … Through ages" (8.782–83) and what more could be done. He looks upon it as a "Chronicle" (8.749) that is still being written.

Notes

Introduction

1. See Simon P. Hull, *Charles Lamb, Elia and the London Magazine: Metropolitan Muse* (London: Pickering & Chatto, 2010); Daniel Sanjiv Roberts, "The Janus-Face of Romantic Modernity: Thomas De Quincey's Metropolitan Imagination," *Romanticism* 17.3 (2011): 299–308; David Stewart, *Romantic Magazines and Metropolitan Literary Culture* (New York: Palgrave Macmillan, 2011); Kevin Gilmartin, *William Hazlitt: Political Essayist* (Oxford: Oxford University Press, 2015), 233–305; and works cited later in this volume.
2. James K. Chandler and Kevin Gilmartin, eds., *Romantic Metropolis: The Urban Scene of British Culture, 1780–1840* (Cambridge: Cambridge University Press, 2005), 1.
3. Raymond Williams, *The Country and the City* (Oxford: Oxford University Press, 1973).
4. E. P. Thompson, *Customs in Common* (New York: New Press, 1993); Peter Linebaugh, *The London Hanged*, 2nd ed. (London: Verso, 2006).
5. Simon Joyce, *Capital Offenses: Geographies of Class and Crime in Victorian London* (Charlottesville: University of Virginia Press, 2003); Saree Makdisi, *Making England Western: Occidentalism, Race, and Imperial Culture* (Chicago: University of Chicago Press, 2014), xiv, see 39–86. On the disciplining of urban literary culture, see also Ian Newman, "Tavern Talk: Literature, Politics and Conviviality, 1780–1840" (PhD dissertation, UCLA Department of English), 2013.
6. Daniel E. White, *From Little London to Little Bengal* (Baltimore: Johns Hopkins University Press, 2013). Among studies of representations of the imperial metropolis, see Saree Makdisi, *Romantic Imperialism: Universal Empire and the Culture of Modernity* (Cambridge: Cambridge University Press, 1998), 23–44, 154–72; and Jon Klancher, "Discriminations, or Romantic Cosmopolitanisms in London," in *Romantic Metropolis*, ed. Chandler and Gilmartin, 65–82.
7. See James A. W. Heffernan, "Wordsworth's London: The Imperial Monster," *Studies in Romanticism* 37.3 (Fall 1998): 421–43.

8. See John Feather, *The Provincial Book Trade in Eighteenth-Century England* (Cambridge: Cambridge University Press, 1985); Jeremy Black, *The English Press in the Eighteenth Century* (London: Croom Helm, 1987). My association of transformations of urban form with changes in genres was inspired in part by Ian Duncan's remarkable study of the novel in Edinburgh in *Scott's Shadow: The Novel in Romantic Edinburgh* (Princeton: Princeton University Press, 2007).
9. Gillian Russell and Clara Tuite, eds., *Romantic Sociability: Social Networks and Literary Culture in Britain, 1770–1840* (Cambridge: Cambridge University Press, 2002).
10. Jon Mee, *Conversable Worlds: Literature, Contention, and Community 1762 to 1830* (Oxford: Oxford University Press, 2011), 8.
11. See Kevin Gilmartin, "The 'Sinking Down' of Jacobinism and the Rise of the Counter-revolutionary Man of Letters," in *Romanticism and Popular Culture in Britain and Ireland*, ed. Philip Connell and Nigel Leask (Cambridge: Cambridge University Press, 2009), 128–47. The trailblazing works placing Wordsworth and Coleridge in the context of urban radicalism include Nicholas Roe, *Wordsworth and Coleridge: The Radical Years* (Oxford: Oxford University Press, 1988) and Kenneth R. Johnston, *The Hidden Wordsworth* (New York: W. W. Norton, 1998).
12. Jeffrey N. Cox, *Poetry and Politics in the Cockney School: Keats, Shelley, Hunt and Their Circle* (Cambridge: Cambridge University Press, 1998), 28, 29, 60, 50. Gregory Dart recasts the Cockney debate as a conservative reaction to the emergence of the petit bourgeois and its adaptation to a world of commodification and suburbanization that threatened to confound old social distinctions. What the conservative critics found offensive about the figure of the Cockney, Dart argues, was "the Cockney's very modernity." Gregory Dart, *Metropolitan Art and Literature, 1810–1840: Cockney Adventures* (Cambridge: Cambridge University Press, 2012), 6.
13. One sophisticated example is William Chapman Sharpe, *Unreal Cities: Urban Figuration in Wordsworth, Baudelaire, Whitman, Eliot, and Williams* (Baltimore: Johns Hopkins University Press, 1990). Lawrence Manley recognizes patterns from Simmel's work in Renaissance literature in *Literature and Culture in Early Modern London* (Cambridge: Cambridge University Press, 1995).
14. Manuel Castells, *The Urban Question: A Marxist Approach*, trans. Alan Sheridan (London: Edward Arnold, 1977), 83. Castells reviews sociological literature that challenges the "possible causal connections between the spatial forms of the city and the characteristic social content of 'urban culture'" (80). Jan De Vries describes this general category as "behavioural urbanization" in *European Urbanization, 1500–1800* (London: Routledge, 2007), 12.

15. Saree Makdisi's work on Blake demonstrates that such models of urban consciousness are not necessary. See *William Blake and the Impossible History of the 1790s* (Chicago: University of Chicago Press, 2003).
16. See the introductions to recent collections: Gregory Dart's "Preface: Re-imagining the City" to the special issue of *Romanticism* 14.2 (July 2008): v–vi; Larry H. Peer, ed., *Romanticism and the City* (New York: Palgrave, 2011); Jens Martin Gurr and Berit Michel, eds., *Romantic Cityscapes: Selected Papers from the Essen Conference of the German Society for English Romanticism* (Trier: WVT, 2013).
17. Williams, *The Country and the City*, 79, 76, 150, 151.
18. Gerald MacLean, Donna Landry, and Joseph P. Ward revisit Williams's book without proposing an improvement to his method in their edited collection *The Country and the City Revisited: England and the Politics of Culture, 1550–1850* (Cambridge: Cambridge University Press, 1999).
19. Vic Gatrell contrasts the bawdy, rumbustious culture of eighteenth-century satirical prints against the canting seriousness of Romantic-period print culture. Gatrell does not treat the poets as strawman humbugs: while he places Wordsworth and Coleridge on the sober side, he nonetheless identifies Byron and Shelley as "major satirists" in the Augustan tradition. For Gatrell, urban often means urbane. See *City of Laughter: Sex and Satire in Eighteenth-Century London* (New York: Walker & Co., 2007), 461.
20. See Rosemary Sweet, *The Writing of Urban Histories in Eighteenth-Century England* (Oxford: Clarendon Press, 1997).
21. See David Harvey, *The Urbanization of Capital* (London: Basil Blackwell, 1985).
22. David Harvey, *The Urban Experience* (Baltimore: Johns Hopkins University Press, 1989), 83.
23. Harvey, *The Urban Experience*, 54. Harvey's conceptions of space and of the complications of urban administration are indebted to Henri Lefebvre: the best exposition of Lefebvre's urban theory in English – the most concise and best translated – is *The Urban Revolution*, trans. Robert Bononno (Minneapolis: University of Minnesota Press, 2003). Harvey presents his fullest reading of the relation between cultural production and socioeconomic conditions in *The Condition of Postmodernity* (Oxford: Basil Blackwell, 1989). There Harvey highlights correspondences between the logic of a regime of flexible accumulation and the logic of postmodernism on the abstract level of general attitudes toward time, space, and images; he does not consider in depth the mechanism and limits of the process of determination. When Harvey turns to specify the mechanism of cultural determination, he invokes Bourdieu.

24. I draw the statistics in this paragraph from De Vries, *European Urbanization*, 39, 195; Francis Sheppard, *London: A History* (Oxford: Oxford University Press, 1998), 363; and E. A. Wrigley, *People, Cities and Wealth: The Transformation of Traditional Society* (Oxford: Basil Blackwell, 1987), 133–56.
25. Several critics describe Romanticism as a cultural reaction against modernization. See Marshall Berman's reading of Goethe's *Faust, Part Two* in *All That Is Solid Melts into Air: The Experience of Modernity* (New York: Penguin, 1988), 37–86; Robert Sayre and Michael Löwy, "Figures of Romantic Anti-Capitalism," *New German Critique* 32 (Spring–Summer 1984): 42–92, and *Romanticism Against the Tide of Modernity*, trans. Catherine Porter (Durham, NC: Duke University Press, 2001). In *Romantic Imperialism* Makdisi follows Marx's sense of Romanticism as dialectically involved in modernism: the "bourgeois viewpoint has never advanced beyond this antithesis between itself and this romantic viewpoint, and therefore the latter will accompany it as legitimate antithesis up to its blessed end." Karl Marx, *Grundrisse*, trans. Martin Nicholas (New York: Penguin, 1973), 162.
26. See Mark Overton, *Agricultural Revolution in England: The Transformation of the Agrarian Economy, 1500–1850* (Cambridge: Cambridge University Press, 1996), 1–9; M. J. Daunton, *Progress and Poverty: An Economic and Social History of Britain 1700–1850* (Oxford: Oxford University Press, 1995), 49.
27. Harvey remarks, "The history of the urbanization of capital is at least in part a history of its evolving labor market geography" (*Urban Experience*, 19). See Arthur Redford, *Labour Migration in England 1800–1850*, 2nd ed., and rev. W. H. Chandler (New York: Augustus M. Kelley, 1968), 13–18; J. A. Yelling, *Common Field and Enclosure in England, 1450–1850* (London: Macmillan, 1977); Williams, *Country and the City*, 87–107.
28. See Wrigley, *People, Cities and Wealth*, 133–49. For the demand for food and the wares of commerce, see Daunton, *Progress and Poverty*, 35 and 139; on shoemakers see George Rudé, *Hanoverian London, 1714–1808* (London: Secker & Warburg, 1971), 28; on public works projects Andrew Saint, "The Building Art of the First Industrial Metropolis," in *London – World City, 1800–1840*, ed. Celina Fox (New Haven: Yale University Press, 1992), 51–76. Saint cites, for example, the construction of the London Docks (1800–05), the West India Docks (1800–06), and the Regent's Canal (1812–20).
29. Rudé, *Hanoverian London*, 30: London's share "of the tonnage of ships entering English ports had already declined from 59 [per cent] in 1686 to 54 in 1718, and would decline to 49 in 1772; while her share of the nation's foreign trade fell from 77 per cent in 1700 to 67 per cent in 1737 and 65 per cent in 1792."
30. Harvey, *Urban Experience*, 80. "In 1750 a fast coach covered the 114 miles from London to Bristol in 40 hours; by 1811 the journey could be completed in 11 hours 45 minutes." Daunton, *Progress and Poverty*, 306.

31. William Cobbett, "Summary of Politics," *Cobbett's Political Register* 19.20 (March 9, 1811), 589. Cobbett's emphasis. See also Cobbett's refusal to ride on turnpike roads in *Rural Rides*, ed. Ian Dyck (London: Penguin, 2001), 36–37.
32. Peter Borsay, *The English Urban Renaissance: Culture and Society in the Provincial Town 1660–1770* (Oxford: Clarendon Press, 1989), 20.
33. Daunton, *Progress and Poverty*, 163.
34. John Summerson, *Georgian London* (London: Barrie & Jenkins, 1970), 25; Roy Porter, *London: A Social History* (Cambridge: Harvard University Press, 1995), 8.
35. Donald Low, *Thieves' Kitchen: The Regency Underworld* (London: J. M. Dent, 1982), 19. See also Steen Eiler Rasmussen, *London: The Unique City* (Cambridge: MIT Press, 1967), 37; Makdisi, *Making England Western*, 47–48.
36. "Almost all domestic building in London and its immediate outskirts, that is to say perhaps 90 per cent of all building activity, took place on the speculative leasehold method." Saint, "Building Art," 70.
37. Sheppard, *London: A History*, 179.
38. Sheppard, *London 1808–1870: The Infernal Wen* (London: Secker & Warburg, 1971), 94; Porter, *London*, 217.
39. Sheppard, *London 1808–1870*, 94 (cf. 102); Summerson, *Georgian London*, 25.
40. Daunton, *Progress and Poverty*, 258.
41. Saint, "Building Art," 54; John Barrell, "London in the 1790s," in *The Cambridge History of English Romantic Literature*, ed. James K. Chandler (Cambridge: Cambridge University Press, 2009), 131–32.
42. William Cobbett, "Sussex Journal," *Cobbett's Weekly Register* 41.3 (January 18, 1822), 155. Cobbett's emphasis.
43. Letter to Robert Dodge, February 29, 1792; Edmund Burke, *The Correspondence of Edmund Burke, Vol VII*, ed. P. J. Marshall and John A. Woods (Cambridge: Cambridge University Press, 1968), 85; Porter, *London*, 124.
44. Friedrich Engels, *The Condition of the Working Class in England*, ed. David McLellan (Oxford: Oxford University Press, 2009), 57.
45. Jeffrey G. Williamson refers to underinvestment as an "ugly-city" strategy of development. *Coping with City Growth during the Industrial Revolution* (Cambridge: Cambridge University Press, 1990), 220.
46. Rosemary Sweet, *The English Town, 1680–1840* (Singapore: Longman, 1999), 177.
47. Arthur Young, *The Farmer's Letters to the People of England* (London: Nicoll, 1768), 338; Thomas Malthus, *An Essay on the Principle of Population* (London: J. Johnson, 1803), 307–10.
48. Rasmussen, *London*, 274.
49. Barrell, "London in the 1790s," 136.

50. J. G. A. Pocock, *Virtue, Commerce, and History* (Cambridge: Cambridge University Press, 1985).
51. James Mackintosh, "Speech of Lord John Russell in the House of Commons on the 14th Dec. 1819, for Transferring the Elective Franchise from Corrupt Boroughs to Unrepresented Great Towns," *Edinburgh Review* 34 (1820): 478.
52. H. T. Dickinson, "Radical Culture," in *London – World City*, ed. Fox, 209–10.
53. N. McKendrick, J. Brewer, and J. H. Plumb, *The Birth of a Consumer Society* (London: Europa, 1982); Peter Clark, *British Clubs and Societies 1580–1800: The Origins of an Associational World* (Oxford: Clarendon Press, 2000), 142–44.
54. Sweet, *English Town*, 182.
55. Borsay, *English Urban Renaissance*, 257. Borsay's emphasis.
56. Gillian Russell, *Women, Sociability and Theatre in Georgian London* (Cambridge: Cambridge University Press, 2007).
57. David Hume, "Of Refinement in the Arts," *Political Essays*, ed. Knud Haakonssen (Cambridge: Cambridge University Press, 2006), 107.
58. Robert Raikes, describing the origin of what he claimed to be the first Sunday school, cited by Thomas Walter Laqueur, *Religion and Respectability: Sunday Schools and Working Class Culture 1780–1850* (New Haven: Yale University Press, 1976), 23. On town literacy rates, see Wrigley, *People, Cities and Wealth*, 139.
59. See William St. Clair, *Reading Nation in the Romantic Period* (Cambridge: Cambridge University Press, 2004), appendix 10; Borsay, *English Urban Renaissance*, 133.
60. William Wordsworth, *The Thirteen Book* Prelude, ed. Mark L. Reed, 2 vols. (Ithaca: Cornell University Press, 1991), volume 1, book 8, lines 747–48. All subsequent quotations from *The Prelude* will conform to the text in this edition.
61. Ian Watt, *The Rise of the Novel: Studies in Defoe, Richardson and Fielding* (Berkeley: University of California Press, 1971), 35–60. For the interrelation between the theory of the novel and the cultural logic of nineteenth-century capitalism expressed in the urban environment, see Franco Moretti, *Signs Taken for Wonders: Essays in the Sociology of Literary Forms*, trans. Susan Fischer, David Forgacs, David Miller (London: NLB, 1983), 109–56; *Atlas of the European Novel, 1800–1900* (New York: Verso, 1999), 75–140. Robert Alter examines the influence of the nature of urban space on the form of the nineteenth- and twentieth-century novel in his *Imagined Cities: Urban Experience and the Language of the Novel* (New Haven: Yale University Press, 2005).
62. Stuart Curran refers to the Romantic culture as "simply mad for poetry" in *Poetic Form and British Romanticism* (New York: Oxford University Press, 1986), 15. This madness may be as much a matter of production as of consumption and

the volume of poetry printed pushed by supply as much as pulled by demand: Chandler notes in his "Introduction" to the *Cambridge History of English Romantic Literature* that "Britons talented in other ways consistently gravitated toward writing as the primary work of their lives in this period, precisely out of a sense that writing had become a medium of extraordinary potency" (7).

63. Gilmartin, "The 'Sinking Down' of Jacobinism," 128–47.
64. See E. P. Thompson, *The Making of the Working Class* (London: Victor Gollancz, 1963), 616.
65. Cobbett, *Rural Rides*, 37. Cobbett's emphasis. See Sheppard, *London 1808–1870*, 96.

Chapter 1

1. Georg Simmel, "The Metropolis and Mental Life," in *On Individuality and Social Forms*, ed. Donald N. Levine, trans. Edward A. Shils (Chicago: University of Chicago Press, 1971), 325.
2. Louis Wirth, "Urbanism as a Way of Life," *The American Journal of Sociology* 44.1 (July 1938): 11–13, 23, 15–17.
3. Claude S. Fischer, *The Urban Experience* (New York: Harcourt Brace Jovanovich, 1976), 180.
4. Castells, *The Urban Question*, 4, 86.
5. Castells, *The Urban Question*, 47, 73.
6. Simmel, "Metropolis and Mental Life," 337.
7. Castells, *The Urban Question*, 83.
8. Castells, *The Urban Question*, 81.
9. Williams, *The Country and the City*, 142, 46.
10. Sharpe, *Unreal Cities*; William B. Thesing, *The London Muse: Victorian Poetic Responses to the City* (Athens: University of Georgia Press, 1982); Max Byrd, *London Transformed* (New Haven: Yale University Press, 1978); Brean Hammond, "The City in Eighteenth-Century Poetry," in *The Cambridge Companion to Eighteenth-Century Poetry*, ed. John Sitter (Cambridge: Cambridge University Press, 2001), 84–103. Markman Ellis highlights stylistic continuities between eighteenth-century and Romantic-period poetry, such as the use of lists, in "Poetry and the City," in *A Companion to Eighteenth-Century Poetry*, ed. Christine Gerard (Oxford: Blackwell, 2006), 534–48.
11. Sheppard, *London: A History*, 131.
12. Porter, *London*, 113.
13. Manley, *Literature and Culture in Early Modern London*, 485.
14. Manley, *Literature and Culture in Early Modern London*, 486; see 481–530.
15. Richard Sennett, *The Fall of Public Man* (New York: Knopf, 1977), 19.

16. John Brewer, *The Pleasures of the Imagination* (Chicago: University of Chicago Press, 1997), 1–55.
17. Cynthia Wall, *The Literary and Cultural Spaces of Restoration London* (Cambridge: Cambridge University Press, 1998), ix.
18. Peter Stallybrass and Allon White, *The Politics and Poetics of Transgression* (London: Methuen, 1986), 83, 88. Stallybrass and White's emphasis.
19. See J. A. Downie, "Gay's Politics," in *John Gay and the Scriblerians*, ed. Peter Lewis and Nigel Wood (New York: St. Martin's Press, 1989), 44–61.
20. John Barrell and Harriet Guest have argued that such hybrid genres "certainly *facilitated* the utterance of contradictions." "On the Use of Contradiction: Economics and Morality in the Eighteenth-Century Long Poem," in *The New Eighteenth Century: Theory, Politics, English Literature*, ed. Felicity Nussbaum and Laura Brown (New York: Methuen, 1987), 132. Barrell and Guest's emphasis.
21. Ellis, "Poetry and the City," 539.
22. See Alison O'Byrne, "The Art of Walking in London: Representing Urban Pedestrianism in the Early Nineteenth Century," *Romanticism* 14.2 (July 2008): 94–107.
23. Philip Carter, "Faces and Crowds: Biography in the City," in *Walking the Streets of Eighteenth-Century London: John Gay's* Trivia, ed. Clare Brant and Susan E. Whyman (Oxford: Oxford University Press, 2007), 33. Other critics also follow the determinist line: Flavio Gregori, "The 'Audacious' Art of Walking: The Metropolis and the Proto-Flâneur in John Gay's *Trivia*," *South Atlantic Review* 70.1 (Winter 2005): 71–96; Clare Brant, "Artless and Artful: John Gay's *Trivia*," in Brant and Whyman, eds., *Walking the Streets of Eighteenth-Century London*, 105–19.
24. John Gay, *Poetry and Prose of John Gay*, ed. Vinton A. Dearing with Charles E. Beckwith, 2 vols. (Oxford: Clarendon Press, 1974), book 2, line 405. All references to the text of *Trivia* will be cited internally by book and line number in the first volume of this edition, and all emphasis is Gay's. Dearing and Beckwith use the first edition (1714) as their copy text.
25. Sven Armens notes the rare exception that rural life seems healthier. *John Gay: Social Critic* (New York: Octagon, 1954), 85.
26. John Chalker, *The English Georgic: A Study in the Development of a Form* (London: Routledge, 1969).
27. Stephen Copley and Ian Haywood, "Luxury, Refuse and Poetry: John Gay's *Trivia*," in *John Gay and the Scriblerians*, ed. Lewis and Wood, 77.
28. Gay jokes to Thomas Parnell, "What I got by walking the streets I am now spending in riding in Coaches." Letter from Gay to Thomas Parnell, March 26, 1716, cited in Susan Whyman, "Sharing Public Spaces," in Brant and Whyman, eds., *Walking the Streets of Eighteenth-Century London*, 55.

29. Dianne S. Ames, "Gay's 'Trivia' and the Art of Allusion," *Studies in Philology* 75.2 (Spring 1978): 199–200.
30. Joanna Picciotto, "Optical Instruments and the Eighteenth-Century Observer," *Studies in Eighteenth-Century Culture* 29 (2000): 124.
31. Tom Woodman, "'Vulgar Circumstance' and 'Due Civilities': Gay's Art of Polite Living in Town," in *John Gay and the Scriblerians*, ed. Lewis and Wood, 86.
32. Gay gives contradictory instructions. He mocks those who ride in coaches for "trust[ing] their Safety to another's Feet" (2.514), but he asks his reader to heed his poetic feet and pedestrian experience and asks the goddess to guide his steps. The conflict between the ethics of the gentleman and of the middle-class professional ramifies into the tension between deference to authority and the empiricist's *nullius in verba*.
33. Carter, "Faces and Crowds," 40.
34. Miles Ogborn, *Spaces of Modernity: London's Geographies, 1680–1780* (New York: Guilford Press, 1998), 78.
35. Critics cite Mandeville as a context for Gay's interest in the dirt and refuse of London. See Copley and Haywood, "Luxury, Refuse, and Poetry," 68, and David Nokes, *John Gay: A Profession of Friendship* (Oxford: Oxford University Press, 1995), 214. Swift seems to be a closer source for Gay's interest in filth: in the preface to the poem, Gay says he "*owe*[s] *several Hints of it to Dr. Swift*" (134). While the *Fable of the Bees* was published in 1714, it was not widely read until Mandeville was prosecuted for immorality after the release of the 1723 edition. Armens argues, "It might be more accurate to say that Swift, Pope, and Gay, although they never mention him, actually shared the belief promoted by the Earl of Shaftesbury that there was essential good in human nature" (*John Gay*, 52–53).
36. Ogborn, *Spaces of Modernity*, 87.
37. Pope, *Essay on Man*, 3.318. Alexander Pope, *The Poems of Alexander Pope: A One-Volume Edition of the Twickenham Text with Selected Annotations*, ed. John Butt (New Haven: Yale University Press, 1963). On Shaftesbury and Mandeville, see Basil Willey, *The Eighteenth Century Background* (London: Chatto & Windus, 1941), 57–75, 95–100.
38. Alison Stenton, "Spatial Stories: Movement in the City and Cultural Geography," in Brant and Whyman, eds., *Walking the Streets of Eighteenth-Century London*, 62–73. Stenton quotes Lewis Mumford to good effect by reanimating the dead metaphor of "movement": "If the individual would participate at all in the social, political and economic life of the city, he [*sic*] must subordinate some of his individuality to the demands of the larger community and in that measure immerse himself in mass movements" (66).

39. Dryden, *Annus Mirabilis*, 5–6. John Dryden, *The Works of John Dryden*, ed. Edward Niles Hooker and H. T. Swedenberg, vol. 1 (Berkeley: University of California Press, 1956), 59.
40. Woodman, "'Vulgar Circumstance,'" 85.
41. Downie, "Gay's Politics," 55.
42. Dianne Dugaw, *"Deep Play" – John Gay and the Invention of Modernity* (Newark: University of Delaware Press, 2001), 113–14.
43. Copley and Haywood, "Luxury, Refuse, and Poetry," 77.
44. Clare Brant and Susan E. Whyman, "Introduction," in Brant and Whyman, eds., *Walking the Streets of Eighteenth-Century London*, 7; Tim Harris, "Perceptions of the Crowd in Later Stuart London," in *Imagining Early Modern London: Perceptions and Portrayals of the City from Stow to Strype, 1598–1720*, ed. J. F. Merritt (Cambridge: Cambridge University Press, 2001), 254.
45. Jürgen Habermas, *Structural Transformation of the Public Sphere*, trans. Thomas Burger (Cambridge: MIT Press, 1991), 46.
46. Leonore Davidoff and Catherine Hall, *Family Fortunes: Men and Women of the English Middle Class, 1780–1850* (London: Hutchison, 1987), 165, 166.
47. James Thomson, *The Seasons*, ed. James Sambrook (Oxford: Clarendon Press, 1981), Summer, lines 1458–63.
48. Williams, *Country and City*, 68–69.
49. Dustin Griffin, "Redefining Georgic: Cowper's *Task*," *ELH* 57.4 (Winter 1990): 876, 877.
50. Thomas Pfau, *Wordsworth's Profession* (Stanford: Stanford University Press, 1997), 17–87.
51. William Cowper, *The Poems of William Cowper*, ed. John D. Baird and Charles Ryskamp, 3 vols. (Oxford: Clarendon Press, 1980–95), 2.136, book 1, line 749. All subsequent quotations from Cowper's poetry will conform to the text in this edition and will be cited internally by line number.
52. Martin Priestman, *Cowper's* Task*: Structure and Influence* (Cambridge: Cambridge University Press, 1983), 12.
53. William Cowper, *The Letters and Prose Writings of William Cowper*, ed. James King and Charles Ryskamp, 4 vols. (New York: Oxford University Press, 1979–84). All subsequent quotations from Cowper's letters will be cited by addressee, date, and page number in this edition. Letter to Rev. William Unwin, October 10, 1784, 2.285. Letter to Rev. John Newton, November 27, 1784, 2.301.
54. Williams, *Country and the City*, 50–54.
55. Marshall Brown discusses Cowper with Locke and Kant in *Preromanticism* (Stanford: Stanford University Press, 1991), 58–81, and Baird and Ryskamp cite a few references to Locke in their edition of the poems. On Cowper and Beattie see George MacLennan, *Lucid Interval: Subjective Writing and Madness in*

History (Leicester: Leicester University Press, 1992), 109–10; James King, *William Cowper: A Biography* (Durham: Duke University Press, 1986), 140–43.

56. Cowper refers to Hume only twice in his letters and does not mention his philosophical works. He tells Unwin he has read "3 volumes of Hume's History" and notes he read a review of "Hume's essays on suicide." Letter to William Unwin, May 8, 1780, 1.340; Letter to William Unwin, July 12, 1784, 2.263. Cowper would have had Hume secondhand through Beattie's *Essay* and contemporary periodicals.
57. David Hume, *A Treatise of Human Nature*, ed. L. A. Selby-Bigge, rev. P. H. Nidditch, 2nd ed. (Oxford: Clarendon Press, 1978), 252. Hume's emphasis.
58. Hume, *Human Nature*, 253.
59. Hume, *Human Nature*, 3. Hume's emphasis.
60. Kant offers a transitional account of urban experience overwhelming the mind's ability to process sensations. After positing consciousness as a transcendental ground for the comprehension of intuitions, he considers what would happen if consciousness were unable to synthesize appearances: "Unity of synthesis in accordance with empirical concepts would be entirely contingent, and, were it not grounded on a transcendental ground of unity, it would be possible for a swarm of appearances to fill up our soul [so würde es möglich seyn, das ein Gewühle von Erscheinungen unsere Seele anfüllete] without experience ever being able to arise from it. But in that case all relation of cognition to objects would also disappear, since the appearances would lack connection in accordance with universal and necessary laws, and would thus be intuition without thought, but never cognition, and would therefore be as good as nothing for us." Immanuel Kant, *Critique of Pure Reason*, trans. Paul Guyer and Allen W. Wood (New York: Cambridge University Press, 1998), 234; German from the first edition, Immanuel Kant, *Critik der reinen Vernunft* (Riga: Verlegts J. F. Hartknoch, 1781), 111. Transcendental apperception relates intuitions to the self, and the self's sense of its own identity grounds its ability to unify and understand intuitions. As Norman Kemp Smith glosses this section of Kant's *Critique*, intuitions "must be so related to one another that, notwithstanding their variety and diversity, the self can still be conscious of itself as identical throughout them all. In other words, no intuition can be related to the self that is incapable of being combined together with all the other intuitions to form a unitary consciousness." See Norman Kemp Smith, *A Commentary to Kant's 'Critique of Pure Reason'* (New York: Humanities Press, 1950), 252 and, more generally, 250–54. The failure of intuitions to relate sufficiently to one another would therefore entail the self's failure to perceive its own integrity and to serve as a ground for knowledge. The project would collapse back into Humean skepticism. The image Kant uses for this failure is that of a

"swarm"; in Smith's translation, the image is of a "crowd." Immanuel Kant, *Critique of Pure Reason*, trans. Norman Kemp Smith (New York: St. Martin's Press, 1963), 138. Kant's word is "Gewühle," a milling crowd or throng. When searching for an experience in which a surplus of perception exceeds the mind's ability to apprehend it, Kant imagines the seething turmoil of a city crowd. This sort of argument appears ready-to-hand in Nietzsche's account of modernity, which in turn anticipates Simmel's blasé attitude: "Sensibility immensely more irritable ... the abundance of disparate impressions greater than ever ... The tempo of this influx *prestissimo*; the impressions erase each other; one instinctively resists taking in anything, taking anything deeply ... A kind of adaptation to this flood of impressions takes place. ... They spend their strength partly in assimilating things, partly in defense, partly in opposition." Friedrich Nietzsche, *The Will to Power*, trans. Walter Kaufmann and R. J. Hollingdale (New York: Vintage, 1967), 47.

61. See MacLennan, *Lucid Interval*, 98; Deidre Lynch, "On Going Steady with Novels," *The Eighteenth Century* 50.2–3 (Summer/Fall 2009): 208; Vincent Newey, *Cowper's Poetry: A Critical Study and Reassessment* (Liverpool: Liverpool University Press, 1982), 63–64.
62. Letter to Lady Hesketh, January 16, 1786, 2.456. Cowper's emphasis.
63. For a reading of the digressive structure of the poem, see Richard Terry, "Transitions and Digressions in the Eighteenth-Century Long Poem," *Studies in English Literature, 1500–1900* 32.3 (Summer 1992): 495–510.
64. Brown, *Preromanticism*, 64. Priestman reads the poem as a search for psychological stability. Priestman, *Cowper's* Task, 4.
65. John Locke, *An Essay Concerning Human Understanding*, ed. Peter H. Nidditch (Oxford: Oxford University Press, 1975), 112.
66. Letter to William Unwin, June 8, 1783, 2.139.
67. William Cowper, *Memoir of the Early Life of William Cowper, Esq.* (London: R. Edwards, 1816), 71.
68. Letter to Joseph Hill, November 5, 1772, 1.258.
69. Letter to Joseph Hill, March 16, 1780, 1.324.
70. Fredric Jameson, "Postmodernism, or The Cultural Logic of Late Capitalism," *New Left Review* 146 (July–August 1984): 73.
71. Newey, *Cowper's Poetry*, 70. Max Byrd, *Visits to Bedlam: Madness and Literature in the Eighteenth Century* (Columbia: University of South Carolina Press, 1974), 152.
72. Paolo Virno, "The Ambivalence of Disenchantment," in Michael Hardt and Paolo Virno, eds., *Radical Thought in Italy: A Potential Politics* (Minneapolis: University of Minnesota Press, 1996), 28.

73. Kevis Goodman, *Georgic Modernity and British Romanticism: Poetry and the Mediation of History* (Cambridge: Cambridge University Press, 2004), 98. Goodman's emphasis.
74. See Johnson's "London": "Here malice, rapine, accident, conspire . . . And here the fell attorney prowls for prey; / Here falling houses thunder on your head" (13–17). Samuel Johnson, *The Poems of Samuel Johnson*, ed. David Nichol Smith and Edward L. McAdam (Oxford: Clarendon Press, 1951). The tradition, however, extends back at least to Davenant's *Gondibert* (1653). Davenant observes that "here the early Lawyer mends his pace; / For whom the earlier Cliant waited long; / Here greedy Creditors their Debtors chace, / Who scape by herding in th'indebted Throng" (2.1.67–70). William Davenant, *Sir William Davenant's* Gondibert, ed. David F. Gladish (Oxford: Clarendon Press, 1971).
75. Julie K. Ellison, "News, Blues, and Cowper's Busy World," *MLQ* 62.3 (September 2001), 228.
76. Goodman, *Georgic Modernity*, 86. Lucretius, *The Way Things Are: The De Rerum Natura of Titus Lucretius Carus*, trans. Rolfe Humphries (Bloomington: Indiana University Press, 1968), 2.1–5.
77. Richard Feingold, *Nature and Society: Later Eighteenth-Century Uses of the Pastoral and Georgic* (New Brunswick: Rutgers University Press, 1978), 139.
78. Letter to Rev. John Newton, June 12, 1780, 1.351 and June 23, 1780, 1.357.
79. Letter to Mrs. Cowper, July 20, 1780, 1.369.
80. Letter to Lady Hesketh, December 1, 1792, 4.248.
81. Newey, *Cowper's Poetry*, 175.
82. Alexander Gilchrist, *The Life of William Blake*, ed. W. Graham Robertson (London: John Lane the Bodley Head, 1922), 36.
83. Jacob Bronowski, *William Blake: Man Without a Mask* (London: Secker and Warburg, 1947), 36.
84. David V. Erdman, *Blake: Prophet Against Empire* (Princeton: Princeton University Press, 1977), 9.
85. William Blake, *The Complete Poetry and Prose of William Blake*, ed. David V. Erdman, commentary Harold Bloom, rev. ed. (New York: Anchor, 1988), 671. All references to Blake's texts will be to this edition, by line number for short poems, by abbreviation, plate, line number, and page for major works, and by page number for prose works.
86. Jon Mee, *Dangerous Enthusiasm: William Blake and the Culture of Radicalism in the 1790s* (Oxford: Oxford University Press, 1992), 51, cf. 214–26. On Blake and the Johnson circle, see also Erdman, *Prophet Against Empire*, 152–62.
87. On Blake and antinomianism see Makdisi, *Impossible History*, 16–77; E. P. Thompson, *Witness against the Beast* (New York: The New Press, 1993); A. L. Morton, *The Everlasting Gospel* (London: Lawrence and Wishart, 1958).

88. Mee, *Dangerous Enthusiasm*, 220.
89. David Punter, "Blake and the Shapes of London," *Criticism* 23.1 (Winter 1981): 6.
90. Makdisi, *Impossible History*, 38.
91. Kenneth R. Johnston, "Blake's Cities: Romantic Forms of Urban Renewal," in *Blake's Visionary Forms Dramatic*, ed. David V. Erdman and John E. Grant (Princeton: Princeton University Press, 1970), 423.
92. Williams, *The Country and the City*, 148.
93. Gavin Edwards, "'Mind-Forg'd Manacles': A Contribution to the Discussion of Blake's 'London'," *Literature & History* 5 (1979): 95–96.
94. Makdisi, *Romantic Imperialism*, 157.
95. Makdisi, *Impossible History*, 11.
96. Simmel, "Metropolis and Mental Life," 326.
97. E. P. Thompson, "'London,'" *Interpreting Blake*, ed. Michael Phillips (Cambridge: Cambridge University Press, 1978), 12.
98. Thompson, "'London,'" 21.
99. Punter, "Shapes of London," 15.
100. Heather Glen, "The Poet in Society: Blake and Wordsworth on London," *Literature and History* 3 (1976): 7, 9, 12.
101. Michael Ferber, "'London' and Its Politics," *ELH* 48.2 (Summer 1981): 323.
102. Makdisi, *Impossible History*, 34–35.
103. Steve Vine, "Blake's Material Sublime," *Studies in Romanticism* 41.2 (Summer 2002): 255.
104. I decline to refer to Golgonooza as a Foucauldian "heterotopia," though it fits Kevin Hetherington's definition of heterotopia "as spaces of alternate ordering. Heterotopia organize a bit of the social world in a way different to that which surrounds them. That alternate ordering marks them out as Other and allows them to be seen as an example of an alternative way of doing things. . . . Heterotopia, therefore, reveal the process of social ordering to be just that, a process rather than a thing." Kevin Hetherington, *Badlands of Modernity: Heterotopia and Social Ordering* (London: Routledge, 1997), viii–ix. David Harvey provides a sharp critique of the concept: it "has the virtue of insisting upon a better understanding of the heterogeneity of space but it gives no clue as to what a more spatiotemporal utopianism might look like. Foucault challenges and helps destabilize . . . but provides no clue as to how any kind of alternative might be constructed." David Harvey, *Spaces of Hope* (Berkeley: University of California Press, 2000), 185.
105. Makdisi, *Impossible History*, 5.
106. Sarah Haggarty, *Blake's Gifts: Poetry and the Politics of Exchange* (Cambridge: Cambridge University Press, 2009), 35.

107. See Nicholas M. Williams, *Ideology and Utopia in the Poetry of William Blake* (Cambridge: Cambridge University Press, 1998), 170–206.
108. Morton Paley argues "Golgonooza is the realization of the city envisaged by Milton in Areopagitica: 'Behold now this vast City, a city of Refuge, the mansion house of liberty'," in *The Continuing City: William Blake's* Jerusalem (Oxford: Clarendon Press, 1983), 166.
109. Wordsworth, *Thirteen Book* Prelude, 2.324.
110. Wordsworth, *Thirteen Book* Prelude, 2.324, 2.322.
111. Williams, *The Country and the City*, 150–51. Glen, "The Poet in Society," 4.
112. Glen, "The Poet in Society," 4, 18.
113. See David Simpson, *Wordsworth and the Figurings of the Real* (London: Macmillan, 1982), 49–60; *Wordsworth's Historical Imagination* (London: Methuen, 1987), 56–78; Pfau, *Wordsworth's Profession*, 362–82; Makdisi, *Romantic Imperialism*, 23–31. In *Making England Western* (65–66) Makdisi revisits his earlier argument about Book 7 and finds Wordsworth critical of the temporality of modernization.
114. For Wordsworth's involvement with the hegemonic radicals, including Coleridge, Thelwall, Godwin, Joseph Fawcett, and others, see Roe, *Wordsworth and Coleridge*, 145–98; Johnston, *The Hidden Wordsworth*; and Judith Thompson, *John Thelwall in the Wordsworth Circle* (New York: Palgrave Macmillan, 2012).
115. John Thelwall, *The Politics of English Jacobinism: The Writings of John Thelwall*, ed. Gregory Claeys (University Park: Pennsylvania State University Press, 1995), xxv.
116. Ross King, "Wordsworth, Panoramas, and the Prospect of London," *Studies in Romanticism* 32.1 (Spring 1993): 73.
117. Simmel, "Metropolis and Mental Life," 336.
118. Reed does not split the verse paragraphs, but the Norton Critical (among several other editions) does. William Wordsworth, *The Prelude 1799, 1805, 1850*, ed. Wordsworth, Abrams, and Gill (Norton: New York, 1979).
119. Richard D. Altick, *The Shows of London* (Cambridge: Harvard University Press, 1978), 95.
120. Timothy Webb, "Dangerous Plurals: Wordsworth's Bartholomew Fair and the Challenge of an Urban Poetics," *London in Literature: Visionary Mappings of the Metropolis*, ed. Susana Onega and John A. Stotesbury (Heidelberg: C. Winter, 2002), 56–57.
121. Wordsworth, *Thirteen Book* Prelude, 2.351, 2.354.
122. The Den of Yordas simile has been a crux in these arguments. In his early book, *Figurings of the Real*, David Simpson argues that the passage undermines Wordsworth's affirmation in Book 8 that his imagination can function in London: the "image of the cave yet remains . . . suggestive

of a privileged perception which cannot tend to flourish in the city" (57). But Wordsworth does not present the simile as a model of poetic perception, and it follows an account of his first entry into London that corrects the way of seeing represented in Book 7. Tim Fulford has shown, furthermore, that Yordas was at the time "reduced to being an exhibition of magic tricks, a dazzling but ultimately unfulfilling visual playground . . . Yordas was a commercial show cave in which the guide, in return for the tourist's shillings, illuminated the interior with torches and likened its features to everyday objects in the world outside." *The Late Poetry of the Lake Poets* (Cambridge: Cambridge University Press, 2013), 241. If the cave and city present disappointing shows, the fault lies in the guides and in commodification, something that, the structure of the simile implies, can spoil the experience of nature as much as the experience of the metropolis.

123. Hugh Sykes Davies, "Wordsworth and the Empirical Philosophers," in *The English Mind: Studies in the English Moralists Presented to Basil Willey*, ed. Hugh Sykes Davies and George Watson (Cambridge: Cambridge University Press, 1964), 163.
124. Jonathan Wordsworth contrasts the mystery of the faces of strangers in London against the poet's description of Hawkshead, where "The face of every neighbour whom I met / Was as a volume to me" (4.58–59). *William Wordsworth: The Borders of Vision* (Oxford: Clarendon Press, 1982), 302. But the passage should also be read alongside the "wondrous power of words" passage and his image of a parade of soldiers in a French town in which his eye catches "here and there a face / Or person singled out among the rest, / Yet still a stranger and beloved as such" (9.284–86).
125. William Wordsworth, *The Prose Works of William Wordsworth*, ed. W. J. B. Owen and Jane Worthington Smyser, 3 vols. (Oxford: Clarendon Press, 1974), 1.103. All quotations from Wordsworth's prose will conform to the texts in this edition.
126. Edmund Spenser, *The Faerie Queene*, ed. A. C. Hamilton (London: Longman, 2001), book 1, canto 1, stanzas 20 and 22.

Chapter 2

1. Raymond Williams, *Culture and Society, 1780–1950* (New York: Columbia University Press, 1983), 31–32.
2. Williams, *Culture and Society*, 62. Williams's emphasis.
3. See Jon Klancher, *The Making of English Reading Audiences, 1790–1832* (Madison: University of Wisconsin Press, 1987), 47–49, 150–70; Paul Magnuson, *Reading Public Romanticism* (Princeton: Princeton University Press, 1998), 68–94; Lucy

Newlyn, *Reading, Writing, and Romanticism* (Oxford: Oxford University Press, 2000), 49–90; Jon Mee, *Romanticism, Enthusiasm, and Regulation* (Oxford: Oxford University Press, 2005), 131–72. For Coleridge's Cambridge and London milieu, see Roe, *Wordsworth and Coleridge*; for his Bristol milieu, see White and Kitson cited in note 6 of this chapter. For Coleridge amid the London cultural scene, see Jon Klancher, *Transfiguring the Arts and Sciences: Knowledge and Cultural Institutions in the Romantic Age* (Cambridge: Cambridge University Press, 2013), 153–81. On Coleridge's lecturing, see Peter J. Manning, "Manufacturing the Romantic Image: Hazlitt and Coleridge Lecturing," in *Romantic Metropolis*, ed. Chandler and Gilmartin, 227–45; Sarah M. Zimmerman, "Coleridge the Lecturer, a Disappearing Act," in *Spheres of Action: Speech and Performance in Romantic Culture*, ed. Alexander Dick and Angela Esterhammer (Toronto: University of Toronto Press, 2009), 46–72.

4. Kevin Gilmartin, "Sinking Down." Only a few critics have studied Coleridge's representations of cities. In *The Country and the City*, Williams reads "Dejection: An Ode" as a lamentation of Coleridge's "lonely creative imagination" (132), always alienated in the crowd and incapable of finding succor in nature. The division between Williams's reading of Coleridge's poetry and prose shows the persistent difficulty of finding consistency between his early and later writings and between his works in different literary kinds. Nicola Trott captures Coleridge's ambivalence toward cities by juxtaposing his aversion to smoke and crowds with his penchant for flirting with London's fashionable ladies. "Coleridge's City," *Coleridge Bulletin* 19 (Spring 2002): 41–57.
5. Perry sees in Coleridge "a genuine pattern of oppositions, a consistent double-mindedness." Seamus Perry, *Coleridge and the Uses of Division* (Oxford: Clarendon Press, 1999), 3.
6. Daniel E. White, *Early Romanticism and Religious Dissent* (Cambridge: Cambridge University Press, 2006), 119–51; Peter J. Kitson, "Coleridge's Bristol and West Country Radicalism," in *English Romantic Writers and the West Country*, ed. Nicholas Roe (London: Palgrave Macmillan, 2010), 115–28; Mike Jay, *The Atmosphere of Heaven: The Unnatural Experiments of Dr Beddoes and His Sons of Genius* (New Haven: Yale University Press, 2009).
7. Wrigley, *People, Cities and Wealth*, 133–56.
8. de Vries, *European Urbanization*, 255.
9. See Daunton, *Progress and Poverty*, 285–307; Harvey, *The Urban Experience*, 80. Urbanization entails "the creation of a material physical infrastructure for production, circulation, exchange, and consumption" (*Urban Experience*, 71–72). This process breaks down barriers to trade between regions while at the same time entailing "the production of new geographical differentiations which form new spatial barriers." David Harvey, *The Limits to Capital* (New York: Verso, 2006), 417; on infrastructure, see 232–35, 395–98.

10. "The more production comes to rest on exchange value, hence on exchange, the more important do the physical conditions of exchange – the means of communication and transport – become for the costs of circulation. Capital by its nature drives beyond every spatial barrier. Thus the creation of the physical conditions of exchange – of the means of communication and transport – the annihilation of space by time – becomes an extraordinary necessity for it." Marx, *Grundrisse*, 524.
11. Wrigley, *People, Cities and Wealth*, 160.
12. Borsay, *English Urban Renaissance*, 9. See Kenneth Morgan, *Bristol and the Atlantic Trade in the Eighteenth Century* (Cambridge: Cambridge University Press, 1993), 89–127.
13. See John Evans and John Corry, *The History of Bristol, Civil and Ecclesiastical*, 2 vols. (Bristol: W Sheppard, 1816), 2.307–11; and Julius Caesar Ibbetson, et al., *A Picturesque Guide to Bath, Bristol Hot-Wells, the River Avon and the Adjacent Country* (London: Hookham and Carpenter, 1793), 157. Morgan adds "smaller enterprises in bricks and tiles, soap, leather, earthenware, chocolate, porter brewing, ceramics, and clay-tobacco pipe making." *Bristol and the Atlantic Trade*, 97.
14. See Morgan, *Bristol and the Atlantic Trade*, 31–32; Wrigley, *People, Cities and Wealth*, 160.
15. Samuel Taylor Coleridge, *The Friend*, ed. Barbara E. Rooke, 2 vols. (Princeton: Princeton University Press, 1969), 1.230.
16. James Raven notes that limited financial services in provincial towns complicated provincial publishing for much of the eighteenth century, making it "usually impractical to do anything other than negotiate terms with a single London wholesale bookseller who then acted as a middleman in dealings with other London suppliers." *The Business of Books: Booksellers and the English Book Trade* (New Haven: Yale University Press, 2007), 228.
17. Klancher, *Reading Audiences*, 34.
18. In this chapter, I aim to fill in a gap between Pierre Bourdieu's model of the literary field and David Harvey's model of the production of urban space by the drive for progressive accumulation. In *Rules of Art*, Bourdieu studies the historical emergence and internal dynamics of the literary field, but he pays little attention to the definition of the boundaries of markets and fields. By focusing on Paris, he effectively brackets the influence of geography. See Pierre Bourdieu, *Rules of Art*, trans. Susan Emanuel (Stanford: Stanford University Press, 1992).
19. Borsay, *English Urban Renaissance*, 129, 221. See also Geoffrey Alan Cranfield, *The Development of the Provincial Newspaper, 1700–1760* (Oxford: Clarendon Press, 1962).

20. Richard Wilson, "Newspapers and Industry: The Export of Wool Controversy in the 1790s," in *The Press in English Society from the Seventeenth to Nineteenth Centuries* (Cranbury, NJ: Associated University Presses, 1986), 81.
21. Black, *English Press in the Eighteenth Century*, 57.
22. Letter to Thomas Poole, April 11, 1796. Samuel Taylor Coleridge, *Collected Letters of Samuel Taylor Coleridge*, ed. Earl Leslie Griggs, 5 vols. (Oxford: Clarendon Press, 1956), 1.202. All subsequent quotations from Coleridge's letters will conform to the text in this collection and will be cited by addressee, date, and volume and page number.
23. See Letter to the Rev. John Edwards, February 4, 1796, 1.182.
24. Samuel Taylor Coleridge, *Lectures 1795 on Politics and Religion*, ed. Lewis Patton and Peter Mann (Princeton: Princeton University Press, 1971), 313.
25. Bourdieu largely omits geography from his account of habitus. He briefly refers to "*socially ranked geographical space*" that stratifies groups according to their access to prestigious cultural resources and that marks populations with local identifiers such as pronunciation. Pierre Bourdieu, *Distinction: A Social Critique of the Judgement of Taste*, trans. Richard Nice (Cambridge: Harvard University Press, 1984), 124. Bourdieu's emphasis. Harvey uses Bourdieu's habitus in his analysis of the self-reproduction of the cultural and spatial logic of capitalism in *The Condition of Postmodernity*. But Harvey assumes rather than analyzes a correspondence between the logics of the regime of capital accumulation, the structure of social geography, and the dominant mode of cultural production. He does not mediate the relation through the field of cultural production.
26. See Roe, *Wordsworth and Coleridge*, 145–56.
27. White, *Early Romanticism and Religious Dissent*, 142–43, quoting from Peter Marcy, "Eighteenth-Century Views of Bristol and Bristolians," in *Bristol in the Eighteenth Century*, ed. Patrick McGrath (Newton Abbott: David & Charles, 1972), 38. Writing in 1816, historian John Evans considers the "intense application to trade" in the "pursuit of wealth" to be "the characteristic" of Bristol; and while this may be true of many cities, "in few have its effects been more conspicuous than in Bristol." Evans and Corry, *The History of Bristol*, 2.230.
28. Quoted in John Colmer, *Coleridge: Critic of Society* (Oxford: Clarendon Press, 1967), 26.
29. Romaine Joseph Thorn, *Bristolia, A Poem* (Bristol: Rees, 1794), lines 7–8, 29; Robert Lovell, *Bristol: A Satire* (London, 1794), lines 200–01.
30. Letter to Horace Walpole Bedford, December 11, 1793; Robert Southey, *New Letters of Robert Southey*, ed. Kenneth Curry, 2 vols. (New York: Columbia University Press, 1965), 1.37. J. G. A. Pocock studies an example of a dispute within Dissenting ranks, or what Edmund Burke refers to as "the very dissidence of dissent" in *Virtue, Commerce, and History*, 159–88 (173).

31. See Patton's "Introduction" in *Lectures*, xlvii, John Morrow, *Coleridge's Political Thought* (London: Macmillan, 1990), 33, 29.
32. Colmer, *Coleridge: Critic of Society*, 25–26; Jay, *Atmosphere of Heaven*, 110–42.
33. See Joseph Priestley, *Hartley's Theory of the Human Mind* (London: Joseph Johnson, 1775).
34. David Hartley, *Observations on Man, His Frame, His Duty, and His Expectations*, 2 vols. (London: S. Richardson, 1749), 1.420.
35. Letter to George Dyer, March 10, 1795, 1.154.
36. Coleridge, *Lectures*, 224.
37. Letter to George Dyer, March 10, 1795, 1.154.
38. Coleridge, *Lectures*, 224–25.
39. Morrow, *Coleridge's Political Thought*, 33; *cf. Lectures*, xlvii. For the sources of Coleridge's *Lectures*, see *Lectures* liv–lxxx; Morrow, *Coleridge's Political Thought*, 29–33; Nigel Leask, *Politics of Imagination in Coleridge's Critical Thought* (Basingstoke: Macmillan, 1988), 28–35. On the connection between Dissent and Commonwealth political philosophy see Caroline Robbins, *The Eighteenth-Century Commonwealthman* (Cambridge: Harvard University Press, 1959), 223–370.
40. See Morrow, *Coleridge's Political Thought*, 57.
41. Daniel S. Malachuk, "Coleridge's Republicanism and the Aphorism in *Aids to Reflection*," *Studies in Romanticism* 39.3 (Fall 2000): 397–417. See also Pocock, *Virtue, Commerce, and History*.
42. Letter to John Thelwall, May 13, 1796, 1.214. Coleridge's emphasis. In "Coleridge's Bristol," Kitson distinguishes Coleridge's politics from both Thelwall's and the Bristol Dissenters' on the grounds of his leveling (116). According to Peter Mann, Priestley "believed in equality of rights but not in equality in private property, far less in the abolition of it." Coleridge, *Lectures*, lxiv.
43. Coleridge, *Lectures*, 350, 219; *cp* 130.
44. Coleridge, *Lectures*, 350.
45. Coleridge, *Lectures*, 223–24.
46. Letter to Robert Southey, July 13, 1794, 1.88; Coleridge, *Friend*, 2.146.
47. For the intellectual history of the "four stages theory," see Ronald L. Meek, *Social Science and the Ignoble Savage* (Cambridge: Cambridge University Press, 1976).
48. Southey, *New Letters*, 1.72.
49. Nicholas Roe, *Politics of Nature* (London: Macmillan, 1992), 50.
50. Letter to Robert Southey, September 1, 1794, 1.99. Coleridge's emphasis.
51. George Whalley, "Coleridge and Southey in Bristol, 1795," *RES* n.s. 1 (1950), 327.
52. Leask, *Politics of Imagination*, 34, 38, 13.

53. Tim Fulford, *Landscape, Liberty and Authority* (Cambridge: Cambridge University Press, 1996), 216, 215. Kelvin Everest also places Coleridge's poetry in a tradition of retirement extending back from Cowper and Bowles. See Kelvin Everest, *Coleridge's Secret Ministry: The Context of the Conversation Poems 1795–1798* (New York: Barnes & Noble, 1979), 156.
54. Richard Holmes, *Coleridge: Early Visions* (London: Hodder & Stoughton, 1989), 176. Jack Stillinger exaggerates the claim in *Romantic Complexity: Keats, Coleridge, and Wordsworth* (Urbana: University of Illinois Press, 2006). Stillinger generalizes that Coleridge wrote "practically all of the good poems he ever produced" during "two distinct periods when he was away from the cities that . . . were an impediment to his union with nature" (161). The claim seems weaker if we distinguish between the influence of nature and the influence of Wordsworth. It also has factual limits. Coleridge wrote poetry in the city throughout his career – he probably composed at least part of "The Eolian Harp" and "Reflections" in Bristol – and he later published *The Friend* while living in Keswick.
55. Bourdieu, *Rules of Art*, 115.
56. Edward Glaeser, *The Triumph of the City* (New York: Penguin, 2011), 10. Living in the city may improve a poet's chances of acquiring a patron, though the chances decrease as patronage declines and market relations become more typical. See Marilyn Butler's discussion of Chatterton's career in *Mapping Mythologies: Countercurrents in Eighteenth-Century British Poetry and Cultural History* (Cambridge: Cambridge University Press, 2015), 98–122.
57. See Richard Holmes, *Coleridge: Darker Reflections* (New York: Pantheon Books, 1998), 317–21, 465–68, 322, 425.
58. Letter to George Dyer, March 10, 1795, 1.155. He expressed similar concerns when thinking about moving to Stowey. See Letter to Thomas Poole, December 12, 1796, 1.270.
59. Coleridge sees newspapers squeezed by advertisements and bound up in quick turnover. Letter to Daniel Stuart, June 4, 1811, 3.332–34.
60. Bourdieu, *Rules of Art*, 120–21.
61. Samuel Taylor Coleridge, *Poetical Works I: Poems (Reading Text): Part I*, ed. J. C. C. Mays (Princeton: Princeton University Press, 2001), lines 6, 4. All quotations from Coleridge's poems conform to the text in Mays's edition of the poems and will be cited internally by line number.
62. Trott, "Coleridge's City," 46.
63. Samuel Taylor Coleridge, *The Watchman*, ed. Lewis Patton (Princeton: Princeton University Press, 1970), 9.
64. Coleridge, *The Watchman*, 139. Coleridge continues, "There is one criterion by which we may always distinguish benevolence from mere sensibility – Benevolence impels to action, and is accompanied by self-denial" (140).

65. Mays follows the 1797 text. After 1828, the line reads: "Praise, praise it, O my Soul! oft as thou scann'st" (55).
66. Coleridge, *Poems*, 261. Paul H. Fry argues Coleridge "repudiates, or wants to repudiate, precisely, *poetry*. Poetry, an outmoded way of life in an increasingly industrial, urban, and politicized world, is at most a Sabbath recreation." "Time to Retire? Coleridge and Wordsworth Go to Work," *The Wordsworth Circle* 41.1 (Winter 2010): 24. Fry's emphasis. Timothy Corrigan is less stark: "Coleridge's departure from the bucolic world does not mean he must forsake poetry, but perhaps only a kind of poetry." See *Coleridge, Language, and Criticism* (Athens: University of Georgia Press, 1982), 44.
67. Letter to Thomas Poole, October 7, 1795, 1.161.
68. Letter to the Rev. John Edwards, March 20, 1796, 1.192. Rent was not the problem: the rent in Clevedon was only £5 per annum and he kept the cottage after moving back to Bristol. In the ninth number of *The Watchman*, Coleridge projected starving poets as his doubles: "Who has not sighed over the fates of [starved poets] Otway, Collins, and Chatterton . . . He [Boissy] laboured incessantly for uncertain bread. Alas! I have yet mentioned but a small part of his miseries; the most heart-breaking calamity follows – *he had a Wife and Child*." *Watchman*, 313–14. Coleridge's emphasis.
69. Paul Magnuson, *Coleridge's Nightmare Poetry* (Charlottesville: University of Virginia Press, 1974), 24.
70. Jon Mee, *Romanticism, Enthusiasm, and Regulation*, 155–57.
71. Coleridge, *The Watchman*, 224. Coleridge reproduces "A Retrospect of the Active World," *The English Review* 27 (March 1796): 281–300 (292).
72. Coleridge, *Lectures*, 43. Coleridge's emphasis.
73. Coleridge, *Lectures*, 114.
74. Newlyn, *Reading, Writing, and Romanticism*, 74.
75. See Letter to the Rev. John Edwards, March 20, 1796, 1.192: "Yesterday Mrs Coleridge miscarried. . . . I think the subject of Pregnancy the most obscure of all God's dispensations . . . the pangs which the Woman suffers, seem inexplicable in the system of optimism."
76. For discussions of Coleridge's Unitarianism, see, for example, Mann's Introduction to Coleridge, *Lectures*, liii–lxvii; William A. Ulmer, "Virtue of Necessity: Coleridge's Unitarian Moral Theory," *Modern Philology* 102 (2005): 372–404. On the Unitarian background of "Reflections," see H. W. Piper, *Singing of Mount Abora: Coleridge's Use of Biblical Imagery and Natural Symbolism in Poetry and Philosophy* (Rutherford, NJ: Fairleigh Dickinson University Press, 1987), 34–36.
77. Years later, Coleridge facetiously returns to the notion of the divine presence in the city. "My Spinosism . . . disposed me to consider this big City as that

part of the Supreme *One*, which the prophet Moses was allowed to see." Letter to Robert Southey, December 24, 1799, 1.551. Coleridge's emphasis.

78. Lucy Newlyn, *Coleridge, Wordsworth, and the Language of Allusion*, 2nd ed. (Oxford: Oxford University Press, 2001), 207. See also Lucy Newlyn, "'In City Pent': Echo and Allusion in Wordsworth, Coleridge, and Lamb, 1797–1801," *The Review of English Studies*, n.s. 32.128 (November 1981): 408–28.
79. William A. Ulmer, "The Rhetorical Occasion of 'This Lime-Tree Bower My Prison,'" *Romanticism* 13.1 (2007): 26.
80. Letter to Coleridge, June 10, 1796, in Charles and Mary Lamb, *The Letters of Charles and Mary Anne Lamb*, ed. Edwin W. Marrs, Jr., 3 vols. (Ithaca: Cornell University Press, 1975–78), 1.23. Lamb's emphasis. Writing to a friend after the publication of "This Lime-Tree Bower," Lamb commented, "For my part, with reverence to my friends northward, I must confess that I am not romance-bit about *Nature*." Letter to Manning, November 29, 1800, Marrs, 1.248. Lamb's emphasis.
81. Coleridge, *Poems*, 350.
82. Coleridge compares the action of the imagination to the movement of a "small water-insect" that "*wins* its way up against the stream" in Samuel Taylor Coleridge, *Biographia Literaria*, ed. James Engell and W. Jackson Bate, 2 vols. (Princeton: Princeton University Press, 1983), 1.124.
83. Coleridge, *Poems*, 350. Mays adopts the text from *Sibylline Leaves* (1817).
84. Carl R. Woodring, *Politics in the Poetry of Coleridge* (Madison: University of Wisconsin Press, 1961), 68.
85. Nicholas Mason, *Literary Advertising and the Shaping of British Romanticism* (Baltimore: Johns Hopkins University Press, 2013); Raven associates this commercial development of the book trades with "the reshaping of the whole system of trade in London, exacerbated by demographic shifts and the increase in population outside the walls," and therefore beyond the reach of guild restrictions. Raven, *The Business of Books*, 204.
86. Klancher, *Transfiguring the Arts and Sciences*, 180.
87. Samuel Taylor Coleridge, *Essays on His Times*, ed. David V. Erdman, 3 vols. (Princeton: Princeton University Press, 1978), 2.76.
88. Coleridge, *The Friend*, 1.508. Coleridge's emphasis.
89. Coleridge, *The Friend*, 1.507. Coleridge's emphasis.
90. Coleridge, *Essays on His Times*, 2.431. Coleridge's emphasis.
91. Coleridge, *The Friend*, 1.233. Coleridge's emphasis.
92. Coleridge, *The Friend*, 1.35–36.
93. Coleridge, *The Friend*, 1.59–60. Coleridge's emphasis.
94. Coleridge, *The Friend*, 1.36.
95. Coleridge, *The Friend*, 1.494.

96. Samuel Taylor Coleridge, *Lay Sermons*, ed. R. J. White (Princeton: Princeton University Press, 1972), 189.
97. Bourdieu, *Rules of Art*, 120.
98. Coleridge, *Biographia Literaria*, 1.38–39. Coleridge's emphasis.
99. Jerome Christensen, *Coleridge's Blessed Machine of Language* (Ithaca: Cornell University Press, 1981), 161–78.
100. Samuel Taylor Coleridge, *On the Constitution of the Church and State*, ed. John Colmer (Princeton: Princeton University Press, 1976), 24.
101. Coleridge, *Church and State*, 27.
102. Coleridge, *Lay Sermons*, 33, 181.
103. Coleridge, *Lay Sermons*, 206, 223. Coleridge's emphasis.
104. Coleridge, *Lay Sermons*, 169.
105. Religion and poetry both appear to bring the whole soul of man into activity. See Coleridge, *Lay Sermons*, 90 note 6, and 62, 169.
106. Coleridge, *Lay Sermons*, 196–97.
107. Samuel Taylor Coleridge, *Table Talk*, ed. Carl Woodring, 2 vols. (Princeton: Princeton University Press, 1991), 1.284–85.
108. Coleridge, *Church and State*, 50.
109. Coleridge, *Essays on His Times*, 2.470. Coleridge's emphasis.
110. Quoted in Leask, *Politics of Imagination*, 211.
111. Coleridge, *The Friend*, 1.231. Coleridge's emphasis.
112. Samuel Taylor Coleridge, *Lectures 1808–1819 On Literature*, ed. R. A. Foakes, 2 vols. (Princeton: Princeton University Press, 1987), 1.515–16.
113. Coleridge, *Lectures on Literature*, 1.186. Coleridge's emphasis.
114. Manning, "Manufacturing the Romantic Image," 239.
115. Zimmerman, "Coleridge the Lecturer," 69, 61–62. Letter to William Godwin, November 12, 1811, 3.345.
116. Coleridge, *Lectures on Literature*, 1.391.
117. Coleridge, *Lectures*, 43.
118. Gilmartin, "Sinking down," 133–34, quoting Letter to Robert Southey, May 12, 1812, 3.410. In *The Watchman*, Coleridge imagines "great numbers" of laborers assembled in "towns and cities," "spending their last sixpence in an alehouse" listening to screeds of radicalism (224).
119. Klancher, *Reading Audiences*, 169.

Chapter 3

1. See F. B. Pinion, *A Wordsworth Chronology* (London: Macmillan, 1988), 85–87.
2. Letter from Wordsworth to Mary Wordsworth, May 16, 1812, *The Letters of William and Dorothy Wordsworth*, ed. Ernest de Selincourt, 8 vols. (Oxford:

Clarendon Press, 1967), 8.79. All quotations from Wordsworth's letters will conform to the text in this collection and will be cited in the notes by addressee, date, and volume and page number.

3. Linebaugh, *The London Hanged*, xix. In court, Bellingham described the damages as petty highway robbery, a capital crime, measured against Perceval's denial of his petitions for release from imprisonment as "no more than a mite to a mountain." He called on "the superior classes" not to neglect the grievances of the oppressed. Despite Bellingham's comparison of political acts to ordinary thefts and his warning to the upper classes, he insisted he shot Perceval to redress a personal grievance. "Correct Likeness of Bellingham, with an Accurate Report of his Trial," *Universal Magazine* 17.102 (May 1812): 434. According to *The Examiner* report, the crowd at his execution was orderly. When Bellingham ascended the scaffold, "a confused noise arose among the mob, from the desire and attempts of some to huzza him, counteracted by a far greater number who called 'Silence!'" "Execution of Bellingham," *The Examiner* 230 (May 24, 1812): 335.
4. Letter from Wordsworth to Mary Wordsworth, May 23, 1812, 8.92.
5. Wordsworth, *Prose Works*, 1.128. Subsequent references to this edition will be cited internally by the page number in the first volume.
6. Letter from Wordsworth to Catherine Clarkson, June 4, 1812, 3.21.
7. Thompson, *Customs in Common*, 7, 2.
8. Thompson, *Customs in Common*, 395. Thompson's emphasis.
9. Linebaugh, *London Hanged*, 440.
10. Critics have chided Thompson for simplifying class relations. They observe his tendency to identify market mentalities with a patrician class, to identify customary culture with a plebian order, and to efface the role of the middle classes. Thompson acknowledges his model may appear "bi-polar." He sees the middle classes as aligned with the upper ranks through the "controls of clientage, of patronage and 'interest.'" Thompson, *Customs in Common*, 88–89. I follow Thompson's binary division rather than his critics' request for subtler distinctions. Wordsworth appears to focus on the sharper, tenser division between polite and popular culture rather than on the divisions within polite culture.
11. "It is only the expression of equivalence between different sorts of commodities which brings to view the specific character of value-creating labour, by actually reducing the different kinds of labour embedded in the different kinds of commodity to their common quality of being human labour in general." Karl Marx, *Capital: Volume One*, trans. Ben Fowkes (New York: Penguin, 1990), 142. The money commodity in the form of the wage directly accomplishes and depends on this abstraction.

12. Manley, *Literature and Culture in Early Modern London*, 16. What Deleuze and Guattari say of the nomad applies to figures in Wordsworth's poetry: he "reterritorializes on deterritorialization itself. It is the earth that deterritorializes itself." See *A Thousand Plateaus: Capitalism and Schizophrenia*, trans. Brian Massumi (Minneapolis: University of Minnesota Press, 1987), 381.
13. Henri Lefebvre, *The Production of Space*, trans. Donald Nicholson-Smith (Oxford: Blackwell, 2009), 307, 49, 51.
14. Anthony Giddens, *The Consequences of Modernity* (Stanford: Stanford University Press, 1990), 20.
15. Deleuze and Guattari, *A Thousand Plateaus*, 10.
16. Raymond Williams, *Marxism and Literature* (Oxford: Oxford University Press, 1977), 132.
17. Sianne Ngai, *Ugly Feelings* (Cambridge: Harvard University Press, 2005), 7.
18. Virno, "The Ambivalence of Disenchantment," 13, 12. All emphasis is Virno's.
19. G. J. Barker-Benfield, "Sensibility," in *An Oxford Companion to the Romantic Age*, ed. Iain McCalman (Oxford: Oxford University Press, 2001), 104. See also John Brewer, "Sensibility and the Urban Panorama," *Huntington Library Quarterly* 70.2 (June 2007): 243.
20. See Michelle Faubert, "Nerve Theory, Sensibility, and Romantic Metrosexuals," in *Romanticism and the City*, ed. Larry H. Peer (New York: Palgrave, 2011), 9–24.
21. Pfau, *Wordsworth's Profession*, 248, 251.
22. Pfau, *Wordsworth's Profession*, 243, 240.
23. Rowan Boyson, *Wordsworth and the Enlightenment Idea of Pleasure* (Cambridge: Cambridge University Press, 2012), 1; Adela Pinch, *Strange Fits of Passion: Epistemologies of Emotion, Hume to Austen* (Stanford: Stanford University Press, 1996), 72–110. On concepts of affect without subjects, see Rei Terada, *Feeling in Theory: Emotion after the 'Death of the Subject'* (Cambridge: Harvard University Press, 2001).
24. Adam Smith, *The Wealth of Nations* (New York: Bantam, 2003), 987.
25. Simpson, *Wordsworth's Historical Imagination*, 3. Simpson focuses on epistemological rather than affective concerns. His model of the "second look," in which Wordsworth appears to find urban environments too busy to allow the mind to digest sensory information, sees Wordsworth subscribing to urban ideology. For a concise summary of the "second look," see *Wordsworth's Historical Imagination*, 60.
26. Adam Ferguson, *An Essay on the History of Civil Society*, ed. Fania Oz-Salzberger (Cambridge: Cambridge University Press, 1995), 173, 180.

27. Adam Smith, *The Theory of Moral Sentiments*, ed. Ryan Patrick Hanley (New York: Penguin, 2009), 235.
28. Simpson, *Wordsworth and the Figurings of the Real*, 142.
29. In a letter to Rev. Francis Wrangham from June 5, 1808, Wordsworth contrasts the situation of the "labouring man in agriculture," who "finds a hundred little jobs which furnish him with a change of employment, which is grateful and profitable" against "The situation of Manufacturers ... The monotony of their employments renders some sort of stimulus, intellectual or bodily, absolutely necessary for them" 2.247–48.
30. Alan Bewell, *Wordsworth and the Enlightenment: Nature, Man, and Society in the Experimental Poetry* (New Haven: Yale University Press, 1989), 5.
31. Klancher, *Making of English Reading Audiences*, 144, 17, 143.
32. Klancher, *Making of English Reading Audiences*, 147, 17.
33. Simpson, *Wordsworth's Historical Imagination*, 69, 61.
34. Newlyn, *Reading, Writing, and Romanticism*, 102, 101.
35. John Guillory, *Cultural Capital: The Problem of Literary Canon Formation* (Chicago: University of Chicago Press, 1994), 127.
36. Williams, *Marxism and Literature*, 130.
37. Simpson, *Wordsworth's Historical Imagination*, 6–7. Simpson's emphasis. My argument treats class not as a category of identity but as a construct within a relation to the means of production or consumption.
38. Simpson, *Figurings of the Real*, 168.
39. St. Clair, *The Reading Nation in the Romantic Period*, 244, 241.
40. See Douglas Milburn Jr., "The Popular Reaction to German Drama in England at the End of the Eighteenth Century," *Rice University Studies* 55.3 (Summer 1969): 149–62.
41. Simpson, *Wordsworth's Historical Imagination*, 62.
42. William Wordsworth, *Lyrical Ballads and Other Poems, 1797–1800*, ed. James Butler and Karen Green (Ithaca: Cornell University Press, 1992), 307–08. All quotations from Wordsworth's poetry from 1797 to 1800 conform to the texts and manuscript transcriptions in this edition. Published poems will be cited internally by line number, manuscript poems by page number.
43. Ferguson, *Essay on the History of Civil Society*, 177.
44. Letter to John Wilson, June 7, 1802, 1.355.
45. Letter to John Wilson, June 7, 1802, 1.355.
46. Letter to Francis Wrangham, June 5, 1808, 2.248.
47. Letter to John Taylor, April 9, 1801, 1.325–26.
48. Robert Mayo, "The Contemporaneity of the *Lyrical Ballads*," *PMLA* 69.3 (June 1954): 486.
49. Pfau, *Wordsworth's Profession*, 249.

50. Hilary A. Zaid, "Wordsworth's 'Obsolete Idolatry': Doubling Texts and Facing Doubles in 'To Joanna'," *Studies in Romanticism* 36.2 (Summer 1997): 205.
51. Thomas H. Schmid describes a critical consensus that remarks Wordsworth's "aggression and defensiveness" in his representation of Joanna. "Strained Tenderness: Wordsworth, Joanna Hutchinson, and the Anxiety of Sisterly Resistance in 'To Joanna,'" *Studies in Romanticism* 40.3 (Fall 2001): 412.
52. Zaid, "Wordsworth's 'Obsolete Idolatry'," 207.
53. Marjorie Levinson, *Wordsworth's Great Period Poems* (Cambridge: Cambridge University Press, 1986), 58–79.
54. Levinson, *Wordsworth's Great Period Poems*, 73, 67.
55. Mark Jones, "Double Economics: Ambivalence in Wordsworth's Pastoral," *PMLA* 108.5 (October 1993): 1099, 1105–06.
56. Simpson, *Wordsworth's Historical Imagination*, 7; see Jones, "Double Economics," 1109.
57. My sense of Wordsworth's treatment of pastoral most closely resembles Jones's. Most criticism on *Michael* and pastoral was written before the early 1990s and sees Wordsworth celebrating rural life while reconfiguring the generic repertoire. See Stephen M. Parrish, *The Art of the Lyrical Ballads* (Cambridge: Harvard University Press, 1973), 167; Sydney Lea, "Wordsworth and His 'Michael': The Pastor Passes," *ELH* 45.1 (Spring 1978): 55–68; Annabel Patterson, *Pastoral and Ideology: Virgil to Valéry* (Berkeley: University of California Press, 1987): 272–78; W. Thomas Pepper, "The Ideology of Wordsworth's 'Michael: a Pastoral Poem,'" *Criticism* 31.4 (Fall 1989): 367–82; Bruce Graver, "Wordsworth's Georgic Pastoral: *Otium* and *Labor* in 'Michael,'" *European Romantic Review* 1.2 (1991): 119–34.
58. Lore Metzger, *One Foot in Eden: Modes of Pastoral in Romantic Poetry* (Chapel Hill: University of North Carolina Press, 1986), 143.
59. Mark Schoenfield, *The Professional Wordsworth: Law, Labor & The Poet's Contract* (Athens: University of Georgia Press, 1996), 50. The speaker does not fall into a linear narrative under the crisis related to urban commerce. Luke, for example, works endlessly in the third verse paragraph, arrives at his "eighteenth year" (125) in the fourth, appears as an infant in the fifth, and ages back to eighteen over the next three paragraphs.
60. Simpson, *Wordsworth's Historical Imagination*, 145.
61. Wordsworth prefers houses that keep with the geological character of the region. See *A Guide through the District of the Lakes* (*PrW* 2.214–15).
62. Schoenfield, *The Professional Wordsworth*, 43–44.
63. Letter from Wordsworth to Charles James Fox, January 14, 1801, 1.314–15. Coleridge wrote the letter; Wordsworth signed it.

64. Thomas Pfau, *Romantic Moods: Paranoia, Trauma, and Melancholy, 1790–1840* (Baltimore: Johns Hopkins University Press, 2005), 193.
65. Schoenfield, *The Professional Wordsworth*, 36.
66. See Penny Fielding, *Scotland and the Fictions of Geography, North Britain, 1760–1830* (Cambridge: Cambridge University Press, 2008), 2, 3, 186.
67. *Paradise Lost*, 1.680–83. John Milton, *Complete Poems and Major Prose*, ed. Merritt Y. Hughes (Indianapolis: Hackett, 2003). All subsequent quotations from *Paradise Lost* will be cited internally.
68. See Sally Bushell, "The Mapping of Meaning in Wordsworth's 'Michael': (Textual Place, Textual Space and Spatialized Speech Acts)," *Studies in Romanticism* 49.1 (Spring 2010): 53.
69. Berman, *All That Is Solid Melts into Air*, 66–71.
70. Letter from Wordsworth to Charles James Fox, January 14, 1801, 1.315.
71. See William Wordsworth, *Poems, in Two Volumes, and Other Poems, 1800–1807*, ed. Jared Curtis (Ithaca: Cornell University Press, 1983), 21: "Dancers / Star gazer / Fiddler / Westminster bridge." All subsequent quotations from poems in the 1807 volume conform to the reading texts in this edition and will be cited internally. Wordsworth moved the "Westminster Bridge" sonnet to the "Miscellaneous Sonnets" section. In the title in the first edition, the sonnet gave the year as 1803; I follow his later correction to 1802. I use the title "Stray Pleasures," which Wordsworth introduced only after 1820, because scholarship tends to be indexed by that title.
72. Letter to Lady Beaumont, May 21, 1807, 2.147.
73. Bewell, *Wordsworth and the Enlightenment*, 41.
74. Simpson, *Wordsworth's Historical Imagination*, 140; David Simpson, *Wordsworth, Commodification, and Social Concern* (Cambridge: Cambridge University Press, 2009), 84.
75. Klancher, *The Making of English Reading Audiences*, 150.
76. See Pfau, *Wordsworth's Profession*, 17–140.
77. Altick, *Shows of London*, 128–32. On Wordsworth on panoramas, see King, "Wordsworth, Panoramas, and the Prospect of London"; Tanya Agathocleous, "Wordsworth at the Panoramas: The Sublime Spectacle of the World," *Genre* 36.3–4 (Fall–Winter 2003): 295–315; Jennifer J. Jones, "Absorbing Hesitation: Wordsworth and the Theory of the Panorama," *Studies in Romanticism* 45.3 (Fall 2006): 357–75. On affect and panoramas, see Brewer, "Sensibility and the Urban Panorama."
78. Paul Fry, "The Diligence of Desire: Critics On and Around Westminster Bridge," *The Wordsworth Circle* 23.3 (Summer 1992): 162–64.
79. Williams, *The Country and the City*, 152.
80. Alan Liu, *Wordsworth: Sense of History* (Stanford: Stanford University Press, 1989), 461.

81. Peter Ackroyd remarks that by 1800 Lambeth was "acquiring the characteristics of a peculiarly repellent urban slum with wretchedly built and undrained houses." *Blake* (New York: Knopf, 1995), 128.
82. Quoted in Stephen Gill, *William Wordsworth: A Life* (Oxford: Clarendon Press, 1989), 349.
83. Charles Molesworth, "Wordsworth's 'Westminster Bridge' Sonnet: The Republican Structure of Time and Perception," *Clio* 6.3 (Spring 1977): 262.
84. Letter from Dorothy and William Wordsworth to Catherine Clarkson, March 28, 1806, 2.19. Wordsworth stayed several months.
85. Newlyn, *Reading, Writing, and Romanticism*, 15. The few other critics who consider "Star Gazers" read it for Wordsworth's attitudes toward astronomy or science.
86. Ngai, *Ugly Feelings*, 14. Ngai's emphasis.
87. Simon Jarvis, *Wordsworth's Philosophic Song* (Cambridge: Cambridge University Press, 2007), 105.
88. W. A. Speck, *Robert Southey: Entire Man of Letters* (New Haven: Yale University Press, 2006), 115.
89. Robert Southey, *Letters from England by Don Manuel Alvarez Espriella*, 2nd ed., 3 vols. (London: Longman, Hurst, Rees and Orme, 1808), 3.179–81.
90. Jarvis, *Wordsworth's Philosophic Song*, 105.

Chapter 4

1. Not much has been written on Shelley's representations of cities or urbanization. Raymond Williams includes Shelley along with Blake and Wordsworth among those in whom he hears "a Romantic structure of feeling." *Country and the City*, 79. Other studies address single works or representations of specific cities. See, for example, Karl Kroeber, "Experience as History: Shelley's Venice, Turner's Carthage," *ELH* 41.3 (Autumn 1974): 321–39; Douglas Thorpe, "Shelley's Golden Verbal City," *Journal of English and Germanic Philology* 86.3 (April 1987): 215–27; Michael Gassenmeier and Jens Martin Gurr, "The Experience of the City in British Romantic Poetry," in *Romantic Poetry*, ed. Angela Esterhammer (Philadelphia: John Benjamins, 2002), 319–22; Jonathan Sachs, "'Yet the Capital of the World': Rome, Repetition, and History in Shelley's Later Writings," *Nineteenth-Century Contexts* 28.2 (June 2006): 105–26.
2. David Harvey assesses the relation between the urban, regional, national, and global levels of politics and economic activity in *Urban Experience*, 125–64. But his critical apparatus cannot be transposed to the present analysis. The situation at issue – the effects of rapid urbanization on a democracy that does not redistribute representation – is a historically

peculiar one. Shelley limits it to Britain after the Civil War, and it closes with the Reform Act of 1832.

3. Williams, *The Country and the City*, 279.
4. James Chandler, *England in 1819* (Chicago: University of Chicago Press, 1998), 516–17. Chandler's emphasis.
5. Percy Bysshe Shelley, *Complete Poetry of Percy Bysshe Shelley*, ed. Donald Reiman and Neil Fraistat, 4 vols. to date (Baltimore: Johns Hopkins University Press, 2000). *Queen Mab*, 2.110, 121–22. Quotations from Shelley's poetry will conform to the texts in this edition, when available, and when not available, to the texts in Percy Bysshe Shelley, *Shelley's Poetry and Prose*, ed. Reiman and Fraistat, 2nd ed. (New York: Norton, 2002). Nahoko Alvey touches on the persistent motif of ruined cities in her readings of *Queen Mab*, "Mont Blanc," and *Prometheus Unbound* in *Strange Truths in Undiscovered Lands: Shelley's Poetic Development and Romantic Geography* (Toronto: University of Toronto Press, 2009).
6. Anne Janowitz, *England's Ruins: Poetic Purpose and the National Landscape* (Cambridge: Blackwell, 1990), 118.
7. Alan Bewell, *Romanticism and Colonial Disease* (Baltimore: Johns Hopkins University Press, 1999), 209, 217. Bewell's emphasis.
8. Percy Bysshe Shelley, *The Complete Works of Percy Bysshe Shelley*, ed. Ingpen and Peck, 10 vols. (New York: Charles Scribner's Sons, 1926–30), 7.22. In the absence of a complete standard critical edition of Shelley's prose, I cite Reiman and Fraistat's Norton edition for *A Defence of Poetry*, E. B. Murray's Oxford edition when possible, and the Julian edition for all other prose texts. All subsequent citations to this edition will be to this volume and will be cited internally by page number. Reiman determines Shelley most likely wrote the *View* between November 1819 and January 1820. See Donald H. Reiman, ed., *Shelley and His Circle, 1773–1822*, 8 vols. (Cambridge: Harvard University Press, 1973), 6.954.
9. Reiman and Fraistat, *Shelley's Poetry and Prose*, 530–31. All subsequent quotations from *A Defence of Poetry* will be cited internally by the page number to this edition.
10. Cited in Kenneth Neill Cameron, "Shelley, Cobbett, and the National Debt," *The Journal of English and German Philology* 42.2 (April 1943): 198.
11. Kevin Gilmartin, *Print Politics: The Press and Radical Opposition in Early Nineteenth-Century England* (Cambridge: Cambridge University Press, 1996), 61.
12. Donald H. Reiman, *Romantic Texts and Contexts* (Columbia: University of Missouri Press, 1987), 263. Reiman bases his argument heavily on the *View* and claims Shelley "ignored the Corn Laws" (263). Shelley does not discuss the Corn Laws in the *View*, but he hardly ignores them. In *The Mask of*

Anarchy, he begins his definition of "Freedom" (209) by saying, "For the labourer thou art bread" (217), a direct reference to the artificially high price of grain propped up by the Corn Laws. So too, Shelley pointedly refers to taxes on "bread" (177) in *Peter Bell the Third* and shows the urban denizens of "The Tower of Famine" (1820) "rave" for "bread" (*Works* 4.61–62).

13. "Disturbances at Manchester," *The Examiner* 608 (August 22, 1819), 529.
14. "Description of a Part of Manchester," *The Examiner* 609 (August 29, 1819), 558.
15. See Engels, *Condition of the Working Class*, 36–86. Engels refers to the "money aristocracy" (58), discusses "St. Giles" (39) and Manchester's "Irish Town" (66), and scorns "narrow self-seeking" as a "fundamental principle of our society everywhere" (37).
16. Cobbett, "Sussex Journal," 155. Cobbett's emphasis.
17. R. J. White, *Waterloo to Peterloo* (London: William Heinemann, 1957), 12.
18. White, *Waterloo to Peterloo*, 77, 184.
19. In *The London Hanged* Linebaugh shows that innovations in policing were inspired less by the growth of cities than by the realignment of class relations, though the two are interrelated. For a history of the evolution of policing in London, see Elaine A. Reynolds, *Before the Bobbies: The Night Watch and Police Reform in Metropolitan London, 1720–1830* (Stanford: Stanford University Press, 1998), especially 84–125.
20. Thompson, *English Working Class*, 608, 600.
21. See White, *Waterloo to Peterloo*, 130–31; Thompson, *English Working Class*, 608–10.
22. White, *Waterloo to Peterloo*, 121.
23. See White, *Waterloo to Peterloo*, 137–38; Thompson, *English Working Class*, 616.
24. Steven E. Jones, *Shelley's Satire: Violence, Exhortation, and Authority* (DeKalb: Northern Illinois University Press, 1994), 39.
25. Thomas Chalmers, *The Works of Thomas Chalmers* (Philadelphia: Hogan & Thompson, 1833), 348, 459.
26. White, *Waterloo to Peterloo*, 98.
27. Percy Bysshe Shelley, *The Letters of Percy Bysshe Shelley*, ed. Frederick L. Jones, 2 vols. (Oxford: Clarendon Press, 1964). 1.197. Letter to Thomas Charles Medwin, November 26, 1811. Shelley's emphasis. All quotations from Shelley's letters conform to the text in this collection and will be cited in the notes by addressee, date, and volume and page number.
28. Thompson, *English Working Class*, 676–77.
29. Donald Read, *Peterloo: The 'Massacre' and its Background* (Manchester: Manchester University Press, 1958), 3.

30. Kenneth Neill Cameron, *Shelley: The Golden Years* (Cambridge: Harvard University Press, 1974), 123.
31. See, for example, Mr. Brand's proposal in Commons to transfer "to those towns that were most populous and were not now represented" members from uninhabited but represented places such as "Gatton, St Mawes, Old Sarum," transcribed in "Imperial Parliament," *The Examiner* 126 (May 27, 1810), 324. See also Lord John Russell, *Speech of Lord John Russell in the House of Commons, On December 14th, 1819* (London: Longman, Hurst, Rees, Orme, 1820). Russell notes that before the reign of Charles the Second, the king would routinely relieve sparsely populated villages of the cost of sending a representative to Parliament and would invite representatives from towns as they rose in importance. Shelley's language in the *View* resembles that of Sir James Mackintosh's review of Lord Russell's speech in *Edinburgh Review* 34 (November 1820): 461–501. Mackintosh refers to "Lord Clarendon's commendation of the constitution of Cromwell's parliament, to which Manchester, Leeds and Halifax, then towns of moderate size, sent representatives" (473). Shelley read Clarendon's *History of the Rebellion and Civil Wars in England* from October 2 through November 9, 1819. See Mary Shelley, *The Journals of Mary Shelley, 1814–1844*, ed. Paula R. Feldman and Diana Scott-Kilvert (Baltimore: Johns Hopkins University Press, 1995), 654. Mackintosh notes that after the prerogative to enfranchise towns had fallen into disuse, "Villages have since sprung up into immense cities" (478). Shelley, however, stands securely on the radical side of the Whigs. He does not share Mackintosh's proposals that representation be "proportioned to their share of property" (478) or allotted on the basis of representing "interest[s]" (479).
32. On Edmund Burke's complex negotiation between the notion that each member of Parliament virtually represents the whole nation and that members can represent specific interests, see Hanna Fenichel Pitkin, *The Concept of Representation* (Berkeley: University of California Press, 1967), 168–89.
33. "On the Game Laws," in Percy Bysshe Shelley, *The Prose Works of Percy Bysshe Shelley*, ed. E. B. Murray (Oxford: Clarendon Press, 1993), 280.
34. Percy Bysshe Shelley, *The Mask of Anarchy Draft Notebooks: A Facsimile of Huntington Ms. HM 2177*, ed. Mary A. Quinn (New York: Garland Publishing, 1990), 85–87. Shelley sustains the figure of a revitalized necropolis in "Ode to Naples."
35. "Numerous large bodies of Reformers continued to arrive … from the different towns in the neighbourhood of Manchester, all with flags, and many of them drawn up five deep, and in regular marching order," "Dispersal of the Reform Meeting at Manchester by a Military Force," *The*

Examiner 608 (August 22, 1819), 539. The conservative press seized on the "flags and banners, and array and organization" as "overt acts of high treason"; see "Disturbances at Manchester and Matters Connected with Them," *The Examiner* 609 (August 29, 1819), 546.

36. Steven Goldsmith, *Unbuilding Jerusalem: Apocalypse and Romantic Representation* (Ithaca: Cornell University Press, 1993), 214, 215.
37. William Keach sees no contradiction between revolutionary and progressive impulses in Shelley in "Shelley and the Revolutionary Left," *Evaluating Shelley*, ed. Timothy Clark and Jerrold Hogle (Edinburgh: Edinburgh University Press, 1996), 75–90.
38. Fredric Jameson, *Valences of the Dialectic* (New York: Verso, 2009), 413, 415. Here Jameson gives an abstract of the argument in his *Archaeologies of the Future* (New York: Verso, 2005). Jameson uses an image of urban development as his example: "If we think of historically new forms of space – historically new forms of the city, for example – they might well offer new models for urbanists and in that sense constitute a kind of method" (410). The genealogy of Jameson's example and logic might include Shelley. Jameson quotes Brecht's *Hollywood Elegies*: "God / Requiring a heaven and a hell, didn't need to / Plan two establishments but / Just the one: heaven. It / Serves the unprosperous, unsuccessful / As hell" (410). Brecht likely owes the figure of infernal Hollywood in part to Shelley. Brecht translated *The Mask of Anarchy* and worked closely with Walter Benjamin, who planned to incorporate Shelley's allegory of Hell as London from *Peter Bell the Third* into his *Arcades Project*. On Shelley and Brecht, see Robert Kaufman, "Intervention and Commitment Forever! Shelley in 1819, Shelley in Brecht, Shelley in Adorno, Shelley in Benjamin," *Reading Shelley's Interventionist Poetry* ed. Michael Scrivener. May 2001. *Romantic Circles Praxis Series* 5 May 2010 www.rc.umd.edu/praxis/interventionist/kaufman/kaufman.html; Richard Cronin, *Shelley's Poetic Thoughts* (London: Macmillan, 1981), 42–43. See also Walter Benjamin, *The Arcades Project*, trans. Howard Eiland and Kevin McLaughlin (Cambridge: Harvard University Press, 2002), 351, 370, 449–50.
39. Hume affirms of causation "that the knowledge of this relation is not, in any instance, attained by reasonings *a priori*; but arises entirely from experience, when we find, that any particular objects are constantly conjoined with each other." David Hume, *An Enquiry Concerning Human Understanding*, ed. Eric Steinberg (Indianapolis: Hackett, 1993), 17. See also C. E. Pulos, *The Deep Truth* (Lincoln: University of Nebraska Press, 1962), 17–18. Where Hume seems comfortable relying on custom in the absence of sure knowledge, Shelley exploits the absence of sure knowledge as an inherent fracture in custom.
40. Jon Klancher, "Godwin and the Genre Reformers: On Necessity and Contingency in Romantic Narrative Theory," *Romanticism History, and the*

Possibilities of Genre: Re-forming Literature 1789–1837, ed. Tilottama Rajan and Julia M. Wright (Cambridge: Cambridge University Press, 2006), 29.

41. Jerome Christensen argues that Hume's principle of induction "naturaliz[es] power into a Newtonian force" and "impos[es] rule as if it were a natural necessity." What "'Hume calls a general rule,'" Christensen quotes from Deleuze, "'is an institution.'" Jerome Christensen, *Practicing Enlightenment: Hume and the Formation of a Literary Career* (Madison: University of Wisconsin Press, 1987), 42.
42. Goldsmith, *Unbuilding Jerusalem*, 222.
43. Shelley, *Prose*, 261.
44. Francis Bacon, *The New Organon*, ed. Lisa Jardine and Michael Silverthorne (Cambridge: Cambridge University Press, 2000), 46. Bacon's emphasis.
45. Stuart Curran, "Shelley and the End(s) of Ideology," in *The Most Unfailing Herald: Percy Bysshe Shelley 1792–1992*, ed. Alan M. Weinberg and Romaine Hill (Pretoria: Unisa Press, 1996), 24, 26. In his chapter on the *View*, Hogle describes Shelley's mode of social agency as "Transforming the verbal orders that configure thought" and "altering . . . the discourse systems or institutions that determine the way we now see our personal identities and social functions." *Shelley's Process: Radical Transference and the Development of His Major Works* (New York: Oxford University Press, 1998), 223.
46. Edward John Trelawny, *Records of Shelley, Byron, and the Author* (New York: New York Review of Books, 2000), 162.
47. Letter to Leigh Hunt, September 27, 1819, 2.121. Shelley's emphasis.
48. Kim Wheatley, *Shelley and His Readers: Beyond Paranoid Politics* (Columbia: University of Missouri Press, 1999), 3.
49. Chandler, *England in 1819*, 516–17.
50. Michael Warner, *Publics and Counterpublics* (New York: Zone Books, 2005), 14, 12.
51. Habermas, *Structural Transformation*, 185, 195. "Public opinion," Warner summarizes, "comes less to generate ideas and hold power accountable and more simply to register approval or disapproval." Warner, *Publics and Counterpublics*, 50.
52. Thompson, *English Working Class*, 677.
53. Klancher, *Transfiguring the Arts and Sciences*, 220. Klancher's emphasis.
54. Michael Henry Scrivener, *Radical Shelley* (Princeton: Princeton University Press, 1982), 222.
55. Richard Cronin, "Peter Bell, Peterloo, and the Politics of Cockney Poetry," *Percy Bysshe Shelley: Bicentenary Essays*, ed. Kelvin Everest (Cambridge: D.S. Brewer, 1992), 81.
56. Letter to Peacock, January 23–24, 1819, 2.75; Letter to Peacock, June 20–21?, 1819, 2.99.

57. Thompson, *English Working Class*, 627, 611. Thompson notes that "money-matters" and "vanity" (626) were sources of squabbles among radicals. Cobbett proposed in late 1819 and early 1820 to raise a fund of £5,000 for his own use. Thompson refers to this as a "politically discreditable incident" (699).
58. Paula R. Backscheider, *Spectacular Politics: Theatrical Power and Mass Culture in Early Modern England* (Baltimore: Johns Hopkins University Press, 1993), xi–xv.
59. G. M. Matthews, "A Volcano's Voice in Shelley," *ELH* 24.3 (September 1957): 191–228.
60. Cromwell attempted to demolish Pembroke Castle's towers with gunpowder after Pembroke turned for the Royalists. See E. Donovan, *Descriptive Excursions through South Wales and Monmouthshire*, 2 vols. (London: Rivingtons, 1805), 2.306–12. Gunpowder had also been used for demolition during the Great Fire and the Peninsular Campaign.
61. Thomas R. Edwards, *Imagination and Power: A Study of Poetry on Public Themes* (London: Chatto & Windus, 1971), 163–64.
62. Susan J. Wolfson, *Formal Charges: The Shaping of Poetry in British Romanticism* (Stanford: Stanford University Press, 1997), 195, 287. Wolfson notes that Mary Shelley "frankly conceded" that the poem "was not publishable in 1819" (288) in her note to the poem in Moxon's 1839 volume of Shelley's *Political Works*. Mary's notes notoriously sanitize Shelley's radicalism and should be read skeptically. And while Hunt's testimony is no more reliable than Mary's, he says in his preface to the 1832 edition of the *Mask* that he refrained from publishing it in 1819 not out of fear of prosecution but out of fear of its effect on the people: "I thought that the public at large had not become sufficiently discerning to do justice to the sincerity and kind-heartedness of the spirit that walked in this flaming robe of verse" (v). Percy Bysshe Shelley, *The Masque of Anarchy: A Poem* (London: Moxon, 1832).
63. Letter from Leigh Hunt to Percy Shelley, December 2, 1819. Reiman, ed., *Shelley and His Circle, 1773–1822*, 6.1090.
64. See Letter to the Editor of *The Examiner*, November 3, 1819, 2.142–43.
65. Letter to the Editor of *The Examiner*, November 3, 1819, 2.148.
66. Letter to Charles Ollier, September 6, 1819, 2.117.
67. Chandler, *England in 1819*, 31. Chandler's emphasis.
68. Critics less focused on textual agency have compared Shelley's revolutionary philosophy of history to Benjamin's concept of "*weak* messianic power." See Forest Pyle, "'Frail Spells': Shelley and the Ironies of Exile," in *Irony and Clerisy*, ed. Deborah White, *Romantic Circles Praxis Series*, paragraph 14; Marc Redfield, "Masks of Anarchy: Shelley's Political Politics," *Bucknell Review* 45.2 (2002): 102; see Walter Benjamin, *Illuminations*, trans. Harry Zohn (New York: Schocken, 2007), 254. Critics turn to Benjamin's *Theses on the Philosophy of History* because,

like Shelley, Benjamin describes a revolutionary event in apocalyptic discourse. Benjamin concurs with Shelley's sense that the revolutionary event is never total and may be sudden, unforeseen, and capable of creating a new understanding of the past that, in a sense, it redeems. Shelley, however, does not set the apocalypse against gradual progress, as Benjamin defines his notion of messianic intervention against the inclination toward progress in the Second and Third Internationals.

69. Forest Pyle, "'Frail Spells,'" paragraphs 16, 15.
70. Andrew Franta, "Shelley and the Poetics of Political Indirection," *Poetics Today* 22.4 (Winter 2001), 774, 782.
71. Seth T. Reno challenges celebrations of Shelley's supposed nonviolence in "The Violence of Form in Shelley's Mask of Anarchy," *Keats-Shelley Journal* 62 (2013): 80–98. Shelley allows the ends the possibility of justifying the means: "reversing the proverbial expression of Shakespeare, it may be the good which the Revolutionists did lives after them, their ills are interred with their bones" (*Works* 14). See Harry White, "Relative Means and Ends in Shelley's Social-Political Thought," *Studies in English Literature 1500–1900* 22.4 (1982): 613–31.
72. Letter to Thomas Love Peacock, September 9, 1819, 2.119.
73. Shelley's translation of the *Symposium* in James A. Notopoulos, *The Platonism of Shelley* (Durham: Duke University Press, 1949), 435.
74. Wolfson, *Formal Charges*, 197.
75. See Scrivener, *Radical Shelley*, 198–210; Jones, *Shelley's Satire*, 94–123.
76. Chandler, *England in 1819*, 529.
77. Kevin Gilmartin, "Hazlitt's Visionary London," in *Repossessing the Romantic Past*, ed. Heather Glen and Paul Hamilton (Cambridge: Cambridge University Press, 2006), 43.
78. Timothy Webb, *Shelley: A Voice not Understood* (Manchester: Manchester University Press, 1977), 89, 93.
79. Shelley asks about prospective publishers of a volume of popular political songs in a letter to Leigh Hunt, May 1, 1820, 2.191. Shelley's emphasis. Stephen C. Behrendt, *Shelley and His Audiences* (Lincoln: University of Nebraska Press, 1989), 191, 198.
80. Goldsmith, *Unbinding Jerusalem*, 241.
81. St. Clair, *Reading Nation*, 575. Philip Harling, "William Hazlitt and Radical Journalism," *Romanticism* 3.1 (April 1997), 53.
82. Jones, *Shelley's Satire*, 102. Jones's emphasis. Cronin, *Shelley's Poetic Thoughts*, 42.
83. Letter to Leigh Hunt, May 1, 1820, 2.191.
84. Goldsmith, *Unbinding Jerusalem*, 243.
85. Richard Cronin, "Shelley's Language of Dissent," *Essays in Criticism* 27 (1977): 203–15.

86. Letter to the Editor of *The Examiner*, November 3, 1819, 2.148. Shelley's emphasis.
87. Wheatley, *Shelley and His Readers*, 6. Wolfson suggests Shelley deflates poetry's pretension to act in politics by rendering both the oppressive triumph and the concluding revolutionary assembly as specimens of "political art" or "aesthetic spectacle." *Formal Charges*, 200–01.
88. Robert Kaufman, "Legislators of the Post-Everything World: Shelley's *Defence* of Adorno," *ELH* 63.3 (Fall 1996): 707–33. Kaufman notes a "degree of ambivalence" in Shelley's "attack" on reason (708). But much of the controversy evaporates if the *Defence* is read not as an attack on reason per se but a response to its exclusive preeminence in public thought and if the imagination is not read in terms of an ethereal, "inspirational and utopian" (708) or "escapist" (710) faculty.
89. Morton Paley, "Apocapolitics: Allusion and Structure in Shelley's *Mask of Anarchy,*" *Huntington Library Quarterly* 54.2 (Spring 1991): 92.

Chapter 5

1. See Pocock, *Virtue, Commerce, and History*; J. G. A. Pocock, *The Machiavellian Moment: Florentine Political Thought and the Atlantic Republican Tradition* (Princeton: Princeton University Press, [1975] 2003).
2. John Sekora, *Luxury: The Concept in Western Thought, Eden to Smollett* (Baltimore: Johns Hopkins University Press, 1977); Christopher J. Berry, *The Idea of Luxury* (Cambridge: Cambridge University Press, 1994).
3. On the classical concept of luxury, see Berry, *Idea of Luxury*, 45–86, and Sekora, *Luxury*, 29–39. As Sekora remarks, "aspects of change were inherent" in the classical concept of luxury (68).
4. Berry, *Idea of Luxury*, 101–25.
5. Hume, *Political Essays*, 105.
6. Hume, *Political Essays*, 111.
7. Hume, *Political Essays*, 95. Hume's emphasis.
8. Hume, *Political Essays*, 99.
9. The civic humanist concept of luxury always contained an Orientalist association of the East with debilitating idleness, sumptuousness, and despotism. But by associating luxury with productivity, Hume prepares for the remarkable inversion, recorded with historical precision in Makdisi's *Making England Western*, in which the threat to civilization is no longer the indulgent consumption of the rich but the idleness of the poor, who are Orientalized insofar as they are free from luxury.
10. Hume, *Political Essays*, 112.
11. Hume, *Political Essays*, 107.

12. Maxine Berg, *Luxury and Pleasure in Eighteenth-Century Britain* (Oxford: Oxford University Press, 2005), 35.
13. E. J. Clery, *The Feminization Debate in Eighteenth-Century England: Literature, Commerce and Luxury* (Basingstoke: Palgrave Macmillan, 2004), 1–12; see also Philip Carter, "An 'Effeminate' or 'Efficient' Nation? Masculinity and Eighteenth-Century Social Documentary," *Textual Practice* 11.3 (1997): 429–43; Davidoff and Hall, *Family Fortunes*, 111.
14. Russell, *Women, Sociability and Theatre*, 4, 3. Jane Rendell demonstrates how the formation of gendered spaces and gendered divisions of production and consumption inscribed traces of gender on Romantic-period London. *The Pursuit of Pleasure: Gender, Space & Architecture in Regency London* (New Brunswick: Rutgers University Press, 2002).
15. Harriet Guest, *Small Change: Women, Learning, Patriotism, 1750–1810* (Chicago: University of Chicago Press, 2000), 85.
16. Clery, *Feminization Debate*, 12.
17. Paula R. Backscheider, *Eighteenth-Century Women Poets and Their Poetry: Inventing Agency, Inventing Genre* (Baltimore: Johns Hopkins University Press, 2005), 29.
18. Stephen C. Behrendt, *British Women Poets and the Romantic Writing Community* (Baltimore: Johns Hopkins University Press, 2009), 18, 35.
19. Backscheider, *Women Poets*, 7.
20. See Diego Saglia, "The Dangers of Over-Refinement: The Language of Luxury in Romantic Poetry by Women, 1793–1811," *Studies in Romanticism* 38.4 (Winter 1999): 641–72, 644.
21. Backscheider, *Women Poets*, 9; Clery, *Feminization Debate*, 12.
22. Judith Pascoe, "The Spectacular Flâneuse: Mary Robinson and the City of London," *The Wordsworth Circle* 23.3 (Summer 1992), 169; Judith Pascoe, *Romantic Theatricality: Gender, Poetry, and Spectatorship* (Ithaca: Cornell University Press, 1997), 144, 150. The foundational scholarship on women's literary representations of the city circles around debates about the historical possibility of a flâneuse. See Janet Wolff, "The Invisible *Flâneuse*: Women and the Literature of Modernity," *Theory, Culture and Society* 2/3 (1985): 37–46; Griselda Pollock, "Modernity and the Spaces of Femininity," in *Vision and Difference: Femininity, Feminism and the Histories of Art* (London: Routledge, 1988), 50–90; Deborah Epstein Nord, *Walking the Victorian Streets: Women, Representation, and the City* (Ithaca: Cornell University Press, 1995); Deborah L. Parsons, *Streetwalking the Metropolis: Women, the City, and Modernity* (Oxford: Oxford University Press, 2000).
23. Pascoe, *Romantic Theatricality*, 156, 135–38, 169–70.
24. Diego Saglia, "Commerce, Luxury, and Identity in Mary Robinson's *Memoirs*," *SEL: Studies in English Literature 1500–1900* 49.3 (Summer 2009): 727.

25. Jon Klancher, "Discriminations, or Romantic Cosmopolitanisms in London," in *Romantic Metropolis*, ed. Chandler and Gilmartin, 69, 70. The republic of letters is a useful concept for analyzing Robinson primarily in terms of its structure of support for men and women of letters; cosmopolitan intellectual exchange and the advance of knowledge are not Robinson's focus.
26. On Robinson and the Della Cruscans, see Daniel Robinson, *The Poetry of Mary Robinson* (Basingstoke: Palgrave, 2011), 32–61.
27. See Robinson, *Poetry of Mary Robinson*, 31, 68; Robert S. Woof, "Wordsworth's Poetry and Stuart's Newspapers: 1797–1803," *Studies in Bibliography* 15 (1962): 172–74.
28. Mary Robinson, *Selected Poems*, ed. Judith Pascoe (Peterborough: Broadview, 2000), 54. Unless otherwise noted, all quotations from Robinson's works cited internally are from this edition.
29. Ashley J. Cross argues that Robinson's relation to the Lake Poets was "both competitive and nurturing" and conferred "the authority of Robinson's name to Wordsworth's and Coleridge's text." "From *Lyrical Ballads* to *Lyrical Tales*: Mary Robinson's Reputation and the Problem of Literary Debt," *Studies in Romanticism* 40.4 (Winter 2001), 584. But the Lake Poets already had valuable connections and were getting good reviews. There is no record of them mentioning Robinson when pitching and publicizing *Lyrical Ballads*.
30. "Newspapers, considered as poetical repositories, may be compared to pleasure-gardens badly kept; where more nettles appear than roses, and where a beautiful flower often loses the admiration to which it is entitled, in consequence of its being obscured by surrounding weeds. Hence newspaper poetry has sunk under one indiscriminate condemnation." "The Poetry of the World, Vols. III and IV [Review]," *Monthly Review, or Literary Journal* 6 (September 1791): 21.
31. Pascoe, *Romantic Theatricality*, 169–70; Robinson, *Poetry of Mary Robinson*, 18.
32. Chandler, *England in 1819*, 127.
33. Mary Robinson and Adriana Craciun, "Present State of the Manners, Society, Etc. Etc. of the Metropolis of England," *PMLA* 119.1 (January 2004): 108.
34. Harriet Guest, *Unbounded Attachment: Sentiment and Politics in the Age of the French Revolution* (Oxford: Oxford University Press, 2013), 64.
35. Mary Robinson, *A Letter to the Women of England and The Natural Daughter*, ed. Sharon Setzer (Peterborough: Broadview, 2003), 83.
36. Adriana Cracuin, *Fatal Women of Romanticism* (Cambridge: Cambridge University Press, 2003), 17.
37. See Gilmartin, *Print Politics*, 61.
38. Mary Robinson, *Memoirs of the Late Mrs. Robinson*, 4 vols. (London: R. Phillips, 1801), 3.19.
39. Saglia, "Commerce, Luxury, and Identity," 720.

40. Timothy Webb, "Listing the Busy Sounds: Anna Seward, Mary Robinson and the Poetic Challenge of the City," in *Romantic Women Poets: Genre and Gender*, ed. Lilla Maria Crisafulli and Cecilia Pietropoli (Amsterdam: Rodopi, 2007), 109.
41. Daniel E. White, "The 'Joineriana': Anna Barbauld, the Aikin Family Circle, and the Dissenting Public Sphere," *Eighteenth-Century Studies* 32.4 (Summer 1999): 511–33; Angela Keane, "The Market, the Public and the Female Author: Anna Laetitia Barbauld's Gift Economy," *Romanticism* 8.2 (July 2002): 161–78; Saglia, "The Dangers of Over-Refinement"; Kathryn Ready, "Dissenting Patriots: Anna Barbauld, John Aikin, and the Discourse of Eighteenth-Century Republicanism in Rational Dissent," *History of European Ideas* 38.4 (December 2012): 527–49.
42. Maggie Favretti, "The Politics of Vision: Anna Barbauld's 'Eighteen Hundred and Eleven'," in *Women's Poetry in the Enlightenment: The Making of a Canon, 1739–1820*, ed. Isobel Armstrong and Virginia Blain, (Basingstoke: Macmillan, 1999), 99.
43. Jon Mee, *Romanticism, Enthusiasm, and Regulation: Poetics and the Policing of Culture in the Romantic Period* (Oxford: Oxford University Press, 2003), 177, 210.
44. William McCarthy, *Anna Letitia Barbauld: Voice of the Enlightenment* (Baltimore: Johns Hopkins University Press, 2008), 53, quoting Francis Hutcheson, *A Short Introduction to Moral Philosophy* (Glasgow: Robert Foulis, 1747), 81.
45. Francis Hutcheson, *An Inquiry into the Original of Our Ideas of Beauty and Virtue* (London: J. Darby, 1726), 220, 219. Hutcheson's emphasis.
46. Hutcheson, *Short Introduction*, 321, 322.
47. Hutcheson, *Short Introduction*, 321.
48. Anne Janowitz, "Amiable and Radical Sociability: Mrs Barbauld and the Priestleys," in Gillian Russell and Clara Tuite, eds., *Romantic Sociability: Social Networks and Literary Culture in Britain, 1770–1840* (Cambridge: Cambridge University Press, 2002), 62–81.
49. Mee, *Romanticism, Enthusiasm, and Regulation*, 193.
50. See Keane, "The Market," 165; White, "'Joineriana'," 515.
51. Deirdre Coleman, "Firebrands, Letters and Flowers: Mrs Barbauld and the Priestleys," in Russell and Tuite, *Romantic Sociability*, 84. See William McCarthy, "'We Hoped the Woman Was Going to Appear': Repression, Desire and Gender in Anna Letitia Barbauld's Early Poems," in *Romantic Women Writers: Voices and Countervoices*, ed. Paula R. Feldman and Theresa M. Kelley (Hanover, NH: University Press of New England, 1995), 113–37.
52. Janowitz, "Amiable and Radical Sociability," 62.
53. Janowitz, "Amiable and Radical Sociability," 63.

54. Anna Letitia Barbauld, *Selected Poetry and Prose*, ed. William McCarthy and Elizabeth Kraft (Peterborough: Broadview, 2001). Line 1. Unless otherwise noted, all quotations from Barbauld's works cited internally are from this edition.
55. Backscheider observes that "women poets never find that Great Britain's gains [in war] balance the costs at home." *Women Poets*, 21. In *War at a Distance: Romanticism and the Making of Modern Wartime* (Princeton: Princeton University Press, 2010), Mary Favret touches on the weather imagery of *Eighteen Hundred and Eleven* but does not discuss Barbauld's incisive presentation and exploitation of the affective implications of mediation of war.
56. Suvir Kaul, *Poems of Nation, Anthems of Empire: English Verse in the Long Eighteenth Century* (Charlottesville: University Press of Virginia, 2000), 126.
57. Marlon Ross, *The Contours of Masculine Desire: Romanticism and the Rise of Women's Poetry* (Oxford: Oxford University Press, 1989), 224. Ross's emphasis.
58. Anna Letitia Barbauld, *A Legacy for Young Ladies* (London: Longman, 1826), 149.
59. Barbauld, *Legacy*, 126.
60. Barbauld, *Legacy*, 128.
61. See Chandler, *England in 1819*, 115–18. Chandler reads the essay as "Barbauld's attempt to explain to the Crokers of the world all that they failed to comprehend" about the poem (118). I read the essay as part defense and part apology. "Uses" defuses much of the tension of the poem's representation of abstract time and space.
62. Kaul, *Poems of Nation, Anthems of Empire*, 125.
63. Janowitz, "Amiable and Radical Sociability," 78.
64. Barbauld, *Selected Poetry and Prose*, 164.
65. Ready, "Dissenting Patriots," 541.
66. Kaul, *Poems of Nation, Anthems of Empire*, 124.
67. John Aikin, *Letters from a Father to His Son on Various Topics*, 2nd ed. (London: J. Johnson, 1794), 207–08.
68. Aikin, *Letters from a Father*, 212, 217. Aikin's emphasis.
69. William Keach, "A Regency Prophecy and the End of Anna Barbauld's Career," *Studies in Romanticism* 33.4 (Winter 1994): 574.
70. Linebaugh, *The London Hanged*, 409–41.
71. John Bugg, *Five Long Winters* (Stanford: Stanford University Press, 2014), 146–54.

Conclusion

1. Gilmartin, "Hazlitt's Visionary London," 40–62.
2. Edward Glaeser, *The Triumph of the City* (New York: Penguin, 2012), 204, 205.

3. Jonathan Bate, *Romantic Ecology: Wordsworth and the Environmental Tradition* (New York: Routledge, 1991), 4.
4. Gillen D'Arcy Wood, "Leigh Hunt's New Suburbia: An Eco-historical Study in Climate Poetics and Public Health," *Interdisciplinary Studies in Literature and Environment* 18.3 (Summer 2011): 527–52.
5. Cox, *Poetry and Politics in the Cockney School*, 97, 32.
6. Leigh Hunt, "On the Same [On Receiving a Crown of Ivy]" (1818), lines 12–14, in *The Selected Writings of Leigh Hunt*, ed. John Strachan, 6 vols. (Brookfield, VT: Pickering and Chatto, 2003), 5.231.
7. Robert E. Park, "The City: Suggestions for the Investigation of Human Behavior in the Urban Environment," in *The City* (Chicago: University of Chicago Press, 1967), 3.
8. Harvey, *Urban Experience*, 14. In an interview with Michael Schapira for *Full Stop*, Harvey says, "early on I went through my Romantic phase and had great affection for these figures. I got immersed in Keats and Shelley, never took to Byron that much, but Wordsworth to some degree. I think there's a strain of it in Marx; particularly in the early writings you see more of this Romanticist thinking. And it never really goes away. For instance, how can you really talk about notions of alienation without invoking some sense of dispossession and loss, and this search to regain an un-alienated existence? Now there is the big question of whether [such an existence] ever really existed. So if the political project from a Marxist standpoint is to recuperate some kind of un-alienated world of laboring and socializing and so on, then it seems to me that it's very hard to do that without taking some threads from the Romantics as to what might be possible." www.full-stop.net/2012/05/01/interviews/michael-schapira-and-david-backer/david-harvey/.
9. Benjamin, *The Arcades Project*, 231, 968.
10. Williams, *The Country and the City*, 5.

Bibliography

Ackroyd, Peter, *Blake* (New York: Alfred A. Knopf, 1996)

Agathocleous, Tanya, "Wordsworth at the Panoramas: The Sublime Spectacle of the World," *Genre* 36.3–4 (Fall–Winter 2003), 295–315

Aikin, John, *Letters from a Father to His Son on Various Topics*, 2nd ed. (London: J. Johnson, 1794)

Alter, Robert, *Imagined Cities: Urban Experience and the Language of the Novel* (New Haven: Yale University Press, 2005)

Altick, Richard D., *The Shows of London* (Cambridge: Harvard University Press, 1978)

Alvey, Nahoko, *Strange Truths in Undiscovered Lands: Shelley's Poetic Development and Romantic Geography* (Toronto: University of Toronto Press, 2009)

Ames, Dianne S., "Gay's 'Trivia' and the Art of Allusion," *Studies in Philology* 75.2 (Spring 1978), 199–222

Armens, Sven, *John Gay: Social Critic* (New York: Octagon, 1954)

Backscheider, Paula R., *Eighteenth-Century Women Poets and Their Poetry: Inventing Agency, Inventing Genre* (Baltimore: Johns Hopkins University Press, 2005)

Spectacular Politics: Theatrical Power and Mass Culture in Early Modern England (Baltimore: Johns Hopkins University Press, 1993)

Bacon, Francis, *The New Organon*, ed. Lisa Jardine and Michael Silverthorne (Cambridge: Cambridge University Press, 2000)

Barbauld, Anna Letitia, *A Legacy for Young Ladies* (London: Longman, 1826)

Selected Poetry and Prose, ed. William McCarthy and Elizabeth Kraft (Peterborough: Broadview, 2001)

Barker-Benfield, G. J., "Sensibility," in Iain McCalman, ed., *An Oxford Companion to the Romantic Age* (Oxford: Oxford University Press, 2001), pp. 102–14

Barrell, John, "London in the 1790s," in James Chandler, ed., *The Cambridge History of English Romantic Literature* (Cambridge: Cambridge University Press, 2009), pp. 127–58

Barrell, John and Harriet Guest, "On the Use of Contradiction: Economics and Morality in the Eighteenth-Century Long Poem," in Felicity Nussbaum and Laura Brown, eds., *The New Eighteenth Century: Theory, Politics, English Literature* (New York: Methuen, 1987), pp. 121–43

Bate, Jonathan, *Romantic Ecology: Wordsworth and the Environmental Tradition* (New York: Routledge, 1991)

Behrendt, Stephen C., *British Women Poets and the Romantic Writing Community* (Baltimore: Johns Hopkins University Press, 2009)

Shelley and His Audiences (Lincoln: University of Nebraska Press, 1989)

Benjamin, Walter, *The Arcades Project*, trans. Howard Eiland and Kevin McLaughlin (Cambridge: Harvard University Press, 2002)

Illuminations, trans. Harry Zohn (New York: Schocken, 2007)

Berg, Maxine, *Luxury and Pleasure in Eighteenth-Century Britain* (Oxford: Oxford University Press, 2005)

Berman, Marshall, *All That Is Solid Melts into Air: The Experience of Modernity* (New York: Penguin, 1988)

Berry, Christopher J., *The Idea of Luxury* (Cambridge: Cambridge University Press, 1994)

Bewell, Alan, *Romanticism and Colonial Disease* (Baltimore: Johns Hopkins University Press, 1999)

Wordsworth and the Enlightenment: Nature, Man, and Society in the Experimental Poetry (New Haven: Yale University Press, 1989)

Black, Jeremy, *The English Press in the Eighteenth Century* (London: Croom Helm, 1987)

Blake, William, *The Complete Poetry and Prose of William Blake*, ed. David V. Erdman, commentary Harold Bloom, rev. ed. (New York: Anchor, 1988)

Borsay, Peter, *The English Urban Renaissance: Culture and Society in the Provincial Town 1660–1770* (Oxford: Clarendon Press, 1989)

Bourdieu, Pierre, *Distinction: A Social Critique of the Judgement of Taste*, trans. Richard Nice (Cambridge: Harvard University Press, 1984)

Rules of Art, trans. Susan Emanuel (Stanford: Stanford University Press, 1992)

Boyson, Rowan, *Wordsworth and the Enlightenment Idea of Pleasure* (Cambridge: Cambridge University Press, 2012)

Brant, Clare, "Artless and Artful: John Gay's *Trivia*," in Clare Brant and Susan E. Whyman, eds., *Walking the Streets of Eighteenth-Century London: John Gay's* Trivia (Oxford: Oxford University Press, 2007), pp. 105–19

Brewer, John, *The Pleasures of the Imagination* (Chicago: University of Chicago Press, 1997)

"Sensibility and the Urban Panorama," *Huntington Library Quarterly* 70.2 (June 2007), 229–49

Bronowski, Jacob, *William Blake: Man without a Mask* (London: Secker and Warburg, 1947)

Brown, Marshall, *Preromanticism* (Stanford: Stanford University Press, 1991)

Bugg, John, *Five Long Winters* (Stanford: Stanford University Press, 2014)

Burke, Edmund, *The Correspondence of Edmund Burke, Vol VII*, eds. P. J. Marshall and John A. Woods (Cambridge: Cambridge University Press, 1968)

Bushell, Sally, "The Mapping of Meaning in Wordsworth's 'Michael': (Textual Place, Textual Space and Spatialized Speech Acts)," *Studies in Romanticism* 49.1 (Spring 2010), 43–78

Butler, Marilyn, *Mapping Mythologies: Countercurrents in Eighteenth-Century British Poetry and Cultural History* (Cambridge: Cambridge University Press, 2015)

Byrd, Max, *London Transformed* (New Haven: Yale University Press, 1977)

Visits to Bedlam: Madness and Literature in the Eighteenth Century (Columbia: University of South Carolina Press, 1974)

Cameron, Kenneth Neill, "Shelley, Cobbett, and the National Debt," *The Journal of English and German Philology* 42.2 (April 1943), 197–209

Shelley: The Golden Years (Cambridge: Harvard University Press, 1974)

Carter, Philip, "An 'Effeminate' or 'Efficient' Nation? Masculinity and Eighteenth-Century Social Documentary," *Textual Practice* 11.3 (1997), 29–43

"Faces and Crowds: Biography in the City," in Clare Brant and Susan E. Whyman, eds., *Walking the Streets of Eighteenth-Century London: John Gay's* Trivia (Oxford: Oxford University Press, 2007), pp. 27–42

Castells, Manuel, *The Urban Question: A Marxist Approach*, trans. Alan Sheridan (London: Edward Arnold, 1977)

Chalker, John, *The English Georgic: A Study in the Development of a Form* (London: Routledge, 1969)

Chalmers, Thomas, *The Works of Thomas Chalmers* (Philadelphia: Hogan & Thompson, 1833)

Chandler, James K., *England in 1819* (Chicago: University of Chicago Press, 1998)

"Introduction," in James K. Chandler, ed., *The Cambridge History of English Romantic Literature* (Cambridge: Cambridge University Press, 2009), pp. 1–18

Chandler, James K. and Kevin Gilmartin, eds., *Romantic Metropolis: The Urban Scene of British Culture, 1780–1840* (Cambridge: Cambridge University Press, 2005)

Christensen, Jerome, *Coleridge's Blessed Machine of Language* (Ithaca: Cornell University Press, 1981)

Practicing Enlightenment: Hume and the Formation of a Literary Career (Madison: University of Wisconsin Press, 1987)

Clark, Peter, *British Clubs and Societies 1580–1800: The Origins of an Associational World* (Oxford: Clarendon Press, 2000)

Clery, E. J., *The Feminization Debate in Eighteenth-Century England: Literature, Commerce and Luxury* (Basingstoke: Palgrave Macmillan, 2004)

Cobbett, William, *Rural Rides*, ed. Ian Dyck (London: Penguin, 2001)

"Summary of Politics," *Cobbett's Political Register* 19.20 (March 9, 1811), 577–91

"Sussex Journal," *Cobbett's Weekly Register* 41.3 (January 18, 1822), 154–88

Coleman, Deirdre, "Firebrands, Letters and Flowers: Mrs Barbauld and the Priestleys," in *Romantic Sociability: Social Networks and Literary Culture in Britain, 1770–1840* (Cambridge: Cambridge University Press, 2002), pp. 83–103

Coleridge, Samuel Taylor, *Biographia Literaria*, ed. James Engell and W. Jackson Bate, 2 vols. (Princeton: Princeton University Press, 1983)

Collected Letters of Samuel Taylor Coleridge, ed. Earl Leslie Griggs, 5 vols. (Oxford: Clarendon Press, 1956)

Essays on His Times, ed. David V. Erdman, 3 vols. (Princeton: Princeton University Press, 1978)

The Friend, ed. Barbara E. Rooke, 2 vols. (Princeton: Princeton University Press, 1969)

Lay Sermons, ed. R. J. White (Princeton: Princeton University Press, 1972)

Lectures 1795 on Politics and Religion, ed. Lewis Patton and Peter Mann (Princeton: Princeton University Press, 1971)

Lectures 1808–1819 on Literature, ed. R. A. Foakes, 2 vols. (Princeton: Princeton University Press, 1987)

On the Constitution of the Church and State, ed. John Colmer (Princeton: Princeton University Press, 1976)

Poetical Works I: Poems (Reading Text): Part I, ed. J. C. C. Mays (Princeton: Princeton University Press, 2001)

Table Talk, ed. Carl Woodring, 2 vols. (Princeton: Princeton University Press, 1991)

The Watchman, ed. Lewis Patton (Princeton: Princeton University Press, 1970)

Colmer, John, *Coleridge: Critic of Society* (Oxford: Clarendon Press, 1967)

Copley, Stephen and Ian Haywood, "Luxury, Refuse and Poetry: John Gay's *Trivia*," in Peter Lewis and Nigel Woods, eds., *John Gay and the Scriblerians* (New York: St. Martin's Press, 1989), pp. 62–82

Corrigan, Timothy, *Coleridge, Language, and Criticism* (Athens: University of Georgia Press, 1982)

Cowper, William, *The Letters and Prose Writings of William Cowper*, ed. James King and Charles Ryskamp, 4 vols. (New York: Oxford University Press, 1979–84)

Memoir of the Early Life of William Cowper, Esq. (London: R. Edwards, 1816)

The Poems of William Cowper, eds. John D. Baird and Charles Ryskamp, 3 vols. (Oxford: Clarendon Press, 1980–95)

Cox, Jeffrey N., *Poetry and Politics in the Cockney School: Keats, Shelley, Hunt and Their Circle* (Cambridge: Cambridge University Press, 1998)

Craciun, Adriana, *Fatal Women of Romanticism* (Cambridge: Cambridge University Press, 2003)

Cranfield, Geoffrey Alan, *The Development of the Provincial Newspaper, 1700–1760* (Oxford: Clarendon Press, 1962)

Cronin, Richard, "Peter Bell, Peterloo, and the Politics of Cockney Poetry," in Kelvin Everest, ed., *Percy Bysshe Shelley: Bicentenary Essays* (Cambridge: D.S. Brewer, 1992), pp. 62–87

"Shelley's Language of Dissent," *Essays in Criticism* 27 (1977), 203–15

Shelley's Poetic Thoughts (London: Macmillan, 1981)

Cross, Ashley J., "From *Lyrical Ballads* to *Lyrical Tales*: Mary Robinson's Reputation and the Problem of Literary Debt," *Studies in Romanticism* 40.4 (Winter 2001), 571–605

Curran, Stuart, *Poetic Form and British Romanticism* (New York: Oxford University Press, 1986)

"Shelley and the End(s) of Ideology," in Alan M. Weinberg and Romaine Hill, eds., *The Most Unfailing Herald: Percy Bysshe Shelley 1792–1992* (Pretoria: Unisa Press, 1996), pp. 21–30

Dart, Gregory, *Metropolitan Art and Literature, 1810–1840: Cockney Adventures* (Cambridge: Cambridge University Press, 2012)

"Preface: Re-imagining the City," *Romanticism* 14.2 (July 2008), v–vi

Daunton, M. J., *Progress and Poverty: An Economic and Social History of Britain 1700–1850* (Oxford: Oxford University Press, 1995)

Davenant, William, *Sir William Davenant's Gondibert*, ed. David F. Gladish (Oxford: Clarendon Press, 1971)

Davidoff, Leonore, and Catherine Hall, *Family Fortunes: Men and Women of the English Middle Class, 1780–1850* (London: Hutchison, 1987)

Davies, Hugh Sykes, "Wordsworth and the Empirical Philosophers," in Hugh Sykes Davies and George Watson, eds., *The English Mind: Studies in the English Moralists Presented to Basil Willey* (Cambridge: Cambridge University Press, 1964), pp. 153–74

Deleuze, Gilles and Felix Guattari, *A Thousand Plateaus: Capitalism and Schizophrenia*, trans. Brian Massumi (Minneapolis: University of Minnesota Press, 1987)

De Vries, Jan, *European Urbanization, 1500–1800* (London: Routledge, 2007)

Dickinson, H. T., "Radical Culture," in Celina Fox, ed., *London – World City, 1800–1840* (New Haven: Yale University Press, 1992), pp. 209–24

Donovan, E., *Descriptive Excursions through South Wales and Monmouthshire*, 2 vols. (London: Rivingtons, 1805)

Downie, J. A., "Gay's Politics," in Peter Lewis and Nigel Woods, eds., *John Gay and the Scriblerians* (New York: St. Martin's Press, 1989), pp. 44–61

Dryden, John, *The Works of John Dryden*, ed. Edward Niles Hooker and H. T. Swedenberg, vol. 1 (Berkeley: University of California Press, 1956)

Dugaw, Dianne, *"Deep Play" – John Gay and the Invention of Modernity* (Newark: University of Delaware Press, 2001)

Duncan, Ian, *Scott's Shadow: The Novel in Romantic Edinburgh* (Princeton: Princeton University Press, 2007)

Edwards, Gavin, "'Mind-Forg'd Manacles': A Contribution to the Discussion of Blake's 'London,'" *Literature & History* 5 (1979), 87–105

Edwards, Thomas R., *Imagination and Power: A Study of Poetry on Public Themes* (London: Chatto & Windus, 1971)

Ellis, Markman, "Poetry and the City," in Christine Gerard, ed., *A Companion to Eighteenth-Century Poetry* (Oxford: Blackwell, 2006), pp. 534–48

Ellison, Julie K., "News, Blues, and Cowper's Busy World," *Modern Language Quarterly* 62.3 (September 2001), 219–37

Engels, Friedrich, *The Condition of the Working Class in England*, ed. David McLellan (Oxford: Oxford University Press, 2009)

Erdman, David V., *Blake: Prophet against Empire* (Princeton: Princeton University Press, 1977)

Evans, John and John Corry, *The History of Bristol, Civil and Ecclesiastical*, 2 vols. (Bristol: W Sheppard, 1816)

Everest, Kelvin, *Coleridge's Secret Ministry: The Context of the Conversation Poems 1795–1798* (New York: Barnes & Noble, 1979)

Faubert, Michelle, "Nerve Theory, Sensibility, and Romantic Metrosexuals," in Larry H. Peer, ed., *Romanticism and the City* (New York: Palgrave Macmillan, 2011), pp. 9–24

Favret, Mary, *War at a Distance: Romanticism and the Making of Modern Wartime* (Princeton: Princeton University Press, 2010)

Favretti, Maggie, "The Politics of Vision: Anna Barbauld's 'Eighteen Hundred and Eleven,'" in Isobel Armstrong and Virginia Blain, eds., *Women's Poetry in the Enlightenment: The Making of a Canon, 1739–1820* (Basingstoke: Macmillan, 1999), pp. 99–110

Feather, John, *The Provincial Book Trade in Eighteenth-Century England* (Cambridge: Cambridge University Press, 1985)

Feingold, Richard, *Nature and Society: Later Eighteenth-Century Uses of the Pastoral and Georgic* (New Brunswick: Rutgers University Press, 1978)

Ferber, Michael, "'London' and Its Politics," *ELH* 48.2 (Summer 1981), 310–38

Ferguson, Adam, *An Essay on the History of Civil Society*, ed. Fania Oz-Salzberger (Cambridge: Cambridge University Press, 1995)

Fielding, Penny, *Scotland and the Fictions of Geography, North Britain, 1760–1830* (Cambridge: Cambridge University Press, 2008)

Fischer, Claude S., *The Urban Experience* (New York: Harcourt Brace Jovanovich, 1976)

Franta, Andrew, "Shelley and the Poetics of Political Indirection," *Poetics Today* 22.4 (Winter 2001), 765–93

Fry, Paul H., "The Diligence of Desire: Critics on and around Westminster Bridge," *The Wordsworth Circle* 23.3 (Summer 1992), 162–64

"Time to Retire? Coleridge and Wordsworth Go to Work," *The Wordsworth Circle* 41.1 (Winter 2010), 23–29

Fulford, Tim, *Landscape, Liberty and Authority* (Cambridge: Cambridge University Press, 1996)

The Late Poetry of the Lake Poets (Cambridge: Cambridge University Press, 2013)

Gassenmeier, Michael and Jens Martin Gurr, "The Experience of the City in British Romantic Poetry," in Angela Esterhammer, ed., *Romantic Poetry* (Philadelphia: John Benjamins, 2002), pp. 319–22

Gatrell, Vic, *City of Laughter: Sex and Satire in Eighteenth-Century London* (New York: Walker & Co., 2007)

Gay, John, *Poetry and Prose of John Gay*, ed. Vinton A. Dearing with Charles E. Beckwith, 2 vols. (Oxford: Clarendon Press, 1974)

Giddens, Anthony, *The Consequences of Modernity* (Stanford: Stanford University Press, 1990)

Gilchrist, Alexander, *The Life of William Blake*, ed. W. Graham Robertson (London: John Lane the Bodley Head, 1922)

Gill, Stephen, *William Wordsworth: A Life* (Oxford: Clarendon Press, 1989)

Gilmartin, Kevin, "Hazlitt's Visionary London," in Heather Glen and Paul Hamilton, eds., *Repossessing the Romantic Past* (Cambridge: Cambridge University Press, 2006), pp. 40–62

Print Politics (Cambridge: Cambridge University Press, 1996)

"The 'Sinking Down' of Jacobinism and the Rise of the Counter-revolutionary Man of Letters," in Philip Connell and Nigel Leask, eds., *Romanticism and Popular Culture in Britain and Ireland* (Cambridge: Cambridge University Press, 2009), pp. 128–47.

William Hazlitt: Political Essayist (Oxford: Oxford University Press, 2015)

Glaeser, Edward, *The Triumph of the City* (New York: Penguin, 2011)

Glen, Heather, "The Poet in Society: Blake and Wordsworth on London," *Literature and History* 3 (1976), 2–28

Goodman, Kevis, *Georgic Modernity and British Romanticism: Poetry and the Mediation of History* (Cambridge: Cambridge University Press, 2004)

Goldsmith, Steven, *Unbuilding Jerusalem: Apocalypse and Romantic Representation* (Ithaca: Cornell University Press, 1993)

Graver, Bruce, "Wordsworth's Georgic Pastoral: *Otium* and *Labor* in 'Michael,'" *European Romantic Review* 1.2 (1991), 119–34

Gregori, Flavio, "The 'Audacious' Art of Walking: The Metropolis and the Proto-Flâneur in John Gay's *Trivia*," *South Atlantic Review* 70.1 (Winter 2005), 71–96

Griffin, Dustin, "Redefining Georgic: Cowper's *Task*," *ELH* 57.4 (Winter 1990), 865–79

Guest, Harriet, *Small Change: Women, Learning, Patriotism, 1750–1810* (Chicago: University of Chicago Press, 2000)

Unbounded Attachment: Sentiment and Politics in the Age of the French Revolution (Oxford: Oxford University Press, 2013)

Guillory, John, *Cultural Capital: The Problem of Literary Canon Formation* (Chicago: University of Chicago Press, 1994)

Gurr, Jens Martin and Berit Michel, eds., *Romantic Cityscapes: Selected Papers from the Essen Conference of the German Society for English Romanticism* (Trier: WVT, 2013)

Habermas, Jürgen, *The Structural Transformation of the Public Sphere*, trans. Thomas Burger (Cambridge: MIT Press, 1991)

Haggarty, Sarah, *Blake's Gifts: Poetry and the Politics of Exchange* (Cambridge: Cambridge University Press, 2009)

Hammond, Brean, "The City in Eighteenth-Century Poetry," in John Sitter, ed., *The Cambridge Companion to Eighteenth-Century Poetry* (Cambridge: Cambridge University Press, 2001), pp. 84–103

Harling, Philip, "William Hazlitt and Radical Journalism," *Romanticism* 3.1 (April 1997), 53–65

Harris, Tim, "Perceptions of the Crowd in Later Stuart London," in J. F. Merritt, ed., *Imagining Early Modern London: Perceptions and Portrayals of the City from Stow to Strype, 1598–1720* (Cambridge: Cambridge University Press, 2001), pp. 250–72

Hartley, David, *Observations on Man, His Frame, His Duty, and His Expectations*, 2 vols. (London: S. Richardson, 1749)

Harvey, David, *The Condition of Postmodernity* (Oxford: Basil Blackwell, 1989)

Interview with David Schapira and David Backer, *Full Stop*, May 1, 2012, www.full-stop.net/2012/05/01/interviews/michael-schapira-and-david-backer/david-harvey/

The Limits to Capital (New York: Verso, 2006)

Spaces of Hope (Berkeley: University of California Press, 2000)

The Urban Experience (Baltimore: Johns Hopkins University Press, 1989)

The Urbanization of Capital (London: Basil Blackwell, 1985)

Heffernan, James A. W., "Wordsworth's London: The Imperial Monster," *Studies in Romanticism* 37.3 (Fall 1998), 421–43

Hetherington, Kevin, *Badlands of Modernity: Heterotopia and Social Ordering* (London: Routledge, 1997)

Hogle, Jerrold, *Shelley's Process: Radical Transference and the Development of His Major Works* (New York: Oxford University Press, 1998)

Holmes, Richard, *Coleridge: Darker Reflections* (New York: Pantheon Books, 1998)

Coleridge: Early Visions (London: Hodder & Stoughton, 1989)

Hull, Simon, *Charles Lamb, Elia and the London Magazine: Metropolitan Muse* (London: Pickering and Chatto, 2010)

Hume, David, *An Enquiry Concerning Human Understanding*, ed. Eric Steinberg (Indianapolis: Hackett, 1993)

Political Essays, ed. Knud Haakonssen (Cambridge: Cambridge University Press, 2006)

A Treatise of Human Nature, ed. L. A. Selby-Bigge, rev. P. H. Nidditch, 2nd ed. (Oxford: Clarendon Press, 1978)

Hunt, Leigh, *The Selected Writings of Leigh Hunt*, ed. John Strachan, 6 vols. (Brookfield, VT: Pickering and Chatto, 2003)

Hutcheson, Francis, *An Inquiry into the Original of Our Ideas of Beauty and Virtue* (London: J. Darby, 1726)

A Short Introduction to Moral Philosophy (Glasgow: Robert Foulis, 1747)

Ibbetson, Julius Caesar et al., *A Picturesque Guide to Bath, Bristol Hot-Wells, the River Avon and the Adjacent Country* (London: Hookham and Carpenter, 1793)

Jameson, Fredric, *Archaeologies of the Future* (New York: Verso, 2005)

"Postmodernism, or The Cultural Logic of Late Capitalism," *New Left Review* 146 (July–August 1984), 53–92

Valences of the Dialectic (New York: Verso, 2009)

Janowitz, Anne, "Amiable and Radical Sociability: Mrs Barbauld and the Priestleys," in Gillian Russell and Clara Tuite, eds., *Romantic Sociability: Social Networks and Literary Culture in Britain, 1770–1840* (Cambridge: Cambridge University Press, 2002), pp. 62–81

England's Ruins: Poetic Purpose and the National Landscape (Cambridge: Blackwell, 1990)

Jarvis, Simon, *Wordsworth's Philosophic Song* (Cambridge: Cambridge University Press, 2007)

Jay, Mike, *The Atmosphere of Heaven: The Unnatural Experiments of Dr Beddoes and His Sons of Genius* (New Haven: Yale University Press, 2009)

Johnson, Samuel, *The Poems of Samuel Johnson*, ed. David Nichol Smith and Edward L. McAdam (Oxford: Clarendon Press, 1951)

Johnston, Kenneth R., "Blake's Cities: Romantic Forms of Urban Renewal," in David V. Erdman and John E. Grant, eds., *Blake's Visionary Forms Dramatic* (Princeton: Princeton University Press, 1970), pp. 413–42

The Hidden Wordsworth (New York: W. W. Norton, 1998)

Jones, Jennifer J., "Absorbing Hesitation: Wordsworth and the Theory of the Panorama," *Studies in Romanticism* 45.3 (Fall 2006), 357–75

Jones, Mark, "Double Economics: Ambivalence in Wordsworth's Pastoral," *PMLA* 108.5 (October 1993), 1098–113

Jones, Steven E., *Shelley's Satire: Violence, Exhortation, and Authority* (DeKalb: Northern Illinois University Press, 1994)

Joyce, Simon, *Capital Offenses: Geographies of Class and Crime in Victorian London* (Charlottesville: University of Virginia Press, 2003)

Kant, Immanuel, *Critik der reinen Vernunft* (Riga: Verlegts J.F. Hartknoch, 1781)

Critique of Pure Reason, trans. Paul Guyer and Allen W. Wood (New York: Cambridge University Press, 1998)

Critique of Pure Reason, trans. Norman Kemp Smith (New York: St. Martin's Press, 1963)

Kaufman, Robert, "Intervention and Commitment Forever! Shelley in 1819, Shelley in Brecht, Shelley in Adorno, Shelley in Benjamin," in Michael Scrivener, ed., "Reading Shelley's Interventionist Poetry," *Romantic Circles Praxis Series*, May 2001

"Legislators of the Post-everything World: Shelley's *Defence* of Adorno," *ELH* 63.3 (Fall 1996), 707–33

Kaul, Suvir, *Poems of Nation, Anthems of Empire: English Verse in the Long Eighteenth Century* (Charlottesville: University Press of Virginia, 2000)

Keach, William, "A Regency Prophecy and the End of Anna Barbauld's Career," *Studies in Romanticism* 33.4 (Winter 1994), 569–77

"Shelley and the Revolutionary Left," in Timothy Clark and Jerrold Hogle eds., *Evaluating Shelley* (Edinburgh: Edinburgh University Press, 1996), pp. 75–90

Keane, Angela, "The Market, the Public and the Female Author: Anna Laetitia Barbauld's Gift Economy," *Romanticism* 8.2 (July 2002), 161–78

King, James, *William Cowper: A Biography* (Durham: Duke University Press, 1986)

King, Ross, "Wordsworth, Panoramas, and the Prospect of London," *Studies in Romanticism* 32.1 (Spring 1993), 57–73

Kitson, Peter J., "Coleridge's Bristol and West Country Radicalism," in Nicholas Roe, ed., *English Romantic Writers and the West Country* (London: Palgrave Macmillan, 2010), pp. 115–28

Klancher, Jon, "Discriminations, or Romantic Cosmopolitanisms in London," in Chandler and Gilmartin, eds., *Romantic Metropolis* (Cambridge: Cambridge University Press, 2005), pp. 65–82

"Godwin and the Genre Reformers: On Necessity and Contingency in Romantic Narrative Theory," in Tilottama Rajan and Julia M. Wright, eds., *Romanticism History, and the Possibilities of Genre: Re-forming Literature 1789–1837* (Cambridge: Cambridge University Press, 2006), pp. 21–38

The Making of English Reading Audiences (Madison: University of Wisconsin Press, 1987)

Transfiguring the Arts and Sciences: Knowledge and Cultural Institutions in the Romantic Age (Cambridge: Cambridge University Press, 2013)

Kroeber, Karl, "Experience as History: Shelley's Venice, Turner's Carthage," *ELH* 41.3 (Autumn 1974), 321–39

Lamb, Charles and Mary Lamb, *The Letters of Charles and Mary Anne Lamb*, ed. Edwin W. Marrs, Jr., 3 vols. (Ithaca: Cornell University Press, 1975–78)

Landau, Leya, "The Metropolis and Women Novelists in the Romantic Period," *Romanticism* 14.2 (June 2008), 119–32

Laqueur, Thomas Walter, *Religion and Respectability: Sunday Schools and Working Class Culture 1780–1850* (New Haven: Yale University Press, 1976)

Lea, Sydney, "Wordsworth and His 'Michael': The Pastor Passes," *ELH* 45.1 (Spring 1978), 55–68

Leask, Nigel, *Politics of Imagination in Coleridge's Critical Thought* (Basingstoke: Macmillan 1988)

Lefebvre, Henri, *The Production of Space*, trans. Donald Nicholson-Smith (Oxford: Blackwell, 2009)

The Urban Revolution, trans. Robert Bononno (Minneapolis: University of Minnesota Press, 2003)

Levinson, Marjorie, *Wordsworth's Great Period Poems* (Cambridge: Cambridge University Press, 1986)

Linebaugh, Peter, *The London Hanged* (London: Verso, 2006)

Liu, Alan, *Wordsworth: Sense of History* (Stanford: Stanford University Press, 1989)

Locke, John, *An Essay Concerning Human Understanding*, ed. Peter H. Nidditch (Oxford: Oxford University Press, 1975)

Lovell, Robert, *Bristol: A Satire* (London, 1794)

Low, Donald, *Thieves' Kitchen: The Regency Underworld* (London: J. M. Dent, 1982)

Lucretius, *The Way Things Are: The De Rerum Natura of Titus Lucretius Carus*, trans. Rolfe Humphries (Bloomington: Indiana University Press, 1968)

Lynch, Deidre, "On Going Steady with Novels," The Eighteenth Century 50.2–3 (Summer/Fall 2009), 207–19

Mackintosh, James, "Speech of Lord John Russell in the House of Commons on the 14th Dec. 1819, for transferring the Elective Franchise from Corrupt Boroughs to Unrepresented Great Towns," *Edinburgh Review* 34 (1820), 461–501

MacLean, Gerald, Donna Landry, and Joseph P. Ward, eds., *The Country and the City Revisited: England and the Politics of Culture, 1550–1850* (Cambridge: Cambridge University Press, 1999)

MacLennan, George, *Lucid Interval: Subjective Writing and Madness in History* (Leicester: Leicester University Press, 1992)

Magnuson, Paul, *Coleridge's Nightmare Poetry* (Charlottesville: University of Virginia Press, 1974)

Reading Public Romanticism (Princeton: Princeton University Press, 1998)

Makdisi, Saree, *Making England Western: Occidentalism, Race, and Imperial Culture* (Chicago: University of Chicago Press, 2014)

Romantic Imperialism: Universal Empire and the Culture of Modernity (Cambridge: Cambridge University Press, 1998)

William Blake and the Impossible History of the 1790s (Chicago: University of Chicago Press, 2003)

Malachuk, Daniel S., "Coleridge's Republicanism and the Aphorism in *Aids to Reflection*," *Studies in Romanticism* 39.3 (Fall 2000), 397–417

Malthus, Thomas, *An Essay on the Principle of Population* (London: J. Johnson, 1803)

Manley, Lawrence, *Literature and Culture in Early Modern London* (Cambridge: Cambridge University Press, 1995)

Manning, Peter J., "Manufacturing the Romantic Image: Hazlitt and Coleridge Lecturing," in James K. Chandler and Kevin Gilmartin, eds., *Romantic Metropolis* (Cambridge: Cambridge University Press, 2005), pp. 227–45

Marcy, Peter, "Eighteenth-Century Views of Bristol and Bristolians," in Patrick McGrath, ed. *Bristol in the Eighteenth Century* (Newton Abbott: David & Charles, 1972), pp. 11–40

Marx, Karl, *Capital: Volume One*, trans. Ben Fowkes (New York: Penguin, 1990)

Grundrisse, trans. Martin Nicholas (New York: Penguin, 1973)

Mason, Nicholas, *Literary Advertising and the Shaping of British Romanticism* (Baltimore: Johns Hopkins University Press, 2013)

Matthews, G. M., "A Volcano's Voice in Shelley," *ELH* 24.3 (September 1957), 191–228

Mayo, Robert, "The Contemporaneity of the *Lyrical Ballads*," *PMLA* 69.3 (June 1954), 486–522

McCarthy, William, *Anna Letitia Barbauld: Voice of the Enlightenment* (Baltimore: Johns Hopkins University Press, 2008)

"'We Hoped the *Woman* Was Going to Appear': Repression, Desire and Gender in Anna Letitia Barbauld's Early Poems," in Paula R. Feldman and Theresa M. Kelley, eds., *Romantic Women Writers: Voices and Countervoices* (Hanover, NH: University Press of New England, 1995), pp. 113–37

McKendrick, N., J. Brewer, and J. H. Plumb, *The Birth of a Consumer Society* (London: Europa, 1982)

Mee, Jon, *Conversable Worlds: Literature, Contention, and Community 1762 to 1830* (Oxford: Oxford University Press, 2011)

Dangerous Enthusiasm: William Blake and the Culture of Radicalism in the 1790s (Oxford: Oxford University Press, 1992)

Romanticism, Enthusiasm, and Regulation (Oxford: Oxford University Press, 2005)

Meek, Ronald L., *Social Science and the Ignoble Savage* (Cambridge: Cambridge University Press, 1976)

Metzger, Lore, *One Foot in Eden: Modes of Pastoral in Romantic Poetry* (Chapel Hill: University of North Carolina Press, 1986)

Milburn, Jr., Douglas, "The Popular Reaction to German Drama in England at the End of the Eighteenth Century," *Rice University Studies* 55.3 (Summer 1969), 149–62

Milton, John, *Complete Poems and Major Prose*, ed. Merritt Y. Hughes (Indianapolis: Hackett, 2003)

Molesworth, Charles, "Wordsworth's 'Westminster Bridge' Sonnet: The Republican Structure of Time and Perception," *Clio* 6.3 (Spring 1977), 261–73

Moretti, Franco, *Atlas of the European Novel, 1800–1900* (New York: Verso, 1999)

Signs Taken for Wonders: Essays in the Sociology of Literary Forms, trans. Susan Fischer, David Forgacs, David Miller (London: NLB, 1983)

Morgan, Kenneth. *Bristol and the Atlantic Trade in the Eighteenth Century* (Cambridge: Cambridge University Press, 1993)

Morrow, John, *Coleridge's Political Thought* (London: Macmillan, 1990)

Morton, A. L., *The Everlasting Gospel* (London: Lawrence and Wishart, 1958)

Newey, Vincent, *Cowper's Poetry: A Critical Study and Reassessment* (Liverpool: Liverpool University Press, 1982)

Newlyn, Lucy, *Coleridge, Wordsworth, and the Language of Allusion*, 2nd ed. (Oxford: Oxford University Press, 2001)

"'In City Pent': Echo and Allusion in Wordsworth, Coleridge, and Lamb, 1797–1801," *The Review of English Studies* n.s. 32.128 (November 1981), 408–28

Reading, Writing, and Romanticism (Oxford: Oxford University Press, 2000)

Newman, Ian, "*Tavern Talk: Literature, Politics and Conviviality, 1780–1840*" (PhD dissertation, UCLA Department of English), 2013

Ngai, Sianne, *Ugly Feelings* (Cambridge: Harvard University Press, 2005)

Nietzsche, Friedrich, *The Will to Power*, trans. Walter Kaufmann and R. J. Hollingdale (New York: Vintage, 1967)

Nokes, David, *John Gay: A Profession of Friendship* (Oxford: Oxford University Press, 1995)

Nord, Deborah Epstein, *Walking the Victorian Streets: Women, Representation, and the City* (Ithaca: Cornell University Press, 1995)

Notopoulos, James A., *The Platonism of Shelley* (Durham: Duke University Press, 1949)

O'Byrne, Alison, "The Art of Walking in London: Representing Urban Pedestrianism in the Early Nineteenth Century," *Romanticism* 14.2 (July 2008), 94–107.

Ogborn, Miles, *Spaces of Modernity: London's Geographies, 1680–1780* (New York: Guilford Press, 1998)

Overton, Mark, *Agricultural Revolution in England: The Transformation of the Agrarian Economy, 1500–1850* (Cambridge: Cambridge University Press, 1996)

Paley, Morton, "Apocapolitics: Allusion and Structure in Shelley's *Mask of Anarchy*," *Huntington Library Quarterly* 54.2 (Spring 1991), 91–109

The Continuing City: William Blake's Jerusalem (Oxford: Clarendon Press, 1983)

Park, Robert E., "The City: Suggestions for the Investigation of Human Behavior in the Urban Environment," in Robert E. Park, Ernest W. Burgess, and Roderick D. McKenzie, eds., *The City* (Chicago: University of Chicago Press, 1967), pp. 1–46

Parrish, Stephen M., *The Art of the Lyrical Ballads* (Cambridge: Harvard University Press, 1973)

Parsons, Deborah L., *Streetwalking the Metropolis: Women, the City, and Modernity* (Oxford: Oxford University Press, 2000)

Pascoe, Judith, *Romantic Theatricality: Gender, Poetry, and Spectatorship* (Ithaca: Cornell University Press, 1997)

"The Spectacular Flâneuse: Mary Robinson and the City of London," *The Wordsworth Circle* 23.3 (Summer 1992), 165–71

Patterson, Annabel, *Pastoral and Ideology: Virgil to Valéry* (Berkeley: University of California Press, 1987)

Peer, Larry H., ed., *Romanticism and the City* (New York: Palgrave Macmillan, 2011)

Pepper, W. Thomas, "The Ideology of Wordsworth's 'Michael: a Pastoral Poem,'" *Criticism* 31.4 (Fall 1989), 367–82

Perry, Seamus, *Coleridge and the Uses of Division* (Oxford: Clarendon Press, 1999)

Pfau, Thomas, *Romantic Moods: Paranoia, Trauma, and Melancholy, 1790–1840* (Baltimore: Johns Hopkins University Press, 2005)

Wordsworth's Profession (Stanford: Stanford University Press, 1997)

Picciotto, Joanna, "Optical Instruments and the Eighteenth-Century Observer," *Studies in Eighteenth-Century Culture* 29 (2000), 123–53

Pinch, Adela, *Strange Fits of Passion: Epistemologies of Emotion, Hume to Austen* (Stanford: Stanford University Press, 1996)

Pinion, F. B., *A Wordsworth Chronology* (London: Macmillan, 1988)

Piper, H. W., *Singing of Mount Abora: Coleridge's Use of Biblical Imagery and Natural Symbolism in Poetry and Philosophy* (Rutherford, NJ: Fairleigh Dickinson University Press, 1987)

Pitkin, Hanna Fenichel, *The Concept of Representation* (Berkeley: University of California Press, 1967)

Pocock, J. G. A., *The Machiavellian Moment: Florentine Political Thought and the Atlantic Republican Tradition* (Princeton: Princeton University Press, [1975] rpt. 2003)

Virtue, Commerce, and History (Cambridge: Cambridge University Press, 1985)

Pollock, Griselda, *Vision and Difference: Femininity, Feminism and the Histories of Art* (London: Routledge, 1988)

Pope, Alexander, *The Poems of Alexander Pope: A One-Volume Edition of the Twickenham Text with Selected Annotations*, ed. John Butt (New Haven: Yale University Press, 1963)

Porter, Roy, *London: A Social History* (Cambridge: Harvard University Press, 1995)

Priestley, Joseph, *Hartley's Theory of the Human Mind* (London: Joseph Johnson, 1775)

Priestman, Martin, *Cowper's Task: Structure and Influence* (Cambridge: Cambridge University Press, 1983)

Pulos, C. E., *The Deep Truth* (Lincoln: University of Nebraska Press, 1962)

Punter, David, "Blake and the Shapes of London," *Criticism* 23.1 (Winter 1981), 1–23

Pyle, Forest, "'Frail Spells': Shelley and the Ironies of Exile," in Deborah White, ed., "Irony and Clerisy," *Romantic Circles Praxis Series*, August 1999

Rasmussen, Steen Eiler, *London: The Unique City* (Cambridge: MIT Press, 1967)

Raven, James, *The Business of Books: Booksellers and the English Book Trade* (New Haven: Yale University Press, 2007)

Read, Donald, *Peterloo: The 'Massacre' and Its Background* (Manchester: Manchester University Press, 1958)

Ready, Kathryn, "Dissenting Patriots: Anna Barbauld, John Aikin, and the Discourse of Eighteenth-Century Republicanism in Rational Dissent," *History of European Ideas* 38.4 (December 2012), 527–49

Redfield, Marc, "Masks of Anarchy: Shelley's Political Politics," *Bucknell Review* 45.2 (2002), 100–26

Redford, Arthur, *Labour Migration in England 1800–1850*, ed. and rev. W. H. Chandler, 2nd ed. (New York: Augustus M. Kelley, 1968)

Reiman, Donald H., *Romantic Texts and Contexts* (Columbia: University of Missouri Press, 1987)

ed., *Shelley and His Circle, 1773–1822*, 8 vols. (Cambridge: Harvard University Press, 1973)

Rendell, Jane, *The Pursuit of Pleasure: Gender, Space, and Architecture in Regency London* (London: Athlone, 2002)

Reno, Seth T., "The Violence of Form in Shelley's *Mask of Anarchy*," *Keats-Shelley Journal* 62 (2013), 80–98

Reynolds, Elaine A., *Before the Bobbies: The Night Watch and Police Reform in Metropolitan London, 1720–1830* (Stanford: Stanford University Press, 1998)

Robbins, Caroline, *The Eighteenth-Century Commonwealthman* (Cambridge: Harvard University Press, 1959)

Roberts, Daniel Sanjiv, "The Janus-face of Romantic Modernity: Thomas De Quincey's Metropolitan Imagination," *Romanticism* 17.3 (2011), 299–308

Robinson, Daniel, *The Poetry of Mary Robinson* (Basingstoke: Palgrave, 2011)

Robinson, Mary, *A Letter to the Women of England and the Natural Daughter*, ed. Sharon Setzer (Peterborough: Broadview 2003)

Memoirs of the Late Mrs. Robinson, 4 vols. (London: R. Phillips, 1801)

Selected Poems, ed. Judith Pascoe (Peterborough: Broadview, 2000)

Robinson, Mary and Adriana Craciun, "Present State of the Manners, Society, Etc. of the Metropolis of England," *PMLA* 119.1 (January 2004), 103–19

Roe, Nicholas, *Politics of Nature* (London: Macmillan, 1992)

Wordsworth and Coleridge: The Radical Years (Oxford: Oxford University Press, 1988)

Ross, Marlon, *The Contours of Masculine Desire: Romanticism and the Rise of Women's Poetry* (Oxford: Oxford University Press, 1989)

Rudé, George, *Hanoverian London, 1714–1808* (London: Secker & Warburg, 1971)

Russell, Gillian, *Women, Sociability and Theatre in Georgian London* (Cambridge: Cambridge University Press, 2007)

Russell, Gillian and Clara Tuite, eds., *Romantic Sociability: Social Networks and Literary Culture in Britain, 1770–1840* (Cambridge: Cambridge University Press, 2002)

Russell, Lord John, *Speech of Lord John Russell in the House of Commons, On December 14th, 1819* (London: Longman, Hurst, Rees, Orme, 1820)

Sachs, Jonathan, "'Yet the Capital of the World': Rome, Repetition, and History in Shelley's Later Writings," *Nineteenth-Century Contexts* 28.2 (June 2006), 105–26

Saglia, Diego, "Commerce, Luxury, and Identity in Mary Robinson's *Memoirs*," *SEL: Studies in English Literature 1500–1900* 49.3 (Summer 2009), 717–36

"The Dangers of Over-Refinement: The Language of Luxury in Romantic Poetry by Women, 1793–1811," *Studies in Romanticism* 38.4 (Winter 1999), 641–72

Saint, Andrew, "The Building Art of the First Industrial Metropolis," in Celina Fox, ed., *London – World City, 1800–1840* (New Haven: Yale University Press, 1992), pp. 51–76

Sayre, Robert and Michael Löwy, "Figures of Romantic Anti-Capitalism," *New German Critique* 32 (Spring–Summer 1984), 42–92

Romanticism Against the Tide of Modernity, trans. Catherine Porter (Durham: Duke University Press, 2001)

Schmid, Thomas H., "Strained Tenderness: Wordsworth, Joanna Hutchinson, and the Anxiety of Sisterly Resistance in 'To Joanna,'" *Studies in Romanticism* 40.3 (Fall 2001), 401–25

Schoenfield, Mark, *The Professional Wordsworth: Law, Labor & The Poet's Contract* (Athens: University of Georgia Press, 1996)

Scrivener, Michael Henry, *Radical Shelley* (Princeton: Princeton University Press, 1982)

Sekora, John, *Luxury: The Concept in Western Thought, Eden to Smollett* (Baltimore: Johns Hopkins University Press, 1977)

Sennett, Richard, *The Fall of Public Man* (New York: Alfred A. Knopf, 1977)

Sharpe, William Chapman, *Unreal Cities: Urban Figuration in Wordsworth, Baudelaire, Whitman, Eliot, and Williams* (Baltimore: Johns Hopkins University Press, 1990)

Shelley, Mary, *The Journals of Mary Shelley, 1814–1844*, ed. Paula R. Feldman and Diana Scott-Kilvert (Baltimore: Johns Hopkins University Press, 1995)

Shelley, Percy Bysshe, *The Complete Poetry of Percy Bysshe Shelley*, ed. Donald Reiman and Neil Fraistat, 4 vols. to date (Baltimore: Johns Hopkins University Press, 2000–)

The Complete Works of Percy Bysshe Shelley, ed. Ingpen and Peck, 10 vols. (New York: Charles Scribner's Sons, 1926–30)

The Letters of Percy Bysshe Shelley, ed. Frederick L. Jones, 2 vols. (Oxford: Clarendon Press, 1964)

The Mask of Anarchy Draft Notebooks: A Facsimile of Huntington Ms. HM 2177, ed. Mary A. Quinn (New York: Garland Publishing, 1990)

Masque of Anarchy: A Poem (London: Moxon, 1832)

The Prose Works of Percy Bysshe Shelley, ed. E. B. Murray (Oxford: Clarendon Press, 1993)

Shelley's Poetry and Prose, ed. Reiman and Fraistat, 2nd ed. (New York: Norton, 2002)

Sheppard, Francis, *London 1808–1870: The Infernal Wen* (London: Secker & Warburg, 1971)

London: A History (Oxford: Oxford University Press, 1998)

Simmel, Georg, *On Individuality and Social Forms*, ed. Donald N. Levine, trans. Edward A. Shils (Chicago: University of Chicago Press, 1971)

Simpson, David, *Wordsworth and the Figurings of the Real* (London: Macmillan, 1982)

Wordsworth, Commodification, and Social Concern (Cambridge: Cambridge University Press, 2009)

Wordsworth's Historical Imagination: The Poetry of Displacement (New York: Methuen, 1987)

Smith, Adam, *The Theory of Moral Sentiments*, ed. Ryan Patrick Hanley (New York: Penguin, 2009)

The Wealth of Nations (New York: Bantam, 2003)

Smith, Norman Kemp, *A Commentary to Kant's 'Critique of Pure Reason'* (New York: Humanities Press, 1950)

Southey, Robert, *Letters from England by Don Manuel Alvarez Espriella*, 2nd ed. (London: Longman, Hurst, Rees and Orme, 1808)

New Letters of Robert Southey, ed. Kenneth Curry, 2 vols. (New York: Columbia University Press, 1965)

Speck, W. A., *Robert Southey: Entire Man of Letters* (New Haven: Yale University Press, 2006)

Spenser, Edmund, *The Faerie Queene*, ed. A. C. Hamilton (London: Longman, 2001)

Stallybrass, Peter and Allon White, *The Politics and Poetics of Transgression* (London: Methuen, 1986)

St. Clair, William, *The Reading Nation in the Romantic Period* (Cambridge: Cambridge University Press, 2004)

Stenton, Alison, "Spatial Stories: Movement in the City and Cultural Geography," in Clare Brant and Susan E. Whyman, eds., *Walking the Streets of Eighteenth-Century London: John Gay's Trivia* (Oxford: Oxford University Press, 2007), pp. 62–73

Stewart, David, *Romantic Magazines and Metropolitan Literary Culture* (New York: Palgrave Macmillan, 2011)

Stillinger, Jack, *Romantic Complexity: Keats, Coleridge, and Wordsworth* (Urbana: University of Illinois Press, 2006)

Summerson, John, *Georgian London* (London: Barrie & Jenkins, 1970)

Sweet, Rosemary, *The English Town, 1680–1840* (Singapore: Longman, 1999)

The Writing of Urban Histories in Eighteenth-Century England (Oxford: Clarendon Press, 1997)

Terada, Rei, *Feeling in Theory: Emotion after the 'Death of the Subject'* (Cambridge: Harvard University Press, 2001)

Terry, Richard, "Transitions and Digressions in the Eighteenth-Century Long Poem," *Studies in English Literature, 1500–1900* 32.3 (Summer 1992), 495–510

Thelwall, John, *The Politics of English Jacobinism: The Writings of John Thelwall*, ed. Gregory Claeys (University Park: Pennsylvania State University Press, 1995)

Thesing, William B., *The London Muse: Victorian Poetic Responses to the City* (Athens: University of Georgia Press, 1982)

Thompson, E. P., *Customs in Common* (New York: New Press, 1993)

"'London,'" in Michael Phillips, ed., *Interpreting Blake* (Cambridge: Cambridge University Press, 1978), pp. 5–31

The Making of the English Working Class (London: Victor Gollancz, 1963)

Witness against the Beast (New York: The New Press, 1993)

Thompson, Judith, *John Thelwall in the Wordsworth Circle* (New York: Palgrave Macmillan, 2012)

Thomson, James, *The Seasons*, ed. James Sambrook (Oxford: Clarendon Press, 1981)

Thorn, Romaine Joseph, *Bristolia, A Poem* (Bristol: Rees, 1794)

Thorpe, Douglas, "Shelley's Golden Verbal City," *Journal of English and Germanic Philology* 86.3 (April 1987), 215–27

Trelawny, Edward John, *Records of Shelley, Byron, and the Author* (New York: New York Review Books, 2000)

Trott, Nicola, "Coleridge's City," *Coleridge Bulletin* 19 (Spring 2002), 41–57

Ulmer, William A., "The Rhetorical Occasion of 'This Lime-Tree Bower My Prison,'" *Romanticism* 13.1 (2007), 15–27

"Virtue of Necessity: Coleridge's Unitarian Moral Theory," *Modern Philology* 102 (2005), 372–404

Vine, Steve, "Blake's Material Sublime," *Studies in Romanticism* 41.2 (Summer 2002), 237–57

Virno, Paolo, "The Ambivalence of Disenchantment," in Paolo Virno and Michael Hardt, eds., *Radical Thought in Italy* (Minneapolis: University of Minnesota Press, 1996), pp. 13–36

Wall, Cynthia, *The Literary and Cultural Spaces of Restoration London* (Cambridge: Cambridge University Press, 1998)

Warner, Michael, *Publics and Counterpublics* (New York: Zone Books, 2005)

Watt, Ian, *The Rise of the Novel: Studies in Defoe, Richardson and Fielding* (Berkeley: University of California Press, 1971)

Webb, Timothy, "Dangerous Plurals: Wordsworth's Bartholomew Fair and the Challenge of an Urban Poetics," in Susana Onega and John A. Stotesbury, ed., *London in Literature: Visionary Mappings of the Metropolis* (Heidelberg: C. Winter, 2002), pp. 53–79

"Listing the Busy Sounds: Anna Seward, Mary Robinson and the Poetic Challenge of the City," in Lilla Maria Crisafulli and Cecilia Pietropoli, eds., *Romantic Women Poets: Genre and Gender* (Amsterdam: Rodopi, 2007), pp. 79–111

Shelley: A Voice not Understood (Manchester: Manchester University Press, 1977)

Whalley, George, "Coleridge and Southey in Bristol, 1795," *RES* n.s. 1 (1950), 324–40

Wheatley, Kim, *Shelley and His Readers: Beyond Paranoid Politics* (Columbia: University of Missouri Press, 1999)

White, Daniel E., *Early Romanticism and Religious Dissent* (Cambridge: Cambridge University Press, 2006)

From Little London to Little Bengal (Baltimore: Johns Hopkins University Press, 2013)

"The 'Joineriana': Anna Barbauld, the Aikin Family Circle, and the Dissenting Public Sphere," *Eighteenth-Century Studies* 32.4 (Summer 1999), 511–33

White, Harry, "Relative Means and Ends in Shelley's Social-Political Thought," *Studies in English Literature 1500–1900* 22.4 (1982), 613–31

White, R. J., *Waterloo to Peterloo* (London: William Heinemann, 1957)

Whyman, Susan E., "Sharing Public Spaces," in Clare Brant and Susan E. Whyman, eds., *Walking the Streets of Eighteenth-Century London: John Gay's Trivia* (Oxford: Oxford University Press, 2007), pp. 42–60

Willey, Basil, *The Eighteenth Century Background* (London: Chatto & Windus, 1941)

Williams, Nicholas M., *Ideology and Utopia in the Poetry of William Blake* (Cambridge: Cambridge University Press, 1998)

Williams, Raymond, *The Country and the City* (Oxford: Oxford University Press, 1973)

Culture and Society: 1780–1950 (New York: Columbia University Press, 1983)

Marxism and Literature (Oxford: Oxford University Press, 1977)

Williamson, Jeffrey G., *Coping with City Growth during the Industrial Revolution* (Cambridge: Cambridge University Press, 1990)

Wilson, Richard, "Newspapers and Industry: The Export of Wool Controversy in the 1790s," in Michael Harris and Alan Lee, eds., *The Press in English Society from the Seventeenth to Nineteenth Centuries* (Cranbury, NJ: Associated University Presses, 1986), pp. 81–112

Wirth, Louis, "Urbanism as a Way of Life," *The American Journal of Sociology* 44.1 (July 1938), 1–24

Wolff, Janet, "The Invisible *Flâneuse*: Women and the Literature of Modernity," *Theory, Culture and Society* 2/3 (1985), 37–46

Wolfson, Susan J., *Formal Charges: The Shaping of Poetry in British Romanticism* (Stanford: Stanford University Press, 1997)

Wood, Gillen D'Arcy, "Leigh Hunt's New Suburbia: An Eco-historical Study in Climate Poetics and Public Health," *Interdisciplinary Studies in Literature and Environment* 18.3 (Summer 2011), 527–52

Woodman, Tom, "'Vulgar Circumstance' and 'Due Civilities': Gay's Art of Polite Living in Town," in Peter Lewis and Nigel Wood, eds., *John Gay and the Scriblerians* (New York: St. Martin's Press, 1989), pp. 83–93

Woodring, Carl R., *Politics in the Poetry of Coleridge* (Madison: University of Wisconsin Press, 1961)

Woof, Robert S., "Wordsworth's Poetry and Stuart's Newspapers: 1797–1803," *Studies in Bibliography* 15 (1962): 172–74

Wordsworth, Jonathan, *William Wordsworth: The Borders of Vision* (Oxford: Clarendon Press, 1982)

Wordsworth, William, *Lyrical Ballads and Other Poems, 1797–1800*, ed. James Butler and Karen Green (Ithaca: Cornell University Press, 1992)

Poems, in Two Volumes, and Other Poems, 1800–1807, ed. Jared Curtis (Ithaca: Cornell University Press, 1983)

The Prelude 1799, 1805, 1850, eds. Wordsworth, Abrams, and Gill (Norton: New York, 1979)

The Prose Works of William Wordsworth, eds. W. J. B. Owen and Jane Worthington Smyser, vols. (Oxford: Clarendon Press, 1974)

The Thirteen Book Prelude, ed. Mark L. Reed (Ithaca: Cornell University Press, 1991)

Wordsworth, William and Dorothy Wordsworth, *The Letters of William and Dorothy Wordsworth*, ed. Ernest de Selincourt, 8 vols. (Oxford: Clarendon Press, 1967)

Wrigley, E. A., *People, Cities and Wealth: The Transformation of Traditional Society* (Oxford: Basil Blackwell, 1987)

Yelling, J. A., *Common Field and Enclosure in England, 1450–1850* (London: Macmillan, 1977)

Young, Arthur, *The Farmer's Letters to the People of England* (London: Nicoll, 1768)

Zaid, Hilary A., "Wordsworth's 'Obsolete Idolatry': Doubling Texts and Facing Doubles in 'To Joanna,'" *Studies in Romanticism* 36.2 (Summer 1997), 201–26

Zimmerman, Sarah M., "Coleridge the Lecturer, A Disappearing Act," in Alexander Dick and Angela Esterhammer, eds., *Spheres of Action: Speech and Performance in Romantic Culture* (Toronto: University of Toronto Press, 2009), pp. 46–72

"Correct Likeness of Bellingham, with an Accurate Report of his Trial," *Universal Magazine* 17.102 (May 1812), 428–36

"Description of a Part of Manchester," *The Examiner* 609 (August 29, 1819), 558

"Dispersal of the Reform Meeting at Manchester by a Military Force," *The Examiner* 608 (August 22, 1819), 539–43

"Disturbances at Manchester," *The Examiner* 608 (August 22, 1819), 529–31
"Disturbances at Manchester and Matters Connected with Them," *The Examiner* 609 (August 29, 1819), 545–47
"Execution of Bellingham," *The Examiner* 230 (May 24, 1812), 334–36
"Imperial Parliament," *The Examiner* 126 (May 27, 1810): 323–28
"The Poetry of the World, Vols. III and IV [Review]," *Monthly Review, or Literary Journal* 6 (September 1791), 21–24

Index

CAMBRIDGE STUDIES IN ROMANTICISM

General Editor: JAMES CHANDLER, *University of Chicago*

1. *Romantic Correspondence: Women, Politics and the Fiction of Letters*
   MARY A. FAVRET
2. *British Romantic Writers and the East: Anxieties of Empire*
   NIGEL LEASK
3. *Poetry as an Occupation and an Art in Britain, 1760–1830*
   PETER MURPHY
4. *Edmund Burke's Aesthetic Ideology: Language, Gender and Political Economy in Revolution*
   TOM FURNISS
5. *In the Theatre of Romanticism: Coleridge, Nationalism, Women*
   JULIE A. CARLSON
6. *Keats, Narrative and Audience*
   ANDREW BENNETT
7. *Romance and Revolution: Shelley and the Politics of a Genre*
   DAVID DU
8. *Literature, Education, and Romanticism: Reading as Social Practice, 1780–1832*
   ALAN RICHARDSON
9. *Women Writing about Money: Women's Fiction in England, 1790–1820*
   EDWARD COPELAND
10. *Shelley and the Revolution in Taste: The Body and the Natural World*
    TIMOTHY MORTON
11. *William Cobbett: The Politics of Style*
    LEONORA NATTRASS
12. *The Rise of Supernatural Fiction, 1762–1800*
    E. J. CLERY
13. *Women Travel Writers and the Language of Aesthetics, 1716–1818*
    ELIZABETH A. BOHLS
14. *Napoleon and English Romanticism*
    SIMON BAINBRIDGE
15. *Romantic Vagrancy: Wordsworth and the Simulation of Freedom*
    CELESTE LANGAN
16. *Wordsworth and the Geologists*
    JOHN WYATT
17. *Wordsworth's Pope: A Study in Literary Historiography*
    ROBERT J. GRIN
18. *The Politics of Sensibility: Race, Gender and Commerce in the Sentimental Novel*
    MARKMAN ELLIS

19. *Reading Daughters' Fictions, 1709–1834: Novels and Society from Manley to Edgeworth*
CAROLINE GONDA
20. *Romantic Identities: Varieties of Subjectivity, 1774–1830*
ANDREA K. HENDERSON
21. *Print Politics: The Press and Radical Opposition in Early Nineteenth-Century England*
KEVIN GILMARTIN
22. *Reinventing Allegory*
THERESA M. KELLEY
23. *British Satire and the Politics of Style, 1789–1832*
GARY DYER
24. *The Romantic Reformation: Religious Politics in English Literature, 1789–1824*
ROBERT M. RYAN
25. *De Quincey's Romanticism: Canonical Minority and the Forms of Transmission*
MARGARET RUSSETT
26. *Coleridge on Dreaming: Romanticism, Dreams and the Medical Imagination*
JENNIFER FORD
27. *Romantic Imperialism: Universal Empire and the Culture of Modernity*
SAREE MAKDISI
28. *Ideology and Utopia in the Poetry of William Blake*
NICHOLAS M. WILLIAMS
29. *Sexual Politics and the Romantic Author*
SONIA HOFKOSH
30. *Lyric and Labour in the Romantic Tradition*
ANNE JANOWITZ
31. *Poetry and Politics in the Cockney School: Keats, Shelley, Hunt and Their Circle*
JEREY N. COX
32. *Rousseau, Robespierre and English Romanticism*
GREGORY DART
33. *Contesting the Gothic: Fiction, Genre and Cultural Conflict, 1764–1832*
JAMES WATT
34. *Romanticism, Aesthetics, and Nationalism*
DAVID ARAM KAISER
35. *Romantic Poets and the Culture of Posterity*
ANDREW BENNETT
36. *The Crisis of Literature in the 1790s: Print Culture and the Public Sphere*
PAUL KEEN
37. *Romantic Atheism: Poetry and Freethought, 1780–1830*
MARTIN PRIESTMAN
38. *Romanticism and Slave Narratives: Transatlantic Testimonies*
HELEN THOMAS

39. *Imagination under Pressure, 1789–1832: Aesthetics, Politics, and Utility*
JOHN WHALE
40. *Romanticism and the Gothic: Genre, Reception, and Canon Formation, 1790–1820*
MICHAEL GAMER
41. *Romanticism and the Human Sciences: Poetry, Population, and the Discourse of the Species*
MAUREEN N. MCLANE
42. *The Poetics of Spice: Romantic Consumerism and the Exotic*
TIMOTHY MORTON
43. *British Fiction and the Production of Social Order, 1740–1830*
MIRANDA J. BURGESS
44. *Women Writers and the English Nation in the 1790s*
ANGELA KEANE
45. *Literary Magazines and British Romanticism*
MARK PARKER
46. *Women, Nationalism and the Romantic Stage: Theatre and Politics in Britain, 1780–1800*
BETSY BOLTON
47. *British Romanticism and the Science of the Mind*
ALAN RICHARDSON
48. *The Anti-Jacobin Novel: British Conservatism and the French Revolution*
M. O. GRENBY
49. *Romantic Austen: Sexual Politics and the Literary Canon*
CLARA TUITE
50. *Byron and Romanticism*
JEROME MCGANN AND JAMES SODERHOLM
51. *The Romantic National Tale and the Question of Ireland*
INA FERRIS
52. *Byron, Poetics and History*
JANE STABLER
53. *Religion, Toleration, and British Writing, 1790–1830*
MARK CANUEL
54. *Fatal Women of Romanticism*
ADRIANA CRACIUN
55. *Knowledge and Indifference in English Romantic Prose*
TIM MILNES
56. *Mary Wollstonecraft and the Feminist Imagination*
BARBARA TAYLOR
57. *Romanticism, Maternity and the Body Politic*
JULIE KIPP
58. *Romanticism and Animal Rights*
DAVID PERKINS

59. *Georgic Modernity and British Romanticism: Poetry and the Mediation of History*
KEVIS GOODMAN
60. *Literature, Science and Exploration in the Romantic Era: Bodies of Knowledge*
TIMOTHY FULFORD, DEBBIE LEE, AND PETER J. KITSON
61. *Romantic Colonization and British Anti-Slavery*
DEIRDRE COLEMAN
62. *Anger, Revolution, and Romanticism*
ANDREW M. STAUER
63. *Shelley and the Revolutionary Sublime*
CIAN DUY
64. *Fictions and Fakes: Forging Romantic Authenticity, 1760–1845*
MARGARET RUSSETT
65. *Early Romanticism and Religious Dissent*
DANIEL E. WHITE
66. *The Invention of Evening: Perception and Time in Romantic Poetry*
CHRISTOPHER R. MILLER
67. *Wordsworth's Philosophic Song*
SIMON JARVIS
68. *Romanticism and the Rise of the Mass Public*
ANDREW FRANTA
69. *Writing against Revolution: Literary Conservatism in Britain, 1790–1832*
KEVIN GILMARTIN
70. *Women, Sociability and Theatre in Georgian London*
GILLIAN RUSSELL
71. *The Lake Poets and Professional Identity*
BRIAN GOLDBERG
72. *Wordsworth Writing*
ANDREW BENNETT
73. *Science and Sensation in Romantic Poetry*
NOEL JACKSON
74. *Advertising and Satirical Culture in the Romantic Period*
JOHN STRACHAN
75. *Romanticism and the Painful Pleasures of Modern Life*
ANDREA K. HENDERSON
76. *Balladeering, Minstrelsy, and the Making of British Romantic Poetry*
MAUREEN N. MCLANE
77. *Romanticism and Improvisation, 1750–1850*
ANGELA ESTERHAMMER
78. *Scotland and the Fictions of Geography: North Britain, 1760–1830*
PENNY FIELDING
79. *Wordsworth, Commodification and Social Concern: The Poetics of Modernity*
DAVID SIMPSON

80. *Sentimental Masculinity and the Rise of History, 1790–1890*
MIKE GOODE
81. *Fracture and Fragmentation in British Romanticism*
ALEXANDER REGIER
82. *Romanticism and Music Culture in Britain, 1770–1840: Virtue and Virtuosity*
GILLEN D'ARCY WOOD
83. *The Truth about Romanticism: Pragmatism and Idealism in Keats, Shelley, Coleridge*
TIM MILNES
84. *Blake's Gifts: Poetry and the Politics of Exchange*
SARAH HAGGARTY
85. *Real Money and Romanticism*
MATTHEW ROWLINSON
86. *Sentimental Literature and Anglo-Scottish Identity, 1745–1820*
JULIET SHIELDS
87. *Romantic Tragedies: The Dark Employments of Wordsworth, Coleridge, and Shelley*
REEVE PARKER
88. *Blake, Sexuality and Bourgeois Politeness*
SUSAN MATTHEWS
89. *Idleness, Contemplation and the Aesthetic*
RICHARD ADELMAN
90. *Shelley's Visual Imagination*
NANCY MOORE GOSLEE
91. *A Cultural History of the Irish Novel, 1790–1829*
CLAIRE CONNOLLY
92. *Literature, Commerce, and the Spectacle of Modernity, 1750–1800*
PAUL KEEN
93. *Romanticism and Childhood: The Infantilization of British Literary Culture*
ANN WEIRDA ROWLAND
94. *Metropolitan Art and Literature, 1810–1840: Cockney Adventures*
GREGORY DART
95. *Wordsworth and the Enlightenment Idea of Pleasure*
ROWAN BOYSON
96. *John Clare and Community*
JOHN GOODRIDGE
97. *The Romantic Crowd*
MARY FAIRCLOUGH
98. *Romantic Women Writers, Revolution and Prophecy*
ORIANNE SMITH
99. *Britain, France and the Gothic, 1764–1820*
ANGELA WRIGHT

100. *Transfiguring the Arts and Sciences*
JON KLANCHER
101. *Shelley and the Apprehension of Life*
ROSS WILSON
102. *Poetics of Character: Transatlantic Encounters 1700–1900*
SUSAN MANNING
103. *Romanticism and Caricature*
IAN HAYWOOD
104. *The Late Poetry of the Lake Poets: Romanticism Revised*
TIM FULFORD
105. *Forging Romantic China: Sino–British Cultural Exchange 1760–1840*
PETER J. KITSON
106. *Coleridge and the Philosophy of Poetic Form*
EWAN JAMES JONES
107. *Romanticism in the Shadow of War: Literary Culture in the Napoleonic War Years*
JEREY N. COX
108. *Slavery and the Politics of Place: Representing the Colonial Caribbean, 1770–1833*
ELIZABETH A. BOHLS
109. *The Orient and the Young Romantics*
ANDREW WARREN
110. *Lord Byron and Scandalous Celebrity*
CLARA TUITE
111. *Radical Orientalism: Rights, Reform, and Romanticism*
GERARD COHEN-VRIGNAUD
112. *Print, Publicity, and Popular Radicalism in the 1790s*
JON MEE
113. *Wordsworth and the Art of Philosophical Travel*
MARK OORD
114. *Romanticism, Self-Canonization, and the Business of Poetry*
MICHAEL GAMER
115. *Women Wanderers and the Writing of Mobility, 1784–1814*
INGRID HORROCKS
116. *Eighteen Hundred and Eleven: Poetry, Protest and Economic Crisis*
E. J. CLERY
117. *Urbanization and English Romantic Poetry*
STEPHEN TEDESCHI

Lightning Source UK Ltd.
Milton Keynes UK
UKHW020604070719
345681UK00018B/367/P

9 781108 402637